A DECADE OF
REVOLUTION

1789-1799

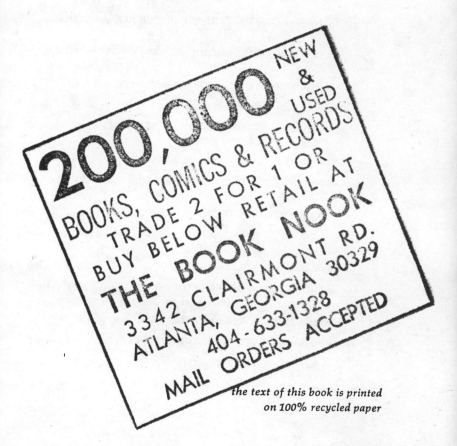
*the text of this book is printed
on 100% recycled paper*

THE RISE OF MODERN EUROPE

Edited by WILLIAM L. LANGER
Harvard University

* In preparation

A DECADE OF REVOLUTION

1789-1799

BY CRANE BRINTON

HARPER TORCHBOOKS
Harper & Row, Publishers
New York, Evanston, San Francisco, London

A DECADE OF REVOLUTION

Copyright, 1934 by Harper & Row, Publishers, Incorporated
Printed in the United States of America

*This book was originally published in 1934 by Harper & Brothers
in The Rise of Modern Europe series, edited by William L. Langer.*

First paperback edition published 1963 by Harper & Row,
Publishers, Incorporated.

75 76 77 78 79 80   12 11

TABLE OF CONTENTS

LIST OF ILLUSTRATIONS

The illustrations, grouped in a separate section, will be found following page 142.

INTRODUCTION

Our age of specialization produces an almost incredible amount of monographic research in all fields of human knowledge. So great is the mass of this material that even the professional scholar cannot keep abreast of the contributions in anything but a restricted part of his general subject. In all branches of learning the need for intelligent synthesis is now more urgent than ever before, and this need is felt by the layman even more acutely than by the scholar. He cannot hope to read the products of microscopic research or to keep up with the changing interpretations of experts, unless new knowledge and new viewpoints are made accessible to him by those who make it their business to be informed and who are competent to speak with authority.

These volumes, published under the general title of *The Rise of Modern Europe*, are designed primarily to give the general reader and student a reliable survey of European history written by experts in various branches of that vast subject. In consonance with the current broad conceptions of the scope of history, they attempt to go beyond a merely political-military narrative, and to lay stress upon social, economic, religious, scientific and artistic developments. The minutely detailed, chronological approach is to some extent sacrificed in the effort to emphasize the dominant factors and to set forth their interrelationships. At the same time the division of European history into national histories has been abandoned and wherever possible attention has been focussed upon larger forces common to the whole of European civilization. These are the broad lines on which this history as a whole has been laid out. The individual volumes are integral parts of the larger scheme, but they are intended also to stand as independent units, each the work of a scholar well qualified to treat the period covered by his book. Each volume contains about fifty illustrations selected from the mass of contemporary pictorial material. All non-contemporary illustrations have been excluded on principle. The bibliographical note appended to each volume is designed to facilitate further study of special aspects touched upon in the text. In general every effort has been made to give the reader a clear idea of the main movements in European history, to embody the monographic contributions of research workers, and to present the material in a forceful and vivid manner.

.   .   .

In this volume Professor Brinton has essayed the difficult task of presenting in limited scope at once the salient facts of the French Revolution and the repercussions of that epoch-making event upon European affairs at large. He has long been a student of the period and has made some valuable contributions to our understanding of the stormy course of the great overturn. In keeping with the spirit of this history he has tried to put the Revolution into its general European setting, and to take account of the international aspects of revolutionary ideology and revolutionary organization. While many short histories of the period bring the narrative to a close with the downfall of Robespierre, this volume continues the story to *coup d'état* of Brumaire which put Napoleon Bonaparte firmly in the saddle. It will be seen that Professor Brinton looks upon the interlude of the Directory as in a sense the consummation of the Revolution and that he has a more favorable impression than many other writers of the accomplishments of that period. In general he has given a broad, fresh and incisive analysis of forces and personalities, of movements of opinion and of literary and artistic currents. Special attention may be called to the illuminating discussion of various interpretations of the Revolution, and to the author's general estimate of the period, in which he attempts something like a reconciliation between widely divergent viewpoints.

WILLIAM L. LANGER

Preface

The account of my indebtedness for the writing of this book ought to be at least as long as its bibliography. I must, however, single out the late R. M. Johnston, with whom I began the study of the French Revolution, and the late Albert Mathiez, who gave me freely of his time and knowledge. I have profited greatly from the labors of my American co-workers in the field, and especially from those of Messrs. L. Gershoy, L. R. Gottschalk, and T. H. Thomas—though none of these gentlemen should be held responsible for the weaknesses and heresies of this book. I wish to thank my cousin, Miss Eunice Barrows, for help in preparation of the manuscript. To Mr. Penfield Roberts I am as usual indebted for constant help. Finally, I wish to thank Mr. W. L. Langer for editorial suggestions made rather as a friend than as an editor.

CRANE BRINTON

Peacham, Vermont
June 15, 1934

For help in the complete revision of the bibliography of this book I am particularly indebted to Mrs. Charles Drekmeier and to Miss Elizabeth F. Hoxie.

CRANE BRINTON

Cambridge, Massachusetts
October 16, 1958

Map of
EUROPE
IN 1799

— Holy Roman Empire

Scale in Miles
0   100   200   300   400   500

THE MAPDRAFT CO. N.Y.

Chapter One

THE MONARCHICAL EXPERIMENT: THE SETTING

THE FRENCH REVOLUTION is one of the few events of modern history towards which, even today, a man may entertain a feeling of awe. To the theological temperament the Revolution was, of course, proof that neither God nor Satan had abandoned the heroic battleground of this earth. But for the common man in the contemporary world the scientist has taken the place of the theologian. Our undiminished faith attaches itself to the hypotheses of science, and transforms them into laws if not into dogmas. Our sense of awe, perhaps a trifle weakened, invests these laws, these regularities, with a meaning denied the particular, the accidental, the picturesque detail. Thus the modern mind is attracted to the French Revolution, not by its melodramatic variety of incident, but by the startling finality of what seems to be its plan. That plan may be as obvious to the dramatist as to the sociologist, but in these days it is the sociologist who, not altogether unwillingly, shoulders the responsibility for history. Now for the sociological historian the French Revolution is almost too tempting a field. Let him seek his analogy in human pathology: the Revolution is a fever, with recognizable symptoms, a crisis, a period of convalescence. Let him look to psychology: the Revolution exhibits to perfection the phenomena of mass delusion, religious emotion, stereotypes, pressure groups, personal maladjustment. Let him use more purely political terms: the Revolution is a series of shocks, each shock displacing power from Right to Left, from larger groups to smaller and more determined groups, each shock taking on more and more the aspect of a *coup d'état*, less and less that of a widespread, spontaneous outbreak of the people, until finally, in a commonplace *coup d'état* hardly worthy of a good operetta, power comes to rest in the hands of the dictator Bonaparte.

Now the spirit of an age, the sum of its hopes and fashions, must appear at all times a little ridiculous. But, for those who are its subjects in space and time, it is a compelling force; and through this very compulsion it attains an elevation, almost a nobility. The man who writes of past ages is subject to the spirit of his own age. No one could now write of the French Revolution as did Carlyle, and no wise man would try to write of it as did the late M. Aulard. Sociological history must be written. But perhaps history will manage to survive this fashion, as it has survived others. Perhaps, indeed, there is something more fundamental than fashion. Women have been lovely in bustles, and hotels comfortable in Anglo-Venetian Gothic.

One must, then, approach the study of the French Revolution with certain definite questions not to be answered wholly by simple narration. The first of these questions is an obvious one: why did the constitutional monarchy, auspiciously begun by a revolution hardly scandalous even to an Anglo-Saxon, fail after three short years of experiment, and give place to a truly scandalous innovation, a French republic? The answer is unfortunately far from obvious.

II. ESTATES OR NATION?

At Versailles on May 5, 1789, the king formally opened the first States-General called since 1614. Both this ceremony and the religious ceremonies of the previous day went off most impressively in the grand manner, with royal pageantry, processions, carpeted streets, flowers, banners, choruses, lovely women, and gaping crowds. They seem to have produced in those who shared them an extraordinary exhilaration, a communion in hope and love, never wholly to be lost by the elect in the bitterest days of the Terror. Thus at its outset the French Revolution bore the unmistakable imprint of religious emotion. Ferrières, deputy of the nobility of Saumur, wrote in a letter which, since it was directed to his wife, ought at least to be free from the more public kinds of insincerity: "My country, my fellow citizens, the monarch, God himself, all became me. I rested sweetly and peacefully on so many objects; they were alive in me, I was alive in them. The same feelings penetrated everyone; and, far from weakening as they spread, acquired a strength which could hardly be resisted."[1]

Such sentiments, especially if they are genuine, are too exhausting for daily use. Even during the formal opening of May 5 there were minor difficulties. The commoners had not wholly enjoyed the contrast between the somberness of their official costume and the relative splendor of the nobles and the clergy. The ceremony did not begin on time. The acoustics of the *salle des menus plaisirs* were very bad indeed; no one had heard a word of the speech of Barentin, the Keeper of the Seals, and many had not been able to hear the king and Necker, the financial genius who was to save the country. None of the speakers had been clear about the necessary next step, the organization of the States-General according to proper parliamentary procedure. Necker had taken three hours to explain away most of the deficit, but had failed to dwell at length on the exciting subject of constitutional reform. Naturally enough the States soon became a warring ground of interests; but these interests, complex like all human interests, were under the circumstances subject in an unusual degree to the transfiguring—or warping—influence of ideas and emotions.

The essentials of the situation during the next six weeks are clear, however obscure the intrigues of the court, however confused the goings and comings of the deputies. It is a situation which will appear again and again during the Revolution. On one side there is a hesitant, heterogeneous group, well-meaning, without organization though not without guile, and desirous on the whole of keeping things as they are; on the other side there is a determined group, united at least for a given end, well-organized despite the surface babel of its ranks, and desirous of achieving a new order.

On the hesitant, conservative side must be numbered the king and court, most of the nobility and upper clergy, some of the bankers and business men, a scattering of humbler men and women, who do not always behave as the Marxians would have them. These people thought the States-General had been called primarily to devise a way to stop the deficit and avoid a state bankruptcy. Many of them felt that there was a good deal wrong with France, and

[1] Marquis de Ferrières, *Correspondance inédite,* ed. H. Carré (Paris, 1932), 44.

that something might well be done about it, though preferably not by the commons. But these people—headed by the king himself—did not work out anything like a program. They failed even to rally around a simple central issue—the retention of the feudal organization of the States-General—until after the meeting of May 5. The States-General had always deliberated and voted in three separate bodies, clergy, nobles, and commons, and a measure passed in two of these bodies was considered by the crown as approved. With characteristic good intentions, and, it must be admitted, after a good deal of pressure from the now quite vocal French public, the king and Necker had decided that in the new States-General the Third Estate, or commons, was to have a representation numerically equal to that of the other two orders combined. But no definite provision was made, either for a new and radical meeting of the three orders in a single body or for the old meeting in separate bodies.

Barentin on May 5 announced that the king graciously allowed the States themselves to settle that question. Naturally the nobles and the clergy voted to continue separate meetings—though thanks to the popular sympathies of many of the lower clergy the vote of the latter was close, 133 to 114. The commons resolutely refused to consider the possibility of separate meetings, invited the other orders to join them, and settled down to particularly empty, but in this instance particularly useful, debates. The longer the commons did nothing, the better for them. In the long run they wore down the patience of the other orders. In the meantime, the king also did nothing, with results hardly satisfactory to himself. Not until June 23 did he take a definite stand on an issue which stood out clearly on the very first day. Pressed by Marie Antoinette and by his brother, the Comte d'Artois, Louis decided in a critical royal council of June 22, and against the advice of Necker and the majority of the ministry, to order the commons to abandon their pretensions and to accept the separate meeting of the three orders.[2]

The commons meanwhile had assumed, on June 17, the effective title of "National Assembly" and, shut out by royal tactlessness

[2] Necker, offering his resignation, was told by Artois, "No, Monsieur, we are keeping you as a hostage." J. Flammermont, "Le second ministère de Necker," *Revue Historique* (1891), XLVI, 55.

from their regular meeting place, had on June 20 reassembled in the Tennis Court and taken their famous oath not to separate until they had given France a constitution. These now powerful and self-assured commons listened to the king in the royal session of June 23 order them to abandon all that they had done towards creating a National Assembly. With relatively few histrionics, they refused. On the next day they met again, and were joined by a majority of the clergy. On the day after, forty-seven nobles and some more of the clergy came over. On June 27, Louis himself wrote formally requesting the two upper houses to merge with the lower to form a National Assembly.

This, rather more than the lurid later affair of the Bastille, was a revolution. The men who made it were not altogether political innocents. They undeniably represented the opinions and desires of the majority of articulate Frenchmen at the time. For over a generation Frenchmen had been talking and writing about political ideas. Phrases like "law of nature," "constitutional rights," "separation of powers" had become the ordinary coin of conversation. Men were organized in literary societies, smoking clubs, Masonic lodges, where the remaking of human society was an accepted goal. Finally, the actual elections to the States-General of 1789, especially in the Third Estate, give surprising evidence of the existence of a "reform" party with a pretty definite platform and an almost precocious aptitude for realistic methods of getting itself in power.[3]

The failure of the king to decide the question as to how the States-General should be organized provided this reform party with an invaluable rallying point, the demand for a single National Assembly. But back of this demand lay the real point at issue between the court party and the reformers: should these deputies, however they might organize themselves, be limited to the task of filling the treasury by devising new taxes, or should they take upon themselves the task of giving France a written constitution? Upon that

[3] See A. Cochin, *Les sociétés de pensée et la Révolution en Bretagne* (Paris, 1925); and also the chapter "Comment furent élus les députés aux États généraux" in the same author's *Les sociétés de pensée et la démocratie* (Paris, 1921). Cochin was a royalist. Republican historians have until very recently been unwilling to entertain the thesis that the Revolution was in any sense "planned" or "prepared." A great advance in this respect is made in G. Martin, *La franc-maçonnerie française et la préparation de la Révolution* (Paris, 1926).

magic word "constitution" were centered the most varied, and even contradictory, hopes. But there can be no doubt that, save for the relatively small group of nobles, higher clergy, and other *privilégiés*, most of France wanted a constitution. To no eighteenth-century Frenchman could it have occurred that France already possessed one. Constitutions were understood to be written documents, preferably like the excellent and up-to-date ones with which the thirteen former British colonies had recently provided themselves. Or at the very worst, if a constitution were not in one document, at least it must be capable of such clear statement as Montesquieu and De Lolme had given the English constitution. France was a constitutionless despotism, definitely behind the times, and the real solution to her financial difficulties lay in the radical reform of her government.

This reform party numbered practically the whole of the 600 deputies of the Third Estate; well over 100 of the 300 deputies of the clergy; over 50 of the 300 deputies of the nobility, led, at least in public opinion, by the young paladin Lafayette. It had solid roots in the population of France. When the deputies had been selected in various local assemblies these assemblies, following feudal custom, had drawn up *cahiers*, statements of what they wished their deputies to try to do. These *cahiers* exist in great numbers and length.[4] Many of them are quite specific, even parochial, in their grievances; and, though the peasants' requests show little interest in general ideas, any considerable reading in the general body of the *cahiers*, and especially in those from the urban areas, leaves the definite impression that there was a widespread popular demand for a constitution. That demand was, inevitably, couched in terms of the natural rights philosophy of the century. Here again at the very outset is discernible a condition to be found throughout the Revolution: specific, worldly aims dictated by individual interests and appetites, and generalized, abstract political principles derived from further ethical abstractions—Nature, Right, Justice. The true study of the Revolution, it would seem obvious, is the study of the inter-

---

[4] A most useful and complete bibliography of the *cahiers*, both in print and in manuscript, is Miss B. F. Hyslop's recent *Répertoire critique des cahiers de doléance pour les États généraux de 1789* (Paris, 1933).

action of these concrete appetites and abstract principles. The Revolution seen exclusively as the product of definite, worldly, realistic, economic aims, or exclusively as a noble crusade to realize in France a Utopia synthesized from the writings of the *philosophes*, is a pure myth. Though history must indeed study myths, it ought to create as few of them as possible.

By the end of June, then, the first great step in the Revolution was achieved. The 1,200 deputies of the States-General were meeting together in one great new body, the National Assembly, with the avowed purpose of making France a limited monarchy by giving her a written constitution. And this had come about without bloodshed, without violence, with the full consent, even with the blessing, of a Bourbon king. It is no wonder that Europe and America were astounded, that men could speak only of the reforms of Solon, of the best days of the Roman Republic. For two years this assembly was to play a double rôle: first, as an ordinary parliament governing the country in collaboration with the executive; second, as a constitutional convention—it is often called the Constituent Assembly—elaborating a definite constitution. For one year the constitutional monarchy constructed by this assembly endured, and then the monarchy collapsed, to give place to a new constitutional convention which decreed France a republic. The explanation of the failure of this experiment, so warmly acclaimed by all the world in 1789, must, like all historical explanations, be clothed ultimately in narrative form. But such a narrative will be clearer and more satisfactory if it is preceded by a more analytic statement of the underlying factors in the situation.

III. LEADERS

Only for certain dialectic structures like that of Marx are important men unimportant. (Of course, in his own life men were singularly important to Marx himself.) Common sense certainly rejects the notion that the character of Louis XVI, for instance, had little to do with the course of the Revolution. The first step in an analysis of the France of 1789 must be a consideration of the men in whom the interests and aspirations of thousands of nameless, and perhaps even insignificant, Frenchmen were centered. "Gods, what a theatre this is for a first-rate character!"[5] wrote Gouverneur Morris, newly arrived from America early in 1789. Morris himself never found that character. Even Mirabeau asserted, with becoming modesty, that "we live in a time of great events but little men."[6] For Maistre the most striking proof that God made the Revolution was the insignificance of the men who seemed to have made it. At any rate, it is clear that in 1789 France was ruled by a monarch incapable of dominating the situation.

As to Louis XVI historians have been in rare agreement. Royalist and republican alike assign to him the ordinary private Christian virtues, and alike they grant that he was a poor king. He was fat, awkward according to the standards of the minuet, slow-witted in a way that showed not merely in his face, but in his gestures, in his whole body. Yet he was not unkingly. He had, on the contrary, a presence invaluable to a constitutional monarch. His manners and his character gave dignity to his bulk. Indeed, bulk and stupidity, properly corseted by etiquette and training, seem in some indefinable way assets for a purely ornamental royalty. Louis was loved by his people, loved as the "Restorer of French Liberty," loved through the imprisonment, trial, and execution brought upon him by a fanatical minority.[7] In all the bitter mouthings against the "tyrant" so fashionable during the Terror there is an added fury of emptiness as if the speakers felt their rhetoric beating against a reality for once simple. Yet Louis's failings were obvious, and not unrelated to his virtues. His emotions were the emotions of a just man. He wished, in the plainest common sense of the phrase, always to do the right thing. But his advisers were numerous, and each gave different advice. Louis thought slowly, took a long time to sort conflicting evidence and arrive at a decision, and then, untrue to the cliché whereby slow men, once they make up their minds, hold fast to a decision, was perfectly capable of abandoning that decision with disconcerting rapidity. Now it is true that will-

[5] G. Morris, *Diary and Letters* (New York, 1888), I, 56.

[6] *Correspondance entre le comte de Mirabeau et le comte de La Marck,* ed. Bacourt (Paris, 1851), I, 423.

[7] The Jacobins did not dare accept the proposed plebescite on Louis's fate in 1793. Saint-Just virtually admitted their reason: "We are asked to refer the matter to the people; what other language would be used if it were wished to save the king?" Saint-Just, *Œuvres complètes,* ed. Vellay (Paris, 1908), I, 397.

ingness to change one's mind is sometimes taken to be the highest mark of statesmanship. But throughout his life Louis always changed his mind at the wrong time. He was one of those men whom folk-wisdom singles out as especially unlucky, as always backing the wrong horse, as born with two left hands, and so on. Yet even folk-wisdom commonly doubts its own explanation of such men.

Louis's failure probably lay as much in this as in anything, that he judged in accordance with the moral categories of Christianity in a time of revolutionary stress when those categories have even less than their customary validity. More simply, he did not understand the character and motives of the men with whom he dealt. Certainly Louis was unlucky to have been king of France during so troubled an epoch; but there is little use in attempting history in the subjunctive, and speculating on whether, had he been a stronger and more intelligent man, the experiment of constitutional monarchy might not have succeeded. It is sufficient to state that Louis's weakness, and especially that weakness which lay in the failure of his understanding, made it almost certain that the experiment could not withstand a determined attack.

Of none of the other members of the court party may it be said that their personalities played a decisive part in events. It is true that the queen had a great influence upon her husband, and that she certainly did not share his hesitations. But the direction in which she pushed him was the direction in which his brothers and, indeed, the whole of the court, were pushing him. Marie Antoinette's true importance lies rather in the fact that she formed an excellent focus for anti-monarchical sentiment. The "Austrian bitch" —her enemies found even lower terms than that for her—had never been popular. Her Austrian origins could easily be reproached her by patriots of the pro-Prussian school. And it was, of course, quite obvious that she would not hesitate to betray France in case of war. She certainly had no great social conscience, and never tried to cultivate popularity among the common people. The famous story of how, told that the people had no bread, she remarked "let them eat cake," though presumably, like most such stories, a fabrication, does—again like most such stories—show how people felt

about her and is therefore in a very real sense "true." Finally, she
was a beautiful woman in a leisured and privileged society. That
is, she must clearly be an adulteress. There is a nice, and pretty
much unsolved, problem for social psychology in the attitude of
the masses towards the sex morals of their betters. French people
undoubtedly expected Versailles to be highly, even heroically, promiscuous in matters of love, much as modern Americans expect
Hollywood to be promiscuous in such matters. Normally it would
seem that the people are pleased enough when concrete evidence
arises that their expectations have been realized. Normally a privileged class would seem to exist partly for the spectacle it affords
to those condemned to duller lives. Yet even in normal times public
opinion will, for reasons difficult to state, occasionally seize upon
one individual and damn him, pillory him for violations of sex
taboo, violations it finds amusing in others. Something like this
happened to Marie Antoinette even before the Revolution. The
affair of the diamond necklace showed that Frenchmen already
thought the worst of their queen. The Revolution found in the brilliant Marie Antoinette a source for effective anti-monarchical propaganda wholly lacking in the stolid Louis.

The great man of the monarchical experiment was Mirabeau.
Yet even Mirabeau failed to mold events, and when he died on
April 2, 1791, the radical movement he had once led had far out-
run his control. "His destiny," concludes a recent biographer, "was
inferior to his genius."[8] It is worth while to try to find the reasons
for this failure, since Mirabeau's is almost a test case for the rôle
of leaders in the French Revolution. He had many and great assets.
He was a large man, with a pockmarked face of compelling ugli-
ness, a grand pair of lungs, and abounding energy. He had the gift
of bringing all the forces of his personality to bear in externalizing,
so to speak, that personality so that it could captivate the common
man. He was an excellent orator, and, what was more important
in the confused early days of the Assembly, a good debater. One
example must suffice. The commons were growing restless during
the long stalemate over the question of organizing the Estates by
order. On May 18, Mirabeau rallied the doubtful in a speech full

[8] L. Barthou, *Mirabeau* (Paris, 1920), 315.

of salient strokes like this: "Already people are saying that it is better to accept voting by order than to expose ourselves to a schism (which amounts to saying, *let us separate for fear of separation*)."[9]

Mirabeau was a political realist. He knew the value as well as the danger of abstract terms in politics. There is no sign that he was ever the dupe of the fashionable theories of the Rights of Man; but he was aware that only by some concession to fashion could he attain specific reforms. He was willing to have a Declaration of Rights attached to the constitution, but only after the constitution had been made. To build such a declaration out of thin air was dangerous. It amounted to denying, as he later said, that France was "an old nation," that it had "a preëxisting government, a preëxisting king, preëxisting prejudices."[10] He saw very clearly, indeed, that the first few months of the Revolution had swept away all the complicated checks and balances of the old régime, its guilds and corporations, its administrative hierarchy, its feudal limitations. He saw that some group within the French state would fall heir to these powers. He wished that heir to be the crown, governing in close alliance with an enlightened bourgeoisie. He saw that, thanks to a natural distrust of the executive produced by the very fact that the movement was a movement against the crown, thanks also to the prestige of Montesquieu's theory of the separation of powers, the heir actually was an unwieldy assembly of 1,200 men. Power finally, he feared, would go to the most determined, the most ruthless, the most fanatically democratic group represented in that assembly. To prevent that, he wished by introducing ministerial responsibility to allow executive and legislature to coöperate, to permit an able minister to maintain the true balance of power between the central government and local assemblies. This was a moderate program, and one very close to what the average French bourgeois wanted.

Mirabeau's liabilities are as clear as his assets. He had had a shady career under the old régime. He had been a disobedient son—always a most serious offense in a land where moral traces of the Roman *paterfamilias* still exist—he had carried adultery to the un-

[9] P. Buchez et P. Roux, *Histoire parlementaire de la Révolution française* (Paris, 1834), I, 402.
[10] Speech of August 17, 1789, *Moniteur* (*réimpression*) I, 338; Barthou, *Mirabeau*, 177.

pardonable length of elopement, he had had suspicious relations with the world of stock-jobbing and international finance, he was known for his debts and his vices. In other times and places, all this need not have hurt him. Fox was loved for some of the things for which Mirabeau was distrusted. But the French Revolution had from its start a Puritanical tinge. Mirabeau's reputation as a rake handicapped him at every stage. Again, though he was obviously the natural leader, in the parliamentary sense, of the National Assembly, that body was never willing to trust him. In spite of his eloquent opposition, it decided in November, 1789, that the functions of minister and deputy were incompatible. Nor could Mirabeau find solid support in the king, to whom he later turned. Louis secretly corresponded with Mirabeau, and paid him for his advice. But he did not use it. Suspected by both sides, Mirabeau dragged out the last few months of his life in a pretty complete political impotence. His fate suggests the limitations, during so unusual a time as that of the French Revolution, of even extraordinary political sagacity. Had his moral reputation been better, had his king been more intelligent and more determined, had Lafayette and a few others been willing to coöperate, and had he lived, Mirabeau might have saved France from the madness of the Terror. Yet after all, the impression remains that Mirabeau failed precisely because of his common sense. It is not always true that in the kingdom of the blind the one-eyed man is king.

Only one other figure seemed for a time to be capable of sustaining the monarchical experiment. Yet Lafayette was to the keenest of his contemporaries never more than a man of straw. "He is on the other side of the line where one is marked an intelligent man. In his desires and methods of distinguishing himself there is something learned, acquired. What he does seems not to belong to his true nature. He seems always to be following advice."[11] His romantic American experience, his carefully cultivated opposition to the court, his dignity and presence raised him high in the eyes of the people. But he was no orator, and his influence in the Assembly was slight. Outside, his position as commander-in-chief of the Parisian national guard gave him a moment of pres-

11 Talleyrand, Mémoires, ed. Broglie (Paris, 1891), I, 69.

tige. He had no very clear ideas as to his political goal, and was as much lacking in power of decision as Louis himself. He had a simple love of glory which his enemies called vanity. Witness the curious letter he wrote Washington from Albany in 1778, complaining bitterly, not that the failure of his Canadian expedition to materialize would hurt the American cause, but that all Europe would laugh at him, ingloriously rusting away on the Hudson.[12] Had he been able to get along with Mirabeau, something might have been done. Mirabeau's brains and Lafayette's prestige seem a combination capable of altering the course even of so fatally mad a movement as the French Revolution. Mirabeau was willing, and made advances. But Lafayette was probably envious of Mirabeau's superior powers; he himself asserts that he was shocked by Mirabeau's "immorality."[13]

IV. PARTY ORGANIZATION

Neither king nor queen, Mirabeau nor Lafayette, nor any other outstanding person dominated the situation in the early days of the Revolution. What they were and what they did are important, actually, only as indications of the failure of the constitutional monarchy. It remains to consider another element in the situation: the National Assembly, its organization, its procedure, its parties. Between the nameless mass of Frenchmen and the few figures singled out as conspicuous leaders, the deputies form a natural link. They are not quite nameless, some, indeed, are well-known, and they are direct participants in events, not mere spectators.

Much of what has been written about this Assembly is, of course, true. The traditional view runs somewhat as follows: Its membership of 1,200 was much too large for proper deliberations. Neither at Versailles nor at Paris, whither it moved after the "October days," was it ideally housed either for acoustical or for ceremonial purposes. It was a noisy, disorderly body, disrespectful of its own rules of procedure, and usually poorly presided over by a succession of presidents whose terms were too brief for them to learn their job. It was the victim of the rule opening its galleries to the public,

[12] Quoted in B. Whitlock, *Lafayette* (New York, 1929), I, 127-128.
[13] Lafayette, *Mémoires* (Paris, 1837), II, 365.

to whom it permitted all kinds of manifestations of approval or disapproval, and of its absurd patience with almost daily popular delegations. Its debates were often no debates at all, but a mere succession of dull speeches, prepared in advance and read by their authors from a central pulpit. Its members were mostly lawyers, at least so far as the Third Estate went, and educated in an apparently futile dialectic based on the natural rights philosophy. All of its members were soaked in that philosophy, and therefore incapacitated for hard, practical politics. All were inexperienced, for the old régime had been governed, not by the people, but by a bureaucracy. Finally, the assembly never succeeded in adapting itself to the two-party system orthodox in England. Its party divisions were numerous and unstable, their natural development checked but not prevented by the current philosophical notion that parties are factions, and dangerous to the state.

There must, however, occur to a modern historian at least two qualifying remarks which considerably alter the significance of the traditional picture sketched above. First, it is pretty clear now that parliamentary government never really worked in the way hopeful nineteenth-century political writers assumed that it worked. The real work of government, under the parliamentary as under any other system, is done in the direct contact of man and man, in committee, in informal talk, in a hundred ways, and a hundred places, not all of which are dignified. Through some variant of the party system, with caucuses, local committees and bosses this *immediacy* of personal government is possible over the wide area of the modern state. The parliament itself is useful, first, as providing a means of deciding peacefully what group of men are to do the actual governing, second, as the decorative, but none the less indispensable, medium by which the actions of the true governors are dramatized, made part of the psychological reality which is the general will. Now in the French Revolution parliaments commonly failed to perform the first function. But the important reasons for this failure are to be found largely outside the field of of parliamentary organization. The second function they performed very well indeed, all the more because of the non-British features of their procedure previously outlined. The real work of the Constituent Assembly was not done in its formal sessions. These, with their read speeches, delegations, perpetual hubbub gave just the dramatic touch the French wanted. Abstract ideas expressed in the Assembly were a happy complement to the quite concrete interests which were struggling for the real government of France. No doubt certain features of the organization of the Assembly—notably the uncontrolled behavior of the public in its galleries—did contribute to the failure of the monarchical experiment. But their importance has been much exaggerated by historians who take parliamentary government at its face value—in English.

Secondly, the two-party system may now be seen to have been an ideal generalization derived from certain dramatic moments of English and American history—the struggle between federalist and anti-federalists, the followers of Gladstone and those of Disraeli. Even in Anglo-Saxon countries the ideal has been altered by "third parties," blocs, bolts and other variations. The almost immediate adoption by the National Assembly of a rough organization according to groups, and the subsequent recurrence of this method in most countries under parliamentary rule, certainly suggest that the group system is at least a viable one. It may well be argued that if the main function of a parliament is not to govern, but to provide a focus for public opinion for the guidance of the governors, then the group system, since it frankly accepts existing diversity of opinion, is better than a two-party system which tries to gloss over such a diversity. It is true that the French revolutionists were always condemning, while practicing, political organization by what they called "faction"; but the real function of parties was almost as much misunderstood by eighteenth-century publicists in England and America as in France.

Certainly if the National Assembly be regarded as primarily a body for discussion, there can be no point in calling it inexperienced. Frenchmen had been discussing politics for years under the stimulating irregularity of the inefficient despotism of the old régime. Nor, if one considers the effective way in which elections to the Third Estate were managed, the capable negotiations which brought the clergy over to the commons, the successful defiance of the king, the early organization of propaganda, is one inclined to deny the presence in the Assembly of many skillful practitioners of the art of government. But in the National Assembly—and this is a fact of great importance—the most able organizers, the most practical politicians, were either identical in person with the most extreme and violent political theorists, or else worked with these theorists in the same group. The great paradox of the French Revolution lies here: That until the fall of Robespierre in 1794 the most tender-minded were consistently the most hard-headed; the most doctrinaire, the most pliable. Historians, as a class rightly distrustful of paradox, have concluded, in spite of the evidence, that the combination is impossible. Royalist historians in general conclude that the revolutionists were impractical theorists, and fail to explain their success, except as the accidental triumph of villainy; republican historians conclude that the revolutionists were practical, far seeing men, and fail to explain either their ideology or their failure in 1794, except that the latter is always attributable to the villainy of their enemies. A true explanation must accept the facts, even though the facts are shocking to preconceived notions.

There is certainly little trace of political acumen in the extreme Right of the Assembly, and in the court party which it represented. Its ablest orator was the Abbé Maury, son of a cobbler, conservative with the interests of a self-made man, a good fighter, but utterly tactless and without any program. The Vicomte de Mirabeau, from his corpulence called Barrel Mirabeau, was an able obstructionist, especially when interrupting his brilliant brother. Outside the Assembly the queen, the king's brothers, most of the Versailles nobility formed a group with a definite aim: no concessions. It was a group scornful of propaganda, for the very reason that it denied public opinion, in the modern sense, any place in government. It was, of course, destined to failure from the simple fact that public opinion was already in 1789 a factor in government. Many of its members lived up to the middle-class notion of an aristocrat; that is, they were proud, haughty, dissolute, contemptuous of those immediately beneath them in the social scale. But as a class they were hardly the vicious and irresponsible tyrants revolutionary propaganda made them out. They were certainly among the most intellectual of aristocracies. It may well be argued that part of their impotence lies here. Morally they were no doubt as willing to stoop to low tricks as their opponents, but intellectually they could not degrade themselves to revolutionary tastes, could not make their tricks effective. A glance at one of their newspapers —the *Actes des Apôtres,* for instance—is convincing. Clever, witty, learned in an unpedantic way, bitter, indecent, violent, but never vulgar, it can have done the party nothing but harm and certainly made no converts. An epigram never yet shook a conviction.[14]

A similar ineptness for practical politics runs through the next parliamentary group, the advocates of a constitutional monarchy on the English pattern, with a House of Lords and a House of Commons, ministerial responsibility, a strong royal prerogative. Composed chiefly of liberal noblemen like Clermont-Tonnerre, and well-balanced, essentially reflective and critical bourgeois like Mounier and Mallet du Pan, this small group lacked brilliance, lacked roots in the country, and suffered from the accusation of Anglomania, no longer a compliment in a nation becoming daily more aware of its own civilizing mission. From this group have come many of the soundest contemporary commentaries on the revolution; but the comments were written from exile, and the wisdom of the commentators was characteristically divorced from action. Indeed, one consistent cause for the impotence of parliamentary opposition during the whole course of the Revolution was the emigration, at first, certainly, without the menace of the guillotine, of many of the abler moderates. The Anglophil or "constitutional" group suffered especially in this way, its ablest leader, Mounier, emigrating in 1789.

The majority of the Assembly may be classed simply as the patriotic party. At the start it formed a solid body against the court, and won its aim; France was to have a new constitution. Very shortly the Anglophil constitutionals broke away in opposition. The patriots, however, were at least united in favor of a unicameral government. But there is not much point in talking about a patriotic party in 1790 and 1791 as if it were a unified whole. That party

[14] The first number of the *Actes des Apôtres* is November, 1789, the last October, 1791. The last numbers are more serious and less witty than the first, and much very sentimental poetry about the queen, the old days, etc., has crept in. The romantic legend of the lost cause is already beginning.

had at least three fairly clear subdivisions: a majority group of prosperous, educated bourgeois, definitely children of the age (the philosophical) but still cautious, moderate, by no means doctrinaire, for it included men like Lanjuinais, Siéyès, Lafayette, Talleyrand; a smaller and more radical group, headed by the famous triumvirate of Barnave, du Port, and Charles de Lameth; a left wing group, not yet powerful, but with its mind made up, with increasingly good connections with Paris municipal politicians, a group containing men like Prieur (de la Marne), Dubois-Crancé, Pétion, and Robespierre, already Jacobins in the making.

Now thanks to the work of the *sociétés de pensée* and similar clubs, there was already in existence a rudimentary political organization, covering most of the country, an organization which was potentially a powerful political machine. The next two years saw the capture of that organization by the above-mentioned left wing of the Assembly, and its use to bring pressure on the Assembly itself to secure radical legislation. This fact is one of the keys to the failure of the monarchical experiment.[15] No other group succeeded in building up such organized support in the country at large. The conservatives seem to have assumed that local government would continue in the hands of professional agents of the central government, and therefore failed to see the necessity of building up an organization independent of the governmental hierarchy. But this hierarchy, like most of the old régime, was swept away in 1789, and a very decentralized system of local government substituted. Even had the Assembly tried to restore something like the old professional centralized bureaucracy, real power must have gone, for some time at least, to the only national organization existing during the inevitable hiatus—and that organization was the network of political societies known as the Jacobin clubs, a network which can be traced back to the *sociétés de pensée*. The conservatives, then, were hardly aware of the necessity of using new methods until it was too late. When they attempted to organize, they failed

15 Albert Mathiez, who always fell into a fury at the notion of a deliberately planned revolutionary campaign in 1789, yet admitted that the bourgeois took over the control of these local societies from the nobility of the Gown (members of the *parlements,* judges) at that time. *Annales historiques de la Révolution française* (1931), VIII, 451.

completely. Witness the moderate Friends of Peace and similar monarchical societies organized in 1791 to hold back the republican movement. All display excellent intentions and political ineptness. The Paris Club attempted charitable distribution of bread during a food shortage. They were accused of trying to corrupt the poor, of "chucking bread down our throats as if we were dogs."[16] Had they not done this, they would have been accused of stony indifference to the lot of the poor. All sorts of pressure were brought to bear on the authorities, and most of these monarchical clubs were closed by official order, often for "disturbing the peace."

The Jacobin organization, then, was first in the field, and never abandoned this dominating position until, with the fall of Robespierre, the great experiment of the Revolution came to an end. It will be necessary to recur to the rôle of the Jacobins during the Terror. Here it will suffice to consider them briefly as a pressure group. The transition from the *sociétés de pensée* to the Jacobin machine was effected through the Club Breton, an informal caucus of radical Breton deputies to the States-General, which soon absorbed other radical deputies, began to take in outsiders, and when the Assembly moved to Paris, joined with Parisian radicals to form the Society of Friends of the Constitution, called the Jacobin club because it met in the library of a Jacobin monastery. The Paris Jacobins early began to correspond with literary societies in the larger provincial towns, urging common action on the *assignats*, on the new religious laws, and so on. These provincial societies, anxious to be as Parisian as possible, soon took over the title of Friends of the Constitution. New societies were founded, and the whole tied together by formal affiliation, by correspondence, junketing trips, and district meetings into an effective network over France. The Jacobins very soon displayed in actual practice many of the political arts familiar to the twentieth century: highly efficient use of various instruments of propaganda, the newspapers, the pamphlet, the pulpit, the theater, even the school; direct interference in elections, all the easier because the electoral assemblies deliberated in public; indirect pressure of all sorts directed towards influencing the vote of the deputies in Paris and the members of local governing boards;

[16] A. Aulard, *La Société des Jacobins de Paris* (Paris, 1889-1897), II, 134.

use of violence, especially in street manifestations, breaking windows of monarchical clubs, beating obnoxious conservatives, and so on; outright nullification of laws disagreeable to them, especially laws protecting the Roman Catholic clergy; and other acts which will be recognized by the student of the Anti-Corn Law League, the Ku Klux Klan, and Tammany Hall.

The actual composition of these Jacobin clubs varied surprisingly little, so far as the social strata from which they were recruited goes, during the whole course of the Revolution. Variation as to the individuals who made them up there was, though perhaps rather less than is commonly thought. A kernel of some one-third to one-half of the membership of the average club remained through all the vicissitudes of monarchy and republic. The membership over the whole period was consistently middle class, with a sprinkling of nobles and clergy, and an increasingly large, but never dominant, representation from the artisan class. These Jacobins, by and large, were prosperous, educated, quite ordinary business and professional men; a study of the amount they paid in direct taxes under the old régime shows that they formed a body definitely more wealthy than the average of their communities.[17]

What did these men want? To what end was this elaborate and effective organization directed? The answer surely is, to the creation of a French republic. Aulard, who as first professor of the history of the Revolution to hold a chair at the Sorbonne gave a decisive direction to the work of the "official" school, insisted all his life that no one wanted a republic in France until the flight of the king in June, 1791, that the republic was not planned and fought for by men brought up in the political philosophy of the century, that, in fact, the republic was an accident, the outgrowth of Louis's stupidity and the French failure in the war of 1792. Obviously the emotions of the official historians are strongly, if to an outsider rather inexplicably, bound up with this thesis, as though an accidental republic were more pure, more desirable than a republic achieved by political intrigue. The First Republic, according to the freethinker Aulard, must enjoy the prestige of a virgin birth. To one not sharing these emotions, the evidence of the words

[17] C. Brinton, *The Jacobins* (New York, 1930), Appendix II.

and acts of the Jacobins does not sustain Aulard. Much, though not all, of the quarrel here is a matter of words. Aulard himself admits that the word "republican" was applied to all sorts of Frenchmen long before 1789, and explains that "there had formed, among these Frenchmen who did not want a Republic, a republican state of mind, which was expressed in republican words and attitudes."[18]

Doubtless few members of the Jacobin Clubs in 1790 were prepared to overthrow the existing monarchy. Yet they already had a program involving the elimination of all civil and political distinctions, a lay state, lay education, legislative supremacy in government, and most of the rest of what by 1848 passed as good republican tradition. The point is that in 1790 their heads and hearts were already filled with aims quite inconsistent with the perpetuation in office of a monarch like Louis, reverently Catholic, devoted to his proud and headstrong wife, determined at bottom, in spite of his hesitancies, his indolence, his dislike of ceremony, his very real sympathy for his people, to be a king. The monarchical experiment did not fail solely because of the war, or Louis's indecisions, or the evil plots of the former privileged classes. The experiment failed even more because a well-organized pressure group very early decided that it could not get what it wanted under the constitutional monarchy. Had Louis been willing to turn Voltairean as regards the church, to accept the position of first *citizen* of a land of equals, to repudiate his family and his friends, had he, in short, turned Jacobin, the Jacobins might have accepted the monarchy. In reality, the Jacobins were almost from the first working towards a republic.

V. THE PEOPLE

There still remains, in this brief sketch of the setting for the monarchical experiment of 1789-1792, to consider the people at large, the nameless millions who made France. What did they want? How were their desires to influence the situation?[19] From these

---

[18] A. Aulard, *Histoire politique de la Révolution française* (Paris, 1901), 6.

[19] This chapter will not attempt a survey of the condition of France in 1789. That will be done in the preceding volume of this series, dealing with the period 1763-1789. The problem here is simply, how far did the condition of France affect the situation after the successful formation of the National Assembly?

millions one may subtract the 300,000 noblemen. *As a class* they were no longer seriously to influence the Revolution from within after the summer of 1789. They had had their moment of importance. In the complex goings and comings, the negotiations of all sorts which produced the National Assembly out of the States-General, a critical factor had been the indifference of many of the provincial noblemen towards the fate of their order. Throughout the century the dislike of these country noblemen, most of them poor and unknown, had been centered on the nobility of Versailles, resplendent and outwardly prosperous. Many of these poorer noblemen came to feel that the domination of the Third Estate was no worse than that of Versailles.[20] Many such men acquiesced willingly in the absorption of their order in the National Assembly. But once absorbed, they were impotent.

The great majority of Frenchmen—from twenty to twenty-two millions out of twenty-six millions—were engaged in agriculture.[21] They are commonly lumped together as "peasants"; but the word should connote an occupation, not a class in the Marxian sense. Some of the peasants were already capitalist landowners, to whom the Revolution gave an excellent chance for expansion. Nearly half of them owned some land, though often an amount inadequate to support themselves. Such peasants supplemented their income by cottage industry or by hiring themselves out as laborers. At the bottom of the social scale were a certain number of landless laborers. There undoubtedly existed a rural proletariat in France in 1789, though it is doubtful whether it was relatively as large as the English rural proletariat of the time. Now in terms of purely material aims, the Revolution meant very different things to different groups among the peasantry. To most peasants it meant the abolition of the annoying remnants of the feudal system. As the news of the great Revolution at Versailles seeped into the villages, the event was universally interpreted as meaning the abolition of feudal obligations. A short, sharp rural revolution followed in July, 1789, when in all parts of France isolated but somehow united

[20] One of them, a deputy, wrote, "all in all, I prefer that Coucaud (i.e., John Jones) should consider himself my equal, than to see a great noble regard me his inferior, and assimilate me to the people he pays and feeds." Ferrières, *Correspondance*, 120.
[21] E. Levasseur, *La population française* (Paris, 1889), I, 217,226.

risings of peasants burnt châteaux, destroyed title deeds, shot formerly protected game with a sense of joyful release. It is true that the National Assembly, in setting the sanction of law on this abolition of feudal dues, distinguished between dues originating in violence done the individual, or *personal* dues, which were abolished without compensation to the owner, and dues originating merely in feudal land law, or *real* dues, which were abolished subject to compensation to the owner in a series of installment payments. But here as elsewhere in the Revolution, the important question is, what was actually done? The answer is that the law was usually disregarded, that the peasants simply did not pay.[22] There were sporadic rural uprisings in 1790 and 1791, some of which were protests against this legislation. But on the whole it is safe to say that rural discontent with respect to feudal dues was not a factor in making the rural classes desire the downfall of the monarchy.

To some peasants the sale of the lands of the clergy, which were confiscated by the Assembly to fill the deficit and put on the market late in 1790, gave an opportunity to enrich themselves, to lift themselves to the level of the bourgeois. No doubt to many of these peasants events like the flight of the king to Varennes, the bitterness of the royalists against the extreme and increasingly successful Jacobins brought the fear that even a moderate reaction would mean the loss of their new lands, that the only safe thing for them was to follow the lead of the urban radicals. Yet, in the absence of facts, of a study of the opinions of these rich peasants, the above is a mere deduction. It would be at least as safe to insist that these men were grateful to the monarchical revolution for giving them their chance, that they had no complaint as to the way the public sales of these lands were run, that they would naturally distrust the egalitarian aims of the extremists, that, unless they were very sure indeed that only a republic could guarantee them their lands, they would prefer a monarchy.

On the other hand, it is clear that the rural populations were almost closed to the world of ideas. Village *cahiers* almost wholly eschew, not only metaphysics, but all general ideas; they demand concrete, specific reforms—abolition of various dues, which are

[22] S. Herbert, *The Fall of Feudalism in France* (London, 1920), 175.

named (almost never do they ask for the abolition of the feudal system as a whole), abolition of game laws, monopolies, and so on. The Jacobins of the towns were always talking of the necessity of "enlightening" the countryside; during the Terror they felt obliged to send "missionaries" to explain to the country people just what the republic meant. A special newspaper, *La feuille villageoise,* was devoted by certain Paris radicals to the task of awakening the peasants. Its first number, in an address to the "virtuous people of the countryside," lists among the difficulties facing any such republican missionary work "your lack of preliminary knowledge, which obliged us to go back to the very elements of ideas and grammar."[23] Not only was this peasantry, rich and poor alike, attached to old habits, land hungry but not daring nor speculative, financially cautious, saving, intellectually torpid, but it was loyal to Roman Catholic Christianity as seen in the parish church and the village priest. The corruption of the upper clergy, which so scandalized the radical, literate townsmen, was hardly known to the peasants. When tithes were abolished with the rest of the feudal system—and abolished without compensation—the peasant had no longer any reason to quarrel with his priest. For centuries the rites of the church had touched with grace and eternity the brief moments of crisis in peasant life—birth, marriage, death. Rural France was Christian, not in any profound theological sense, nor at all heroically, but Christian in the deep routine of unimportant things.[24] The Jacobins began very early to show their animosity towards the church, their desire to destroy it. Here is an added reason why the peasantry should not as a whole welcome further revolution after 1789. To sum up, it may be concluded that the peasantry did not, as a group, play an important part in the overthrow of the monarchy. By the summer of 1789 they had secured their *material* aims; there is no sign that they were capable of nourishing *spiritual* aims towards a republic. In the long run, the peasantry was to exercise an undoubted influence on nineteenth century France. But on the

[23] *La feuille villageoise,* no. I, September 29, 1791.
[24] P. de la Gorce, *Histoire religieuse de la Révolution française* (1917-18), I, 415 ff. This book is commonly dismissed by republican, anti-clerical historians with something between a sneer and an apology on the ground that its author is a Catholic. For the view that Christianity was but shallowly rooted among the peasantry, see A. Aulard, *Christianity and the French Revolution,* trans. Lady Frazer (London, 1927),

foundation of the Jacobin republic their influence was negligible, if not, indeed, negative.

The urban proletariat—the "working class"—was numerically insignificant, either as compared with the peasantry of 1789 or with the French urban proletariat of today. Industry was barely leaving what Mr. Mumford calls the eotechnic stage. Important industries like that of silk at Lyons made no great use even of the large workshop. Yet in many—perhaps most—industries there was already in 1789 a gap between masters and men. Paris with some 650,000 inhabitants, Marseilles with 90,000, Bordeaux with 76,000, Rouen with 72,000, and some dozen other considerable cities, numbered a proletarian population capable of making itself a force.[25] Now these workingmen of the cities, though they were perhaps almost as illiterate in a bookish way as their brothers of the country, had at least the urban facility with catchwords and fashions. They had that capacity for mass suggestion and mass movement which seems especially high among French crowds. They had, or were soon to have, a definite grievance against the monarchical experiment. For in the name of liberty the old guilds were destroyed, and, by the Le Chapelier law of June 14, 1791, combinations of all kinds among workmen, and strikes, were prohibited. This law, put through in the spirit of nineteenth century capitalism, had an ascertainable effect in creating a class-conscious workers' group hostile to the monarchy.[26] These workers suffered as a class more than any other from seasonal variations in employment and prices, from actual food shortages, from all the dislocations of economic life, frequently enough in normal times, but tremendously intensified by the uncertainties, and even by the plots of the Revolution. They formed the necessary element in street-risings and manifestations. But it is important to note that this urban proletariat was not in itself an active, creative, guiding element in the downfall of the monarchy. The republican leaders were almost all bourgeois. Their aims were a middle-class republic resting on free competition and natural rights, including the right of private property. They organized the workmen in various popular

[25] E. Levasseur, *Population française*, 227, 228 and note 1.
[26] E. Soreau, "La Loi Le Chapelier," *Annales historiques de la Révolution française* (1931), VIII, 310.

societies, especially in Paris, but they were careful to maintain the distinction between their own Jacobin club, middle class and indeed upper middle class in membership, and these clubs of humble folk.[27] Later on, the rôle of these workingmen becomes in part an active one. But it is safe to conclude that, though they helped overthrow the monarchy, the impulsion did not come from them, that their condition is not in itself an important element in the failure of the monarchical experiment.

There remains only the bourgeoisie. Now the Revolution of 1789 was made by the middle class—aided, indeed, by members of the upper classes converted to the new ideas. The writers and the talkers of the literary societies, the deputies of the Third Estate, the local leaders, all were working for a bourgeois domination, for that triumph of natural rights over prescription which meant the triumph of the business man over the gentleman. But surely by the summer of 1789 these men had all they could reasonably want, had at least an immediate and peaceful prospect of such reasonable satisfaction? Their pride need no longer suffer from their inferior place in the hierarchy of classes. In the eyes of the law, there were no longer nobles and commoners, but only Frenchmen. In eyes more discerning of simple things than those of the law, a marquis was no doubt still a marquis, though he were called Motier instead of Lafayette, Riquetti instead of Mirabeau. Perhaps even the distinction of citizen-king was an invidious one among freemen. If the French middle class was to be moved to overthrow the limited monarchy, it must be either through pressure of circumstances or through some such motives as envy of the upper classes and the monarch or attachment to abstract principles of equality and republicanism. Certainly no crude economic motive is discernible. The French middle class had already in 1789 secured the reality or the promise of economic reforms sufficient to allow business to expand freely: a uniform system of taxation; abolition of the old guilds, internal tariffs, and other survivals of medieval restraint of trade; complete freedom of competition in trade and industry (patents and copyrights, of course, protecting for a period the

---

[27] A. Mathiez, "Marat père des sociétés fraternelles," *Annales Révolutionnaires* (1908), I, 661.

results of mechanical or literary invention); individual ownership of property, stocks and bonds as well as land, incorporated into the metaphysical bases of the government in the shape of the Declaration of the Rights of Man; and even so up-to-date a business man's appurtenance as a uniform protective tariff.[28] By the time the Constituent Assembly had finished its work, it had elaborated a code perfectly suited to the modern business man, the economic man of Adam Smith and Karl Marx.

To sum up what may be called a static view of the situation at the outset of the monarchical experiment: there was a disgruntled but ineffective minority of former nobles and other *privilégiés*, a mass of land-hungry and ignorant peasants with no very defined *political* aims, an irresponsible though numerically small group of town laborers almost as ignorant politically as the peasants, but far more easily organized, a middle class which had won the peaceful revolution of May-June at Versailles, and which was about to make over the kingdom in its own image. There would seem every reason, in 1789, to predict the success of the monarchical experiment. The first step, proverbially the most difficult, had not been so hard after all. No supremely great leader, it is true, had yet appeared; but that was perhaps a good sign—the Revolution wanted no Cromwell. There were plenty of troublesome problems, especially financial ones, but the whole country was behind its representatives, willing to trust them to solve these problems. There was in the early days of the Revolution an almost universal access of hope, a communion of joy and optimism extending far down into social strata quite ignorant of the reasons for their elation. The new régime was starting with a tremendous fund of popular goodwill to support it. Indeed, at the time, foreign observers, who might be supposed to possess a certain detachment, almost unanimously agreed that the Revolution was over, that it had done its work. Only Burke, very early indeed, predicted otherwise. He thought that certain men in France, men of political importance, had set out to build a perfect republic on a plan deduced from abstract principles of right and wrong, that these men were quite willing to

---

[28] This tariff of March 15, 1791, of course abrogated the special treaty of 1786 with England, which had seemed to Pitt an entering wedge for something like free trade.

wreck an imperfect but attainable limited monarchy for the sake of a perfect and unattainable philosophic Utopia. Possibly Burke's reasons for his prediction were sound; possibly his prediction was simply lucky. Certainly the only group in France that seemed both discontented and competent in the sphere of politics was the Jacobin group. They alone seemed capable of disturbing the balance of interests and institutions in the process of building a successful constitutional monarchy.

But no static analysis can explain the fall of the monarchy. It is necessary to consider the complicated pattern of the events of the next three years, to trace the impact of ideas and interests on the situation evolving out of the pacific revolution of Versailles, to consider in detail the effect on the social equilibrium of certain key measures passed by the National Assembly, finally, to weigh the influence on events in France of events outside of France. For France, unfortunately, was ultimately, indissolubly, bound to the Western world. The great experiment, to the confusion of subsequent sociologists, was not to be made in isolation, was, indeed, quite inextricably to mingle itself with older and unexperimental realities.

Chapter Two

THE MONARCHICAL EXPERIMENT

I. THE CRISIS OF 1789

BY THE FIRST of July, 1789, the States-General, now become by the peaceful revolution of May-June the National Assembly, was ready to give its undivided attention to the "regeneration" of France. Its attention was soon distracted by the violence which culminated in the fall of the Bastille. At the very outset of the monarchical experiment something went wrong.

The facts are as clear as they will ever be. The wheat crop of 1788 had been poor—and wheat in France was the indispensable food of the people, by no mere metaphor the staff of life. The political uncertainties of the winter of 1788-89 had produced commercial hesitations. By the summer of 1789 there was a shortage of food over much of France, high prices, bewilderment, and in some places active discontent at the prospect of complete freedom of the grain trade. In July bread in Paris cost 4 sous the pound, double what was considered the normal price. There is then a genuine background of economic misery in 1789, affecting especially the lower classes in the cities and towns. M. Lefebvre regards this fact as absolutely decisive. "If bread had been cheap, the brutal intervention of the people, which was indispensable to assure the destruction of the old régime, would perhaps not have occurred, and the bourgeoisie would have triumphed less easily."[1] Protests indeed had already come from Paris. As early as April a riot had cost the life of the manufacturer Reveillon.

It is also clear that an extraordinary concentration of troops was going on about Paris and Versailles. By July 13 there had arrived in the region some eighteen or twenty thousand men in excess of the

[1] G. Lefebvre, *Documents relatifs à l'histoire des subsistances . . . à Bergues* (Lille, 1914), I, xxxviii.

normal garrison of Paris.[2] Many of these soldiers were foreigners little susceptible to revolutionary propaganda. This movement of troops provoked the wildest alarm among the patriotic party. The rumor spread that Louis was planning a military *coup d'état* to dissolve the National Assembly. Good republican historians have since fixed that rumor into their pattern of historical fact, and still commonly assert that Louis intended violence against the Assembly as a whole. On July 8, Mirabeau in the Assembly brought the rumor into full political action by denouncing the troop movements and requesting the king to stop them. The king replied that the military measures were designed to protect the Assembly, not to menace it. On July 11, Necker was summarily dismissed, and a new ministry constituted with such obviously court party men as Breteuil and Broglie.

The dismissal of Necker, unless Louis intended an immediate *coup d'état* against the Assembly, was a blunder. Necker still symbolized for the French people the hope of a new order. His dismissal, following on the concentration of troops in the region of Paris, was taken by the agitated patriots to mean that the king was determined to prevent by force the establishment of such an order. Force was the reply evoked by the threat of force. For the next few days Paris was pandemonium. On the 12th a great procession carried crape-covered busts of Necker and of Orléans (the popular duke was said to have been banished) through the streets to the Place Louis XV, where the crowd jostled the reluctant soldiers of Besenval. Normal business was suspended. Crowds still rather excited than nasty in mood paraded up and down the streets, were held up in little eddies of excited debate at cafés and public squares, filled the garden of the Palais Royal, broke windows, jostled sedan chairs, fêted and cheered such soldiers as would declare against the king. Hundreds of nameless but scarcely unpremeditated agitators held forth wherever listeners could be got. The old feudal structure of city government broke down. Police power there was none. Someone started the tocsin, age-old signal of alarm, and soon all the bell towers of Paris were repeating it. The electors of Paris, the

[2] P. Caron, "La tentative de contre-révolution de juin-juillet 1789," *Revue d'histoire moderne* (1906), VIII, 14. Some excitable patriots at the time estimated as many as 80,000!

official college which had made final choice of Parisian deputies to the Third Estate, met on their own initiative, and took revolutionary steps to form a bourgeois police force—the famous national guard—and a new city government. But these steps could not be effective until the existing crisis was over. Meanwhile the crowd was milling about aimlessly, not too furiously, no doubt mostly to its own great enjoyment. Somehow—probably at the instigation of the patriots at Versailles—from the hundreds of cross-purposes and no-purposes animating it there emerged a single dramatic aim: To the Bastille![3]

The Bastille, long used as a prison, was a feudal fortress on the eastern edge of the city, between the old walls and the newer suburbs. Popular imagination and philosophic propaganda had already made it a symbol of royal tyranny. In its dungeons were supposed to be languishing, consigned by *lettres de cachet*, the virtuous defenders of an oppressed people. On July 14 it was held by Governor de Launay, with a garrison of eighty retired soldiers and thirty Swiss. A crowd began gathering in the small square before its outer gate early in the morning. Deputations passed to and fro. De Launay consented to withdraw the cannon from the walls, now manned only by troops with small arms. The crowd grew in numbers and in excitement. De Launay was on the point of surrendering the fortress, and had there been an obvious authority at hand— had the provisional government of Paris been more enterprising— bloodshed might have been avoided. But arms and munitions had been procured by a raiding party at the Invalides. The whole quarter was black with people pushing towards the great gate. Adventurous patriots climbed up and cut the chains to the drawbridge, giving the attackers access to the outer court. The inner court, the fortress itself, was still unforced, was, indeed, impregnable save to heavy artillery, which the besiegers did not have. The defenders apparently first fired upon the crowd in the courtyard, and attempted to hem them in by raising the drawbridge again. The Bastille cannon came into play, and the crowd (a remarkably able

[6] The schoolbook story of how Camille Desmoulins climbed to a table top in a café in the Palais Royal, stuck a horse-chestnut leaf in his hat and cried "à la Bastille," has now gone the way of most such good old tales. Historians admit that no one knows who started the attack on the Bastille. R. Farge, "C. Desmoulins au jardin du Palais royal," *Annales révolutionnaires* (1914), VII, 646.

crowd, for the cowards and the incompetent had fled by now) sustained the attack from places of cover, and actually brought up some small cannon. De Launay, despairing of relief, consented to parley with self-appointed leaders of the mob, and finally to surrender on terms of safe withdrawal for himself and his men. The gates were opened, the attackers swept into the inner court, and, uncontrolled by their leaders, seized de Launay and shortly afterwards murdered him. Some hundred of the attackers appear to have been killed. The dungeon gave up seven victims of tyranny, five ordinary criminals and two madmen. No patriotic men of letters were to be found among the prisoners.

July 14, 1789, is a sacred day in the cult of the present republic. But it is a little surprising to see how rapidly the consecration of the attack on the Bastille came, how soon the somewhat sordid facts were transmuted into heroic truths. Willing volunteers began the demolition of the Bastille. Its stones were soon spread far and wide over France, and indeed over Europe, in the shape of souvenirs. Thousands of heroes of the actual attack appeared before the public in the Jacobin clubs, in electoral assemblies, in theatrical representations of the Fall of the Bastille, in all the astonishingly modern aspects of revolutionary ballyhoo. Songs, plays, pamphlets, and orations poured forth in praise of this street-riot which had brought about the fall of a fortress. July 14, 1790, the first anniversary of the glorious day, was chosen for a national festival. The symbolism was complete.

Not only as a symbol was the fall of the Bastille important. The confused Parisian risings of July 12-14 defeated the court party. The king appeared in person before the assembly on the 15th and promised to withdraw the troops. Necker was recalled, and the king made a courageous expedition to Paris where he recognized the revolutionary municipal government and national guard, and appeared before the Parisians with Bailly, the new mayor, and Lafayette, commander of the national guard. Louis had voluntarily accepted the union of the three orders in the National Assembly. He now publicly identified himself with the Revolution, pledged himself to further its work. His vacillating will (so runs the republican myth) had, under the urgings of the reactionaries, hit upon a military concentration and subsequent dissolution of the Assembly as a means of maintaining the old régime. In the crisis which his action had evoked, the people of Paris had risen in favor of the threatened Revolution, had beaten the king at his own game, and forced him to return to his former position as a supporter of the new order, a position in which now again, under new advisers, he was for the moment sincere.

Such at least is the account which has been built into the fabric of French history as seen by republicans, an account accepted in its main outline from almost the day the Bastille fell. In one obvious sense of the word, that account is therefore pragmatically "true," since many people have incorporated it into their lives. Yet the historian who is curious about the technique of revolution must push his inquiry a bit further. The official republican account makes out the king the aggressor, the people the injured innocent. M. Caron admits that there is no documentary evidence of a royal plot, that "we are reduced to disengaging, among the different plausible hypotheses, the most likely one."[4]

Now among these hypotheses there is a simple one worth a moment's notice: that the king was in earnest when he told the Assembly that the troop movement was intended to preserve public order, and therefore to protect, not to menace, the Assembly. The revolutionists and their historians assumed kings to be, from nature and office, liars, and the opponents of kings, equally *ex officio,* to be honest men. Neither one assumption nor the other need have much validity now. The dismissal of Necker accords badly with the hypothesis of a royal plot: nothing was done to follow up the dismissal with a *coup d'état* against the Assembly. And not even Louis and his advisers were inept enough to have left so deliberate a gap between the signal for an attack and the attack itself. Here again the explanation may well be a simple one. Louis had realized that Necker was a stuffed shirt rather sooner than the revolutionists were to realize that truth. He dismissed him as he had dismissed many a minister before, from Turgot on. This is perfectly consistent with the hypothesis that Louis was persuaded to try a somewhat more conservative ministry, that he resented the extremists

[4] P. Caron, *Revue d'histoire moderne,* VIII, 20.

of the Assembly. Finally, the astonishing ease with which the Bastille riot attained its goal is suspicious. If Louis really were armed to the teeth, morally as well as physically, against his people, if he had determined to use force against them, he missed an excellent opportunity on July 14. As it was, he did not even try to use the famous foreign regiments against rebellious Paris.

On the side of the innocent people, certain observations also must be made. The July agitation in Paris was a genuinely popular agitation. The manifestations of July 12-14 were too extensive, too aimless, too sporadic to be described as a plot. But it is not unlikely that at first this excitement was aroused by the conscious efforts of relatively few men who knew what they wanted. That agents of the king's cousin, the ambitious Duc d'Orléans, were stirring up trouble in a hundred ways in the hope that their master might succeed to a genuinely "popular" throne, seems incontestable.[5] More important, perhaps, hundreds of nameless Jacobins-to-be, men who had been following excitedly the course of events in Versailles, men for whom Mirabeau was a demigod (and note that Mirabeau in person had made the protest of July 8 against the troop movements)—hundreds of these men fanned the excitement in Paris, led the crowds, produced a movement spontaneous but not unintentional. The simple maneuver by which the electoral college of Paris turned itself into a revolutionary municipal government is further proof that Paris was not politically a mere inchoate mass. The Parisian uprising of July was a folk-movement, spontaneous only in the sense that folk-music is spontaneous. In neither one case nor the other do we know the authors; but we do know the results could not have been produced by the mere collective initiative of thousands of men.

The net effect of the Parisian uprising was to make the break with the old régime catastrophic. The erection of the States-General into the National Assembly had left intact the fabric of local government; indeed, the Assembly had decreed that temporarily the

---

[5] N. Webster, *The French Revolution* (London, 1919), 9-19; 60-99. Mrs. Webster's judgment is not to be trusted. She is as emotionally sure of the plot theory as republican historians are of the spontaneous rising theory. But she has assembled under one cover most of previous literature on the so-called Orléans plot, a literature so extensive that one feels obliged, on the common-sense ground of the adage about smoke and fire, to admit it has a basis of truth.

old taxes and the old administration were to continue as before. Now Paris had given itself overnight an entirely new administrative system directed by the same men who had engineered the choice of the Paris delegation to the Third Estate. Thus arose that self-governing municipality which, as the Commune, was to play at crucial moments a decisive part in swinging the national government towards revolutionary extremes. In a similar fashion the important cities of France now replaced their old machinery of government with new; some cities, like Dijon, did this simultaneously with Paris, before they could possibly have heard the news of the revolt of the capital.[6] Such identity of action in all parts of France can plausibly be interpreted as an indication of widespread organization of the revolutionary party—not organization in the sense of plotting, but political organization of an active minority with a definite program.

Meanwhile in the countryside the only real agrarian movement of the revolutionary period in France was running its brief and successful course. There had been isolated peasant uprisings all spring. Scarcity of grains had occasioned attacks on the great wagon-trains of wheat which crossed the country in the days before the railroads. In Provence, in the Cambrésis, in the Île-de-France peasants anticipated the requests in their *cahiers* and went shooting partridges, refused to pay dues, menaced the châteaux. But the news of July 14 brought matters to a head. The trouble started in one of the most extraordinary mass-delusions history records. At its root seems to have been a widespread fear of a "counter-revolutionary plot" nourished by the concentration of troops near Paris and by the excited rumors produced in that disturbed city. Somehow, somewhere, violence was to be exerted to save feudal privilege. The specific form taken by the rumor was that "the brigands" were coming. No one knew who the brigands were, nor how they had assembled in menacing numbers. Old France had on the whole been an orderly country, well-policed and certainly not prey to wholesale brigandage. It is difficult to escape the conclusion that the rumors had an interested origin, though the old account of how the fear radiated from Paris in methodical waves has had to be

[6] H. Millot, *Le comité permanent de Dijon* (Dijon, 1925).

abandoned in the face of recent detailed study. There were six or eight independent centers of disturbance, and the fear was propagated very irregularly, some regions escaping altogether.[7]

Whole villages went suddenly and completely crazy; that diurnal regularity of little things on which civilization is based was dissolved, and men were faced with chaos—not with the metaphysical figure of speech usually implied by that word, but with its psychological reality. A simple narrative is here worth a host of generalizations. The scene is Creil, then a farming village, now a railway junction some forty-five miles north of Paris; the narrator is describing the "great fear" of her childhood days: "They rang the tocsin, beat the general alarm, took up the stones in the courtyards and filled the rooms with them, intending to hurl them at the heads of the enemy. Some of the women began boiling oil, other collecting ashes from the hearth to throw in the eyes of the first to push into their houses. The men armed themselves with scythes, pitchforks, hoes, and rushed about the surrounding country in squads, hunting for the enemy which each man, fleeing from one hamlet to another, had sworn he had seen in his own. . . . Suddenly there arose a great shout at the sight of some women and children running from the direction of Pont Sainte-Maxence, six miles away. They swore they had seen their husbands killed at their feet. . . . Mother gave the three of us girls a fifteen pound loaf of bread and a quarter of Brie cheese, and barricaded us up in the attic." Next day the little girl was released. No enemy was ever seen, and the women of Pont Sainte-Maxence returned to their unharmed husbands.[8]

The Great Fear was but the start. It was easy for the knowing to profit from this senseless disorder, easy to direct the now aroused peasantry against the tangible enemy, the owner of the château, the *seigneur*. Sometimes violence was not necessary. The *seigneur* peacefully harangued his peasants, promised relief, gave up his feudal titles. Brittany as a whole was unaffected by the movement. Sometimes the château was burned, the hated records on which the dues were based burned up with it. As with all local move-

[7] G. Lefebvre, *La Grande Peur* (Paris, 1932).
[8] "Les souvenirs d'une femme du peuple, 1777-1802," *Société . . . de Senlis; Comptes Rendus et Mémoires* (1925-26), 6me série, I, 68-69.

ments of the Revolution, there is the greatest possible diversity. The impression left by Taine, of a countryside in flames, of a universal and bloody *Jacquerie*, is misleading. Violence, and especially murder, was the exception and not the rule. The peasants had a specific concrete aim—the abolition of feudalism—and when this had been attained they were willing to quiet down. This concreteness of aim, and also an obvious lack of organization, differentiate the agrarian movement of 1789 from the Terror of 1793-94.

As news of these local troubles filtered into Versailles, the Assembly grew more and more alarmed. On the night of August 4, it listened to Target report from committee a project for calming the country by proclaiming that, until the Assembly had made new laws, the old ones should be sacred. At once the Vicomte de Noailles, who had served with Rochambeau in America, arose and in a very practical, unrhetorical speech pointed out that in their *cahiers* the peasants had asked for relief from specific grievances, that these same peasants had now waited three months while the Assembly continued to debate the public good, that for them, however, "the public good is, above all, the definite objects they desire," that the Assembly could calm them by giving them, not mere words, but the legal abolition of the feudal system.[9] He was followed by the Duc d'Aiguillon, another liberal noble, who concurred in urging the voluntary abandonment of feudal revenues by the privileged classes. So began the night of August 4; before it was over dozens of deputies had appeared at the orator's desk and given up privilege after privilege—some of which, indeed, they had hardly been authorized by their constituents to give up. When early in the morning of the 5th the tired president succeeded in stopping the flow of sacrifices, the old régime had been in principle destroyed, equality of taxation and equality of opportunity had been in principle established. In subsequent sessions specific decrees were passed incorporating most of these general principles. But feudal dues seemed too much like economic rent not to be considered property, and property the Assembly was unanimous in considering sacred. Hence in the cold decrees into which the warmth of the night of the 4th was translated, provision was made for compensation to prop-

[9] *Archives parlementaires*, VIII, 43.

erty owners; the peasants were to buy their emancipation from most of these feudal dues in a series of direct payments to their former *seigneurs*.[10]

Significantly enough, the Assembly did not trouble to provide any credit machinery for this transaction. Granted that the members were full of Adam Smith and the Physiocrats, that they were morally convinced of the virtues of self-help, it is none the less true that the form this feudal legislation took is evidence that its sponsors thought the peasants were *economically prosperous enough to pay*. Now the Assembly was by no means ignorant of local conditions, and it had had ample time to sober down from the session of August 4. Possibly the assumption that the peasants could pay was not so far wrong. If, as actually happened, the peasants did not pay, it is quite likely that their successful revolt in the summer of 1789 encouraged them in the belief that they need not pay.

The last of the revolts which formed the crisis of 1789 was the march on Versailles of October 4 and 5. Though the new grain crop had been good, little of it was yet on the market. Unsettled conditions in the provinces had kept the price up and made deliveries irregular. Paris suffered from a food shortage throughout the summer and early autumn, and the bakeries had had to be given police protection. Even the relatively moderate patriots distinguished in this shortage "the deliberate withholding of grains by the great landed proprietors."[11] The popular orators of Paris had no difficulty in discerning the hand of the court, especially after a military banquet at Versailles had provided them with some effective, if irrelevant, material. In the expansive tenderness induced by good wines, officers had put on Bourbon white instead of revolutionary red, white and blue, had toasted the queen, had sung *O Richard, o mon roi*. Finally, the king had not yet approved the work of August 4, and the subsequent Declaration of the Rights of Man; rumor had it that he would refuse to sanction these measures.

On October 5 a crowd of women assembled at Paris, shouting for bread. (The rumor that they were men disguised as women

[10] See above, p. 23.
[11] *Révolutions de Paris*, September 20, 1789.

has never been wholly downed; yet it seems unlikely that the affair was quite so wholesalely epicene as that.) At their head was a certain Maillard, a man not without the somewhat specialized talents, partly those of an actor, partly those of an executive, required for leading revolutionary crowds. After a while the procession started towards Versailles to get bread from the king. A crowd of curious and idle followed after them, and towards evening Lafayette and his national guard set out, a trifle late, to preserve order. At the very moment Lafayette was leaving Paris the head of the column of women was marching in to Versailles, twelve miles away, in the pouring rain. The women invaded the courtyard of the Assembly, and conducted themselves very freely in word and deed, being especially disrespectful towards the "whore" their queen. Maillard and a deputation of women appeared before the Assembly, and complained that the aristocrats were starving them. The Assembly, greatly disturbed, and indeed horrified—the women were in no sense ladies—hastily got rid of its guests by naming a deputation to accompany them to the palace to see the king. Louis temporized, and courageously embraced the youngest of the delegation, a seventeen-year-old *ouvrière en sculpture*, Louison Chabry. More and more people crowded in to Versailles. Finally Lafayette arrived, to the relief of the sober inhabitants of town and palace.

Louis, after much conferring, and some temptation to flight, yielded completely, promising to take special measures to provision Paris, to accept a bodyguard loyal to the new régime, to approve the abolition of the feudal system and the Declaration of Rights. All was apparently over, and everyone lay down to get a little rest in what was left of the night. At sunrise, and under mysterious circumstances, rioting broke out at one of the gates, the palace entrance was forced, the queen obliged to flee in haste, and the whole royal family surrounded. The cry arose that the king must come to Paris. Again he consented, and accompanied by the queen and the dauphin, took the road to Paris, his coach surrounded by an ever-renewed crowd, still a bit damp, but very cheerful and quite unrefined. They were bringing back to Paris "the baker, the baker's wife, and the baker's little boy." They were, as a matter of fact, bringing back even more important prey. The

Assembly, not to be deserted in Versailles, voted to follow the king to Paris. Whether king or assembly was sovereign, Paris possessed them both.

Here, as with the Bastille riot, historians are agreed on the facts, at complete odds as to the meaning of those facts. The aims of the October rising seem to be singularly definite, the whole undertaking to rest less in popular agitation than the July uprising. Much of the groundwork, preparing public opinion, getting the idlers and busybodies who followed after the women into the proper frame of mind, was undoubtedly the work of the newspapers, which by this time were in full blast. Orléans, now perhaps working through Mirabeau, may have had a hand in organizing the march. Certainly the original gathering of women was not accidental. The Venetian ambassador Capello wrote, "Lack of bread was the pretext and not the true cause of this uprising." The Commune of Paris itself wrote the Assembly on October 5 that "this insurrection was premeditated." The march once started, a large part was left to accident, to the enthusiasm of the augmented crowd, to spontaneity. But its beginnings were planned, its development controlled as much as possible, by radical journalists and leaders, Loustalot, Fournier l'Américain, Saint-Huruge, and others.[12]

II. THE CONSTITUTION IN THE MAKING

The October Days close the first period of revolutionary violence. Not for another three years was there a successful insurrection. But the period was only superficially one of quiet. The conflict of parties grew more and more bitter. Violence in word and print presaged violence in deed. Memory of the successful violence of the summer of 1789 was never far from the minds of the radicals. Above all, as the constitution was elaborated, it was put into effect piecemeal, a measure at a time, entangled with current legislation. Certain of these constitutional reforms served to focus specific discontents, to embroil group with group, to make the existing order impossible. Six great measures may be singled out as summing up in themselves this aspect of the problem of the fall of the monarchy

---

[12] Quotations from A. Mathiez, "Les journées des 5 et 6 octobre 1789," *Revue historique* (1899), LXIX, 47.

—the Declaration of Rights; the royal veto; the suffrage; the new system of local government; the attempted financial rehabilitation by means of the *assignats*; the civil constitution of the clergy. All six in one form or another occupied the Assembly until its dissolution, and were inherited as unsolved problems by its successor.

The Assembly could hardly avoid issuing some kind of Bill of Rights; English and American precedent worked here with overwhelming insistence. Mirabeau, Malouet, and a few other moderates did, indeed, urge that such a Declaration of Rights must in the France of 1789 promise more than could be achieved, that it might well stir up, rather than calm, discontent. Grégoire, later the sturdy upholder of the Constitutional Church, wished to declare the duties, as well as the rights, of man. But the majority, in spite of a great deal of debate and project-making, saw the declaration through with surprising rapidity, and on August 27 it was passed in its final form, waiting only the king's approval to become law of the land. This Declaration of the Rights of Man and the Citizen in seventeen brief articles and a preamble is a neat summary of eighteenth-century political ideas. Its first article announces the fact that "men are born and remain free and equal in rights." The rest of the declaration, after a preliminary narrowing of rights to "liberty, property, security and resistance to oppression," proceeds to define them so abstractly that the declaration as a whole has seemed to some men to deliver the individual completely into the hands of the state, and to others to cripple the state by giving the individual irresponsible and anarchic freedom. The truth is that the declaration, though historically explicable as first of all a gesture of defiance against the existing feudal, monarchic society, has become simply a piece of semi-religious symbolism, a sort of nineteenth-century bourgeois credo. Notably the rights of property and security have proved in practice a perfectly adequate conservative ballast. The document as a whole is not revolutionary in the sense of acting as a dissolvent upon social equilibrium. Jefferson, too, asserted certain self-evident truths which sound remarkably like the words of the French Assembly, and which so far have not made American society notably unstable. The "natural" right of property, buttressed by Supreme Court traditions, is still, in spite of recent decisions, deeply rooted in American life. Equality is, of course, a dangerous word, and to Marx might mean something it did not mean to Jefferson or to Lafayette, Barnave, and Siéyès. But the eighteenth century did not invent the word. Christ would seem to have used it not infrequently. His Church, however, proved to be a quite reasonably conservative institution.

The question of the royal veto over legislation had occupied the Assembly from the very first. To those in favor of a strong executive the veto seemed indispensable. English precedent and the more recent work of the American Constitutional Convention concurred in giving the executive this power. Mirabeau eloquently and courageously defended the absolute veto, a step which lost him much of his popular following. On the other hand, to the patriotic the veto meant the return of the old régime. The triumvirate—Barnave, du Port, Lameth—united with Lafayette to procure a compromise which was really no compromise at all. On September 11 a suspensive veto was granted the king. His refusal would block a measure for the duration of two legislatures—four years. The third legislature might pass the measure over his head by a majority vote. The whole debate had been conducted in the press, the clubs, and in Paris as much as in the assembly. The royal office itself was attacked. King and queen were christened M. et Mme. Veto, names which clung to them to the end. Yet with all this damaging publicity, the king received a power which amounted to nothing but the power to annoy his opponents. Given his strong, simple conscience, Louis was bound to use the veto, especially in matters of religious legislation. The veto could postpone everything but settle nothing.

The suffrage provisions of the new constitution show clearly the moderate character of the majority in the Assembly. All male Frenchmen over twenty-five were citizens. Those who paid no direct taxes, or direct taxes less than the value of three days' wages of unskilled labor in their district, or who were servants or bankrupts, were "passive" citizens, and though enjoying civil and natural rights, might not vote. Those who paid such taxes to the amount of at least three days' wages, and were neither servants nor bankrupts, were "active" citizens, and could vote in the primary assemblies. For eligibility to the secondary assemblies, which actually elected deputies, and to all local offices in general an active citizen had to pay direct taxes to the amount of ten days' wages. Finally, for eligibility to the national assembly itself, an active citizen must pay a tax of fifty days' wages—the so-called silver mark—and possess landed property. This was a suffrage with property qualifications, a typical middle-class system of the kind that was to work well enough at later periods in French history. But the Assembly had freshly proclaimed in its Declaration of Rights that "men are born and remain equal in respect to their rights." Now it sorted adult Frenchmen into some 4,000,000 whose income made them full citizens, and 2,000,000 whose lack of income made them incomplete citizens.[13] The new legislature would actually be elected by a suffrage less universal than that by which the deputies of the Third Estate had been chosen in 1789. Skillful exegesis could, and later did, reconcile the contradiction; but many Frenchmen in 1790 were still in such matters in the literal-minded state of converts to a new faith. For the true believers, this artificial distinction between active and passive citizens was a most shocking evasion of the Word.

The uprisings of July had destroyed the old machinery of urban government, and replaced it with a number of autonomous, self-chosen bourgeois governments. The night of August 4 wiped out feudalism in private relations. The old framework of local government, developed directly out of feudalism, could hardly be maintained in the face of other changes. The Assembly set to work to provide France with a complete, rational, and simple administrative framework. Geographically, all the old, varied and frequently overlapping subdivisions, from provinces to *seigneuries*, were legally abolished, to live on in tradition and tourists' handbooks. In their place an ordered series of subdivisions was carved out. First came the eighty-three departments, named from rivers, mountains or other natural features, pieced together chiefly with this in mind, that the capital at the center of each department should be accessible from any point in the department in one day's travel. Each department was divided into districts—usually five or six—each

---

[13] Figures from P. Sagnac, *Histoire de France contemporaine*, ed. E. Lavisse (Paris, 1920), I, 165.

district into cantons, each canton into communes. The canton was never a very important unit. If it be omitted, the hierarchy of department-district-commune is, on a smaller scale, very much like the American hierarchy of state-county-town. There is no doubt that the Assembly set up these tradition-free subdivisions partly because it distrusted local patriotism, Norman, Breton, Provençal, and wished to make all Frenchmen as much alike as possible. But for these men who had tried to get things done under the incredibly entangled local jurisdictions of the old régime, the main motive was to provide France with a single series of coördinated local subdivisions.

These artificial units were endowed with almost complete self-government.[14] Hatred of the old régime and admiration for English and American practice determined the Assembly to strike out on new lines. Each commune was to elect a municipal council, a *procureur*, and a mayor; each district a council, an executive directory, and a *procureur général syndic*; each department a similar council and directory, and a *procureur général syndic*. The *procureurs* were not genuine executives like American governors; the ideal executive was significantly enough considered as always in commission. The *procureurs* were presidents of their councils, and something like solicitors-general for their jurisdictions. All these officials were elected by the active citizens of municipality, district or department from those who paid at least the value of ten days' wages in direct taxes.

In the letter of the law, there was a regular subordination of commune to district, of district to department, of department to the central government at Paris. This sort of subordination had under the old régime been roughly—more roughly, indeed, than most nineteenth-century historians thought—achieved by the royal bureaucracy centering around the appointed *intendant*. Under the new régime the bureaucracy was suddenly swept away, and a series of elective councils substituted. Tied together by no bonds of experience and personal subordination, tied together only by the bonds of interest, so curiously fragile in this Revolution, these local

[14] At the very bottom of the scale the 44,000 communes, from Paris to the tiniest hamlet, were not artificial, but very old indeed.

units soon fell apart. Broadly speaking, it may be said that the village governments possessed hardly any political life. When the new priest at Chaulgnes took his oath the report bore only his signature and the remark "the mayor, the municipal council and the *procureur* of the commune don't know how to sign their names."[15]

Now an illiterate peasant might have been a wise peasant about many matters but he was sure to have been hopelessly lost among the phrases indispensable to the new governance of France. The larger towns and the cities, however, exhibited a very active political life. Since they lived among their constituents, and since the power of the working class was greatest in the towns, the municipal officers in such places tended to be fairly radical. The district governments also leaned towards the popular side. The department governments, chosen in 1790 at a peaceful time, composed of better-known, wealthier men, more removed from their constituents, were a conservative force during the monarchical experiment. The tactics of the Jacobins was to set municipal and departmental governments to quarreling, to back up the municipal government noisily, and thus discredit the more conservative department. When the Assembly refused Mirabeau's plan of ministerial responsibility, it virtually emasculated any ministry of the interior, the natural arbiter of such disputes. If a department did appeal to the ministry, the recalcitrant municipality simply appealed to the National Assembly, and usually won its case. But the various governments showed a tendency to quarrel without outside aid. The vanity of new men, the bursting confidence of emancipated men, the love of intrigue common to all men, were brought to play upon this excellent structure devised by the Assembly and completely warped it. In the partial paralysis resulting from the conflict of authority, the excellent Jacobin organization could work steadily to promote the democratic republic. With the destruction of the old governmental hierarchy, and the failure of the new governmental machinery, the Jacobin organization became the only nation-wide, centrally-administered group in France. The transformation of the whole Jacobin organization into the government of republican France was therefore a simple, and indeed inevitable, thing.

[15] *Bulletin de la Société nivernaise* (1908), XXII, 512.

The National Assembly failed utterly to improve the financial situation of the government. Its attempted solution of the financial problem led straight to a religious schism which finally broke down the monarchical experiment. The historian cannot in fairness blame the Assembly after the manner of Taine, and assert that a cocksure rationalism, a shallow faith in planning, led to bad measures and financial ruin. It is extremely difficult, even with the wisdom of after the event, to see what else the Assembly could have done. Certainly no historian writing in the 1950's should affect virtuous horror at the spectacle of the *assignats,* or reproach the Assembly with failure to maintain an even price-level and balanced budget.

The *cahiers* had been full of protests against the many and irregular taxes of the old régime. The disorders of 1789 gave taxpayers everywhere the opportunity to refuse to pay their taxes. The Assembly was faced with a definite condition: the old taxes were unpopular and were not to be collected. A new system was essential. The Assembly, after much debate, concluded in March, 1790, to suppress most of the old indirect taxes, *gabelle, octroi,* and so on, and not to supplant them with new indirect taxes. It is all very well to remark that indirect taxes are the easiest to collect, since the taxpayer rarely knows he is paying them, and that the Assembly should have maintained them. But public opinion was very roused, indeed, against indirect taxes because in the past they had been farmed out, and the tax farmers had got very rich. To have revived them in 1790, even under good disguise, would simply have given the Jacobins another hold. In place of the old direct taxes, *taille, capitation, vingtième,* a single direct tax was imposed of which 240 millions was to be laid on income from land, 60 millions on income from other sources, judged by the amount paid for rent. The tax was eventually to be partitioned among the departments according to their wealth and population. Until adequate statistics could be drawn up, it was apportioned according to direct taxes paid by each department under the old régime. This apportioning was done very slowly indeed by the departments and the municipalities. Many an ignorant peasant really thought the Revolution meant no more taxes; many less ignorant citizens all over France simply acted as though taxes need no longer be paid. The result was a steadily increasing deficit in the national treasury. The gap between the old taxes and the new was hardly completely bridged until the time of the Directory. By the end of 1792, taxes due in 1791 were only one-third paid up.[16]

A pathetic series of efforts to fill the treasury was made in 1789. Necker appealed to the country for "patriotic loans," at 4½ and 5 per cent interest. But capital was actually leaving the country for safer homes abroad, a phenomenon familiar enough in the twentieth century. The loans were complete failures. A "patriotic tax" was next voted, a sort of voluntary capital levy, each individual giving one-quarter of a year's income, payments to be spread over three years. Without any provision for governmental inquiry or compulsion, this failed also. Finally, amid public manifestations before the Assembly, ladies brought earrings or other golden trinkets to be melted, gentlemen brought shoe-buckles, all sorts of people brought all sorts of things, not as a rule anonymously. But the sum total of these strange "patriotic gifts" was as nothing compared with the needs of the government.

Obviously the government had to have money quickly. It could not, in the existing state of the country, raise great sums by taxation; it could not, born of revolution as it was, expect to entice great sums from the kind of people normally willing and able to lend money to governments. It could not admit bankruptcy, for the people who composed it, the respectable bourgeois of the Assembly, had been trained in a school of morals which regards bankruptcy as a last disgrace. It might, of course, and eventually did, inflate the currency by issuing inconvertible paper money. It might simply confiscate certain riches, for the country itself was far from poor. But the government dared not offend its creators of the Third Estate by confiscating private property, had, indeed, declared such property sacred. Perhaps, however, a kind of property could be found that was not sacred, that did not conform to the economist's definition of property. Such was at hand, the property of the church, a fictitious person, a corporation, and hence not protected by the guaranty of property afforded the individual by the Declaration of

[16] P. Sagnac, *Histoire de France contemporaine*, I, 158.

Rights.[17] Such, a bit later, was the property of the professed enemies of the new state, the *émigrés*. Taken together, the property of the clergy and of the *émigrés* amounted to no inconsiderable part of the French national wealth. This property was almost wholly in land and buildings, since tithes and feudal dues had been abolished. In the department of the Nord such clerical and aristocratic property amounted to nearly one-quarter of the land of the department. At the other extreme, in the district of Saint-Gaudens, it amounted to but 3.5 per cent of the whole.[18] Averaging together the scattered statistical studies hitherto made, one may hazard the assertion that from all France such property must have been not less than 12 per cent of the national wealth, and not more than 20 per cent.

Land is not, of course, in itself a medium of exchange. Having decided on November 2, 1789, that the goods of the clergy were at the disposition of the nation (subject, of course, to the nation's supporting the daily expenses of officiating priests), the Assembly had to devise a way to pay the government's bills with these immovable goods. This is the origin of the *assignat*, the paper money of the Revolution. At first only 400 million francs were issued, bearing 4 per cent interest and having certain privileges in the purchase of church lands. These first *assignats* were not legal tender. As the treasury remained empty, and the debt continued pressing, this issue was not enough. In August, 1790, the decisive step was taken. The amount was carried to 1,200 million francs, and the notes ceased to bear interest and became legal tender. They were still supported by the value of the confiscated lands, however, and were to be burned as they came back to the treasury in payment for these lands. Since most historians of finance have been *rentiers*, the *assignats* have been commonly considered as one of the great missteps of the revolution, as the inevitable start of a senseless and dishonest inflation. As a matter of fact, the *assignats* hardly merit these strictures. The church lands were adequate security. The demand for land in France was so surprisingly great, the confidence engendered in this unorthodox tying of land and paper money together so considerable, the whole financial device so thoroughly

<hr>

[17] Speech of Thouret, *Moniteur*, II, 85.
[18] G. Lefebvre, "Recherches relatives à la vente des biens nationaux," *Revue d'histoire moderne* (1928), III, 207.

worked into the fabric of revolutionary hopes and fears, that the *assignat* was at first an unqualified success.[19]

If later, in the hands of a desperate government fighting off foreign and domestic foes, it became a mere instrument of inflation, even then it served the cause of the Revolution. For the buyer of national lands who paid in *assignats* got credit for their face value though he had acquired them at their depreciated value, and ought certainly to have been correspondingly grateful to the Revolution. The *assignats* permitted the new régime to liquidate the old. Inflation injured the quiet, the sedentary, the possessors of fixed incomes and limited ambitions; it benefited the lively, the enterprising, the innovating, the business man of the new era—surely an end quite consistent with the Revolution?

The creation of the *assignats* and their subsequent administration strengthened, rather than weakened, the constitutional monarchy. But the creation of the *assignats* led the Assembly to another step which did seriously injure the monarchy. The capital wealth of the church had been confiscated to secure the *assignats*. How were the daily expenses of the cult to be met? What might seem now the simple solution, to let the contributions of the faithful support priests and maintain churches, was then probably impossible. In the first place, the Assembly was troubled in conscience over its seizure of sacred property—sacred not because it was Christian, but because it was property—and had insisted that the nation be responsible for the maintenance of the cult. Secondly, the idea of a complete separation of church and state was still a startlingly new one, an idea with no precedents in French history. Therefore, the Assembly proceeded to bind church and state together in the Civil Constitution of the Clergy, completed July 12, 1790. The monastic clergy had previously been disposed of by a law providing that existing monastic vows had no civil standing, that such vows could not be taken at all in the future, that monks and nuns who wished to repudiate their vows might return to private life on a state pension, that those who wished to continue monastic life should be segregated into a few monasteries, that most of the monasteries and their lands be sold as national property.

[19] S. E. Harris, *The Assignats* (Cambridge, Mass., 1930), 90.

The Civil Constitution of the Clergy provided for the election of the parish priest by the electoral assembly of the district, that of the bishop by the electoral assembly of the department. The old dioceses were abolished, and the new ones were made to coincide with the departments. The pope was to have no jurisdiction in France; newly elected bishops were simply to notify the pope of their election. Bishops and priests were to be paid by the state like any other civil servants, 50,000 francs per year for the bishop of Paris, 20,000 to 12,000 francs for other bishops, 4,000 to 1,200 for the parish priests. The bureaucratic note appears time and again. No priest is to absent himself from his cure for more than fifteen days in a year, save with written authorization from the departmental directory. Dogma the Assembly considered had not been touched by these provisions; that was the affair of the faithful. In all this the Assembly had not deigned to negotiate directly with the pope. The king, through the French ambassador at Rome, Bernis, had sought counsel of Pius VI, and throughout the summer of 1790 complicated negotiations took place. Of course, no successor of St. Peter could possibly have accepted the Civil Constitution as actually voted, but Pius probably, and Louis certainly, hoped that accommodations could be made. Meanwhile the Assembly was getting impatient, and on November 27 decided to exact from every public servant an oath of fidelity to the constitution, including the Civil Constitution of the Clergy, and to go ahead with the election of new priests if the old ones refused the oath. Very reluctantly, and after much torturing of his upright and orthodox conscience, Louis signed this decree—and promised himself to escape from the badgerings of the Assembly as soon as possible, even though escape meant flight. When in March and April next the pope officially condemned the principles of the Revolution and the Civil Constitution, Louis, like all good Catholics of the realm, was given the choice of abandoning either the Revolution or his faith.

The Civil Constitution of the Clergy thus drove Louis to flee to Varennes, and Varennes made the monarchy impossible. But the religious legislation of the Assembly had far deeper effects, effects still evident in twentieth-century France. The Civil Constitution of the Clergy made it impossible for an orthodox Catholic to accept the Revolution. The new church was indeed inaugurated and, thanks to Talleyrand, bishop of Autun under the old régime, who consecrated bishops under the new régime, it might even claim apostolic succession. But all over France priests refused the oath, quietly resigned their official cures, and retired to the more effective post of martyr.[20]

The government supported the new church against the old, the "constitutional" priest against the "refractory" priest. But the people, and especially the womenfolk, were in many a parish bitterly resentful of the "intruded" priest brought them by Parisian legislation. In a thousand parishes a tangible, vivid, real quarrel arose, with all the bitterness of an immediate, family quarrel, where previously men had rhetorically disputed over philosophical abstractions, or struggled decently over material interests. In support of the new church, the Assembly and its successor were forced into a series of measures hostile to the non-juring priests and to freedom of worship, until finally the orthodox Catholics were a proscribed sect, its priests hunted down, exiled and murdered, its ceremonies banished to woods and cellars. It is impossible, above all if one keeps in mind the attitude of the French eighteenth-century thought to organized Christianity, not to feel that this result was consciously desired by certain men of the Assembly. Yet doubtless the majority who put through the Civil Constitution had no such desires, foresaw no such result. Many were good pious Christians, who really thought they were restoring the church to its primitive simplicity; many were Gallicans, seizing the opportunity to free the church of France from what they regarded as papal usurpation; some were Jansenists, avenging themselves and their God on the old régime; most were simply unimaginative, well-intentioned gentlemen of the middle class caught sufficiently in the fashionable irreligion of the day not to be able to realize how profoundly religious they themselves were. Time, indeed, was to teach them better. The nineteenth-century bourgeois was usually quite able to reconcile himself to the Catholic Church. Those who

[20] Though local variations were great—some regions accepting the new church pretty completely, others rejecting it—a fair estimate for all France is that 52 to 55 per cent. of the secular clergy refused the oath. P. de la Gorce, *Histoire religieuse*, I, 399.

could not became sectaries of a new religion, a modified Jacobin faith born out of the conflict of the French Revolution.

Of the last few months of the National Assembly but two events need be singled out, both of which contributed to undermining its work. On June 20, 1791, the royal family, aided by the romantic Swedish Count Fersen, succeeded in escaping from the closely guarded Tuileries, and started out in a coach for the eastern frontier, where were the loyal troops of Bouillé, and, a bit farther, in Luxemburg, the sure Austrians of the queen's brother, the Emperor Leopold. They were recognized at Sainte-Menehould, and brought back from Varennes in the Argonne, almost within sight of safety. The Assembly had carefully built up its scheme of limited monarchy; opposition to that monarchy was growing more and more radical in tone, seemed even to threaten measures to promote economic equality. The moderates who had made the constitution simply dared not turn over the government to the radicals, and they were convinced that a republican form of government would involve just such a step. A most amusing fiction was adopted, that the king had been kidnapped against his will, and the new constitution promulgated as if there had never been a Varennes. A radical meeting held in the Champ de Mars to demand that Louis be held to have abandoned the throne, and that a new executive be chosen, was broken up by force, and enough of the radicals shot to provide the party with an excellent grievance. The Jacobins now became for the most part out-and-out republicans, no longer mere republicans of the salon and of Plutarch. They abandoned their vague and inconsistent ideal of a monarchical republic with Louis as a Jacobin citizen-king. Exhausting all one's ingenuity in the service of history-as-it-might-have-been, one cannot conceive, after Varennes, a successful constitutional monarchy in France at that time. Varennes made the First Republic certain.

Finally, the Assembly executed a grand gesture in the best style of the copy-books. In order to prove its disinterestedness, to show that men of virtue are not bitten with the love of power, to give an illustration of the democratic virtues of rotation in office, the Assembly decreed that none of its members should be eligible to sit in the new assembly. This self-denying ordinance has often been taken as irrefutable proof that the members of the Constituent were impractical idealists living in an unreal Utopia. In some measure the charge is true. But the Assembly was liable to sudden gusts of foolishness. Its whole career is hardly to be judged by the above ordinance. Nor were the practical consequences of the self-denying rule as serious as some historians have made out. At any rate, if one agrees with Taine that the men of the Assembly were a pack of fools, one certainly ought not in the next breath to explain that their absence from the new assembly was a great loss in accumulated wisdom. But the whole elaborate constitution, the product of three years' labor, was already condemned. The self-denying ordinance was not a major influence in French history.

III. THE NEW LEGISLATURE

The new Assembly, known in history as the Legislative, met on October 1, 1791. Its brief career of less than a twelvemonth is hardly more than a prolongation of the legislative career of the Constituent Assembly. The extreme Right of the older body, mostly recruited from the former Estates of nobles and clergy, could hardly perpetuate itself in the new. No successor to the Abbe Maury, to Barrel Mirabeau or even to the competent monarchist Cazalès, could have braved the public elections of 1791. All of the 745 new legislators would have been listed as "patriots" in 1789. The new Right, sincerely attached to the monarchical experiment, represented the perpetuation of the Lafayette-triumvirate coalition, and had recently left the Jacobin club to form a schismatic club of their own, the Feuillants. A brief war of pamphlets, correspondence, and personal intrigue for the control of the Jacobin network of affiliated clubs had resulted in a clear victory for the "mother society." The Feuillants, without a machine, remained a mere parliamentary caucus. The new Left was the Jacobin group, already determined to make an end of the monarchy. Neither Left nor Right could count on 200 determined votes; the bulk of the Legislative, like the bulk of the famous Convention which was to follow, was composed of a hesitating mass of deputies, usually elected with the support of the Jacobins of their constituencies, and hence far from royalist, but also usually representing districts where revolutionary passions had not developed, and hence not decisively republican, not, as the phrase went, "up to the height of circumstances." This Center, or Plain, or Marsh as it was derisively called during the Convention, would vote in a crisis with the minority it feared most, the minority best organized to make political pressure effective. That minority, for three more years, was to sit on the Left.

The members of the Legislative were local leaders who had carried on in the provinces the work initiated by the National Assembly. They were apprentices, but apprentices of several years' training, and generally respectful of their masters. Thanks to the Jacobin organization, such former members of the National Assembly as Robespierre, Pétion, and Buzot were able to hand on the reality as well as the tradition of revolutionary methods. On the other hand, Lafayette and his group, without such an organization, were to a much less degree influential in the politics of 1791-92. Certain new reputations were made in the Legislative, but none that are not better to be considered as decisive factors under the Convention. In general it is enough to say that the Legislative pursued a policy much like that of the Constituent Assembly in respect to the exasperating problems which were dividing Frenchmen into groups too hostile to endure a common political organization. The Legislative continued to have its hands full adjusting quarrels between local governmental units, and it continued to adjust such quarrels in favor of the unit which could best rally to its support the press, the professional troublemakers of the clubs, the lobbyists, and the politicians. It continued to issue *assignats*, and at the beginning of 1792 the first real depreciation began. The depreciation was not yet great—perhaps 15 per cent before war was declared in April, 30 per cent afterwards; moreover, in a country where communication was still slow and financial centralization hardly begun, the degree of depreciation varied enormously, and in some regions the *assignat* remained nearly at its old level in terms of purchasing power. A definite improvement in the tax-yield set in early in 1792, and continued throughout the year.[21]

The religious policy of the Legislative continued that of the Constituent. The latter had granted the "refractory" Roman Catholics

[21] S. Harris, *The Assignats*, ch. V, and pp. 48-49.

the right to lease property and hold services, provided the premises were duly marked and no attacks were made on the new régime during the services. Attempts to hold such services were made in Paris, and provoked disorders as the radicals crowded around the chapels and jostled the worshipers. Sardonic anti-clericals were delighted at the spectacle of the Church of Rome appealing to the doctrine of religious toleration, at phrases like the following from a petition of the conservative department of Paris: "Can then an entire century of philosophy but have led us back to the religious intolerance of the sixteenth century, and by the very road of liberty itself?"[22] By a law of November 29, 1791, the Legislative required non-juring priests to take a civic oath of allegiance or else subject themselves to the danger of being expelled from their place of residence as intriguers. Louis vetoed this law, but it was commonly enforced by local authorities, and even by Jacobin clubs. So clearly by the beginning of 1792 had the government at Paris lost control of the country.

One very important matter did, indeed, come to a head under the Legislative. The war, certainly a major factor in the downfall of the monarchy, was the great contribution of this assembly to the revolutionary cause. There will hardly be need here to state that the war guilt of 1792 falls on no one party. In so far as the war was a product of high European politics, it will be considered in a subsequent chapter. Here it can be treated briefly as a part of French internal politics. On May 22, 1790, in the course of a debate as to whether king or assembly should have the right to declare war, the Constituent formally renounced in the name of the French nation all wars of conquest, and promised never to employ French forces against the liberty of a people. The tone of this declaration is already a bit self-righteous, and there is an obvious loophole for employing French forces *for* the liberty of a people. From this declaration to the famous decree of November 19, 1792, whereby the Convention promised French aid to all peoples wishing to regain their natural liberty, there is a steady development of the crusading spirit among the French revolutionaries. By the spring of 1792 this spirit had already developed so strongly that it must be regarded as an im-

[22] *Moniteur*, X, 571.

portant element in the war. Moreover, the affairs of Avignon offered an early test of French pacifism. Avignon with the Comtat Venaissin was the center of a papal enclave in French territory, an enclave wholly French by race, language, and geography. In June, 1790, the radicals of Avignon voted themselves annexed to France. The matter was complicated by the fact that part of the papal territory, and especially the city of Carpentras, was much less radical than Avignon, and did not wish annexation. The whole enclave, like France itself, was divided by partisan quarrels. The Constituent Assembly hesitated, debated, tried various solutions, and finally, after some especially atrocious massacres in the Comtat, annexed it to France in September, 1791. The new France had made its first conquest, which was, of course, but the peaceful reunion of true Frenchmen with the mother country.

The spirit of proselytism did not long remain a vague, general sentiment. It became part of a deliberate party program, and as such was directed towards a specific end: war with Austria and Prussia. The party more particularly associated with the war policy now first appears in revolutionary politics as an organized group. The Girondins were not, of course, organized as efficiently as a modern party. They first appear as a group within the Jacobin societies, and only after the fall of the monarchy do they split away from the Jacobins. Historians are now pretty universally agreed that the Girondins, once the mild, gentlemanly, almost English liberals of Lamartine's fancy, deliberately egged the French people on to war. No doubt the Girondins, now the dominant group in the Legislative, and powerful in the Jacobin club, were sincere in their republican zeal. "You embrace the cause of other peoples in embracing your own; 'tis for them too that the Declaration of Rights is written. . . . No danger should make the French nation forget that the law of equality should be universal."[23] Genuine hypocrisy, always a rare thing, is especially rare in the French Revolution. The Girondins believed they were heralds and missionaries of a new world-order. They were also convinced that war would consolidate their own position in French politics, enable them to dominate both ministry

[23] Vergniaud, Condorcet, reported in *Révolutions de Paris*, January 7, 1792, XI, 9, 12.

and assembly, to supervise closely, or even to get rid of, the king. For months they egged the Assembly on towards war, and won their end against the opposition of Robespierre and the nascent extremist group which was to make the Terror.

The Girondins had more than mere words to work upon; there were two quite concrete quarrels capable in the long run of producing a war without much fanning. First, there was the question of the *émigrés*. Thousands of members of the old court party had left France, and were scattered over Europe. Their chief center, however, was Coblenz, a Rhenish town dependent on the Archbishop (Elector) of Trier, which was a sort of capital for the king's brothers and their retinues. Many of the *émigrés* were intriguing with most of the courts of Europe. The king and queen were suspected of negotiating with the emperor, of being hand-in-hand with the *émigrés*. The former suspicion was quite justified, the latter not at all. The exaggerated claims of the *émigrés* undoubtedly harmed the king at home. The whole situation was a dangerous one and was played up to the hilt by the Girondins. Second, there was the problem of the lands possessed by German princes in Alsace. This highly complicated legal question might possibly have been solved on juridical principles, but in essence it was a quarrel over things, and was solved by force. Many German princes held Alsatian lands as feudal *seigneurs*. The legislation abolishing the feudal system applied to these lands. But the German princes were not French citizens, and held these lands under guaranties renewed in the Treaty of Westphalia. The Assembly was willing to compensate them, as it was willing to compensate French feudal owners under the same circumstances. Perhaps the Germans feared this willingness would never be translated into cash. At any rate some of them refused compensation, and insisted on their rights. The subject was, therefore, kept alive and served as one of the pretexts for the actual declaration of war.

IV. THE FALL OF THE MONARCHY

On April 20 the Legislative Assembly almost unanimously declared war on Austria and thereby hastened its own end. Prussia at once came in on the side of its Austrian ally. It seems probable that internal stress would have destroyed the constitution of 1791 in a fairly short time. The external stress of the war was far more than the constitution could bear. In a military way France was unprepared. The application of the principles of Liberty, Equality, and Fraternity to the old professional army had disrupted it. Many of its officers had emigrated. Those who stayed were distrusted by their men. The enemy had an easy time in the first encounter when, on April 28, French troops under Dillon broke and fled at the sight of Austrians. All the hatreds nourished for years by the extreme revolutionaries were now concentrated in the cry of treason. The whole work of the Revolution was in jeopardy, the king was treasonably egging on the enemy, the aristocrats at home were stabbing the patriots in the back. On June 20 a crowd invaded the Tuileries, swarmed into the royal apartments, forced Louis XVI to wear a red liberty cap, but did him no violence. This curious episode remains a mystery. Was it an uprising intended to destroy the monarchy, and did it therefore fail? Was it merely a sort of dress rehearsal for the final "day," and therefore rather a success? The former seems the likelier hypothesis.

The war continued to go badly. The Duke of Brunswick, commanding the Prussian contingent, had been charged with what then seemed the easy task of marching straight on Paris from the east. In July the duke was persuaded to sign the manifesto which goes by his name, a proclamation asserting that the Allies intended to restore Louis to full liberty and threatening vengeance on the city of Paris if harm came to any of the royal family. The news of this manifesto helped those who were plotting to bring about precisely such an end. A badly managed return to Paris of Lafayette, now a general on the eastern front, had previously provided the Jacobins with a chance to stir up excitement. Bad news from the front had drawn from the Assembly the decree that the fatherland was in danger. To all this Brunswick's manifesto came as a final touch. A Prussian army marching steadily on Paris; a French general apparently rehearsing for the rôle of Cromwell; a French king betraying his people; priests and aristocrats lurking about ready to strike down patriots, seize their goods, restore the old order; fiat paper money decreasing in value almost daily; general financial uncertainty; and finally, a governing body which was doing nothing, but saying a great deal, and very excitedly—here were elements sufficient to maintain in Paris that extraordinary state of collective tension in which almost anything might happen. For the first time since July 14, 1789, thousands of normally quiet, respectable Parisians were stirred out of the daily round of private lives into an apprehensive participation in the common thing, an apprehensiveness which success might make vengeful.

Yet mere popular excitement would never have brought the fall of the monarchy. The events of August 10 were carefully planned and admirably carried out. No one man can be singled out as an archplotter. Danton certainly acquired at the time a reputation as the "man of August 10" and seems in perspective, in spite of Mathiez's attacks on him, to have borne a leading rôle in crucial moments of the insurrection. The monarchy was overthrown by a group of Parisian politicians working through the peculiar local machinery of government in that city. Thanks to Jacobin propaganda, which had prepared people in advance, and to the general state of patriotic fervor produced by the invasion, this act of Parisian politicians was accepted, welcomed, by existing organs of government and of public opinion. The action itself was planned and executed by a minority of Parisians—to that extent it may even be called a plot. But it was an action which, successful, commended itself to those articulate, propertied, middle-class Frenchmen who ultimately determined French politics.

Paris was divided into forty-eight *sections*, or wards, in each of which a popular assembly of the "active" citizens met to elect representatives to the city council, and to administer the affairs of the ward. Paris, in other words, was governed by forty-eight groups of men assembling in something like New England town meetings. Now most citizens were too busy with private matters, or too bored with politics, or too lazy to attend these meetings, especially after their novelty wore off. Gradually the assemblies of the *sections* became mere political clubs, and the same men, chiefly small merchants or political adventurers, turned up day after day. The adventurers, who had nothing to lose, usually drew the merchants into radical courses.[24]

Once a *section* had acquired a firm radical tone, it became almost impossible for the conservatives, even though in a majority, to recapture it. By a hundred devices, many of which would be familiar to small-town New Englanders, the group in power held control of the *section*. Republican propaganda spread rapidly here, especially in the poorer quarters of the city. By the spring of 1792 it was clear that the leaders of the *sections* were determined on action. June 20, for some reason, was a failure. No slips were made on August 10. The process was simple enough. Danton's own *section*, that of the Théâtre Français, declared on July 30 that it had abolished the legal distinction between "active" and "passive" citizens. Other *sections* followed suit, and by this concession were able to rally the popular forces necessary to make the insurrection a success. Few workmen actually debated in the *sections*, or took part in the higher politics of the insurrection, which was wholly bourgeois in leadership and inspiration. On July 31 the Mauconseil *section* decreed that it would transport itself in a body on Sunday, August 5, to the hall of the Legislature, and declare that it no longer recognized Louis XVI. Other *sections* were invited to join in this action. Pétion, mayor of Paris, actually appeared before the Assembly and requested that Louis be suspended from his functions. Meanwhile in each *section* delegates had been chosen to form a revolutionary central government, or Commune, for the whole of Paris. On the night of August 9, after the tocsin had been sounded and the national guard assembled, this revolutionary committee met at the Paris city hall in a room next to the one in which the legal Commune was meeting. The crux of the matter now, of course, was control of the national guard. Its commander, Mandat, taking orders from the legal Commune, prepared to defend the king and queen in the Tuileries. After several hours of confusion and talking at the city hall, the revolutionary Commune invaded the hall where the legal Commune was sitting, ejected its members by force, sent for loyal Mandat, removed him, and put in his place the brewer Santerre, one of the very group of Parisian politicians who were en-

[24] F. Braesch, *La commune du 10 août* (Paris, 1911), II, 72.

gineering the insurrection. The national guard, reinforced with the pick of provincial radicals who had come up to Paris to celebrate the "federation" of July 14, and who had remained about, armed and supported by the Jacobins, for just such an emergency, were now directed to the attack on the Tuileries instead of to its defense. To this semi-military force of guards and *fédérés* was added an unstable mass of patriots, idlers, adventurers, men of much the same stamp as those who had attacked the Bastille. Against them were only the Swiss guard of the palace, and the king's gentlemen. Louis decided not to resist, took refuge with the Assembly, and ordered the Swiss to withdraw. But firing had commenced, and the Swiss had no choice. They fought bravely, but were beaten back, and the palace taken and ransacked. The invaders, now become a mob, ran wild, butchering the Swiss, aristocrats, suspects, even, it is claimed, certain porters simply because in eighteenth-century Paris they were known as "suisses."

The monarchy had fallen. No more hedging, as after the flight to Varennes, was possible. The frightened Assembly set up a provisional executive, in which Danton appears as the strong man, and ordered the election, by universal manhood suffrage, of a new assembly to provide a new constitution. This was the famous Convention.

V. SUMMARY

Louis, taking refuge with the Assembly, had for the moment saved his life; but he had lost his throne. The "Restorer of French Liberty" was a prisoner of those whose liberties he had restored. The monarchical experiment had failed. No simple economic motive lay behind the discontents that found action on August 10. There is ample evidence that the fiscal situation was actually improving in 1792. No downtrodden and oppressed class rose on August 10 against intolerable conditions of life. The constitution of 1791 was made for the economic man of the current classical economics. No simple explanation of any sort is available for the downfall of the monarchy. But the elements of such an explanation are clear. Louis was too undecided and too virtuous—the adjectives are perhaps not quite synonymous—to stamp out opposition by force, too unintelligent to convert it to his own ends. He gambled on the flight to Varennes, and lost. The Civil Constitution of the Clergy, the product, not of idealists, but of men too practical to understand the illusions of their fellows, yet not practical enough to understand their own, made a rift in French life which could be closed only by force. And the only organized force in France in 1792 was the Jacobin machine, already directed towards realizing on earth the "heavenly city of the eighteenth century philosophers."[25] The war, opening disastrously for France, unquestionably set the stage for August 10, unquestionably made that insurrection popular in Paris and acceptable in the provinces. But the monarchy did not fall simply because it was unlucky in war. The republic was no accident, unless all history is accident. The desires and the interests of a relatively small number of politically active men, known to history as the Jacobins, ripened amid the confusions of 1792 into the ephemeral and enduring First French Republic.

That republic was, then, willed, planned, intrigued for, even, in the end, fought for, by men whose scale of values ranged into heights or depths—at any rate into extremes—most uncomfortable, indeed, quite uninhabitable, for ordinary men. Yet these heroes, or demons, attained power only because moderate men failed to hold it. Some sociological law making the failure of the moderates inevitable in time of revolution would be very convenient here. Although such a law has plausibility, as well as convenience, it can hardly be invoked by the historian to answer a challenge to his common sense. Perhaps the men who made the monarchical experiment were not really moderates after all. They had the social position, the wealth, the manners, and Anglo-Saxon notions to the contrary notwithstanding, the experience of this world of political animals, which normally make a moderate. They had moderate desires, moderate temperaments, yet much of their work—their plan of local self-government, their religious measures, their jealous separation of the powers—bears, if not the crazily aspiring touch of the true fanatic, at least the steady yet curiously unreliable hand of the doctrinaire. For in the persons of the patriots of the Constituent

[25] C. Becker, *The Heavenly City of the Eighteenth Century Philosophers* (New Haven, 1932), ch. IV.

Assembly is to be discerned a milder form of that extraordinary gap between interests and ideas which was to appear at its fullest with the Montagnards, and which has always seemed an impossible, and therefore non-existent, gap to men of little imagination or of strong faith—that is, to the majority of historians. The interests of the patriots of this first Assembly were the interests of moderate men; their ideas were largely the ideas of immoderate men, of men determined once and for all to bring to earth those fair abstractions of Justice and Happiness, so dear to the race, so distant, so unattainable, so essential, so inevitable. Their ideas, fitfully but unmistakably, triumphed over their interests, made their constitutional monarchy impossible, and prepared for the first republic. The conduct of these patriots was, then, because of the lack of equilibrium between their ideas and their interests, more revolutionary than they possibly could have intended. Normally when men say one thing and intend another, word and intention are in a working, if illogical, agreement, and something approximating the intention gets itself realized. When, however, the word perversely prevails over, and distorts, the intention, then you have a revolution. This, and not the confusion and bloodshed, is the true horror of revolutions, that they put a stop, for a while, to the comforting cheats which alone make life long endurable.

Chapter Three

EUROPE AND THE REVOLUTION: PEACE

I. GENERALIZATIONS

EUROPE in the eighteenth century is more than a geographical expression; it is a universal. Now though philosophers still dispute, even in the latest terminologies, over the problem of universals, the historian may perhaps here be permitted to fall back on common sense. To men who wrote and talked about philosophy, science, art, and politics in the eighteenth century the words "European" and "Europe" suggested certain patterns which could be woven satisfactorily in with the general pattern of their thought. Europe was not a state, but it was certainly a state of mind. Nor is this common-sense notion of Europe as a whole at all a denial of the separate existences of European societies, of the widest variations in the conditions of life within Europe. Europe is as real, *within its proper conceptual framework,* as Prussia is within its proper conceptual framework. The historian ought not to "emphasize the national point of view," or the European, as the case may be; he should simply keep them decently apart.

Some such preface is peculiarly necessary in a study of Europe between 1789 and 1799. In sheer dramatic looming up, in what may crudely be called publicity value, the French Revolution crowds out everything else in the period. No doubt life in Bradford, in Helsingfors, in Belgrade, even in Berlin, went on much as it always had, though a king of France died on the scaffold. No doubt in England, in Russia, in Germany, in other countries, these ten years saw the slow growth of institutions, measures, habits, fashions, deeply rooted in the national past. Yet it is difficult to assign to these precise ten years any exact part of the development of such important elements of European life as the industrial revolution, for instance, or the romantic movement. Inevitably a history of Europe during the French Revolution must be centered on the influence of the French Revolution in Europe. Such a centering need not lead to false simplification, nor to an exaggerated estimate of the rôle of France. Sometimes the influence of the French Revolution will be a positive one, as in the building up of a new Rhineland from the feudal patchwork of the left bank; sometimes it will be a negative one, the product of a recoil from things French, as in the fixation of Tory rule in England. Sometimes, indeed, the influence of the French Revolution will be but slight, or at any rate inadequate for purposes of explanation, as in the marked decline of Prussia under Frederick William II.

The European war which began in 1792 and which was to last until 1815 is in one sense a successor to previous great wars, a product of rivalries and tensions of long standing. Yet even here the French Revolution brought something new. Though the governments who made the first coalitions against France were seeking simply to manipulate the balance of power in their own favor, they came to regard themselves as defending a European order, a social system based on the continuing power of the successors to the warrior and priestly classes of the Middle Ages. Talleyrand later found them a word for it—Legitimacy. France was not only trying to upset the balance of power, to gain her "natural frontiers"; she was freeing the peoples of Europe from kings, priests, and nobles, preparing them for self-government. Almost from the beginning of that struggle, there began to be visible on both sides an intensification of popular feeling, a more widely spread patriotism, the complex phenomena now so familiar as "nationalism." The wars of the French Revolution involved almost every European country. The old appetites and interests of the men who fought these wars were sharpened, twisted, exalted into something almost new by the abstractions born of that Revolution. The history of no European country at this period, then, can be written in terms of its own peculiar social and political structure, and in neglect of the generalizations of European politics.

II. THE FIRST NEWS

"One of the greatest nations in the world, the greatest in general culture, has at last thrown off the yoke of tyranny. . . . Without doubt God's angels in heaven have sung a Te Deum."[1] The first news of the French Revolution brought joy to thousands of homes throughout Europe, a joy reflected in many familiar quotations from literary sources, Fox's "how much the greatest event that has ever happened in the world, and how much the best," Wordsworth's "Bliss was it in that dawn to be alive . . . ," Goethe's

> Denn wer leugnet es wohl, dass hoch sich das Herz ihm erhoben,
> Ihm die freiere Brust mit reineren Pulsen geschlagen,
> Als sich der erste Glanz der neuen Sonne heranhob,
> Als man hörte vom Rechte der Menschen. . . .

Perhaps most impressive, since least literary, is the description Steffens gives of how his father came home one night in Copenhagen, gathered his sons about him, and with tears of joy told them that the Bastille had fallen, that a new era had begun, that if they were failures in life they must blame themselves, for henceforth "poverty would vanish, the lowliest would begin the struggles of life on equal terms with the mightiest, with equal arms, on equal ground."[2] In the quiet Danish capital the gospel was received with no less fervor than in Paris.

It is almost impossible for the twentieth century to realize the stir the French Revolution made in the eighteenth-century world. For one thing, sensations of all kinds are now too easily produced and spread. It would seem that even the Russian Revolution, though it may ultimately have results even more important than the French, has not yet impressed itself so thoroughly on the Western consciousness as did the French. English and German newspapers reported at length the proceedings of French parliamentary bodies. The terms of French politics—Feuillant, Jacobin, Brissotin, veto, refractory priest, and such like—had surprising currency outside France. Among the literate classes of western and central Europe, one loathed or worshiped the Revolution; the indifferent were few, the wholly ignorant almost none.

The reasons for this widespread, direct interest in the Revolution are not far to seek, and they help throw light on the whole process

---

[1] Schlözer, quoted in A. Stern, *Der Einfluss der Französischen Revolution auf das deutsche Geistesleben* (Stuttgart, 1928), 4.
[2] H. Steffens, *Was ich erlebte* (Breslau, 1840), I, 363.

of change in late eighteenth-century Europe. France was still, in spite of her military defeats under Louis XV, "la grande nation"; her language and arts were still imitated through most of Europe. The middle classes in England, in much of urban Germany and in the Rhineland, in northern Italy, in Holland, Belgium, Switzerland, in much of Scandinavia had already worked out a way of life similar to that of the French middle class, and above all had similar ambitions and interests, similar grievances against the privileged classes. The climate of opinion, the ideology of the *philosophes*, of the *Aufklärung*, of the deists was almost uniform in western and central Europe. Interests and ideas blended curiously, but almost identically, in the different countries. Witness the mixture of benevolence and bourgeois aggressiveness in the above-quoted encouragment of the elder Steffens to his boys. Finally—and this is an important distinction from the Russian Revolution—the French Revolution began in hope, in a country economically prosperous, in a Europe which had been reasonably long at peace, or at any rate without major international wars, in an atmosphere of confidence rare in the history of revolution.

The French Revolution, then, must be studied as a European phenomenon. But such a study must, in dealing with modern Europe, accept the framework of the only society which is also a state—the nation-state.[3]

III. GREAT BRITAIN

The English Channel is by no means impassable. There is, however, enough truth in the notion that the peoples of Great Britain are not quite like the peoples of the Continent so that one should take care not to bury the truth in exaggerations. English writers, notably during the last century, were apt to delight overmuch in what they regarded as the isolation of England. The Channel was never a *cordon sanitaire* against the infection of foreign ideas. Many an English writer rather perversely insisted on dressing his ideas— or his desires—in good homely English dress, and then damned the

[3] Again it must be noted that this is simply a study of the impact of the Revolution upon European states. For a general view of the condition of Europe on the eve of the Revolution, see the preceding volume in this series, dealing with the period 1763-1789.

same ideas and desires in foreign dress. Bentham supported democratic institutions in the name of "utility," and attacked those same
institutions when they were supported in the name of "natural
rights." So, too, nineteenth-century Englishmen were unduly com-
placent over the stability of their state, over the absence of revolutionary violence from their annals. They passed hastily over the be-
heading of one king and the ejection of another in the seventeenth
century, a long series of riots and mob violences in the eighteenth.
Yet in 1789, England had the reputation for political instability
which France had acquired by 1889. Elie Halévy wrote that during
the whole eighteenth century England was regarded as "the classical
country of political insurrection."[4]

The real and valid difference between England and France in
1789 is just this: thanks to the English political revolutions of the
seventeenth century, to the defeat of George III by Wilkes and
Washington, to the growth of commercial enterprise, England enjoyed in 1789 most of what France gained by her first revolution, by
the monarchical experiment. Since the ruling classes of England,
the Whig oligarchy, the London bankers, the middle-class entrepre-
neurs, had had ample time to consolidate their positions, England
could withstand the drive of the democratic republicans, could
oppose her stability to the idealistic, religious crusade of the French
Revolution in its second phase. England had had her 1789 so long
ago that she did not fear 1793-94. She had, indeed, her republicans—
Thomas Paine produced in his *Rights of Man* one of the best
epitomes of that movement. But social, political, and economic conditions in England were against Paine and his fellows. The Channel and English common sense may have contributed to the maintenance of English stability, but they were not the sole, nor even
the most important factors in that stability.

Neglecting for a moment the influence of the French Revolution,
one may say that the last decade of the century witnessed four major
developments in England: enclosure, the transition to the factory
system, the transition to modern business enterprise, the reform
movement. All had begun well before 1789, and all were to continue
after 1799. The decade is not of prime importance in the under-

---

[4] E. Halévy, *Histoire du peuple anglais au XIXme siècle* (Paris, 1913), I, 140.

standing of any of them. The reform movement, indeed, was virtually arrested for a time in 1794 by the reaction to events in France.
A few words, however, must be said on each.

Enclosure was the process of securing through act of Parliament
the partition of commons, pastures, waste lands, bogs, and similar
rural areas owned in common into a series of enclosed fields owned
in severalty. These new fields usually made up fair-sized farms
capable of exploitation by improved capitalistic methods. Those
who had possessed relatively small and unimportant rights in the
old commons were pretty generally compensated in sums too small
to allow them to set up for themselves. The net result of the enclosure movement was no doubt to increase the yield per acre cultivated, but also to throw a large part of the English peasantry into
a wage-economy, to create a large landless rural proletariat. Parliamentary enclosures which under George II had averaged 7 a year,
averaged 47 a year between 1760 and 1765, and 78 a year between
1794 and 1804, so that the last decade of the century represents a
perceptible speeding up of the process.[5] At the very time when the
French Revolution was insuring the persistence and strengthening
in France of a large class of small peasant proprietors—a yeomanry,
England was witnessing the last steps in the extinction of her own
yeomanry. That most English word ceased to describe an English
thing.

This agrarian revolution did not help produce the industrial
revolution by providing a large class of unemployed available as
cheap labor. Silesia in the eighteenth century had a large "surplus"
population, but no industrial revolution. Unlike fifteenth-century
enclosures in England, which were for pasturage, these new enclosures were for tillage, and actually made the land more productive, made it possible to employ more laborers and to support a
larger population. The agrarian revolution is, however, connected
with the industrial revolution in this way: as long as the Corn Laws
protected English agriculture, the improved capitalist methods
of cultivation, by increasing the yield of English farms, enabled
England to feed the workers who ran the mills, enabled her to build
up her industry in the early nineteenth century to a position so com-

[5] M. D. George, *England in Transition* (London, 1931), 115.

manding that she could abandon the Corn Laws and import most of her foodstuffs.

The factory system and the British money market grew together in this period, each one dependent on the other, and by the end of the Napoleonic Wars, England was economically a modern nation. Details, as usual in economic history, are abundant and confusing. Here it is possible only to indicate certain symptoms of this modernization of England. Textile factories, run by water power, had for some time been springing up in the North and Midlands. Samuel Oldknow at Mellow employed 418 workmen in his spinning mill in 1798, and used a method of cost accounting definitely modern, with provisions for what is now called "overhead." He was at all times in close dependence on his bankers, and during the crisis of 1793, finding his assets thoroughly frozen, resorted to scrip to pay his employees.[6] Pitt's policy of paying war expenses by borrowing added greatly to the *rentier* class. There was already a Stock Exchange, a class of merchant-bankers, a certain solidarity in the "City"—in brief, the elements of a money market. In this situation the war acted on the whole as a stimulus both to industrial production and to the credit system. The almost complete economic freedom of English life no doubt made this expansion possible. This same freedom also brought with it the accentuation of commercial crises, of which there were two in the decade, one in 1793, the other in 1797. The business men and bankers who grew rich under these conditions were gradually absorbed into that elastic group known in England as the "ruling classes." "Rentier and squire were assimilated to their financial intermediaries in a new social and political alignment. The City gave its complexion to the New Toryism. And policy which had guided the price of the funds now sought its orders from them."[7]

Reform in England could not be made the dramatic cause it was in France. The English middle class had too much economic freedom to worry overmuch about the exact status of parliamentary representation. Yet there were two strong native reform movements, both of which were well developed before 1789. There was a move-

[6] G. Unwin, "The Transition to the Factory System," *English Historical Review* (1922), XXXVII, 395-397.
[7] L. H. Jenks, *The Migration of British Capital to 1875* (New York, 1927), 19.

ment to reform Parliament—that is, to extend the franchise and to equalize, at least roughly, the constituencies. The House of Commons actually, of course, was chosen in a great majority on a narrow, if varying, franchise, and from borough and county constituencies of varied areas and populations. The most spectacular target for the reformers was the "rotten borough," a somewhat loose term used to designate boroughs where the constituency was so small that its members could be returned by one man. A Society for Promoting Constitutional Information had been founded in 1780, and under the leadership of such men as Major John Cartwright, Sir William Jones, John Jebb, the Duke of Richmond, sought to agitate for reform of Parliament. Major Cartwright, brother of the inventor of the power loom, was a single-minded English gentleman, who sincerely believed that his program of annual Parliaments, universal suffrage, secret ballot, equal electoral districts, and payment of members was a reflection of the historical liberties of England and the native democracy of the Anglo-Saxons. The society as a whole, however, was much less radical, hopeful only of destroying the more shocking inequalities of representation. Pitt himself began as a reformer, and in 1785 introduced a mild scheme of reform involving compensation to borough owners. It was defeated by seventy votes, but since Pitt had not made it a party matter, he did not resign. Pitt did not, however, drop notions of improving the mechanism of English government. He turned to fiscal matters and in 1786 procured a treaty with France which foreshadowed the Free Trade of Cobden.

A second strong current of reform was directed towards humanitarian channels and, as so often in modern England, numbered many political conservatives. The Society for the Abolition of the Slave Trade was founded in 1787, supported by such sober, respectable men as Wilberforce and the Wedgwoods, fired by enthusiasts like Clarkson, and soon launched itself into the campaign which was to culminate in victory in 1807. The society made notable use of the methods of modern pressure groups. Their propaganda was extremely varied—broadsides, pamphlets, public meetings, debates. Cowper wrote a ballad, "The Negro's Complaint," which was set to music and sung in the streets. Wedgwood produced a cameo bearing the seal of the society—a suppliant negro. Clarkson claimed that at one time 300,000 people were boycotting West India sugar.[8] Similar efforts, similar energies were engaged in prison reform, the prevention of cruelty to animals, the care of orphans, in all the great variety of what has since been called social work. Already there is distinguishable that paradox of English civilization which has especially puzzled foreigners: energetic and ruthless pursuit of self-interest in business, equally energetic and ruthless regulation of certain moral aspects of group-life.

In this expanding, generally prosperous England the French Revolution appeared at first but an interesting spectacle. To the political reformers, to the dissenters still legally excluded from full political life by the Test Act, to the humanitarians and to the hopeful, it was a welcome earnest of better things to come. "Look up! look up! O citizen of London, enlarge thy countenance! O Jew, leave counting gold! return to thy oil and wine. O African! black African! Go; winged thought, widen his forehead!"[9] Dissenters formed the greater part of the audience when Dr. Price gave his memorable address before the Revolution Society in November, 1789. Price, Unitarian minister and economist, welcomed the French Revolution as the natural successor of the Glorious Revolution of 1688, as announcing once more the right of resistance to oppression. This address called out in refutation Burke's *Reflections on the Revolution in France*, the first widely read attack on the work of the National Assembly.

The next two years witness the gradual formation of two groups in English public opinion, an anti-revolutionary group centered on Burke, and a much less homogeneous group friendly to the principles of the Revolution. This latter group included the parliamentary Whigs, Fox and his younger allies, Grey, Lambton, Whitbread and others, who in 1792 organized a Society of Friends of the People to spread their views; the old reformers, who now, under the leadership of Horne Tooke, revived the rather somnolent Society for Promoting Constitutional Information; a new and significant group of workingmen, who under the cobbler Thomas Hardy

[8] W. L. Mathieson, *England in Transition*, 1789-1832 (London, 1920), 68-70.
[9] Blake, "A Song of Liberty" (1792), quoted in P. A. Brown, *The French Revolution in English History* (London, 1923), 35.

founded the London Corresponding Society, which soon gathered filiate societies in the provinces into an organization something like that of the French Jacobins. Fox and Burke broke dramatically over the French Revolution in 1791 during a parliamentary debate on a Canadian question. A war of pamphleteers went on, in which Mackintosh, Mary Wollstonecraft and Thomas Paine kept up a running fire on Burke. But not until after the fall of the monarchy in France did the debate in England come to a head in action.

Throughout these years of the monarchical experiment in France, the actual government of England maintained a strict neutrality. As a son of the enlightenment, Pitt was willing to agree that the Revolution was justified; as a British statesman, he was glad to see a state traditionally hostile now for a time disabled by internal difficulties. England in 1789 was allied with Prussia and Holland, an alliance directed primarily against France and Austria. Nothing seemed to Pitt to threaten war for England. He had abandoned his aggressive policy against Russia, had decided to let the Near Eastern and Polish questions be settled among the powers most immediately concerned. Not yet was it possible to alarm a British Parliament over the expansion of Russia. Even after the declaration of war between the German powers and France Pitt hoped that England could remain neutral. Certainly the realistic Pitt was not going to engage England in a romantic crusade to restore the glories of Versailles.

IV. THE GERMANIES

There are for the student of the decade 1789-1799 three Germanies —Austria, Prussia, and the Rhineland. The remaining German states, although they frequently display interesting local variations, can be brought easily enough into the orbits of Austria or Prussia. For the Holy Roman Empire of the German Nation this was to be the last decade. As an institution it was no doubt already dead, and certainly, in the opinion of literary men, buried. Yet it has some claim to be considered a real Germany, a Germany which provided even in the late eighteenth century some sort of focus for patriotic feelings. The Revolution was to destroy the empire as an institution: the nineteenth century was to build up a German nation-state on a pattern quite as modern as that of England and France. Yet the romantic nationalism through which this was achieved "had found in many a place a spiritual ground prepared for it by the old imperial patriotism."[10] Modern Germany was not wholly a product of blood, iron, and romanticism; it owed something to the inefficient common sense of the eighteenth century.

The Rhineland—and especially the left bank—must be considered somewhat apart from the rest of Germany. It was as completely subdivided into little independent units as was southern or central Germany. The electorate of Mainz is a good example of a Rhenish *Kleinstaat*. Technically an archbishopric, and as such one of the three spiritual electorates in the empire, it was administered quite untheocratically by the elector Friedrich Karl von Erthal. Its 350,000 inhabitants were mostly peasants, small landholders, paying feudal dues similar to those paid by French peasants. In the capital was a miniature court, a university, a bench and bar, an army of 2,200 infantry, 120 artillerymen, fifty hussars, one field marshal, twelve generals, one *Hofkriegsrats-präsident* and six *Hofkriegsräte*. By the cannon on the ramparts were piled neat pyramids of cannonballs, which, when the French republican armies approached in 1792, were found to be of the wrong bore.[11] It is quite the Germany of comic opera.

Now this region—the archbishoprics of Mainz, Trier, and Cologne, the Rhenish palatinate, the duchy of Zweibrücken, and many other small states—was influenced first by its very contiguity with France. Even more than the rest of Germany, it had been subjected during the eighteenth century to French cultural and economic penetration. Even before the end of 1792, it had suffered a French invasion and had felt French republican propaganda spread by French soldiers. Mainz provided an excellent center for such propaganda. From its university, merchant, and official circles a Jacobin club was recruited and organized under French supervision, and led by the distinguished savant Georg Forster. This club did much to pave the way for the annexation of the left bank to France, for

[10] A. Berney, "Reichstraditionen und Nationalstaatsgedanke, 1789-1815," *Historische Zeitschrift* (1929), CXL, 66.
[11] K. T. Heigel, *Deutsche Geschichte vom Tode Friederichs d. Gr. bis zur Auflösung des alten Reiches* (1911), II, 53-55.

the introduction of civil equality and the abolition of feudalism. Finally, this whole region was a region of peasant proprietorship, of small farms and vineyards, saddled like France with feudal survivals, but not like eastern and central Germany subject to pretty complete medieval serfdom. "The fate of the Rhenish peasant resembles that of the French peasant. He is a landowner and has enough civil liberty to wish more. The feudal system is sufficiently weakened so that it is possible to conceive of its total abolition."[12] Nor, of course, were those peasants patriotically loyal Germans in the nineteenth-century sense. They welcomed emancipation, even under French auspices and French armies. The Rhineland underwent earlier the influence of the French Revolution, and was more permanently marked by it, than any other part of Germany.

Prussia in 1789 was a kingdom of some 76,000 square miles and 5,500,000 population, of which slightly less than half, both of area and population, was included in the Holy Roman Empire.[13] It had been, under Frederick the Great, the model state of the *philosophes*. After the victories of the Seven Years' War, it enjoyed a reputation in some respects similar to that won by Japan after the Russo-Japanese War. Frederick died in 1786, and the next decade witnessed the disastrous retreat of the admired Prussian army from Valmy, the embarrassment and disorganization of Prussian finances, and abundant signs of the coming collapse of the Prussian state after Jena. The problem of the decline of Prussia is by all odds the outstanding one of German history in this decade.

For one thing, some part of this decline is more apparent than real. Prussia never had quite been able to live up to its Frederician reputation. Still a poor state, with great estates inefficiently run by serf labor, without much industrial development, save in the newly acquired Silesia, Prussia had had to tax itself to the limit to maintain its recently acquired status as a great power. Frederick's parsimony had in his later years gone so far that certain departments of government were starved, and his successor was bound to increase expenses. Moreover, the beautifully organized bureaucracy of the Prussian state was wholly centered on Frederick. "L'état c'est moi,"

---

[12] A. Sorel, *L'Europe et la Révolution française* (Paris, 1885), I, 432.
[13] A. Himly, *Histoire de la formation territoriale des états de l'Europe centrale* (Paris, 1876), II, 83.

quite false as applied to Louis XIV, is as near true as possible when applied to Frederick. Everything depended on his successor. Now Frederick William II was, unlike his uncle, a good man in the modern and sentimental connotation of the phrase. He wanted people to be happy, wanted to be happy himself in a simple, pious, earthy way. His chief delight was in the pleasures of the bed—not by any means limited to the marriage bed—in which he apparently developed considerable skill and endurance. It is perhaps an unprofitable trespass on the none too solid ground of psychology to speculate on whether there is a connection between Frederick William's sensuality and his religious mysticism; but it must be noted that he was by upbringing a good Christian, that organized Christianity frowns with Pauline severity on the pleasures of sex, and that therefore his piety may have been strengthened by his not infrequent need for it. Certainly the slow, well-meaning young man had come to dislike, as well as to admire, his brilliant uncle, and made the latter's death a signal for striking changes.

Frederick had patronized French art and science, wrote in French, saw to it that French was the language of court and academy. Frederick William disliked the French, and particularly the French in Prussia, as a lot of shallow and immoral atheists, incapable of true feeling. He at once made the German language permissible in the Academy of Sciences, appointed Germans to that body, including his favorite, Wöllner, encouraged German literature in the persons of Gleim and Ramler, whom Frederick had never even noticed, revived Bach chorals and patronized contemporary German musicians in preference to foreign-born ones. An edict of July 9, 1788, reinforced in December by a new censorship law, was directed against "Socinians, Deists and Naturalists," and set up the Bible again as part of the law of the land. The Prussian *Aufklärung* was over.

Frederick William had, before his accession, joined under the name of Brother Ormesus Magnus the order of Rosicrucians, one of the numerous secret societies of the time, a society, unlike Freemasons, Illuminati, and so on, highly devoted to Christianity. Here he could give free play to his genius for mysticism and friendship. Now Frederick the Great had had no friends, and his ministers were merely his servants. But they were good servants, and the Prussian bureaucracy worked. Frederick William had favorites—his brother Rosicrucians Bischoffswerder and Wöllner, his beloved Mme. Rietz. Bischoffswerder was a man of rather ordinary capacity, somewhat out of his depth in diplomacy. Wöllner seems to have been a scoundrel and a hypocrite, and, entrusted by his master with complete power over the general administration of the kingdom, succeeded in a very short time in disrupting the bureaucracy. Mme. Rietz, towards whom, according to Dampmartin, Frederick William exhibited "the tenderness of a father, the constancy of a friend, the passion of a lover," was, in spite of being the object of such unpleasant versatility, no Egeria.[14]

The court of Berlin became conspicuous among European courts as a center of intrigue and corruption. Inefficiency and laxness crept into the government departments. Expenses increased, partly because Frederick William's kind heart would not consent to limiting governmental social work—indeed, he notably expanded and improved the common school system, in which the enlightened Frederick had not been interested—partly because of Prussian participation in the war against France. The failure at Valmy did not increase the harmony at Berlin. Indeed, however much one may attempt to analyze the situation in Prussia, one is tempted to assert that here the whole is clearly more than the sum of its parts, that Prussia's decline under Frederick William II is a decline in the efficiency, the equilibrium, the smooth functioning of a complex organism. Modern social science, distrustful of synthesis, has here no adequate terminology; perhaps the nearest one can come to it is to say that Prussian morale had broken down. Prussians collaborating in the running of Prussia had begun to *feel* a lack of confidence in the abstraction, Prussia.

There was little danger that the French Revolution might spread to Prussia. The Pomeranian or East Prussian peasant had not, like the French peasant, enough private property to want more. The middle class was not so near the nobility in wealth, in culture, morals, ambitions, that, like the French middle class, it could find

---

[14] A. H. Dampmartin, *Quelques traits de la vie privée de Frédéric-Guillaume II* (Paris, 1811), 15.

it worth while to fight for equality. The *Aufklärung* had never, as in France, penetrated from fashionable salons to the petty bourgeoisie of provincial towns.[15] The news of the fall of the Bastille was greeted with rejoicing in the circle of the Allgemeine Deutsche Bibliothek. But Nicolai and his friends were already under suspicion as unbelievers, and Wöllner's censorship had little difficulty in suppressing anything that looked like French propaganda. Kant, indeed, who is reported by Nicolovius in 1794 as "a complete democrat," certainly welcomed the Revolution, but he was an old man and a cautious one, and much too complete a metaphysician to worry a censor.[16] It is true that Frederick William himself attempted in 1789-90 through his ambassador Goltz and a special agent, the mysterious Jew Ephraim, to work through the revolutionary party in France towards detaching France from Austria and bringing her into the Triple Alliance. But that was European politics, and no more showed Prussia to be influenced by the Revolution than Richelieu's policy in the Thirty Years' War showed France to be influenced by Lutheranism. As a matter of fact, Frederick William was sadly deceived by his disingenuous ambassador as to the strength of the pro-Prussian party among French radicals. Goltz's reports have been used by French historians to make both Pétion and Barnave Prussian agents, which they never were. Ephraim's mission was a failure from the start.[17] No doubt, however, Frederick William was embittered by his failure, and the subsequent alliance with Austria against revolutionary France made easier.

The Emperor Joseph II died in 1790, having failed in the attempt to rule according to reason a state not constructed according to reason. The hereditary possessions of the house of Hapsburg contained some 256,000 square miles with 24,000,000 inhabitants—quantitatively at least a far stronger state than Prussia. Even if Hungary and the other lands outside the empire are omitted, Austria still counted 10,500,000 people in 88,000 square miles.[18] But the Austrian state lacked racial, linguistic, institutional unity, and the attempts of Joseph II to impose a unified administration resulted

[15] Heigel, *Deutsche Geschichte*, I, 325.
[16] Stern, *Einfluss der Französischen Revolution*, 177-178.
[17] W. Ludtke, "Preussen und Frankreich vom Bastillesturm bis Reichenbach," *Forschungen zur brandenburgischen und preussischen Geschichte* (1929), XLII, 261.
[18] Himly, *Formation territoriale*, I, ch. 441.

in disorganization and revolt, at the very time when his ambitious foreign policy had produced an expensive and unsuccessful war. His brother Leopold, who succeeded him, had had a long training as Grand Duke of Tuscany, and had made his duchy one of the most flourishing states in Italy. He was, like most of his contemporaries, fashionably enlightened; but he was also cautious, almost timid, quite devoid of vanity as well as of principle, intelligent, a sober judge of men and motives. Leopold determined from the first to make foreign and domestic peace, to preserve intact the Hapsburg territories by yielding gladly to unimportant demands, reluctantly to important ones. Leopold's two-year reign was too brief to permit judgment of his statesmanship. It is just possible that, being a sensible, unheroic, and unimaginative person, he could not properly discern what was important and what unimportant in the new nationalism among his subjects, and that therefore he made the wrong concessions. At any rate he did what he set out to do: he pacified a state which, on his accession, seemed about to disintegrate.

Leopold found himself engaged in the war which Joseph and his ally, Catherine of Russia, had begun in 1787 for the partition of Turkey. The Austrian campaign against the Turks, at first a complete failure, had taken a turn for the better in 1789, and Belgrade had been occupied. But Constantinople was still far away, and Austrian finances were incapable of supporting a longer war. Moreover, Prussia had allied herself with Turkey and Poland, mobilized her army in Silesia, and threatened war with Austria. The Austrian Netherlands were in open revolt, Hungary rather more than restive, Bohemia waking at last from the long sleep which had followed the battle of the White Mountain. Prussian agents were stirring up trouble everywhere. Revolutionary France had virtually dissolved the Austrian alliance, and Russia had her own war with Turkey, and another with Gustavus III of Sweden.

Leopold's situation was almost melodramatically insecure. But European diplomacy is, perhaps unfortunately, not quite melodrama, and Leopold escaped his enemies unharmed. In July, 1790, Austria and Prussia at Reichenbach signed an agreement by which Austria was to make peace with Turkey on the basis of the *status quo*, and Prussian and Austrian armies were to be withdrawn from the Silesian frontier. Peace was made between Austria and Turkey at Sistova in 1791. Leopold had saved himself by accepting at the apparent dictatorship of Prussia exactly what he had planned to do himself. Frederick William and his minister Hertzberg had both cherished complicated schemes for Prussian aggression, but they could not, even in the eighteenth century, declare war on Austria for the avowed purpose of despoiling her. Hertzberg's plan in particular has long been famous as a piece of diplomatic folly, of "monstrous impracticability."[19] Briefly, he proposed that Turkey cede what is now Rumania to Austria, Bessarabia and Ochakov to Russia, and in return secure a European guaranty for the integrity of Turkish domains south of the Danube; that Austria, in return for her Turkish gains, retrocede Galicia to Poland; and that Poland then cede Danzig and Thorn to Prussia. Prussia would thus have something for nothing, and only Turkey, her ally, would be the loser. But the Poles obstinately refused, and England and Holland finally decided not to back up their ally Prussia, but to use their influence to secure peace and the *status quo*. Pitt could hardly face the prospect of an Austria completely eliminated from the European balance of power. Deserted by his allies, and not quite strong enough to force a war in the manner of Bismarck, Frederick William was obliged to offer Leopold what the latter wanted. Reichenbach was on the surface an Austrian defeat and a Prussian victory. Acutally it permitted Leopold to pacify his dominions, and thereby perhaps to save the Hapsburg power.

Discontent in Austria itself had not gone beyond grumbling and protest from the Estates, and Leopold was able to restore quiet by abandoning his brother's attempts at religious reform. In Bohemia, concessions such as the establishment of a chair in the Czech tongue at the university in Prague, and a general confirmation of the privileges of the nobles proved sufficient. In Hungary, where the jealously independent counties, controlled by the landed gentry, were in almost open rebellion, greater concessions were necessary. On paper, at least, Leopold granted Hungary complete home rule. A king of Hungary must in the future be crowned within six months,

[19] R. H. Lord, *The Second Partition of Poland* (Cambridge, Mass., 1915), 77.

at Buda, with the holy crown—thus making an abstention like that of Joseph II impossible. As King of Hungary, he must consult Magyar advisers. He may not enforce in Hungary the laws of the rest of his dominions. The Diet must be called at least triennially. It possesses full legislative power, and especially the power of the purse. The Diet, of course, was dominantly noble. What Leopold did was to turn Hungary over to its upper classes. Finally, in the Austrian Netherlands, revolt was complete. A popular uprising had driven the Austrian troops from Brussels back into Luxemburg. The neighboring bishopric of Liège had seen a similar uprising. Delegates to a common meeting of the medieval Estates declared Belgium independent under the name, obviously influenced by American example, of the United Belgian States. Leopold waited quietly until the Belgians had quarreled amongst themselves, and the new government had been proved pretty incompetent, when he made very generous promises of reform and amnesty, and sent his troops to recapture Brussels. By the beginning of 1791 Austrian rule was restored in Belgium.

Several interesting remarks may be made about these internal difficulties of the Hapsburg monarchy. Joseph's attempt to secure uniformity produced the same sort of intense nationalism later called forth in Spain and Germany by Napoleon's aggression. In Hungary one county actually voted to reject all Western civilization and to return to the life of their "Scythian" ancestors.[20] The old heroes of the race, Arpád, Hunyadi János, Rákóczy were sung again, and the Magyar language quite suddenly became universal. Again, though the demands made to Leopold by the rebellious or half-rebellious Estates in Hungary, Bohemia, Belgium were made by privileged classes, and in general involved an extension of privilege, a tightening of medieval survivals, these reactionary demands are almost always couched in the language of the French Revolution. "The Bohemian Estates in 1790 . . . looked only to their medieval past. To them old Bohemia furnished a panacea for all ills. To this ancient source of their political thought they added a few new ideas such as Rousseau's theory of compact government, but only as far

[20] E. Sayous, *Histoire générale des Hongrois* (2nd ed. Budapest, 1900), 417.

as it concerned the sovereign and themselves."[21] A Bohemian noble could say "the essence of a fundamental law, that is to say of a contract, of an alliance between sovereign and people, is that it may not be modified but by mutual consent," but he meant only that noblemen wanted no royal meddling with their peasants. The Moravian nobles in 1791 petitioned Leopold as follows: "As it is certain . . . that all kinds of men, and especially the brutal masses of peasants cannot always be brought to obey by kindness, . . . and that the present insubordination of the rural population is provoked by the numerous formalities exacted, . . . and that, finally, several good blows, inflicted at once, do more good than heavier punishments too much postponed," whipping at will should be restored.[22]

Thanks to Leopold's firmness, this power of punishment was not restored to the nobles. So completely were the French revolutionists themselves fooled by the reactionaries' use of the orthodox eighteenth-century vocabulary of rebellion that, especially in the Belgian revolution, they welcomed as sympathizers men whose aims were wholly different. There was usually a minority in these Hapsburg lands who really did understand revolution in the French sense. They were almost all bourgeois, members of the lower clergy, intellectuals. In Hungary the towns could choose certain members of the Diet, and thanks partly to Leopold's able support, bourgeois interests were not completely overridden. In Belgium, naturally, there was a fairly strong group, known from their leader as the Vonckists, familiar with French radical literature and sympathetic with the radicals of the Assembly. But the Vonckists were in a minority, and were shortly driven into exile by the victorious clerical-noble coalition. In none of these lands do the common people seem aroused by the Francophil party, at least not in its favor. On the contrary, the lower classes not uncommonly sided with the nobles. This is especially true in Belgium, where the Vonckists were known as the "merchants' club," and "considered by the workmen of Brussels as a center of plotting against the people and against the faith."[23]

[21] R. J. Kerner, *Bohemia in the Eighteenth Century* (New York, 1932), 367.
[22] E. Denis, *La Bohème depuis la Montagne Blanche* (New edition, Paris, 1930), I, 615, 619.
[23] H. Pirenne, *Histoire de la Belgique* (Brussels, 1920), V, 483.

V. THE BACKGROUND OF THE WAR

The news of the French Revolution spread all over Europe, wherever men read or talked politics. But its major effects in Italy are later than 1792, while neither Spain nor Russia was really affected by French ideas in this decade. The history of Sweden and its extraordinary king, Gustavus III, is interesting, but unfortunately peripheral to the history of Europe as a whole. Gustavus in a brilliant and personally conducted *coup d'état* in 1789 destroyed the power of the Russian party in the Swedish Riddarhus, and was thus free to carry on his war against Russia with great success in the summer of 1790. This Swedish attack no doubt made the situation at Reichenbach simpler, and it certainly furthered Prussian designs in Poland, since by it Catherine was pretty well kept out of things for a while. Gustavus was a highly romantic, as well as a very capable person, and after having made peace with Catherine —for prolonged war was costly to a poor and minor power like Sweden—he became the chief royal opponent of the French Revolution, and sought in every way to lead a crusade to relieve Louis and his queen. The great powers obviously did not want a crusade, especially since they would have to pay expenses, and Gustavus was rebuffed. In March, 1792, he was assassinated by an agent of the hostile Swedish nobility.

The truth is that, in spite of Burke's pleadings, Gustavus's energy, Artois's intrigues, the conservative powers of central Europe did not want to go to war with France to restore legitimate monarchy and repress the menace of a world-wide revolution. French rhetoric, at the time and since, coupled with the misleading analogy of the Bolshevik Revolution, makes it easy today to consider the war as from the first an attempt by European conservatives to stamp out a social revolution that threatened to spread through all Europe. The men in power in eighteenth-century Europe, however, had no such prescience. To the Hertzbergs, the Kaunitzes, to the William Pitts of a dozen states the French Revolution meant simply that for a while at least France could be counted out of the game. Internal difficulties, ran the axiom, incapacitate a country in foreign affairs. The troubles of the Stuarts, for instance, had made England a negligible factor in the politics of the Thirty Years' War. It is unreasonable to expect these sensible, successful statesmen of routine to realize what such distinguished historians as Aulard and Mathiez did not understand, that the French Revolution was a religious movement, that it aspired to universality, and that this aspiration could be illogically centered on the geographical entity France to make national France far more successfully aggressive than dynastic France had ever been. These statesmen were used to the realities of a struggle for power in which moral ideas were deliberately, and usually without success, employed to deceive one's opponent. They were quite incapable of understanding the workings of democratic nationalism, in which moral ideas enable private citizens as well as statesmen very successfully to deceive themselves. Kaunitz, in November, 1791, composed official "reflections on the pretended dangers of contagion with which the new French constitution menaces other sovereign states of Europe."[24] Catherine, in 1792, thought France so weakened that a corps of 10,000 men would be sufficient to traverse it from one end to the other.[25] It is difficult to get people to exert themselves against a danger they simply do not see to be a danger.

The powers, then, were not to be moved by appeals to stamp out the wicked Jacobins. Nor were they to be persuaded to intervene in French affairs to protect the sacred persons of the king and queen. The word "legitimacy" had not yet become a slogan, and as Sorel has observed, nothing like a Holy Alliance was possible. "The old Europe was incapable of it, and the French Revolution was necessary to give it such a notion."[26] Leopold, brother of the endangered queen, appealed to by the French royal family itself, by the *émigrés*, by the minority of intellectuals already alarmed, finally decided, after Varennes, that at least a gesture was necessary. He met the King of Prussia at Pillnitz in Saxony in August, 1791, and the two sovereigns there issued a joint declaration. They declared French affairs to be the common interest of all Europe, and asserted their willingness to interfere to protect Louis *if* a common agree-

[24] A. von Vivenot, *Quellen zur Geschichte der deutschen Kaiserpolitik Oesterreichs* (Vienna, 1873), I, 285.
[25] C. de Larivière, *Catherine II et la Révolution française* (Paris, 1895), 363.
[26] A. Sorel, *L'Europe et la Révolution française*, I, 71.

ment were obtained from all European powers. Such an agreement was, of course, impossible, if only because England, as Leopold well knew, would not in any case have signed it. Yet Leopold's famous qualifying *if*—"alors et dans ce cas"—was a diplomatic subtlety too great for ordinary Frenchmen. No better illustration of the new importance of public opinion can be had than the reception of this declaration in France. "Then and in that case" was completely neglected by French agitators, and the declaration became for purposes of propaganda an unmitigated threat by Austria and Prussia to crush France. When Louis formally accepted the new constitution—a step which obviously did not alter the realities of the situation—Leopold, alarmed by the belligerent reception of the Declaration of Pillnitz in France, hastily notified the powers that now everything was all right, and the King of France a free man. Catherine, indeed, began a verbal crusade against the "hydra with 1,200 heads" (The National Assembly) comparatively early; but she kept her troops and her money at home for use against the Poles.

There was no concert of Europe in 1789, merely a rough balance of power among competing dynastic groups. If the French Revolution did not immediately arouse a concert of Europe to prevent its spread, it did at least alter the balance of power. Certain areas in Europe had come to be obvious pickings for the great powers of France, Austria, Russia, Prussia (England taking hers outside Europe). Of these areas, Turkey had at the opening of this decade fairly successfully defended herself from the joint attack of Austria and Russia, and was on the point of making peace not altogether without honor. Italy afforded at the moment no obvious openings. There were left only Poland and the minor German states. To these was now added, in the opinion of the central and eastern powers, France. If these powers were unwilling to crusade to save Louis XVI, they were quite prepared for an orthodox eighteenth-century war to acquire French territory. An amazing series of plans for territorial readjustments, of which Hertzberg's Polish scheme is merely the most notorious, went the rounds of the chancelleries. Austria would exchange the Netherlands for Bavaria, or acquire Alsace-Lorraine from France and exchange it for Bavaria. Prussia would let Austria have Bavaria, compensating herself in Luxemburg and Alsace-Lorraine. The Hohenzollern possession of Ansbach-Baireuth had just been acquired by the royal Prussian branch of the family; surely this meant compensation for someone somewhere?

In spite of the confusion of claims and counter-claims, the main lines of diplomatic history are fairly clear. Catherine had already set her heart on acquisitions, or at least a Russian protectorate, in Poland, but wishing to have as free a hand in the matter as possible, did everything in her power to divert the attention of Austria and Prussia towards France. Frederick William, disgruntled by Reichenbach, balked of one chance to emulate his uncle at the head of his army, hesitated between aggression at the expense of Poland and aggression at the expense of France. In either case, he needed a Continental ally. Ephraim's mission in France having failed, and Hertzberg, who like a good Frederician considered Austria the hereditary enemy, out of the way, Frederick William came gradually, under the influence of Bischoffswerder, to favor an alliance with Austria. The notion of permanent, irreconcilable enmities among European powers, like the notion of the biparty system, is a modern myth. Even in the twentieth century, the way from Fashoda to the Entente of 1904 was brief. Under new men like Bischoffswerder, Cobenzl, and Spielmann, the "permanent hatreds" of the Seven Years' War were converted into the Austro-Prussian alliance of February 7, 1792, a defensive alliance into the making of which had gone much discussion about Alsace-Lorraine, the Netherlands, Jülich and Berg.[27] Yet as long as Leopold lived, Austria was unlikely to join voluntarily in an attack on France. Indeed, Leopold did everything in his power to stave off the war, especially by urging the German princes affected by the legislation of August 4 to negotiate for compensation. Bischoffswerder, sent to Vienna in February, 1792 to hasten the declaration of war, found the Austrians anxious to put him off in all possible ways. Then on March 1, Leopold died suddenly of an "inflammatory fever," to be succeeded by his twenty-four-year-old son Francis II.

Meanwhile in France the conciliatory minister de Lessart had been overthrown by Girondin intrigue and oratory, and the king

[27] Heigel, *Deutsche Geschichte*, I, 502.

induced to accept Dumouriez as foreign minister. Dumouriez, like his Girondin supporters, wanted war. No one in Austria now could successfully oppose the drift to war. Kaunitz was still true to his policy of non-interference in France, but with Leopold's death he lost his last shred of influence. Francis, guided by Spielmann, who had made the Prussian alliance on the Austrian side, waited not without eagerness for the war to come. It came by the declaration of the French Assembly on April 20. It was begun, like most wars, with confidence and delight on both sides, with professions of injured innocence on both sides. It is absolutely impossible, again as with most wars, to apportion among the belligerents the responsibility for its outbreak. French historians have commonly blamed the Allies, German historians the French. Anglo-Saxon historians, nourished in a love of freedom, have more often than not sided with free France against despotic Austria and Prussia. Scientifically, the problem is insoluble; morally, it is soluble by faith, and in such matters it is well to be on the side of the angels. But even morally, perhaps the most interesting thing is that, in this first great war of peoples in the modern world, so much effort should be spent to disavow aggressive motives. One is tempted to feel that the very introduction of the issue of war guilt is a sign of progress, unless, indeed, one recalls the strenuous efforts, involving appeals to history, with which the Athenians attempted to blame the Spartans, and the Spartans the Athenians, for the Peloponnesian war.

Chapter Four

THE REPUBLICAN EXPERIMENT

I. A FORETASTE OF TERROR

THREE INFLUENCES, at first sight disparate and even quite separate, in reality, however, so entwined that the artificial analysis of the historian appears to disintegrate them, fill the first months of the French Republic with tragic promise. These are the September Massacres, the preparations for the final partitions of Poland, and the campaign of Valmy.

The cowed Legislative Assembly, with its entire Right and most of its Center absent, set up after August 10 a provisional government of six ministers, Danton, Monge (the great mathematician), Le Brun, Roland, Servan, and Clavière, and ordered the election of a constitutional convention. Until the Convention met on September 22, 1792 and declared France a republic, there was a troubled interregnum of seven weeks when real power lay, if anywhere, with the new revolutionary Commune of Paris. Early in September there occurred in Paris a series of lynchings and jail deliveries known as the September Massacres. The Prussian army was slowly but apparently inexorably approaching the city. Longwy fell, then Verdun, and rumor brought the Duke of Brunswick safely through the Argonne. Paris was still in an excited mood over the attack on the Tuileries, crying with true democratic fury for tenfold vengeance on those who had there massacred the innocent people. With the fall of the monarchy, royalists had become traitors, and political arrests were of daily occurrence. Already the prisons were filled with non-juring priests, long since made traitors by legislation in defiance of the king's veto power. The city was trembling with rumors of treason. Priests and aristocrats in the crowded prisons were said to have hatched a grand plot to break out and attack the patriots in the rear while Brunswick attacked in front. Yet, agitators claimed, the impotent Assembly and its hardly more courageous Executive

Council were doing nothing to foil this horrible plot. Paris was still housing a floating population come to destroy the monarchy. Parisian slums were still filled with hungry and excited men. For the first time since the Bastille fell and the women marched on Versailles, there was to be felt that nameless tension and excitement in which crowds become mobs.

Yet the September Massacres display less spontaneity and more organization than do the events of 1789. The movement was not homogeneous, and at each prison a different set of agitators and butchers seems to have been at work.[1] Those who did the work were, however, a small and compact group, and the populace as a whole seems to have stood by with mixed feelings of horror, curiosity, and sadistic satisfaction. A wagonload of priests, non-juring and suspect, was on September 2 held up on its way to one of the prisons. A small crowd gathered, hauled out the priests and murdered them. As if this were the signal, the massacres began, first at the prison of the Abbaye (near the church of Saint-Germain-des-Prés), extending within the next few days to all the prisons, and ending at the House of Correction at Bicêtre, a prison full of poor proletarian devils hardly in a position to betray the republic.

A fairly consistent pattern of action was followed in each prison. The invaders formed themselves into an impromptu court. At the Abbaye, Usher Maillard, who had led the march on Versailles, set himself up as president of this popular tribunal. One by one prisoners were brought from their cells before this tribunal, sitting in an inner court or hall, summarily charged and tried, and if found guilty, pushed into the street or outer court, where they were killed by a small group of chosen murderers. In a fury of virtue symptomatic of much to come, men and women were tried not merely for treason, but, in prisons like the Grand Châtelet, for thieving, forging, even for prostitution. Death and acquittal were the sole choices before these extraordinary courts.

Around these massacres legend and partisan history have played in freedom, until objective truth is buried even beyond monographic recovery. History, lately at least a chastened muse, doubts

[1] G. Walter, *Les massacres de septembre* (Paris, 1932); review by G. Lefebvre *Annales historiques de la Révolution française* (1933), X, 84.

the story of the courageous daughter who saved the life of her aristocratic father by drinking before her tormentors a glass of human blood. The horrible mutilation of the body of the Princesse de Lamballe, maid of honor to the queen, and its parading before the windows of the prison which held the royal family, is established beyond power of skeptic or republican to deny. The men who directed the massacres could occasionally display fits of sentimental mercy. The Abbé Sicard, known for his humane work with deaf-mutes, was spared, as were the royalists Cazotte and Sombreuil, and Maton de la Varenne, who wrote an excellent contemporary account of the massacres. Some thousand persons perished during these September Days, almost all in or around the prisons.[2] Street-fighting and street-massacres were strangely absent, a fact which reinforces the thesis that the massacres were not the spontaneous product of popular action.

Responsibility for the September Days can never be fixed. Historians have blamed Danton, Marat, Robespierre, the whole Paris Commune, the Jacobin Club, and, of course, the Duc d'Orléans. Clearly the Commune, especially its *comité de surveillance*, on which were Marat, Deforgues, Panis, Sergent, and others, did much to excite the people, to keep the national guard from intervening, and possibly to egg the murderers on. At the time, the confusion of charges and counter-charges was never cleared up, and served chiefly to embitter the quarrel between Girondins and Montagnards. The effect of the massacres on world affairs was critical. Reported in Europe and America in gory detail, commented upon in hundreds of editorial chairs, they accomplished the final discredit of the Revolution in the opinion of the Western world. From this moment only the very doctrinaire would dare defend the conduct of the "French cannibals." With the September massacres, the Revolution in a very real sense enjoyed a foretaste of the Reign of Terror.

II. THE FINAL PARTITIONS OF POLAND

The Republic of Poland, once the most powerful of Slavic states, had already in 1772 been subjected to a partitioning among Russia,

---

[2] Maton de la Varenne, *Histoire particulière des évènements . . . de juin, de juillet, d'août et de septembre* (Paris, 1806), gives an alphabetical list of 1,086 victims.

Prussia, and Austria, which reduced her by nearly one-third of her territory and somewhat more than one-third of her population. The loss of the poorly settled portions of White Russia had not been serious, but Galicia and West Prussia had been vital parts of the republic, the former a rich granary, the latter a last access to the sea. Yet in territory, population, and wealth Poland was still an important country.[3]

The Polish state was constitutionally an aristocratic republic, presided over by an official elected for life and enjoying the title, but hardly the power, of king. Historically the Polish constitution is certainly not unique. It originated in a medieval *Ständestaat*, or state organized by social Orders, and even the famous *liberum veto*, by which a single member of the Polish Diet (that is, the legislative body) could stop its proceedings, has its medieval parallels in Aragon and Catalonia.[4] But whereas in Western Europe the crown had won out over the Orders, and even in Hapsburg lands like Bohemia and Hungary could hold nobles and magnates in some sort of control, in Poland the landed nobility, or *szlachta*, had won a complete victory, and monopolized the machinery of government. Local administration was in the hands of provincial diets, and when the *liberum veto* too completely arrested national affairs there would be arranged by some of these local diets a kind of organized and almost legal *coup d'état* called a Confederation, through which the existing difficulty might be solved. The peasantry was everywhere held in a feudal subjection such as France, for instance, had not known for centuries. The bourgeois class, in the Middle Ages at least well organized as an Order, had been forced to give way to the *szlachta*, and had been excluded from the government. This class, in origin largely of German colonial stock, and the even more alien Jews, bore a relatively unimportant part in the life of eighteenth-century Poland, almost wholly rural and agricultural. The Catholic clergy had been reduced to the rôle of tame subservience to the nobility and squirearchy. The fashions of Versailles and the phraseology and the Encyclopædia penetrated into the nobility and into

---

[3] After the first partition, its population may be estimated at about 7,000,000, and its area at 188,000 square miles. Lord, *Second Partition*, 25, 26, 54. The population of Prussia at the time (1788) was between five and six millions. See above, p. 75.
[4] Lord, *Second Partition*, 8.

the upper circles of the Warsaw bourgeois, but on the whole Poland was economically and politically backward.

A country so poorly organized, without natural frontiers save for the Carpathians, was an easy prey to her ambitious neighbors. The disaster of 1772 stimulated the leaders of the nation, and in 1788 there met the famous Four Years' Diet, under which a plan for reform was finally matured. Not all Poland, nor even politically articulate Poland, was behind these reforms. No doubt the final tragic disaster of Poland's extinction was brought about by the deliberate will of the rulers of Russia, Prussia, and Austria; yet many of the *szlachta*, great nobles like Felix Potocki and Branicki as well as thousands of obscure, almost beggared "noblemen" of the lower economic reaches of the class, really thought their anarchy was liberty, and opposed all change until change came as annihilation. In spite of opposition, in spite of the *liberum veto*, the Four Years' Diet, encouraged by the king, Stanislas, a Pole and a patriot, though somewhat indolent and weak-willed, set about the work of giving Poland a government modeled on more modern lines. In the meantime, Catherine, fearing a reborn Poland, encouraged Polish malcontents with intrigue and even with money. Driven by fear and hatred of Russia, the Poles, after much hesitation, concluded an alliance with Prussia in March, 1790. The Reichenbach agreement reconciled the governments of Austria, Prussia, and Russia—so far at least as these jealous and grasping chancelleries could be reconciled. Meanwhile in Poland real reform was under way. Some French ideas penetrated into Warsaw, where at the "Constitutional Club" in the Radziwill Palace "orators nightly proclaimed the Rights of Man."[5] The actual reformed constitution, voted in an extraordinary access of generosity by the Diet on May 3, 1791, was a moderate document, hardly touched with Jacobinism. It abolished the *liberum veto*, and set up an hereditary monarchy in the Saxon line, a bicameral legislature based on representation of the whole country, not of provincial diets, a cabinet at least potentially subject to the principle of ministerial responsibility. Representation was granted the cities, barriers between nobles and bourgeois partially broken down, and the peasantry brought under

[5] Lord. *Second Partition*, 193.

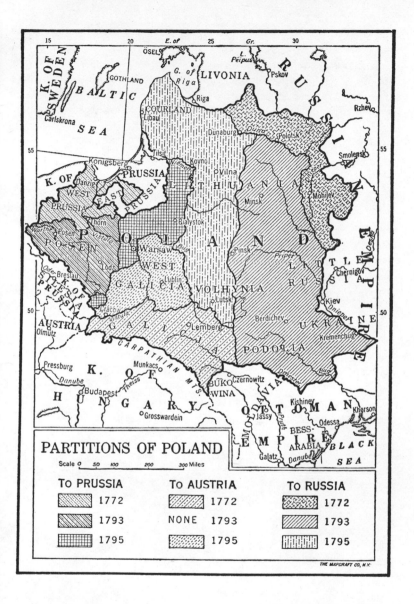

PARTITIONS OF POLAND

Scale 0 50 100 200 300 Miles

To PRUSSIA	To AUSTRIA	To RUSSIA
1772	1772	1772
1793	NONE 1793	1793
1795	1795	1795

THE MAPCRAFT CO., N.Y.

national law. The Third of May promised to do for Poland what the Fourth of August had done for France.

The prospect of a strong Poland alarmed neighboring great powers. The very excellence of the work of the Four Years' Diet brought on the final partitions. Some reactionary Polish nobles, most of them sincerely attached to the old aristocratic republic, formed with Catherine's aid the so-called Confederation of Targowica in May, 1792 (really formed a month earlier at St. Petersburg), and with Russian troops commenced the occupation of Poland. Frederick William, alarmed at the prospect of Catherine's reducing Poland to a Russian protectorate, yet not daring to attack Russia at the very moment he was beginning a campaign in France, finally repudiated his alliance with Poland and signed with Russia a secret agreement for the partition of his recent ally. Prussian troops, which might well have turned the balance against France, were moved into the coveted region of Thorn and Posen (Poznan). The Poles, deserted by everyone, fought courageously but quite uselessly. On September 23, 1793, the Polish Diet, surrounded by Russian troops, gave its consent in the famous "Dumb Session" to the cession of large parts of Lithuania and Ruthenia to Russia, of Thorn and Posen to Prussia. The Austrian government, which had been not unsympathetic towards the Constitution of the Third of May, was shut out from this partition, a fact which hardly contributed to the smooth working of the Austro-Prussian alliance against France.

In what was left of Poland—she was now reduced to less than half her territory of 1773—all the work of the Four Years' Diet was annulled, and the old régime, *liberum veto* and all, restored. Against these indignities the Polish people now rebelled, and brought on the third and final partition, a move which even popular acquiescence in the second partition could hardly have done more than postpone. In the courageous warfare of 1793-1795 the Poles, led by Kosciuszko, gained isolated victories greatly to their credit, and very useful subsequently to their national self-esteem, but the odds against them, isolated from any possible ally, were hopeless, and the Allies were soon in military command of the whole country. This time Austria was in at the kill, and in the third partition what was left of Poland was divided among the three powers of the first. From the three partitions, Russia gained some 180,000 square miles and 6,000,000 people; Austria, 45,000 square miles and 3,700,000 people; Prussia, 57,000 square miles and 2,500,000 people. Prussia had acquired Warsaw and its neighborhood, which after the Napoleonic interlude of the Duchy of Warsaw went to the Russian kingdom of Poland. Otherwise the broad lines of the partitions stood until 1918.

A great state had been wiped off the map, a proceeding unique in the history of a continent hardly ruled in practice by the precepts of its Savior. Even in the cynical world of eighteenth-century international relations, the destruction of Poland appeared a shocking thing, an example to the rising middle classes that kings had little respect for the Legitimacy and Order they preached. Worst of all, a martyred nation had been created, a nation horribly conscious of its past failures and weaknesses, a nation brooding and vengeful. Martyrdom breeds certain virtues, but not comfortable nor peaceful ones. Twentieth-century Poland, restored, is not the Poland of the Third of May. The final legacy of the eighteenth century to the twentieth was the Polish Corridor.

To France, however, the troubles of Poland brought nothing but relief. It was not wholly clear at the time, but we may now discern that France was the chief gainer by the final partitions of Poland. Just how true this apparent paradox is will appear presently.

III. THE WAR

The First French Republic never knew peace. The necessities of war undoubtedly contributed to the administrative centralization which soon supplanted the agreeable anarchy of local government under the monarchical experiment. The inhumanities of war undoubtedly heightened the inhumanities of the Terror. But the war is no full solution of the problems confronting the historian of the Revolution. The war did not make the dictator Napoleon inevitable, for the republic had managed to beat off its enemies and consolidate its gains without his leadership. Nor did the war produce the Terror. The war was an element in the Terror, perhaps even an essential element, but not the characteristic, not the typical element.

War may indeed be, as Madison claimed, the mother of executive aggrandizement, but not all executive powers thus aggrandized have had the same ends. War powers exerted by Pericles did not lead to the same goal as did war powers exerted by Cleon; under pressure of war, both Lincoln and Wilson did extraordinary things, but neither of them exactly imitated the French Committee of Public Safety. It is not the machinery of the Terror that is important—or unique—but the uses to which that machinery was put. The war, for instance, only imperfectly explains why the Terror was directed against Danton, and not at all why it was directed against harlots and gamblers.

If the war is not, then, a ready-made explanation of the Revolution, it is interesting and indeed enlightening in itself, as a good large-scale war fought under modern conditions. Around this war have grown up heroic legends, embroidered by military historians who were also military men, and aware that modern armies fight as much on their illusions as on their bellies. The war is, moreover, a constant accompaniment to the events of the period. It certainly played an important part in the overthrow of the Girondins and in the failure of their experiment in moderate republicanism, and can therefore best be treated in this place.

To many onlookers the events of 1792, as explained in the preceding chapter, were a prelude to a brief, decorous eighteenth-century war and a profitable division of outlying French territories among the other powers. The war of 1792, so lightly begun, was to last, with many shiftings among the combatants, with a few appropriate breathing-spaces, for a quarter of a century. It was not to be a decently orthodox war. Quite apart from any specific effects on tactics and on political events, two far-reaching innovations make it a thoroughly modern one. Eighteenth-century wars had been fought by relatively small professional standing armies, highly trained, expensive, and not easily replaced. Generals made a point of trying to win battles with a minimum loss of men, an endeavor in which the fashionable humanitarianism of the age had perhaps less part than had common sense and the need for economy. The Revolution changed all this. First for France, then for her protégés in the border countries, then, by repulsion, for her enemies, the war became a crusade, a common cause not to be entrusted to mere hirelings. As early as December, 1789, Dubois-Crancé had told the Constituent Assembly "each citizen should be a soldier, and each soldier a citizen, or we shall never have a constitution."[6] In these early days of hope and peace, the citizen-army was to be a volunteer army. In the first years of the war, a levy of 300,000 men was raised by draft. On August 23, 1793, the Convention decreed the portentous *levée en masse*, by which the whole resources of the nation, human and material, were declared subject to use if necessary to win the war, and by which unmarried men and widowers between 18 and 25 years of age were made conscript at once. In actual practice this first wholesale conscription was much less complete than it would appear to be on paper. Exemptions for one cause or another were many. A considerable part of the French population was hostile to the government, some of it in actual revolt. The machinery of the Terror, was never, by modern standards, really efficient. Many men and much wealth escaped the net of the *levée en masse*. The precedent was set, however, for modern democratic national wars; the psychological atmosphere of 1792 is recognizably like that of 1914. At just the moment in history when the state was reluctantly abandoning the claim that citizen and Christian—or some special kind of Christian—are necessarily one, it set up the hardly more gentle claim that citizen and soldier are necessarily one.

A second innovation is a bit less clearly an innovation. Yet the "concert of Europe," hardly more than a phrase if applied to eighteenth-century politics, came during the wars of the French Revolution to stand for a concept, for an order, half-legal, half-ethical, and thanks to the diplomatic negotiations involved in forming the various coalitions against France, not wholly unembodied in the written word. This new concert of Europe, of course, made little attempt to apply the Sermon on the Mount to international politics. Though certain men were religiously exalted for a brief period during the Terror, it is nonsense to regard the Revolution as a moral revolution. Neither kings nor cobblers were, as classes or as individuals, morally altered between 1789 and 1799. If international relations continued to be essentially a dog fight, the vague, ethical generalities used to disguise this fact came under the pressure of maintaining national morale to be even vaguer and more ethical, until they culminated in the Holy Alliance. But the Holy Alliance, like the concert of Europe from which it emerged, was genuinely concerned to protect from liberal contagion a Europe united at least in fear of liberalism. Thus the revolutionary wars not only contributed to the growth of nationalism; they also helped create a new, if not very firm or very forward-looking, internationalism.

The course of the war cannot here be followed in detail. Military history must always be the despair of the sociological historian, for battles are commonly perverse products of chance and confusion, not easily twisted into conformity with law. Rain, fog, the Argonne, dysentery, the enterprising and lucky Dumouriez, the cautious and unlucky Brunswick—this, and much else of Valmy, does not seem to have much to do with the glorious certainties of the Declaration of the Rights of Man and the Citizen, or even with the Industrial Revolution. Yet if particular battles appear the crossroads of chance, the general situation of contending nations in a war seems subject to rational analysis, and the final result of the conflict seems explicable. Certainly reasons enough have been advanced for the ultimate triumph of revolutionary France over a Europe joined against her. Two of these reasons, which have been incorporated into modern democratic mythology, may here be dismissed at once. First, the notion that revolutionary France stamped on the ground and produced a new army, totally independent of the corrupt army of the old régime; second, the allied notion that this new army won victories on patriotic enthusiasm alone, that its victories were those of inspired citizen-soldiers over the stolid mercenaries of despots. Unfortunately both these explanations contain only a modicum of truth—just enough to make their falsity serious.

For the truth is that not French strength, but coalition weakness, affords the best explanation for the military survival of the First Republic in the critical years 1792 to 1794. The First Coalition was not, indeed, completed during the campaign of 1792, which was waged against France by Prussia, with some aid from Austria. The execution of Louis XVI in January, 1793, however, brought in England and Spain and by the summer of that year France was actively at war with Austria, Prussia, the Empire, England, Holland, Spain, Sardinia, and Tuscany—with all Europe, in short, save Scandinavia, Switzerland, Russia, Naples, and Turkey. Now the French, even though gifted with a superhuman will to win in officers and men alike, could not have held out against a united Europe. But Europe was far from united. The concert of Europe was slowly and painfully evolved, was, indeed, not really effective until 1813. The First Coalition, founded on little but a hope for plunder, succumbed early to the mutual jealousies of its members.

In the crucial campaign of 1792, France was unquestionably saved by the second partition of Poland. The possibility of rich gains in Poland kept Catherine altogether out of the war against France, save for an inexpensive—and ineffective—series of verbal attacks, and made Austria and Prussia reluctant to use their full resources in the West. Had the two German powers been willing and able to throw their whole military and economic strength into the campaign of 1792 against France, it is hard to see how the French army, shaken by desertions and rebellious to discipline, could have withstood them. The fine Prussian troops which triumphantly occupied Thorn and Posen might under other circumstances have triumphantly occupied Paris.

Still another German distraction helped save France. Modern governments are habitually in financial difficulties, but there are degrees of insolvency. In general, it may be said that the well-meant efforts of the enlightened despots all over Europe, depending as they did on the extension of the bureaucracies, cost governments more than they brought in. Prussia, notably, had been brought by Frederick the Great to a prestige incommensurate with her real resources, and soon felt the inroads of Frederick William's extravagant favorites. The central government of the Hapsburgs had never been able to carry on war without Spanish, English, or French financial aid. In the first, and in many ways crucial campaign against revolutionary France, that of Valmy, England was not yet paymaster. After England's entry into the war in 1793, the question of subsidies added to the hard feeling between Prussia and Austria, and English suspicion that Prussia was using English money to hold down the Poles (a very justifiable suspicion) was one of the reasons for the break-up of the First Coalition.

Finally, the Prussian army which undertook this invasion of France in 1792 was not, in spite of the enormous prestige it had inherited from Frederick the Great, a good army. Its commander, the Duke of Brunswick, was unenterprising, slow, completely a creature of tradition. The Prussian army was thoroughly trained, capable of undertaking most complex evolutions, always maintaining a perfect dressing of its lines. These evolutions, however, took a very long time to perform, were, indeed, commonly performed the night before a battle, since it was impossible to deploy an army into battle position on short notice. Its officers, save in the fusileers, the hussars, and the artillery, were wholly of the noble caste, mostly good men and patriotic, educated in the superficialities of the Enlightenment, but little capable of initiative. Perhaps in general the criticism, made so often of the Germans in the First World War, holds true of the Prussian army of 1792: its individual members were not encouraged to think for themselves, were not used to relying upon themselves, facing new situations on their own responsibility. Though the cavalry was the best in the world, Prussian artillery was not at all good. Frederick himself had neglected it, and this branch of the army was not sufficiently "ritterlich" to attract ambitious young noblemen. Even the routine services of this army, which ought to have been good, failed to cope with the difficulties of the campaign. In 1792 the sanitary service broke down completely in the face of mud and dysentery. When the army itself was at Valmy in the Argonne, its bakeries were in Verdun and its flour supplies in Trier![7]

On the other hand, the French army possessed certain definite advantages, especially in this campaign of 1792. It was fighting on home ground, it had less serious worries over supplies, and it was on the defensive. It was better commanded. It was fired with patriotism, or ambition, or love of adventure—it was, at any rate, fired with something that made it an active body corporate, not a herd. To explain French victories as wholly the product of some beautiful emotional zeal is nonsense, but it is even greater nonsense

[7] Heigel, *Deutsche Geschichte*, II, 11.

to deny that the republican armies early developed an initiative discernible in the group as well as in the individual, an initiative lacking in their adversaries. "Fricasse, common soldier, in '92 used to pray God in this fashion: 'God of all justice, take into Thy protection a generous nation which fights only for equality.'"[8] In the army, that sense of consecration so obvious in civilian extremists was tempered by the harsh practicalities of military life into efficiency. Finally, and most important, the French army of 1792 was, with regard to the needs of actual warfare, a better trained army than the Prussian, was, from the purely professional point of view, thanks to reforms *before* the Revolution, potentially a very good army.

This last statement will need defense. It is true that the emigration of some six thousand of the nine thousand officers of the old royal army—these *émigré* officers were, of course, noblemen—and the spread of Jacobin propaganda among the rank and file had by 1792 combined to impair the discipline of the army to a dangerous degree. It is true that the new government distrusted the army, created a new one of its own, and strove very hard to keep the two separate. The old army of the line and the new one of volunteers and conscripts were not officially amalgamated until 1794, by which time the older elements were numerically swamped by the newer. Revolutionists then, and revolutionary historians since, insisted that the victorious armies of the republic owed nothing to the monarchy. In truth, however, "the successful armies of the Republic were produced not by the invention of a new organization, but by reversion to the old system."[9]

After the low point of disorganization represented by the disgraceful flight of Dillon's troops in a frontier skirmish with the Austrians in April, 1792, the French army was gradually built up, not on the principles of Liberty, Equality, Fraternity, but on the principles of Saint-Germain, Guibert, Gribeauval and the other reformers of the early years of the reign of Louis XVI. The volunteers of 1791, organized in battalions named after their departments, were on the whole an excellent lot, men who had chosen the mili-

[8] A. Chuquet, *La première invasion prussienne* (Paris, 1886), 62.
[9] R. M. Phipps, *The Armies of the First French Republic* (Oxford, 1926), I, 39.

tary career deliberately, from patriotism or ambition. Brigaded in fact with the army of the line long before legal amalgamation, these volunteers, if at first a trifle unruly, soon became excellent soldiers, and, with the regulars, made a precious leaven among the conscripts of later years. The places of the *émigré* officers were filled with patriots, most of them junior officers or non-commissioned officers of the old army, and therefore men of experience. The career open to talents never worked better than in the revolutionary armies; but it was a career open to *professional* talent, not simply to amateur enthusiasm. Of Napoleon's marshals, nineteen belonged to the old army, nine as officers, ten as non-commissioned officers or privates, and only six were civilians before the revolution.[10] The artillery was untouched by the early revolutionary experiments, and was in 1792 what it had been made by Gribeauval, the best artillery in Europe, with the fastest rate of fire, greatest range, greatest mobility, and best trained officers. The cavalry, too, if not distinguished, had been left pretty much alone by the revolutionists, and was in a serviceable state in 1792. Finally, the French army had, under the leadership of Guibert, adopted a method of drill and field operations far more suited to modern warfare than the ponderous method of the Prussians.

Eighteenth-century warfare, like eighteenth-century poetry, had become a highly formalized art. Soldiers' lives, as has been pointed out already, were valuable, and it was cheaper to maneuver than to charge. Yet when all account is taken of rational motives for eighteenth-century methods of war, there remains much that can only be explained as an irrational adherence to form, custom, decency, discipline, and a dozen other agreeable conventions. On the actual battlefield, convention called for the attacking army to display neatly drawn up lines three ranks deep, composed of men armed with flintlock and bayonet, advancing sedately while volleying, and charging with the bayonet only when very near the enemy. The defending army was similarly drawn up, with its flanks— peculiarly exposed by the line formation—protected by nature or by cavalry. Now an army cannot make long marches across the

[10] Possibly only four, since local report credited Lannes with a brief enlistment in the regulars, and Mortier, by birth a gentleman, was offered a commission in the carabiniers.

country in line; it must march in columns. The great difficulty was to deploy from column formation to line formation on the field of battle, and on that problem professional soldiers spent much loving thought and drill. The Prussian army in particular could maneuver in a plowed field or a rocky pasture with as perfect alignment as on a parade ground. The French army, drilled under Guibert's plan, abandoned this refined perfection, and sought speed above all things. The line was still retained as the normal battle formation, but columns were kept until the very last moment, and the change from column to line was carried out roughly and hastily. If a man got jostled into the wrong place in line he stayed there, and made himself useful. As for parade dressing, that was a useless luxury like overclean uniforms. Provisions were made to render separate commands as self-sustaining as possible, and not too tied down to a given base. The quality of the rank and file was improved by careful recruiting and by attractive conditions for long service. The general staff itself was carefully chosen and given real power to unify operations. By 1792 there was already the nucleus of an excellent army, self-reliant, willing to endure privations, capable of very rapid motion, ably officered by men amazingly openminded for professional soldiers, equipped with a matchless artillery, endowed with ample replacements and recruited cheaply by means of universal service. All that was necessary was a commander willing to abandon the delicate chesslike war of conventional position, to attack where he was not expected, instead of where good manners indicated, to follow the advice of strategists like Saxe and Bourcet and make battle on ground most advantageous to a rapidly moving army, to sacrifice men in the expensive but, especially in surprise, effective attack by column, to adopt, in Guibert's words "la grande tactique, la tactique des mouvements, celle qui fait gagner les combats."[11] But even before Bonaparte, Dumouriez, Jourdan, Hoche, and others gave proof that this newold army was a splendid instrument in capable hands.

The first months of the war were disastrous to France. The steady, if extremely slow, march of the Prussians on Paris helped make the overthrow of the monarchy possible. So slow was the

[11] Quoted by S. Wilkinson, *The French Army before Napoleon* (Oxford, 1915), 74.

Prussian advance, however, that Dumouriez, taken from the War Office and given supreme command, was able to gather together an army of some 60,000 to oppose Brunswick. That army was wholly composed of regulars and the excellent, in large part experienced, volunteers of 1791. Dumouriez, whatever his faults, was a good organizer and a splendid exhorter. From camp to camp he moved, cheering the men, communicating to them his obvious confidence. He had intended to hold the rough forested track of the Argonne, which could be crossed with an army in but five passes (*défilés*). With astonishing carelessness, he neglected one of these, that of La Croix-aux-Bois to the north of his main position at Grandpré, and through this pass, seized a few days before by the Austrians, Brunswick marched his army on September 18. The Argonne was turned, and "Leonidas-Dumouriez" had apparently failed. The road to Paris lay open before Brunswick. The next few days are remarkable, even in military history, for the confusion and uncertainty that prevailed in both armies and in both commanders. Brunswick kept gingerly on towards Paris, and on the morning of September 20 his advance guard just barely sighted, to their south and east, the French outposts on the hills of Valmy.

Dumouriez, after he had allowed his strong position in the Argonne to be turned, had sent for Kellermann, who was protecting Châlons and the road to Paris, and fumbled with these reinforcements into a rather weak position just west of Sainte-Menehould. The two armies were at last face to face—or to be strictly accurate, back to back. The famous battle of Valmy was no battle at all. There was no charge, no bodily contact between troops. There was some artillery exchange, and one Prussian shot struck some French ammunition. The resultant explosion unnerved the nearby infantry, but did not cause them to break. This, after the flight of Dillon's troops in April, was encouraging, and on the French side constitutes the miracle of Valmy. Brunswick studied the ground thoroughly, and finally muttered "Hier schlagen wir nicht." Both armies drew off to more orthodox positions, and waited. Dumouriez, though not a patient man, found waiting easier than Brunswick. Rain and the dysentery, uncertainty and lack of supplies, perhaps old age and disgust, sent Brunswick into retreat. France was saved, Dumouriez a hero, and Valmy a decisive battle. Actually, though the arresting of Brunswick's march was essential to the existence of the new republic, no single stroke of fate or genius, but attrition, stupidity, and accident (so much less dramatic than fate) achieved that end. Yet one need not begrudge the republic its Valmy. Valmy the myth helped in a measure to breed victories that were not myths.

IV. NEW MEN

As the Revolution moved steadily to the Left, its old leaders were stranded on what had now become the Right; and as the Revolution could not admit a constitutional opposition, its old leaders faced exile or the guillotine. Mirabeau, luckier than the others, died in his bed, "of an inflammation of the bowels, caused by excesses."[12] New men came to take the places of Mirabeau, Lafayette, du Port, the Lameths. These new men were not wholly unknown in the days of the monarchy, nor do they in any sense represent a suppressed lower class. Noblemen, it is true, are rare among them. But they are commonly men of education, even of property, trained for public life in the clubs, in the local administrations, in the new and exciting profession of journalism. No one of them seems now quite a hero, no one seems to have mastered events. The twentieth century, however, is hard on heroes. Two of its favorite superstitions, psychology and the economic interpretation of history, are notably hostile to the heroic.

In the early years of the Third French Republic, however, in the seventies and eighties of the last century an urgent need was felt for an adequate patron, preferably to be drawn from the great men of the First. Robespierre's reputation seemed hopelessly sullied by his apparent leadership during the maddest weeks of the Terror; furthermore, he was an austere, rather priggish, person, with no Gallic salt whatever. Danton seemed more promising material, and after a band of official historians, led by Professor Aulard, had got to work upon him, he appeared nicely refurbished, his statue glaring forth audacity and yet more audacity from a pedestal on the Boulevard Saint-Germain. Aulard's successor and former disciple, Professor Mathiez, set to work to attack this new idol, and after

₁₂ Dumont, *Souvenirs sur Mirabeau*, 308.

twenty-four years of research and publishing of articles, has made it pretty clear that Danton was unprincipled, venal, by no means an ardent republican, implicated in what to a rigorous patriot must seem treasonable negotiations with England, Prussia, and Austria, and with all this, no very influential politician after all.[13]

Needless to say, in spite of Mathiez's work, Danton's statue is still firm on its pedestal, his reputation still clear in the school-books of the French Republic. Before the revolution Danton was a briefless barrister at Paris, who had married the daughter of a prosperous restaurant-keeper. A large man, deep-chested, a ready orator, easy and common in commerce with his fellows, endowed with a Rabelaisian feeling for the richness of sense-life, subject to unaccountable fits of laziness, and undisturbed by a desire for justice, his rise in politics was rapid. Half boss, half agitator, he made the radical Club des Cordeliers a starting point for a career in municipal politics, shared in the agitation which led to the insurrection of August 10, and, thanks to the aid of moderates who wished to curb the excesses of the victorious Paris Commune, found himself Minister of Justice in the provisional government. He was elected triumphantly to the Convention, where he became a leading orator if not an influential politician. Like Mirabeau, he did not care enough about principles to maintain himself among men who were foolish enough, or noble enough, to care so much about principles as to do murder in their name. The Third Republic properly made Danton great: in its disabused bourgeois comfort, among its Ferrys, its Mélines, its Poincarés, he would have been quite at home. Morris, who saw so much and so clearly, wrote in 1794 all that need be said of him: "Danton always believed, and, what is worse as to himself at least, always maintained, that a popular system of government for this country was absurd; that the people were too ignorant, too inconstant, and too corrupt to support a legal administration; that, habituated to obey, they required a master. . . . His conduct was in perfect unison with those principles when he acted; but he was too voluptuous for his ambition, too indolent to acquire

[13] Mathiez has conveniently said his last word on Danton in a popular lecture, published in his *Girondins et Montagnards* (Paris, 1930), 260-305.

supreme power. Moreover, his object seems rather to have been great wealth, than great fame."[14]

Brissot is, for the experiment in moderate republicanism, a more important figure than Danton. He was the most conspicuous leader of the moderate Right wing of the new assembly. Indeed, the name Girondins by which that group is known to history was not their contemporary name. To their enemies—until recently parties were usually christened by their enemies—they were known as Brissotins. Brissot de Warville (the "W" to be pronounced in the elegant English manner) was a minor *philosophe*, a publicist or peddler of ideas, who had the misfortune to live on into the revolution he had preached. Not without vanity, envious of the nobility, a born intriguer, who could never quite admit to himself that he was an intriguer, Brissot was yet a not unworthy man. In a time of great opportunities for gaining dishonest wealth—as Danton proved—he lived and died a poor man.[15] He wanted to make over France, and through France the world, into a well-ordered society where the *natural* superiors, the enlightened, tender-hearted men and women should rule for the common good. He did not want to level off society at quite as low a point as did Robespierre. The new world had room for the decently rich. He early identified himself with good causes, such as that of the oppressed negroes, was chosen to the Legislative Assembly, and readily elected to the Convention. Drawn by circumstances into partisan conflict, he showed himself a good, unprincipled fighter, a capable party organizer. No great orator, he left that side to the eloquent men of which his party had, if anything, too many—Vergniaud, Gensonné, Guadet, Barbaroux. His newspaper, the *Patriote français*, was extremely influential, and set a model for personal journalism of opinion. Brissot's faults, like his virtues, are very much those of his party, and any estimate of his position in French history depends on one's estimate of the Girondins.

If one holds that public opinion is the ultimate determining force in politics, then Jean Paul Marat was a very important person indeed. His newspapers, the *Ami du Peuple* and its continuation the

[14] J. Sparks, *Life of Gouverneur Morris* (Boston, 1832), II, 424.
[15] E. Ellery, *Brissot de Warville* (Boston, 1915), 424.

Publiciste, enjoyed in this critical period of 1792-93 an unequaled prestige, were, indeed, among the few papers never sold at cut prices by the hawkers. His martyrdom at the hands of Charlotte Corday in the summer of 1793 gave his words still greater weight, and all through the Terror Marat lived on. Posterity—indeed, his repentant contemporaries of 1795—found in him a perfect scapegoat, and he has ever since been subject to indiscriminate blackening and occasional, rather more discriminating, whitewashing. To discuss Marat without using evaluative terms is even more difficult than with other men of the Revolution. If to call him mad seems to be abusive, it may at least be pointed out that he displayed certain eccentricities the possession of which normally makes a man somewhat trying to his companions. Thwarted in his ambitions to figure as a great scientist, Marat came to the Revolution a middle-aged, disappointed man nourishing a violent hatred of established authority as represented by scientific academies, convinced that he had been oppressed and persecuted. After a beginning as a reasonably moderate pamphleteer, he launched the *Ami du Peuple* in the summer of 1789. From the first, that paper was shrilly extreme, vituperative, bloodthirsty, suspicious of everybody, clamorous for revenge against the foes of the people—successively Constitutionnels, Feuillants, Fayettists, Girondins. Marat's program was simple and imprecise. He wanted a democratic republic, where virtue would triumph over vice. He did not lack cunning, and had a certain sense for political maneuvering. He seemed to enjoy the fight for the fight's sake, to pour his diseased emotions into a mysticism of hatred in which there was no peace. Only as the militant professional radical is Marat to be understood. To condemn him utterly requires a somewhat robust faith in the finalities of this everyday world.

To their contemporaries, it was not Danton nor Marat who stood best for what the Revolution was trying to achieve, but Robespierre. The nineteenth century, trying to forget that the origins of its social order—even in England and Germany—lay in the disreputable confiscations of the great Revolution, preferred to neglect Robespierre, or explain him as a bloodthirsty tyrant, an aberrant fanatic, a malevolent freak of circumstances. Mathiez, who by temperament understood the Terror better than he understood twentieth-century France, sought to rehabilitate Robespierre, to make him, not Danton, the inspiration of modern uncorrupted Frenchmen. Hitherto the Robespierrists have not even achieved a statue for their hero in Paris, a city not at all exacting in the matter of statues. Robespierre before the Revolution was an inconspicuous, but not unsuccessful, provincial lawyer, known as a philanthropist, a correct young bachelor untouched by scandal, a dabbler in literature. Rather surprisingly elected to the States-General by the commons of his native Artois, he early took up a position of resolute radicalism in that assembly. He made a point of speaking—or rather, of reading an appropriate discourse—as often as possible, and though at first derided by an assembly much more jovially opportunist than it is usually supposed to have been, he gradually won a hearing. His real influence in these days, however, lay in the Jacobin Club, where he early became the "Incorruptible" (not *sea-green*, which is a probably unwarranted invention of Carlyle's). Shut out of the Legislative Assembly by the self-denying ordinance, he managed none the less to keep himself in the public eye, and was chosen to represent Paris in the Convention. Here he became at once a leader of the Mountain, and survived the bloody elimination of leaders until, from April to July, 1794, he seemed to have attained a kind of dictatorship.

Why did Robespierre so survive? The answer is, of course, the clue to one's interpretation of his character, and of such interpretations there are, in spite of the objectivity of modern history, a very great many. Mathiez answered simply: because Robespierre was the ablest, most practical, most farseeing of his contemporaries. This answer cannot here be accepted. Robespierre's speeches, his letters and reports are available for all to read, and from their reading no such person as Mathiez imagined can be made out. Robespierre survived because the Terror was in large part a religious movement, and Robespierre had many of the qualities of a second-rate religious leader. His speeches were sermons, edifying to the faithful, quite empty to the unbeliever. His theology was an irresolute theism, in which the Supreme Being reconciled the order of science and the aspirations of humanity after the customary fashion of vulgar theologies with the problem of determinism and free will. His churches were the Jacobin clubs, his congregations the few who were "at the height of revolutionary circumstances." To this religious aspect of the Terror it will be necessary to return. Here it need only be pointed out that Robespierre is less puzzling as a preacher than as a statesman. Intolerant of opponents, very sure of his own righteousness, his own prescience, relishing the forms of ritual, neat, precise, ascetic, wrapped always in the soothing warmth of words that evade definition, partially, and therefore fatally, insulated by these words from the outside world, Robespierre in the end exhibited that extreme inconsistency between thought and action which, in men forced to act, is the mark either of the conscious hypocrite or of the religious fanatic. There is no evidence that Robespierre possessed either the intelligence or the courage necessary for such persistent and large-scale hypocrisy.

V. GIRONDINS AND MONTAGNARDS

In the Legislative Assembly, the Gironde had been the radical party. The elections to the new assembly, held in September, 1792, were, though technically free, subject to such pressure from Jacobin clubs that none of the older conservative elements got a chance to vote. A determined minority of convinced republicans alone voted for members—some 750—of the Convention. In the new assembly, then, the Gironde became naturally the conservative party, and a new radical group, known from its position high up in the amphitheater as the Mountain, arose. The Gironde itself, anywhere else in Europe, would have been a shockingly radical group. In fact, poor Lafayette, become a reactionary in France, was clapped in prison by the Austrians as a dangerous revolutionary when the Tenth of August drove him into exile. Party lines had not, as has already been remarked, anything like the rigor of modern parliamentary practice. Yet these two groups are pretty clearly defined as to membership, their adherents met together outside the assembly, the Girondins socially at various salons, the Montagnards more austerely in the Jacobin club, and they often voted pretty consistently on opposite sides of a given question. Perhaps a hundred to a hundred fifty more or less determined partisans are to be numbered on each side. The remaining four hundred—a majority of the assembly —is the familiar neutral, irresolute group, to be swung by the more aggressive minority, and known as the Plain, the Marsh, or more scornfully yet, as the Belly.

As to the real issues between the Gironde and the Mountain, historians are still at variance. To Aulard, the quarrel was largely an unreal one, enflamed by bitter personal rivalries that ought never to have arisen among virtuous republicans, and reducible solely to the question as to whether Paris should rule France, or France Paris.[16] To Mathiez, on the other hand, the quarrel was the most fundamental one in modern society, the class struggle between bourgeois and proletariat. The Gironde, according to him, was the party of the upper middle class, of the business men and bankers, devoted to a dogmatic laissez-faire in economic life, anxious to maintain a society stratified according to wealth, defenders of the sacredness of private property, partisans of governmental decentralization because distrustful of governmental interference in business. The Mountain, again according to Mathiez, though its parliamentary membership was wholly bourgeois, was compelled by its reliance on the common people, and especially on the common people of Paris, to take up a position much nearer to modern socialism. The Mountain stood for a strong centralized government able to curb the unduly rich, for food-rationing, price-fixing, confiscation of property, progressive taxation, recognition of the right of the individual to the means of subsistence. What gave bitterness to the struggle between the two parties was no mere rivalry of personalities, but this fundamental antagonism of group interests. What gave the Mountain its brief victory was not so much its skill at the game of politics, as its alliance with a proletariat goaded to desperation by war scarcity, and trained for direct political action by the events of July 14, of October 5 and 6, of August 10.

If it cannot finally decide on this matter between Aulard and Mathiez, modern history has at least destroyed for good and all some of the myths attached to the Girondin party. Thanks largely to the work of the poet Lamartine, the Gironde appeared to the

[16] Aulard, *Histoire politique*, 418.

optimistic liberals of the Western world in the nineteenth century as a group of high-minded idealists, doomed in a sordid world to defeat through the very purity of their political lives. Actually the Girondins were quite as unscrupulous as any other revolutionary group. They were not too humane to shed blood; the war was largely of their making. They were not above intrigue; they simply intrigued with the wrong people. They had not always been moderates; against the court, against the Feuillants, they and their journalists had used the language of extreme revolutionaries. They accepted the republic and they judged their king guilty of treason.

On the whole, Mathiez would seem to be right about the Girondins. By the winter of 1792-93 they had got themselves identified with the idea that the Revolution had gone far enough, that somehow the attempt to level off all social differences, even those of wealth, must stop. "Before August 10," wrote Brissot in October, 1792, "the disorganizers were real revolutionists, because a republican had to be a disorganizer. But the disorganizers of today are the real counter-revolutionists. They are anarchists, levelers."[17]

Once in this position, so evident in Brissot's words, the Girondins had to seek allies to the Right, even though the Right was proscribed. Out of natural repulsion from the extremes of their opponents, they were more and more driven to what seemed a reactionary position. The Girondins, wrote Michelet, "were so maladroit that they finally got in a position where they seemed royalists (which they were not)."[18] They lost control of the Jacobin machine, which after December, 1792, is almost wholly identified with the Mountain. This meant that ultimately they lost not only Paris, but even the provinces whose rights they claimed so ardently to defend, and that their downfall was certain. They had not the stuff of revolutionaries, though it is very difficult to put one's finger on just what they lacked. Luck, perhaps. Had the war gone a bit better in the spring of 1793, had Danton been more consistently energetic, had he been willing to work with them, then they might well have brought the bourgeois republic safely through. Until the Gironde fell, there was nothing inevitable about the Terror. But their luck did fail

---

[17] Brissot, quoted in P. A. Kropotkin, *The Great Revolution* (New York, 1909), 358.
[18] J. Michelet, *Histoire de la Révolution française*, 3rd ed. (Paris, 1869), IV, 258.

them. Face to face with unscrupulous opponents they lacked that ultimate unscrupulousness which comes from very high ideals. Lamartine was completely wrong; the Girondins failed, not because they were too unpractical and unworldly, but because, in the rare circumstance of 1793, they were too practical and worldly.

VI. THE FAILURE OF THE MODERATE REPUBLIC

The history of the first eight months of the new republic is the history of the struggle between Gironde and Mountain. That struggle is ceaseless, and takes on a hundred forms. It may easily be quite confused among a host of details, and will appear more clearly, and one hopes no less accurately, if it is seen centered on crucial issues: the September Massacres, the trial of the king, the new constitution, the conduct of the war, the prosecution of Marat, the Commission of Twelve.

In domestic politics, the September Massacres profoundly affected the quarrel between Gironde and Mountain just as it was coming into the open. The quarrel had begun under the Legislative, when the Gironde had been the war party, the Mountain the peace party. Now the Gironde could seize upon the Massacres as a horrible example of "anarchy," and could blame the revolutionary Commune of Paris for permitting, or rather, for promoting them. These tactics drove the Mountain into defending the Commune, and therefore the Massacres. Each side was further committed by its attitude towards the Massacres, the one to deplore violence, the other to extol it.

The trial of the king further separated the Girondins from the revolutionists. For three months the Convention squabbled over what was to be done with the royal family. The Mountain and its Parisian allies were clear from the start. Louis was a traitor: documents discovered in an iron chest in the Tuileries after his fall proved his correspondence with Mirabeau, with the *émigrés*, his desire to subvert the constitution. The excellent example of the English revolutionists and Charles I showed how such kings should be treated. The Girondins here made one of their great mistakes. Never a well-disciplined party, they divided hopelessly on this issue. Some of them urged clemency, others exile. others wished to refer the whole question to a plebiscite. What was perhaps worse, many of them changed their minds, voting finally for the death penalty after having appealed for mercy. Their speeches are appeals to reason, humanity, prudence, dignity, and other favorite abstractions of the century. Their actual motive seems to have been a feeling that the great majority of Frenchmen were still royalist, and that therefore to execute the king would imperil the Revolution. They were right enough in their primary assumption—the majority of Frenchmen were royalist. They were wrong in assuming that in these early days of the Terror the majority counted. The trial itself, before the full Convention as an impeaching body, was a mere formality. Some of the many votes were close, but in the end the parliamentary discipline of the Mountain triumphed, and Louis was condemned to death, 366 to 361, in a vote in which the question of a possible delay complicates the estimate of a majority. A Girondin move to postpone execution was beaten 380 to 310, which may well be considered the decisive majority against the king. He was guillotined on January 21, 1793, dying, as did most men and women publicly executed during the Revolution, courageously.[19]

The Convention had been called together, like the American conventions from which it took its name, primarily to make a constitution for republican France. Actually it became, like its famous predecessor the Constituent Assembly, a supreme governing body. It had, however, at least to make a gesture towards a constitution. The Girondins, masters of the Convention in its early days, secured a majority on the constitutional committee, and on February 15, 1793, Condorcet, their philosopher, presented before the Convention a long and complicated project for a constitution. The document provided for a strong executive council, directly elected by the people, and independent of the legislature, a unicameral legislature, elected annually by a suffrage universal, indeed, but extremely complicated by provisions for what would now be called proportional representation, and a sort of national referendum on certain acts of the central government. It is an interesting scheme; betraying a quite Jeffersonian distrust of the urban proletariat, and a desire to protect the

---

[19] Camille Desmoulins and the du Barry were striking exceptions; both died lamentably.

individual—and his property—from group-interference of any sort. Its machinery and its phraseology are awkward, but the germs of institutions highly popular until quite recently are there—initiative, referendum, recall, proportional representation. Now the project fell very flat indeed, and the whole subject of the constitution went back to committee, where it was kept in the background until the final victory of the Mountain. Condorcet's failure shows how far the Girondins' majority had melted away by February. Their new constitution subjected them to further effective attacks. Now more than ever they could be pointed out as the party of the big propertied interests.[20]

By this time the party struggle had, whatever its origins and its wider implications, attained an intensity where personalities are at least as important as principles, where intrigue counts more than speeches, where the sole desire of the immediate participants is to destroy their opponents. The war had gone nicely for some months after Valmy. French armies had taken the offensive, Custine had captured Mainz, and Dumouriez, after the victory of Jemappes, had overrun Belgium. With the execution of the king, the occupation of Belgium by France, and the consequent opening of the river Scheldt to world commerce, contrary to treaty, England, Holland, and Spain entered the war against France. French conquests had been too ambitious, and French armies were still incompletely consolidated. Supply systems were inadequate, and recruiting by wholesale conscription had not yet brought results. Revolt broke out against the levy of recruits in La Vendée, a rural section in the west where the peasantry had remained loyal to church and king. French armies were beaten in Belgium and the Rhineland. Dumouriez, badly defeated at Neerwinden, attempted in vain to persuade his army to march on Paris and turn the squabbling lawyers out of office. With a handful of officers, including the future king Louis Philippe, he went over to the enemy in March, 1793.

Now Dumouriez had been a great friend of Brissot, and when the news of Dumouriez's treason came to Paris in March, the opposition press, headed by Marat, accused Brissot of treason by proxy. In an atmosphere of fear and suspicion much like that of the sum-

[20] Mathiez, *Girondins and Montagnards,* 93.

mer of 1792, the Gironde was held up in the Paris *sections*, in the Commune, in the Jacobin Club, in the debates in the Convention, as conniving at allied victories, as wishing a royalist restoration, as infamous "moderates" in a time when virtue must be white-hot. The Gironde unluckily chose to strike back at Marat himself. In a desperate effort they pulled together, with the aid of the Plain, enough of their old majority to send him, though as deputy he enjoyed parliamentary immunity, before the newly created Revolutionary Tribunal for having signed, as president of the Jacobin Club, a circular calling on France to arise against a "counter-revolution." The Tribunal, recruited from the orthodox revolutionists of Paris, acquitted Marat, and, crowned with oak leaves, he was carried back to his seat in the Convention. The Gironde had blundered again. They had added luster to the already brightly shining martyr's halo of Marat. They had set a precedent for the abolition of the parliamentary immunity enjoyed by members of the Convention.

The struggle had now gone beyond the possibility of a parliamentary solution. The Girondins had set themselves against the well organized Jacobin minority, and had therefore to be disposed of as other conservative groups in power had previously been disposed of—by direct action. In *sections* and clubs, just as for the Tenth of August, preparations for a rising began. On May 29 delegates from 33 of the more radical *sections* met together to arrange for the final stroke. The Gironde had provided their enemies with a splendid target. On the suggestion of Barère, a peacemaker not perhaps wholly sincere on this occasion, they had accepted the institution of an extraordinary Commission of Twelve to investigate the activities of the *sections*. The Commission, composed wholly of Girondins, was at once accused of plotting a counter-revolution.

On May 31 a huge crowd, composed partly of the organized national guard, surrounded the meeting place of the Convention, and sent in a delegation to demand the dissolution of the Commission of Twelve, the arrest of the Girondin leaders, bread at 3 sous the pound, taxes on the rich, and the creation of a revolutionary army. In spite of this adroit mixture of political and social aims, the Convention— that is, the neutral Plain which determined the balance—refused to act, limiting itself to a suppression of the Commission of Twelve.

On June 2 a more efficiently organized mob, armed by the *sections*, again surrounded the Tuileries, where the Convention met, and demanded the proscription of the Girondins. The Convention made a pathetic attempt to assert its dignity and independence. Headed by their president, Hérault de Séchelles, they marched out of the hall and into the gardens. At the first gate they encountered a firm mass of citizen-soldiers, well-armed and not to be impressed by the majesty of the law. Trooping along after Hérault, the helpless legislators made the circuit of the gardens and were turned away at every gate. To cries of "Vive la Montagne!" and "A bas les traitres!" they went back to their desks and voted the arrest of twenty-nine Girondin deputies. The experiment in parliamentary government had failed. France was under the dictatorship of the Mountain, and the Mountain was under the dictatorship of the organized petty bourgeoisie and artisanry of Paris.

Chapter Five

THE REVOLUTIONARY GOVERNMENT

I. THE CIRCUMSTANCES OF THE TERROR

THE HISTORIAN of the French Revolution may resolutely deny himself to melodrama, but he will not be able wholly to dismiss the Reign of Terror. That tragedy stands proof against statistics. You may, especially if you feel on the whole favorable to the Revolution, point out that the twenty-odd thousand victims of guillotine, *mitraillades,* and *noyades* would hardly equal the casualty list of a sound Napoleonic victory, would be as nothing before the annual list of victims of motor accidents in the modern world. The guillotine is still the symbol of something darker, or brighter, and certainly more moving, than the humble routine of war and chance. To the enemies of the Revolution, as well as to the once numerous historians with a taste for the dramatic, the Terror, of course, is the central theme of the story. Even to the historian attempting to assume the hopeful neutrality of retrospective sociology, the Terror acquires an importance not to be measured by such simple quantitative tests as the number of its victims. For in these few months of 1793-94 the experiment begun in 1789 with confidence and almost with unanimity ended in the unconcealed dictatorship of a minority, in the exaltation of the modest likes and dislikes of ordinary men into the heroic loves and hates of men caught in the absurdities of a Cause. The political overturn of 1789 had developed into the religious movement perhaps miscalled the Reign of Terror.

The actual machinery of the Terror was known to its creators as the "gouvernement révolutionnaire," the abnormal régime necessary to preserve the Revolution from its enemies. This revolutionary government, like the Terror of which it may be said to form the purely political aspect, does not appear at a given moment, full-formed and unprecedented. Just as the Great Fear and the September Massacres anticipate the violence of the Terror proper, so the growth of the Jacobin machine, the establishment of Danton's provisional government in 1792, and the increasing powers of certain committees of the national assemblies anticipate the dictatorship of the revolutionary government. From the establishment of the first Committee of Public Safety in April, 1793, to the decree of December 4 of that year, which codified the various laws creating the new government, the machinery of the Terror was assembled bit by bit.[1] A chronological account of this process is hardly necessary here, the more because the revolutionary government was not, save in minor details, influenced by the accidents of its elaboration. Its six months' growth was not primarily dependent on party struggles, on the clash of leaders nor on the introduction of novel and disturbing factors.

Its defenders, then and since, insist that the revolutionary government is wholly explicable as the desperately centralized rule of men threatened by treason at home and by military defeat abroad. Some of the outlawed Girondins, it is true, escaped to the provinces after June 2, and led abortive risings in Normandy, in Lyons, Marseilles, and Bordeaux. Belgium and the left bank of the Rhine had been evacuated, and midsummer found French armies backed up against their own borders. Wholesale desertions had left the actual fighting forces of the republic far below the numbers officially listed by the bureaucracy of the War Office. In the economically and culturally backward region known as La Vendée, southward from Nantes, the attempt to enforce military conscription had brought the rude and virtuous peasantry, all ignorant of their Rousseau, into open rebellion in support of church and king. Toulon, the important Mediterranean naval base, was betrayed to the English by a royalist faction within the town.

The Girondins, however, were completely repressed by early autumn, and their unsuccessful appeal to the provinces gave the Mountain an opportunity to damn all opponents, indeed, all critics, of the revolutionary government with the epithet "federalist," nowadays innocent and colorless enough, but then charged with the fatal reproach of heresy. Henceforth any group-action outside the new

---

[1] The mechanistic analogy is no mere metaphor. Carnot himself referred to the revolutionary government as "cette machine politique." *Moniteur*, XX, 114.

revolutionary hierarchy could be stopped with a word: "Congresses or joint meetings are forbidden you: they are traps into which the *federalist* seduces the patriot."[2] The allies had been pushed back from the frontier some months before the definite codification of the revolutionary government. Hoche and Pichegru had begun in November to clear the Alsatian frontier and drive the Austrians back again towards Mainz. Even earlier, in September, Houchard at Hondschoote had effectively stopped the Anglo-Austrian invasion from the north, though there the French had not yet reassumed the offensive. Toulon fell to the republicans in December, after a siege in which all historians are obliged to mention the presence, on the republican side, of artillery-captain "Buonaparte." The Vendéens had made a courageous, if not very well coördinated effort to spread their revolt. The "Catholic and royal army" was a loose aggregation of peasants, priests, and country gentlemen, suffering from divided leadership and a highly informal recruiting which made leaves of absence wholly a matter of private convenience. Opposed at first by stupid republican politician-generals and by raw troops, the Vendéens made some headway. In June, though for once in something like their full strength, they were repulsed at Nantes with the loss of their venerated leader, Cathelineau, the "wagoner of Pin-en-Mauges." (The objectives of the "class war" were apparently misunderstood by the proletariat of La Vendée.) Though the war went on throughout the Terror, with an abundance of heroism, savagery and picturesqueness as hardy Vendéens were matched by trained republican troops, the revolt ceased to have national importance. It existed in the background, of course, and could always give material for revolutionary oratory. But it was no longer, after the summer of 1793, a serious menace to the existence of a government armed and organized for ends neither Catholic nor royal.

All in all, the situation from which the revolutionary government emerged was hardly worse than the situation in the summer of 1792 had been: in a military way, things were far better than just before Valmy; internal dissension was a bit more open, but hardly greater; economic conditions, and especially the condition of

[2] *Circulaire du Comité de salut public aux comités de surveillance ou révolutionnaires, portant instructions pour l'application du décret du 14 frimaire*, printed in P. Mautouchet. *Le gouvernement révolutionnaire* (Paris, 1912), 253.

the poor, if slightly worse in the cities than in 1788-89, were far better than they were to be later under the comparatively lax and unrevolutionary government of the Directory. But in the summer of 1792, the Gironde stood in the way of a centralized dictatorship of the Mountain. Now the Gironde had been disposed of, the Mountain could proceed to build up its dictatorship. The stress of circumstances was certainly a powerful argument in the mouths of the organizers of the revolutionary government. But chiefly the Pitts and Cobourgs, the fanatics, traitors, speculators, and federalists—all the bugbears of the Revolution—have the unreal reality of all personifications of evil, from Satan to the Money-Power. For the government of the Terror, if originally directed against real enemies, was in the end almost wholly directed against imaginary ones. That, indeed, is what makes it a Terror instead of a mere government of national defense. Against other men we may fight as men, may even *not* fight against them; against devils we must fight as heroes— or devils.

II. THE MACHINERY OF THE TERROR

After the fall of the Girondins, the Mountain rushed through a constitution of its own, with universal suffrage, an omnipotent unicameral legislature, and a Bill of Rights rather more collectivist than orthodox eighteenth-century Bills of Rights in Europe and America, submitted this constitution to the people, who accepted it 1,801,908 to 11,610, and then, on October 10, 1793, finally suspended its application until the end of the war. The government of France was to be openly and proudly revolutionary. No doubt this so-called Constitution of 1793 could have been made to accord with the aims of the Mountain; it was a vigorously authoritarian document. But its application would have meant a new election, and the Mountain, even though they possessed in the Jacobin clubs an apparently invincible machine for controlling votes, feared that anything resembling a free election would lead to the return of a moderate, and perhaps royalist, legislature.[3] The revolutionary government, however, had a constitution of its own, a definite legal structure, resting

---

[3] Mathiez himself, though a loyal Montagnard, admits this. *Girondins et Montagnards,* 104.

on the famous decree of December 4, 1793, and subsequent amendments. This structure, far from arbitrary or shapeless, must now be analyzed.

At its head were the two great committees of Public Safety and General Security. Chosen by the Convention from its own members, in theory responsible to it, holding their appointment for but one month, the committees from their final constitution in the autumn of 1793 became almost independent executive powers. Each month their membership was automatically renewed, and though they took care to report to the Convention from time to time, their authority was not seriously challenged in open debate until the collapse of the whole system with the fall of Robespierre.

Of the two, the Committee of Public Safety was the more important. Its twelve members were all good Montagnards, radical revolutionaries, educated middle-class men of respectable antecedents—six lawyers, two army officers (both engineers), two men of letters, a civil servant, and a Protestant minister. No one man—and certainly not Robespierre—ever assumed a predominant position among them. The Committee of Public Safety was a sort of dictatorship in commission. So long as its members were held together by that intangible but recognizable relation perhaps too little dignified as teamwork, the Committee was successful. When acute dissensions broke out between the members—broadly speaking, between the ecstatically devout and the less exacting, more worldly men of affairs—the rule of the Great Committee was over. Entrusted by decree of the Convention with complete administrative powers, the Committee soon began to exercise a general supervision over policy. It was at least as unanimous as a modern cabinet in important matters of general concern. In some respects, however, it was a more informal body than a modern cabinet. Each member followed his own interests, took over certain fields, and within them was pretty much his own master. The signature of a single member was sufficient to validate a decree of the Committee, and many of its acts have but one or two signatures, though really important measures were no doubt thoroughly discussed. Barère, a smooth, conciliatory speaker, a man thoroughly at home in parliamentary corridors, commonly reported for the Committee, and served as its chief agent of liaison with the Convention. Carnot and Prieur (de la Côte d'Or), both ex-officers, busied themselves with military affairs, from recruiting men through the manufacture of arms and supplies to the actual tactics of the battlefield. Carnot has emerged in history as the great "Organizer of Victory." Actually Prieur did the more valuable work of organization, but Carnot seems to have had what in modern terms would be called a better publicity. Cambon took over the finances. Jeanbon Saint-André, Prieur (de la Marne), and Saint-Just were frequently away on missions, extending the rule of the Committee to the provinces, the armies, and the navy. Lindet did much of the work of a Minister of the Interior. Robespierre dabbled in most matters, and especially in foreign affairs, but always rather above the level of mere technical knowledge or practical application of details. There is little evidence, save the warm assurances of M. Mathiez, that Robespierre was a great organizer, that like Calvin or Bernard of Clairvaux, he combined spiritual gifts with practical ones. One hardly risks exaggeration to say that during much of its life Robespierre was a sort of "front" for the Committee. The Incorruptible enjoyed a great reputation among the faithful, and his sermons were quite the most popular ones delivered by revolutionary leaders. By an ironical turn not infrequently repeated in modern politics, the maker of phrases survived, both in his own time and with posterity, the makers of things.

The Committee of General Security formed the central administration of the revolutionary police. Most great revolutions—including most emphatically the present Russian Revolution—have created such groups, if only to cater to the popular demand for melodrama, without which revolutions might be mere political changes. The Committee of General Security supervised the police throughout France, issued warrants of arrest unchecked by *habeas corpus* or other limitations, had charge of prisons, administered "revolutionary justice" through *comités de surveillance* in the provinces. Its twelve members lacked some of the personal distinction of the members of the Committee of Public Safety. Neither the violent Amar nor the quietly envious Vadier was a personage of the first rank. Yet the Committee of General Security always held itself to be an organ coördinate with, not subordinate to, the Committee of Public Safety, and within its own elastic police functions certainly acted very independently. At first the two committees coöperated, even meeting together occasionally as one body. But as the Terror became more and more a form of religious intoxication and less and less a government of national defense, dissension broke out between the two committees. The Committee of Public Safety set up its own "bureau de police" to keep watch over the civil servants, later to enforce the decrees of Ventôse.[4] The theoretical unity of the government, never quite perfect in practice, was visibly impaired by the spring of 1794.

Under the two great committees, the ministries and the ordinary committees of the convention were reduced to the position of clerks. So obviously useless was the Executive Council of Ministers—and so hateful still to true republicans was the title of minister—that Carnot on April 1 obtained the suppression of the ministries, and their replacement by twelve "commissions" composed wholly of civil servants and completely without power over policy. Nor was the great Convention itself in a much more powerful position. The decree of December 4 had, indeed, announced that "the national Convention is the unique center of governmental impulsion," but in practice the bulk of the Convention simply submitted to the dictatorship of the Mountain. Parliamentary debates during the Terror were perfunctory. The only striking sessions were those in which reports of the great committees were read by Robespierre, Barère, Amar, Billaud, Saint-Just, or another, and piously accepted. Many of the more active and ambitious Conventionnels were absent for long periods on executive missions and the milder members of the Plain frequently absented themselves to avoid the painful sight of their colleagues acting without benefit of philosophy. Attendance was therefore small, not infrequently falling below one hundred. The Convention was still France, of course, still a symbol, and with no Convention to listen to them the numerous popular delegations, manifesters, and lobbyist groups might actually have annoyed the government.

The indispensable links between this central government and the

---

[4] A. Ording, *Le bureau de police du comité de Salut publique* (Skrifter utgitt av Det Norske Videnskaps—Akademi i Oslo, Hist.—Filos. Klasse, 1930, no. 6), 188.

local administrations were of two sorts: special agents on a definite mission, and a permanent resident *agent national*. The special agents were chiefly the *représentants en mission*. Members, chosen by the Committee of Public Safety and approved by the Convention, were sent out to organize the new revolutionary government in the provinces in accordance with the law of December 4, to supervise the conscription of men and horses, to keep the armies in the field efficient and their generals loyal, in short, to do a specific job. These "proconsuls" were not, however, mere servants of the great committee. Nothing shows better than the great record assembled by Aulard how technically inefficient, at least by modern bureaucratic standards, this revolutionary machine was, how far certain of the representatives on mission set up momentary principalities of their own.[5] Notably in the matter of "dechristianization," representatives like Fouché at Nemours went far beyond the wishes of the Committee of Public Safety. The latter committee was never altogether contented with this form of agency, preferring men without independent status. Occasionally it sent out such humbler men as confidential agents. But the spectacular work was always done by the proconsuls. The best of them—the educator Lakanal, for instance—did very good work, rivaling the more benevolent intendants of the old monarchy. What was done by the worst of them—a Carrier, a Fouché—is pretty well known. As to their achievements with the armies, civilian and military historians have ever since differed. To the former, they were inspiring leaders, enemies of corruption, spiritual mainstays of the common soldier who really wins the battles. To the latter, they were ignorant civilian meddlers, jealous and incompetent.[6] As French armies were victorious both with civilian meddling in 1794 and without it under Napoleon, history can give no satisfactory inductive reply.

The *agents nationaux* were permanent appointive agents of the national government in each local circumscription, municipality or district, charged with the "execution of the laws." In reality, their function was as old as the *missi dominici* of Charlemagne, and is continued today in the prefects of the Fifth Republic. They were

[5] A. Aulard, *Actes du Comité de Salut public*, 26 vols. (Paris, 1889-1923).
[6] Phipps, *Armies of the First Republic*, I, 25-27.

simply the instruments of efficient government from Paris. The monarchical experiment had set up eighty odd departments as little republics, and thousands of communes endowed with more than Anglo-Saxon self-government. Against all this the *agents nationaux* are a reaction towards the French tradition. Actually the revolutionary government lasted for too short a time, and was assembled too rapidly, for this particular form of bureaucracy to reach its full bloom. Notably the use of agents totally strangers in their districts was impossible, and most of the agents were orthodox and even violent local Jacobins who had called attention to themselves in their clubs. A surprisingly large number of them were destined to be respectable Napoleonic bureaucrats. Fire-eaters rarely consume themselves.

The final stage in the purely administrative organization of the revolutionary government is reached with the local units themselves. The law of December 4 left the departments, always a bit less warmly revolutionary than the smaller units, with no real powers, and concentrated authority in the more radical districts and municipalities. To each of these local units was attached an *agent national*, and the entire personnel of each was thoroughly "purified" by the representatives on mission. These purifications, often pretty drastic, were carried through with the advice of local politicians, and resulted in the elimination of all recalcitrant elements. A suitable republican ceremony usually accompanied these arbitrary dismissals and replacements, lending to the whole transaction the grace of the General Will. The local Jacobin club—itself thoroughly purified of priests, aristocrats, federalists, profiteers, lukewarm patriots and other undesirables—would be convoked, commonly in a ci-devant church, listen to a few orations, and finally to a list of local officials worthy of retention, another of the unworthy, a third of the new men suggested to supplant those cashiered. With appropriate shouts and boos the sovereign people—rarely more than a small fraction of the adult male population—would signify its acquiescence.

The Jacobin clubs, now usually called *sociétés populaires*, thus formed the rather narrow base of the pyramid of revolutionary government. Under the Terror they no longer seem like the tireless and remorseless pressure group that destroyed the monarchy. The victorious clubs could hardly attempt to undermine the government they had created, whose leaders indeed were still leaders in the clubs. The *sociétés populaires* served as centers for the new revolutionary cult; they formed a reservoir from which the government could draw civil servants; they managed to get done a certain amount of coöperative work in aid of the beleaguered fatherland—collecting saltpeter, assembling medical supplies, caring for wounded veterans, distributing food, and similar tasks familiar to those who have lived through a good democratic war. But they were tame enough in their relations with constituted authority, and their total active membership was perhaps even smaller than in the days when they were in opposition.

The disputatious course of the ordinary law could hardly suit so convinced an administration as that of the Terror. The judicial organization of the revolutionary government was developed on the same footing as its executive organization. Ordinary cases—even during the Terror there were ordinary cases at law—went through the courts as established by the Constituent Assembly. Any political offense, however, any act, word, or even thought directed against the omnipotent Mountain, came under the jurisdiction of "revolutionary justice." The Supreme Court of the system was the Revolutionary Tribunal of Paris. Established as early as March, 1793, to deal with the enemies of the Revolution more expeditiously than ordinary courts could, this Tribunal took on its final form in October of that year. It had sixteen judges and sixty jurors, both paid by the state, and was by the Law of 22 Prairial[7] divided into four sections to handle the press of constantly increasing business. At first its proceedings were recognizably those of a court of law, with the accused having the right to obtain counsel, to give evidence, to cross-examine. As time went on and men had fewer doubts as to the adequacy of the inner light, the proceedings became mere public pillorying of the already condemned. Death was the only sentence. Occasionally a touch of sentiment—gray hairs, a sobbing daughter

---

[7] The Jacobins had in October, 1793, introduced their new calendar, freed from Christian superstitions. See below p. 150 for an explanation of this type of date. It ᴙ really impossible to avoid this revolutionary nomenclature, confusing though it is.

—would win over the jury, but such touches were rare. Of the 2,559 condemnations pronounced before the Ninth Thermidor, Wallon insists that "you cannot find ten, you cannot find two pronounced for crimes punishable with death in the penal Code."[8]

Similar tribunals were set up in certain provincial centers. Ordinary courts were permitted to try cases *révolutionnairement*, without juries and without appeal. In the disturbed sections, La Vendée, the Lyonnais, the Gironde, special commissions applied what was practically martial law even to non-belligerents. These tribunals and courts were supplied with prisoners by the *comités de surveillance*, commonly known as revolutionary committees, set up in theory at least in every commune, and working under the general direction of the Committee of General Security at Paris. These committees, commonly voluntary in origin, formed by professional agitators and sincere patriots to keep an eye on local enemies of the Revolution, were regularized by the law of March 21, 1793, which ordered their formation in every commune and in every *section* of large towns and entrusted them with the pursuit of "suspects." They were the most efficient agents of the Committee of General Security.[9] They were the real shock troops of the Revolution, and in the closer study of what is left of their papers—a study hitherto neglected—the infinite variety of the Revolution in the provinces will doubtless become more evident.

Now simply as a form of governmental machinery, this *gouvernement révolutionnaire* was far from perfectly designed to further unimpeded centralization. For the separation of powers dear to the theorists of the Constituent Assembly was substituted not a coördination, but a confusion of powers. The dictatorship in commission depended on the steady agreement of twelve men. The functions and mutual relations of the two great committees were never exactly defined. The representatives on mission were constantly exceeding their instructions. There would seem justification for Mathiez's remark that "the dictatorship of the Mountain, individualistic in its essence, was never a complete dictatorship, an organic dictator-

[8] H. Wallon, *Histoire du Tribunal Révolutionnaire de Paris* (Paris, 1882), VI, 145.
[9] G. Belloni, *Le comité de sûreté générale de la Convention nationale* (Paris, 1924), 303; J. B. Sirich, *Revolutionary Committees* (Cambridge, 1943).

ship."[10] Yet the incompleteness of the dictatorship was not very evident to the victims of the guillotine, to the frightened moderates, to the masses who could not maintain their customary indifference to politics. Only in the retrospect of history does the dictatorship seem imperfect. We know now the dissensions which made the fall of Robespierre inevitable. But for the few months of its height, the government of the Terror was far more effectively *one* than would appear from an analysis of its institutions. The clue even to the revolutionary government is not to be found in its machinery, but in the temper of the men who ran it.

III. THE ORGANIZATION OF VICTORY

What did this revolutionary government do? For one thing, it defeated the enemies of the republic. French patriotism reached frantic heights in the famous decree of August 23, 1793, requisitioning in principle every Frenchman and Frenchwoman until the enemy were driven from the land: "Young men will go to the front; married men will forge arms and transport foodstuffs; women will make tents, clothes, will serve in the hospitals; children will tear rags into lint; old men will get themselves carried to public places, there to stir up the courage of the warriors, hatred of kings and unity in the republic."[11] The military conscription fell upon unmarried men and childless widowers between 18 and 25 years of age. No one was permitted to hire a substitute. Detailed provisions organized the whole country as a vast camp. Modern democratic war had begun in earnest.

The application of this decree lay with the revolutionary government, first of all with Carnot and Prieur on the Committee of Public Safety. Science and industry were pressed into service. Monge, Berthollet, Hassenfratz and other distinguished scientists collaborated with the committee to improve the quality and quantity of iron and steel production. Workmen were conscripted from other trades and sent into government armories. Saltpeter, indispensable for the production of gunpowder, and hitherto imported from abroad, was secured in adequate amounts by a sort of saltpeter

[10] A. Mathiez, "La Révolution française," *Annales historiques de la Révolution française* (1933), X, 18.
[11] *Moniteur*, XVII, 478.

"drive." Cellars, walls and similar dark damp spots were scraped by volunteers from the clubs, and hastily trained amateur chemists assembled these raw materials. At Paris alone, 258 forges were erected in the open air, producing some thousand gun barrels a day. Shoes, uniforms, medical supplies in hitherto unheard-of quantities —for armed forces of France now first exceed the million mark, at least on paper—were obtained by means of large-scale business organization.[12] Some scandal there was, some profiteering, some shoes made with paper soles instead of leather, some inefficiency and delay, but on the whole the job was creditably and quickly done. Patriotism would not stand for shirkers. Malingering youths subject to the draft were reported to the authorities. To save leather for the defenders of the fatherland, good citizens clumped to their offices in wooden shoes. To feed the armies, patriots at home abstained from wheaten bread, from sugar and other luxuries.

Under Carnot and Prieur was completed the long-delayed *amalgame* of the various elements of the French armies—professional soldiers of the old royal army, volunteers of '91 and '92, conscripts of '93 and '94. Under the Terror something like stability of discipline was attained, and in all but the highest ranks security of command. In these years the great Napoleonic officers received their training as subalterns. For officers in supreme commands the Terror was, indeed, far from a period of security. Supervised at every point by representatives on mission, constantly hounded by the Committee of Public Safety, subject to the merciless democratic pressure for victory, threatened with the guillotine if defeated, or even if stalemated, the generals in command of the armies of the republic were in no enviable position. Carnot himself can hardly have been a comfort to his generals. He was an impatient man, he lacked experience on the battlefield, and his plans were sometimes a bit too complex for mere three-dimensional battles. "He was never able to adapt his means to his end and to fill the abyss between conception and execution."[13] Yet he forms the necessary link between

---

[12] This emergency organization of industry helped to lay the foundations for the modern French economic state, and seems, indeed, to have been planned partly from the point of view of economic nationalism. G. Richard, *Le comité de salut public et les fabrications de guerre* (Paris, 1922), 804.

[13] General Mangin in *Histoire de la Nation française,* ed. G. Hanotaux (Paris, 1927), VIII, 78.

the ideas of Guibert and the practices of Napoleon. His instructions to the generals insist that the new armies must always assume the offensive, that they must attack in masses, but always at certain specific points, never along a whole line, that they must, if necessary, run certain risks of dispersion in order to converge on the enemy when he least expects them, that they must work swiftly towards decisive victories, never stringing out a war of positions in the eighteenth-century manner.

On the whole, the armies of 1794 achieved his aims. The autumn of 1793, as has already been remarked, saw the advance of the allied armies stopped at the frontiers. All during the bitterest months of the Terror, French armies were fighting victoriously on foreign soil, driving back the allies and spreading the new gospel to conquered peoples. In May the English were thoroughly beaten at Tourcoing, and in June the greatest revolutionary victory, at Fleurus, cleared the way for the reconquest of Belgium. On the Rhine the successes of the winter were continued in the spring. By midsummer the whole left bank was again French, and the Prussians, worried over Poland and facing a cessation of subsidies from England, had made secret overtures for peace. In the Alps and in the Pyrenees slight successes at least paved the way for future French expansion.

Perhaps the Terror had made the victories possible; certainly the victories made the continuation of the Terror impossible. Yet there is possibly less connection between the Terror and the military situation than the school of Aulard has maintained. After all, most of the phenomena of the great national requisition of 1793 are familiar enough to those who lived through the war of 1914-1918. Centralization of power was evident enough then, even in the federal republic of the United States, yet there was no Terror. Something of the explanation of the Terror, indeed, is to be found in the war, but not all. The search must go beyond Aulard.

IV. THE ECONOMIC EXPLANATION

Mathiez extended the search for an explanation of the Terror from military circumstances to economic conditions. To him, the revolutionary government was a premature and incomplete dictatorship of the proletariat: premature, since it had been quite inadequately prepared for by the essentially individualistic ideology of the eighteenth century and since modern industrial society had scarcely yet begun to shape itself in France; incomplete, since it was led and achieved, not by proletarians, but by the middle-class Mountain. An economic dictatorship it was, however, aiming through price-fixing and redistribution of land at a democratic republic without extremes of wealth or poverty.[14] The economic interpretation of history was at its most fashionable peak when Mathiez wrote. The prestige of the theory in its naked form has declined a little, and one may safely suggest that the Terror cannot wholly be explained in terms of the Marxian class struggle, as that struggle appeared to most of the followers of Marx. The economic difficulties facing the revolutionary government, however, if they do not explain the Terror, are certainly part of the whole situation from which the Terror grew, and they are sufficiently similar to modern economic difficulties to be interesting today. A brief outline of the economic activities of the revolutionary government should, on the traditional precedence of induction over deduction, come before an attempt to test the validity of Mathiez's theories in this matter. These may be summarized briefly under the *assignats* and sales of national goods, the *maximum*, and the decrees of Ventôse, year II.

The sale of the confiscated lands of the clergy had been conceived by the Constituent Assembly as a financial measure, as a means of securing the *assignat*, rather than as a means of distributing wealth more evenly, of giving land to the landless peasants. That assembly did indeed admit "the happy increase, above all among the inhabitants of the countryside, of the number of landowners" as an ideal to follow, but the conditions of the sales—competitive biddings, sales in fairly large parcels of land, cash payment of a portion of the purchase price—all favored the capitalist buyer.[15] The Convention really altered these conditions very little. When the goods of the *émigrés* were confiscated and put on the market, an attempt was made to serve the ends of social justice by making it possible for the "poor sans-culottes" to acquire lands. Heads of families in com-

---

[14] Mathiez's ideas on this subject are best summed up in his important *La vie chère et le mouvement social sous la Terreur* (Paris, 1927).
[15] M. Marion, *La vente des biens nationaux pendant la Révolution* (Paris, 1908), 15.

munes where no common lands existed were given the right to pre-empt 500 livres' worth of land without entering the auctions, and given 20 years to pay for it. But very few landless peasants took advantage of this provision.[16] The whole operation served to benefit chiefly the moneyed middle classes, who acquired all the urban properties, and much of the rural properties of the church and emigrant nobles, and exploited these acquisitions as absentee landlords. Where peasants did gain—and over the whole of France their acquisitions were very considerable, exceeding those of the middle classes in some departments—the gains went mostly to already prosperous peasants, men of the middle class in all but manners, men converted by their gains to an economic and political attitude essentially conservative. Division of commons among those who had rights in them, revision of earlier eighteenth-century divisions which had benefited the *seigneur*, above all resales in small lots by capitalists who had bought in big lots, all aided in the process of dividing French soil among small and middling proprietors, in creating the agricultural France which even today contrasts so markedly with industrial England and Germany.[17]

If the sales of national goods, by helping build up a numerous class of urban and rural capitalists, contributed eventually to the stability of a capitalist France, they did not at the moment save the currency, symbol of commercial integrity. Taxes still came in rather slowly, loans were quite impossible, and war expenses were constantly mounting. The government could pay its bills in but one way; it printed *assignats*, printed them without regard to the value of the nationalized lands. Prices rose rapidly, and wages followed them much less rapidly. By the spring of 1793 the general dislocation of economic life had produced actual food shortages. The money incomes of a large number of the working classes in town and country alike were barely adequate to buy bread alone. A continued unchecked rise of prices threatened such people with starvation.

[16] Marion, *Ventes des biens nationaux*, 204.
[17] G. Lefebvre, "Recherches relatives à la vente des biens nationaux," *Revue d'histoire moderne* (1928), III, 214-16. M. Lefebvre will not admit, however, that the Revolution satisfied the peasants. They really wanted, he maintains, some such division of great estates as has recently taken place in parts of Central Europe. This the Convention failed to give them, and they therefore lost interest in the Revolution, abandoning it to the bourgeoisie.

Now no modern government can prosecute a popular war with citizen armies while permitting large numbers of civilians to starve. The logic of the situation established by the decree of August 23, requisitioning all France to beat the enemy, implied that deliberate organization should be substituted for the haphazard play of supply and demand. For months the discontented poor, led in Paris by the party of the Enragés, had been urging the leaders of the Mountain to put a stop to speculation in money and in things, to monopolists and war profiteers, to fix prices so that rich and poor alike could provision themselves in the markets. In May a somewhat reluctant Convention decreed a *maximum* of prices on certain grains. This proved difficult of administration, and annoyed business men without appeasing the workers. After continued agitation, a law was passed on September 23, 1793, setting up a general and consistent *maximum* on all important commodity prices and on wages throughout France. Commodity prices were to be determined in each department on the basis of 1790 prices *plus one-third*; allowance was made for maximum profits for middlemen; wages were similarly fixed at the 1790 level *plus one-half*. The economic dictatorship of the Terror as finally evolved included also government requisition for military purposes at the official *maximum*, municipal or district requisitioning to feed civilians, with suitable apparatus of bread-cards, meat-cards and so on, the establishment of a common *pain d'égalité*, a relatively coarse bread made from mixed flours, the forbidding of fine white bread and *patisserie*, closing of the Stock Exchange, general supervision of foreign trade and foreign exchange by the government at Paris, and a number of similar collectivistic measures. Superficially, at least, economic *laissez-faire* was ended.

Controversy over the results of this economic policy has been fully up to the standard bitterness of historical writing on the French Revolution.[18] The nineteenth century in particular was horrified at the indecent touches of socialism discernible in the work of the Convention, at the scandalous concern of the government for the incompetent poor. In these days of plentiful economic planning one ought to be able to approach the *maximum* with a

[18] For a hostile view, see M. Marion, *Histoire financière de la France* (Paris, 1921), III, 95-116, 199-211: for a favorable view, see J. Jaurès, *Histoire socialiste de la Révolution française*, ed. A. Mathiez (Paris, 1922-1924), VIII, 360-371.

certain degree of detachment. Now the whole price-fixing program was forced on the government by political pressure from the *sans-culottes* of the larger cities, and especially by the organized Commune of Paris and the party of the Enragés; it was never wholeheartedly accepted by the bourgeois of the Mountain. In practice, the *maximum* encountered all kinds of difficulties. An immense amount of bureaucratic labor was necessary to produce the schedules, as the slightest dip into the papers of the committees in charge will show: "*Papiers:* Grand aigle, superfin double; Grand aigle, fin; Grand aigle; Colombier superfin; Colombier; Chapelet; Grand-Jésus superfin; Jésus; Grand raisin; Medien; Carré fin double; Carré fin d'impression; Lombard; Carré moyen; Carré bulle; Ecu; Couronne; Tellière; Romain; Pot; Bas à homme; Gris, pour enveloppe; Raîsin bleu; Raisin en couleur; Carré bleu"—and for each of these in producing departments of France a cost price, a selling price in all departments.[19] Do this for dozens of commodities—the textiles in particular are bewildering—and you will have a mass of papers quite impossible of assimilation by so inexperienced a government as the hastily centralized *gouvernement révolutionnaire*. The *maximum* was simply not rigorously enforceable. Nothing shows how completely modern commercial freedom had already supplanted medieval notions of regulation, how thoroughly the essential spirit and habit of *laissez-faire* had penetrated into eighteenth-century France than the widespread resistance to the *maximum*. Even the petty artisans—shoemakers, milliners, potters, and such like—who had welcomed the *maximum* as a means of cheapening their food, were deeply grieved at the necessity of selling their own products at a fixed price. Secret sales above the *maximum* were common, and the gossip and documents of the time are as full of such violations of the law as was the America of the 1920's of bootlegging. The peasants were particularly aggrieved by the prohibition of special profits accruing to agriculture in war time. They often refused to bring their products to market, stored them, even destroyed them. The government was forced to requisition with troops and special police, and to loosen the bonds of the *maximum*

[19] A. Cochin and C. Charpentier, *Actes du gouvernement révolutionnaire* (Paris, 1920), I, 469.

for farmers. Local application of the various rules differed greatly over France. The *maximum* of wages varied from commune to commune, and occasioned much competition for labor between communes, especially at harvest time. The more one studies local history, the more the efficient economic dictatorship of the government of Paris is seen to be a myth.

Yet the *maximum*, viewed simply as an emergency measure of war rationing, was undoubtedly a successful move in a crisis, and it certainly was an interesting and courageous economic experiment. Thanks to the *maximum*, the *assignat* was saved for the time, and actually *appreciated* somewhat during the Terror. The very lowest classes were able to buy food, were not thrown onto public charity. The government was able to do its own buying in a market fairly completely under its control. The great scandals of army purveying do not date from the height of the Terror. How well, in spite of all difficulties, the *assignat* and *maximum* combined to make possible the success of the *levée en masse* is not fully apparent unless contrasted with the horrible misery of the winters of 1795 and 1796, when with price-fixing abandoned and economic liberty restored the *assignat* fell to one-four-hundredth of its face value, and old misery and new wealth appeared in extremer forms on the streets of Paris.

If the *maximum* was hardly more than a measure of war rationing, comparable to similar measures in unsocialistic America of 1917-18, the decrees of Ventôse are unmistakably attempts to alter the distribution of wealth in a permanent way. A series of decrees passed on the 8, 13, and 23 Ventôse, year 11, on the initiative of Saint-Just and Robespierre, provided that the three hundred thousand "suspects" should be tried as soon as possible by six special popular commissions, that the communes should draw up lists of indigent *sans-culottes*, that the Committee of Public Safety, furnished with lists of the guilty suspects and the innocent poor, should supervise the distribution of the property of the former among the latter. The government, therefore, proposed to attain by direct interference with the distribution of wealth a greater degree of economic equality among its citizens. This has been sufficient to secure for Robespierre praise or blame as a precursor of socialism.

Mathiez is not far from attributing Robespierre's fall to this bold, farsighted, but unhappily premature attempt to found a socialist commonwealth. A coalition of injured capitalist interests brought about the Ninth Thermidor.[20]

The decrees themselves never got much beyond formal enactment. Only two of the popular commissions were set up, and the bureaucracy had barely got to work on the lists of eligible *sans-culottes*, when the fall of Robespierre brought an end to the Terror and to Utopia. Public opinion—that is, the opinion of the Jacobins, the only group allowed to express an opinion—seems on the whole to have been in favor of these decrees.[21] Yet the Jacobins themselves were middle-class property owners. They would certainly not be socialists today. The truth is that they were not socialists then. The French Revolution did confiscate private property and it did fix prices. But it fixed prices largely as a measure of war rationing in the first great modern war to involve civilian as well as military organization; and from the first confiscation of church property in 1789 right through the decrees of Ventôse, its leaders were careful to explain that they were not infringing the sacred right of property. "The revolution brings us to recognize this principle, that he who has shown himself the enemy of his country cannot be allowed to own land . . . *the property of patriots is sacred,* but the goods of conspirators are available for the unfortunate poor."[22] Priests, nobles, federalists, ostentatiously rich men, gamblers, adulterers, misanthropists, men indifferent to politics—these and many others were not members of the French Republic, were, indeed, its enemies, and their property was subject to confiscation just as enemy property is subject to confiscation in war time. The economic ideal of Robespierre and fellows was a sort of greengrocer's paradise, a society of small shopkeepers and landowners, where no one would be very rich and no one be very poor. This rough equality was to be attained

[20] A. Mathiez, *Girondins et Montagnards,* 137-138. M. Lefebvre, on whom Mathiez's mantle has apparently fallen, thinks that the master exaggerated the importance of these decrees of Ventôse. See a review by L. Jacob, *Annales historiques de la Révolution française* (1933), X, 178.

[21] For instance, R. Schnerb, "L'application des décrets de ventôse dans le district de Thiers," *Annales historiques de la Révolution française* (1929), VI, 33. Curiously enough, the indigent themselves were a bit distrustful. Many, according to M. Schnerb, thought the government wanted their names in order to transport them out of France.

[22] Speech of Saint-Just, 8 Ventôse, year II, *Moniteur,* XIX, 68. The italics are mine.

and kept, not by collective ownership of capital, not by government regulation of industry, not even by progressive income taxes, but, once the first lift of the Terror was given, by the force of republican morality among a fit people.

All revolutions are risings of the have-nots against the haves, of the under dog against the upper dog; but not all revolutions are risings of proletarians against capitalists. Recent writers like M. Gaxotte, who see in the Terror a rehearsal for the Commune of 1871 and the Russian Bolshevik Revolution are abusing mere superficial analogies. However accurately the crude economic interpretation of history may apply to the latter movements, it hardly applies at all to the Terror of 1794. The simple fact, and one that needs re-iterating in a time when economic problems seem to many the sole problems, is that the men who made the Terror were not thinking in terms of economics, were not even, incredible though it may seem, lusting in terms of economics.

V. THE STRUGGLE OF THE FACTIONS

They were, of course, lusting partly in terms of power. The actual give and take of daily political struggle cannot wholly be neglected by one who is attempting to explain the Terror. If the machinery of the revolutionary government was already pretty well constructed by the autumn of 1793, the uses to which that machinery would be put depended on who got control of it. Now all political struggle is a struggle among human beings, creatures at times capable of extraordinary consistency of purpose, whether determined by ideas or by interests, but also at times subject to whims, to inconsistencies, above all to the strangest and most inexplicable feelings of attraction or repulsion towards certain of their fellows. The grandest philosophy of history must make room for these personal emotions. The neatest theory of the Terror will fall flat if it omits the crescendos of hatred—hatred of persons, not just hatred of ideas—which accompanied the logical development towards a dictatorship of the elect. Marat, at least, having been raised to the Pantheon by the dagger of Charlotte Corday, no longer complicates the problem. Robespierre, however, undoubtedly felt a contemptuous hatred for Danton, for Hébert a somewhat milder scorn. Mere survival, perhaps, has set Robespierre up as the typical Jacobin, and this survival was perhaps determined more by the definiteness and intensity of his hatreds, and by the strength of his desire to stay in power, than by his typicalness as a Jacobin. History has then read into the ambitious sociological concept of the Jacobin religion what is after all mere ambition and inexplicable individual spite. Such a plight always faces history, and is perhaps less serious in the French Revolution than at other times.

For on the whole its struggles are group struggles; and if the group have any reality at all, that reality must be an objective thing, not something hidden in the consciousness of an individual. It is true that the conflicting groups of 1794 are not great parties nationally organized, but groups so restricted in numbers, so little associated with general ideas and a program that they are commonly called after their leaders—Robespierrists, Dantonists, Hébertists. It is true that since the Jacobin dictatorship had destroyed free speech and the whole apparatus of democratic elections, the political struggle was the peculiarly intense and unabstract struggle of intimates. Yet the eventual triumph of the group whose titular head was Robespierre seems not wholly accidental, not wholly to be dissevered from the curiously logical course which from May, 1789, had successively sacrificed the court, the Constitutionnels, the Feuillants and the Girondins to a group ever smaller, more determined, and more virtuous.

The late autumn of 1793, the winter and early spring of 1794 witness the final shaping of the revolutionary government and the struggle for its control between groups never accurately delimited, never neatly organized, often split up into subgroups, but none the less distinguishable. These may be described as the government, centering in the two great committees (Robespierrists), the "Indulgents" or "citra-revolutionaries" (Dantonists), and the "ultra-revolutionaries" (Hébertists).

Now the government had certain definite assets. It was already in office, had control of the invaluable Jacobin network of popular societies, and was beginning to build up its own provincial bureaucracy. The membership of the two great committees included the most distinguished and capable leaders of the Mountain, and in the

Incorruptible Robespierre the government possessed a leader of great popular prestige, a name which, before the Ninth Thermidor completely blackened it, enjoyed a power comparable to that later given to names like Clemenceau, Winston Churchill. Most important, the government was for the most part composed of earnest Jacobins, men genuinely convinced of their mission to realize a democratic republic, to incorporate on this earth the aspirations of their century of Enlightenment, determined men, religious men. Their rule was brief, for their faith was brief, and without the consecration of a tradition. But their triumph over other groups is at bottom a triumph in public life of qualities which men have commonly regarded as virtues in private life—honesty, conviction, hard work, austerity.

The group loosely held together around Danton were a different lot—political adventurers, journalists, bankers, contractors for army supplies, men of affairs. Most of them perhaps were reasonably decent men, sincerely attached, like Danton himself, to the France of Rabelais if not to the France of Calvin, men of the kind who later gave a characteristic tone to the nineteenth-century democracies of Western Europe, and America, men of the world, which they persist in finding not a bad world. But the Dantonist group included influential men who were outright scoundrels, men who proposed to use the machinery of the Terror to enrich themselves, and these men involved the whole group in ruin. There can be no doubt now that Chabot, Julien of Toulouse, Basire, Fabre d'Eglantine—even Danton himself perhaps—were parliamentary corruptionists, that an affair like that of the *Compagnie des Indes* is comparable to the Panama scandals of the Third Republic, to the Teapot Dome affair in the United States.[23] The inevitable policy towards which such men were drawn was a demand for the abatement of the Terror. The Government was obviously using the Terror as a means of social and political discipline which would make the kind

[23] Mathiez's great work here seems unassailable. In the *Etudes Robespierristes*, I, *La corruption parlementaire sous la Terreur* (2nd edition, Paris, 1927), II, *La conspiration de l'étranger* (Paris, 1918), and in *Un procès de corruption sous la Terreur. L'affaire de la Compagnie des Indes* (Paris, 1920), he has proved that many of the Dantonists were guilty of fraud, forgery, larceny and similar crimes. The most one can now do for Danton himself is to claim, as is sometimes claimed for Warren Harding, that he was an easy-going man misled by his friends, blind to their misdeeds.

of lives these men wished to lead impossible. With the founding of Desmoulins's *Vieux Cordelier* in December, 1793, they began an organized campaign for a reign of clemency. Hesitantly the moderates began to rally to their side. On the streets, in the cafés, even in the Convention, men began to murmur against the dictatorship.

The group known as the Hébertists is even more disparate than the previous group. Its nucleus, centering around Hébert, Ronsin, Momoro, Bouchotte was a rather crudely organized ward machine in certain Paris *sections* which had a particular hold on the war department, and threatened the government's hold over the Paris municipal government, the famous Commune. These men were boisterous patriots, friends of the common man, violent enemies of Christianity, expert mouthers of revolutionary slogans, but astonishingly devoid of social or economic ideas. Many of them were quite as corrupt in morals as any of the Indulgents. Hébert himself, proprietor of the first of yellow journals, the foul-mouthed *Père Duchesne*, was an empty-headed but not empty-handed adventurer. Jaurès himself sums up the program of this friend of the people as "incohérence et néant."[24] Working with the Hébertists, or at least working against the government, was what was left of the group known in 1793 as the Enragés. Led earlier by such men as Varlet and Roux, this Parisian group had imposed the *maximum* on an unwilling Mountain, had announced the overthrow of the rich by the poor, had sketched briefly a program of proletarian revolt much more in accordance with our modern notions of the class struggle than the blusterings of Hébert. Roux himself fell victim to the Hébertist Chaumette, *procureur* of the Commune, but some of the elements of the Enragés group seem to have made common cause with their former enemies in the early spring of 1794. Finally, in this group of ultra-revolutionaries must be numbered a miscellany of cranks, the lunatic fringe represented by the Prussian baron Cloots, the "Ambassador of the Human Race," possibly, too, a certain number of *agents provocateurs* hired by *émigrés* and moderates to stir up revolutionary passions to the pitch of self-destruction. Robespierre at least affected to believe that most of the "ultras" were hired with Pitt's gold to discredit the revolution by

24 J. Jaurès, *Histoire socialiste*, VIII, 267.

their extreme demands. The whole group was distasteful to the government, first because the government was after all composed of educated men never in real sympathy with the noisy proletariat, second because the government was always a bit jealous of the Paris Commune, and third because the government, keenly aware of the religious situation in the country, feared the worst from the intransigent priest-baiting constantly carried on by the Hébertists and their allies among the representatives on mission. Many of the absurdities of social life during the Terror—absurdities to be encountered in the next chapter—are, it must be admitted, Hébertist in origin rather than orthodoxly Jacobin.

Over these two groups the government triumphed in March and April, 1794, by means of a very old political trick; they played one off against the other. First they used Indulgent support to secure from the Convention the indictment of the Hébertists before the Revolutionary Tribunal—an indictment which meant death. Then, within a few weeks, they appealed successfully to the frightened Convention for the indictment and death of Danton and his friends. Against the Hébertists they could rely on the latent but real distrust of the provinces for Paris. The decisive weakness of the "ultras" was their identification with the city of Paris. Against the Dantonists they could and did prove a sufficient number of criminal acts to send, in those uncritical and excited times, the whole lot to the guillotine. Modern democracies, their first fervor gone, no longer punish with death such offenses as larceny, fraud, malfeasance in office; but even modern democracies rarely make permanent heroes of those guilty of such offenses, or keep them forever in office.

The destruction of the two great batches of condemned "ultras" and condemned "citras" did not completely eliminate either of the groups. Indeed, a coalition of what was left of the two groups, with discontented members of the government itself, broke down the whole revolutionary system four months later. But in the meanwhile the opposition was thoroughly cowed. The government of the two great committees was supreme. The greatest of the revolutionary experiments was at its height. The Republic of Virtue had come at last.

Chapter Six

THE REPUBLIC OF VIRTUE

I. THE LITTLE THINGS

THE TERROR does not really seem extraordinary until it is seen to touch ordinary men and common things. Even during years which, like the early eighteenth century, seem in retrospect a bit dull, the great and their associates lead varied and interesting lives. Court intrigue, wars, private adventures furnish excitement and change, and the politest society has a place for surprise. There never was a true aristocracy of neophobes (the Spartan and the British aristocracies were, in different ways, not quite true aristocracies). For common, nameless people—the stuff of social history—life is, however, repetitious and expected, its changes partaking so completely of nature's cycles as hardly to seem changes at all. Not so with the French Revolution. To the humblest cobbler, to the remotest peasant it brought inescapable modifications in the little things which made up their lives. The guillotine, prison, Jacobin clubs, political elections, even political riots—these might all be avoided, especially by the obscure; but no one could altogether avoid clothes, theaters, furniture, cafés, games, newspapers, streets, public ceremonies, birth, death, and marriage. On all this, the Revolution, and especially the Terror, left a mark. It broke in rudely on the accepted ways of millions of humble people, turned their private lives inside out, made them take part in a public life keyed to an amazing pitch of collective activity. This ubiquity of the Terror made its continuation impossible. Men will put up with a certain amount of bloodshed and tyranny for a long time—sometimes for a very long time —but modern men, at least, have hitherto been impatient of too widespread interference with the petty details of their lives, with their habits, vices, furniture, food, and drink.

Nowhere is the revolutionary passion for making this world into the other world more apparent than in the minutiæ of social his-

1. COSTUMES OF THE DEPUTIES OF THE THREE ORDERS CLERGY, NOBILITY, THIRD ESTATE

Bibliothèque Nationale

2. MEETING OF THE PARIS "FRIENDS OF THE CONSTITUTION" IN THE LIBRARY OF A FORMER JACOBIN CONVENT

Musée Carnavalet

3. LOUIS XVI
Boze

4. MARIE ANTOINETTE
Kucharski

These portraits bring out well the contrasting characters of the king and queen

5. THE WOMEN SET OUT FOR VERSAILLES, OCTOBER 5, 1789
Drawing by Massard

6. THE SEPTEMBER MASSACRES: SCENE AT THE ABBAYE
Musée Carnavalet

7. LAFAYETTE AS COMMANDER OF THE NATIONAL GUARD

("He had a canine taste for publicity")

by Dubucourt

8. FREDERICK WILLIAM II OF PRUSSIA

9. GUSTAVUS III OF SWEDEN

10. PAUL I OF RUSSIA

11. LEOPOLD II OF AUSTRIA

European Monarchs of the Revolutionary Period

12. MARAT DEAD IN HIS BATHTUB

Now merely an interesting piece of realism, this was to the true Jacobin a *Pieta*

by David

13. THE ACTOR CHINARD IN THE COSTUME OF A SANS-CULOTTE
by Boilly, Musée Carnavalet

14. BRISSOT
by Billiard

15. CAMILLE DESMOULINS
Contemporary drawing

16. DANTON
Contemporary painting

17. ROBESPIERRE
by Guerin

Moderates and Immoderates

18. FESTIVAL OF THE SUPREME BEING, 20 PRAIRIAL, YEAR II. SYMBOLIC MOUNTAIN SURMOUNTED BY LIBERTY CAP AND TRICOLOR.

Bibliothèque Nationale

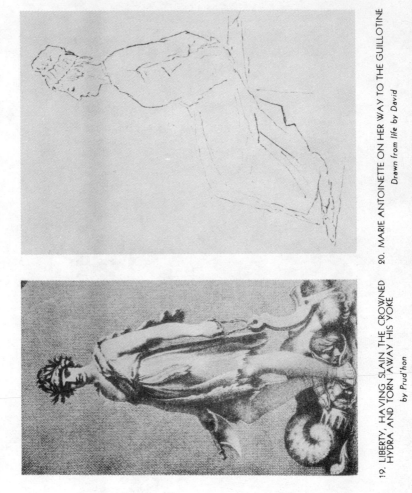

19. LIBERTY, HAVING SLAIN THE CROWNED
HYDRA AND TORN AWAY HIS YOKE

by Prud'hon

20. MARIE ANTOINETTE ON HER WAY TO THE GUILLOTINE

Drawn from life by David

Art in the service of the Revolution

21. MADAME ROLAND
Contemporary Engraving

22. THERESIA CABARRUS (MADAME TALLIEN)
by Isabey

Revolutionary Ladies: Roman and Cyprian

23. A *SECTIONNAIRE* IN REPUBLICAN COSTUME

Bibliothèque Nationale

24. THE PRESIDENT OF A REVOLUTIONARY COMMITTEE RETURNING FROM A SEARCH

Musée Carnavalet

25. REVOLUTIONARY ELECTRICITY OVERTURNING THRONES

(Electricity was then a scientific novelty)

Musée Carnavalet

26. OFFICE OF A REVOLUTIONARY COMMITTEE. BUSTS, PIKES, LIBERTY CAPS, SIMPLICITY

Drawing by Fragonard fils

27. THE JACOBIN BEFORE AND AFTER THE RISING OF PRAIRIAL YEAR III (1795). ALREADY
THE JACOBIN HAS BECOME A SCARECROW

Contemporary caricature

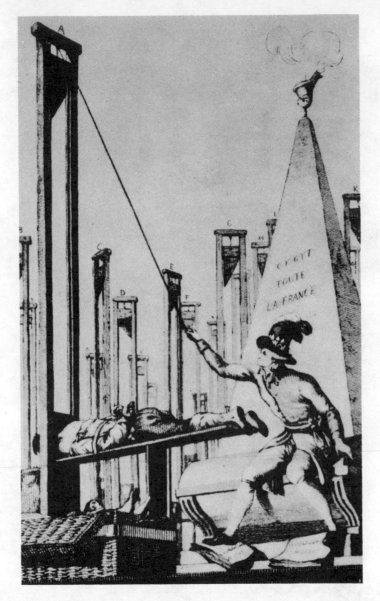

28. ROBESPIERRE GUILLOTINES THE EXECUTIONER AFTER HAVING HAD ALL THE REST OF FRANCE GUILLOTINED

Contemporary caricature

29. BURKE HAS JUST ANNOUNCED A JACOBIN PLOT. PITT AND DUNDAS, ON HIS LEFT,
ARE PROPERLY HORRIFIED; FOX AND SHERIDAN, ON HIS RIGHT, LOOK GUILTY

Caricature by Gilray

30. INCROYABLE AND MERVEILLEUSE

L'arrivée des Remplaçans

Le départ des Remplacés

31. ARRIVAL OF THE NEW DEPUTIES; DEPARTURE OF THE OLD. EVEN TODAY STILL A
FAVORITE THEME OF FRENCH CARICATURE

Caricature of period of the Directory

32. THE YOUNGER PITT
Lawrence

33. GODOY

34. WÖLLNER

35. BISCHOFFSWERDER

European Statesmen of the Revolutionary Period

36. THE FIRST TREE OF LIBERTY AT AMSTERDAM

37. GENERAL BONAPARTE

The handsome young general of the Italian Campaign

Appiani

38. JOSEPHINE
Isabey

40. NELSON
Abbott

39. SUVOROV
Kreuzinger

Heroes of the Second Coalition

41. A MAMELUKE

C. Vernet

42. SOLDIERS OF NAPOLEON'S DROMEDARY CORPS

The Near East

43. SULTAN SELIM III

44. STUDY (CHALK)
Prud'hon

45. THE TENNIS-COURT OATH

David

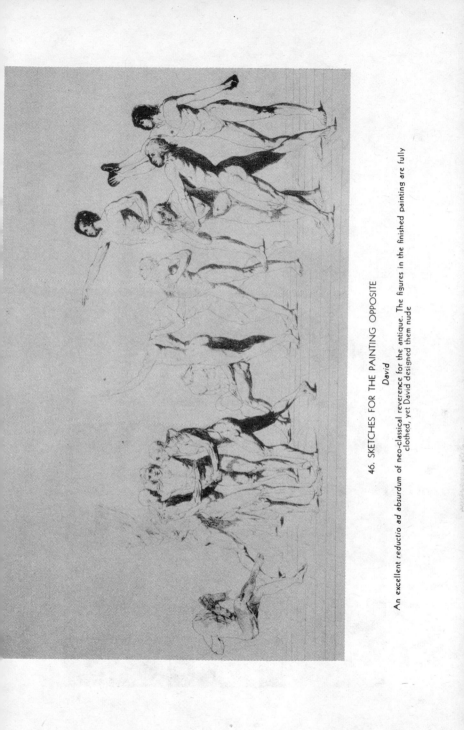

46. SKETCHES FOR THE PAINTING OPPOSITE

David

An excellent *reductio ad absurdum* of neo-classical reverence for the antique. The figures in the finished painting are fully clothed, yet David designed them nude

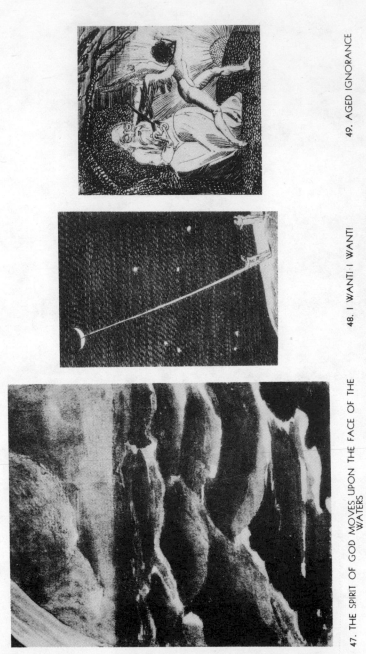

47. THE SPIRIT OF GOD MOVES UPON THE FACE OF THE WATERS

48. I WANT! I WANT!

49. AGED IGNORANCE

Romantic Art—William Blake

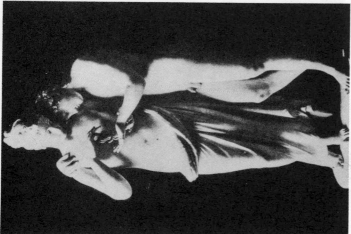

50. CUPID AND PSYCHE WITH BUTTERFLY
Canova

51. HOPE
Thorvaldsen

Neo-classical sculpture

52. BRANDENBURGER GATE, BERLIN

53. CHURCH OF THE MADELEINE, PARIS

Neo-classical architecture

54. ANDRÉ CHÉNIER
Suvee

55. WORDSWORTH
Carruthers

56. SCHILLER
Graff

57. KANT
Döbler

Men of Letters

58. GOETHE IN THE ROMAN CAMPAGNA

Tischbein

tory. Fashion, long powerful and capricious, and the relatively new art of large-scale propaganda were both pressed into service. How much of the result is reasonably spontaneous, how much attributable to the shocking, because disguised, compulsion of propaganda, cannot be decided. It is pretty clear, however, that the element of spontaneity, fairly unmistakable in 1789, diminishes as time goes on, and that under the Terror only the tiny nucleus of genuine Jacobins had their hearts in the thing. And the Jacobins of the Terror were victims, or beneficiaries, of religious auto-intoxication, and utterly unable to distinguish the limitations of propaganda. If much of what follows seems a mixture of absurdity, presumption and cruelty, the explanation lies surely neither in French racial characteristics (which are mostly mythical) nor in French political inexperience (which is greatly exaggerated), but in the fact that true religious convictions embrace a universe well beyond what to the uninspired is absurdity, presumption, and cruelty.

By no mere freak of history does one of the most effective catchwords of the Revolution derive from an article of clothing. The *sans-culottes* wore the honest, long trousers of the workingman, a comfortable garment, and one that made all legs equal by concealment; they repudiated the knee-breeches of the aristocrat, symbol of silken leisure, and no fit refuge for the spindly shank of the counting house or the too sturdy leg of field and ditch. The ardently conformist Jacobin wore, at the height of the Terror, a shirt open at the neck and without cravat, a short jacket (the *carmagnole*), trousers, the red Phrygian bonnet or liberty cap, and, to save leather for the boys at the front, wooden shoes. The whole was to be worn jauntily, a bit carelessly. Neatness and precision were to be avoided as foppish, as unworthy of men whose thoughts were on higher things than dress. The stuffs were woolen, linen, or cotton, and ran to the more subdued shades that have ever since characterized male costume, though an occasional patriot would display on his person a fitting synthesis of the bright national *tricolore*—red, white, and blue. This combination was also popular for ladies' dresses in the earlier days of the movement, but it proved a somewhat exacting one, often failing to set off properly the subdued charms of its patriotic wearers. In general the mode for women ran strongly to the antique, to the flowing white robes of the virtuous females of republican Rome. Both sexes abandoned the artificial distinction acquired by wigs or powdered hair, and made a point of dressing their own hair simply and naturally. The men turned to mustaches, which became a definite, though not universal, symbol of patriotism and virility. Personal ornaments were frowned upon, unless, like tricolor cockades, metal buttons stamped with the head of Brutus or of Marat, pins and brooches in the form of fasces, they were objects of the revolutionary cult. Mere jewelry was unworthy of republican men and women; moreover, its sale to unbelieving foreigners would help the finances of the republic. It was a maxim of the time, repeated in a hundred Jacobin pulpits, that a woman needs no other ornament than her virtue.

Not all Frenchmen adopted these forms of dress. Robespierre himself was a model of neatness in his favorite light blue coat and breeches, clean frilled shirt, and meticulously powdered hair. But the earthly Robespierre was always the little lawyer from Arras, conforming to the habits of his class, and the heavenly Robespierre had fashioned a world for himself where desire was sated not so much in symbols like dress or ornament as in mere words. Many men of temperate conviction were able to avoid the more extreme forms of revolutionary costume. A leading Jacobin of Bourgoin refused to wear the liberty cap on the ground that it didn't become him, and after he had replied to critics that "patriotism does not consist in any particular way of dress, that a true patriot is to be known only by his actions," he actually won from the local club a vote to the effect that each individual was free to dress as he pleased.[1] Yet it was never safe to leave off the revolutionary cockade in public. Women who did so were frequently roughly treated by the patriots, and carelessness with the cockade might well bring one to the list of suspects.

The other decorative arts were soon enlisted in the cause. Revolutionary bric-à-brac of all sorts still remains to adorn historical exhibitions, thought most of it would be out of place in an art exhibition. Stones from the Bastille were suitably inscribed and sold as paper weights. Busts of all sizes and materials brought Brutus,

[1] L. Fochier, *Souvenirs historiques sur Bourgoin* (Vienne, 1880), 476.

Hampden, Sidney, Franklin, Washington, Voltaire, Rousseau, Mably, Mirabeau and Marat to patriotic homes. Pipes, vases, candlesticks, plates, and other objects of domestic use were covered with revolutionary slogans like "Liberté, Égalité, Fraternité ou la Mort!", decorated with the tricolor, stamped with the effigies of the new saints, fashioned into goddesses of Reason, fasces, tables of laws. Miniature guillotines were sold as souvenirs or toys. Playing cards with kings, queens, and knaves could hardly suit a free people. New packs with Liberties, Equalities, Fraternities, Virtues, Reasons, Geniuses, were brought on the market by enterprising men of affairs, one of whom was the future socialist Saint-Simon. The delicate, if already somewhat severely classic, style of furniture known as Louis Seize was judged too corrupting. Republican furniture was more solid, patterned closely after Roman remains, upholstered in harsher shades of brown and yellow. "Patriotic beds" appeared, standing sturdily on legs decorated with fasces, posts capped with liberty bonnets, coverlets embroidered with revolutionary sentiments. "Unité, indivisibilité de la république, liberté, fraternité ou la mort" and similar texts, in painting or needlework, were hung in best rooms as "Home, Sweet Home" used to be hung in American homes. The obviously bosomed, alluringly petticoated ladies and shepherdesses of Boucher, and Fragonard, even the lasciviously innocent maidens of Greuze, went suddenly out of fashion. Painters, led by David, devoted themselves to the two Brutuses, to Mucius Scævola, the Horatii and other Roman heroes. The strumpet Color gave place to Line and Form, always ladies of virtue.

A rage for renaming, such as has accompanied the Russian Revolution, and has not been unknown in America, followed the fall of the monarchy. Unfortunate Leroys, Lévêques, Saint-Jeans, Saint-Pierres changed their surnames to Laloy, Bonhomme, Laliberté, dropped the compromising "Saint." The Christian name of Louis was especially accursed, and often gave place to Brutus, Gracchus, Spartacus. Helpless infants were baptized—civically, not "fanatically"—with names as sincerely barbarous as any English Puritan ever invented—Libre Pétion, Constitution, Montagne, Marat, Chalier. Place names all over France underwent transformations that must have disrupted postal service for some time: Auteuil be-

came Auteuil-sans-culottes; Compiègne, Marat-sur-Oise; Ermenon-
ville proudly took the name of its great hermit, J. J. Rousseau;
Saint-Maximin was transformed into Maximum; Lyons, recaptured
from the royalists, was born anew as Commune Affranchie; Saint-
Péray became Péray-Vin-Blanc; and the little town of Saint-Jean-
aux-Bois took the poetic, but one would think commercially dis-
couraging name of La Solitude. "Royal" was hastily scratched off
the shop signs of former purveyors to his majesty. Street names were
purged of corrupting associations by republican town councils, inn-
keepers obliged to alter their signs. Sometimes one detects a sardonic
humor in these changes, suspects a moderate avenging himself on a
mad world, as when at Breteuil the Rue au Loup became the Rue
Marat, or at Pierrefonds the inn "cidevant nommée L'Enfer" was
changed to "A La République."[2] So went this singular campaign
against what to common sense are mere names, culminating perhaps in the attempt to change the *reine abeille* (queen bee) into the
abeille pondeuse (laying bee)—equality among the bees. Common
sense, however, may here be a bit shortsighted. Words have in this
imperfect world lives of their own, and to kill a word is at least to
acquire some kind of trophy.

The theater was an institution too obviously social, too easily
accessible to the propagandist, to escape the revolutionary contagion.
The Constituent Assembly early abolished the various theatrical
monopolies, such as that held by the Théâtre Français over the
French classics, and decreed complete freedom of competition.
Theaters sprang up all over Paris, ready to please the taste of the
crowd. Overproduction brought its usual result in frantic competition and lowered standards. Plays became mere spectacles, based on
the æsthetic capacities of the virtuous *sans-culottes*. Some of the
older theaters strove to maintain standards, but succeeded only in
amassing an aristocratic clientele which brought them under suspicion. Moreover, as time went on the revolution became more and
more exacting in its orthodoxy. In August, 1793, a modest comedy
called *Pamela*, derived from Richardson through Goldoni, was put

[2] R. Anchel, "Les Jacobins de Breteuil," *Révolution française* (1913), LXV, 494;
M. Dommanget, "Notes et Glanes," *Annales historiques de la Révolution française*
(1924), I, 169.

on at the Théâtre Français, still attempting to live up to its traditions. Patriots raised the objection that Pamela was represented
as a girl of noble blood. The author obligingly made her plebeian.
Even then, at the lines

>   Ah! les persécuteurs sont les seuls condamnables
>   Et les plus tolérants sont les plus raisonnables . . .

one of the audience rose and shouted: "No political toleration. It's
a crime." He was roughly handled in an ensuing riot, and the
upshot of the whole affair was the closing of the theater and the arrest of the actors on suspicion of aristocracy. Henceforth the theater
was simply an instrument of republican propaganda.

Earlier in the Revolution the successful plays had all had a touch
of propaganda. M. J. Chénier's *Charles IX*, a stiff tragedy dealing
with the crowned villain of St. Bartholomew's Day had rallied
patriots, and won for itself the title of "The School for Kings."
Patriotic spectacles with much scenery, marching, music, *tableaux
vivants*, but little dialogue or plot, were popular from the fall of
the Bastille onward. During the Terror, cities and sometimes
Jacobin clubs subsidized edifying performances opened gratis to the
public. The Convention itself on August 2, 1793, decreed that three
times a week at certain designated theaters of Paris should be played
"the tragedies of *Brutus, Guillaume Tell, Caius Gracchus* and other
dramatic pieces retracing the glorious events of the Revolution and
the virtues of the defenders of liberty," one of these performances
each week to be at the expense of the state.[3] Selections from the list
of the plays presented in 1793 and 1794 give a perfectly adequate
idea of the revolutionary theater: *The Victims of the Cloisters, A
Day at the Vatican, or The Pope's Marriage, The Republican's
Widow, The Apotheosis of Marat and Lepeletier, Freedom for
Negroes, The Brigands of the Vendée, The Patriotic Family, The
True Friend of the Law.*[4] A strict censorship prevented the performance of most of the classical repertory, inadequately republican,
trivial, or corrupt. Plays of Molière, Racine, Marivaux, even Diderot

---

[3] *Moniteur*, XVII, 308.
[4] E. and J. de Goncourt, *Histoire de la Société française pendant la Révolution* (3rd
edition, Paris, 1864), 293-294.

were forbidden or permitted only after suitable alterations, such as
that required for Racine's couplet

> Détestables flatteurs, présent le plus funeste
> Que puisse faire aux rois la colère céleste.

Since no republican actor should soil his mouth with the words,
"aux rois" the official version substituted a non-commital "hélas!"

The newspaper press during the Revolution ran a course much
like that of the theater. In 1789 a sudden expansion under complete
freedom of the press, a few years of intense party conflicts, each
paper attached to some political interest, and finally, with the
Terror, a return to censorship, but to a censorship far more efficient
and far more narrow than that of the old régime. As a collection of
gossip, a bulletin of important events, or a literary and scientific
news-letter, the daily or weekly newspaper had existed for over a
century in Western Europe, but it was not yet a major factor in the
life of any people. Politically, the pamphlet was during the eighteenth century a far more important influence, and it is the pamphlet
that dominates the elections to the States-General. But the events of
the spring and summer of 1789 were too crowded for the pamphlet,
and the modern newspaper press came into its own. In these short
months hundreds of newspapers were founded in Paris—heavy collections of information, bright journals of criticism and discussion,
violently radical sheets, satirical weeklies, theatrical dailies, personal
newspapers, party organs, bawdy sheets, yellow journals.[5]

Politically the most influential of these papers were the *Patriote
français* of Brissot, a substantial daily, oriented from the start towards a radical democratic revolution, the *Courrier de Provence* of
Mirabeau, written mostly by its editor's underlings, but influential
and at first radical enough, the *Révolutions de Paris* of Loustalot
and Prudhomme, a serious rival of Brissot's journal, ably edited,
revolutionary but not violent, the *Révolutions de France et de
Brabant* of Camille Desmoulins, a witty and irresponsible weekly,
cruel and puckish at once, completely the expression of its editor,

---

[5] In Paris alone nearly 500 separate titles appear up to August, 1792. M. Tourneux,
Bibliographie de l'histoire de Paris pendant la Révolution française (Paris, 1890-94),
II, nos. 10196-10794. Provincial journalism was somewhat later in its development,
and never as influential as that of Paris. Papers printed in Paris were distributed all
over France.

the *Ami du Peuple* of Marat, as cruel as Desmoulins's paper, but never witty, the watchdog of the Revolution, at times a mad watchdog, the *Père Duchesne* of Hébert, especially addressed to the urban proletariat, spiced liberally with now unprintable oaths, an awkward, tentative prototype of the modern yellow journal. To oppose these the royalists had their *Actes des Apôtres*, a sort of periodical pamphlet of irregular appearance, polished, clever, impotent, the aristocratic wit of the eighteenth century perilously near already to the self-pitying romantic irony of the nineteenth, the *Ami du Roi*, as unbridled and bitter on its side as ever Marat on his, and the *Journal de la Cour et de la Ville*. With the fall of the monarchy, royalist newspapers ceased publication, and gradually political proscriptions eliminated one leader after another from the list of papers, until under the Terror only the *Moniteur*, circumspect, noncommittal register of parliamentary proceedings and foreign dispatches, which stands in lieu of a *Hansard* for historians of the period, the Jacobin organ the *Journal de la Montagne*, and a few other licensed sheets remained.

The total impression left by even a glance at this journalistic output from 1789 to 1795 is one of familiarity. This world is almost a contemporary world. It is true that the papers were small in format, that many were mere four- or eight-page quarto size, that they contained little or no advertising, that they obviously lacked the service of press associations, that they had no skilled reportorial staffs, no feature writing, no illustrations. Yet the essentials of a modern newspaper are all there: a definite political policy, affiliation with a specific political party or bloc, coloration of news to accord with political or moral purposes, a general tone, a corporate character determined partly by its owners and editors, even more, however, by what its owners and editors think the group among whom it circulates want it to be. Most of the striking characteristics of modern journalism are here in embryo: the use of headlines, urban distribution by shouting newsboys, exploitation of public interest in sex-scandal—Marie Antoinette was of great value here—stock market quotations, theatrical information and criticism, and other signs of subdivision into special departments; finally an awareness of having a mission, of being a Fourth Estate, a corporate consciousness balanced between the world of affairs and the world of theory, a proud, sometimes arrogant, spirit touched with envy and graced by doubt. All in all, the step from the *Journal des Savants* or the *Clef du Cabinet des Princes de l'Europe* to the *Révolutions de Paris* or the *Ami du Peuple* is as big a step as any taken during the Revolution.

In other fields, too, the arts were pressed into the service of the Revolution. Patriotic poetry abounds in newspapers, in Jacobin proceedings, in separate printing, usually at the expense of the author. Moral tales, republican catechisms, all sorts of books especially directed towards producing young republicans were poured forth. Music contributed the "Marseillaise," the "Ça ira," and many another useful tune, of which only the "Marseillaise" has endured. Even the dance was made to serve patriotism, and the *carmagnole*, a lively round dance, and other simple democratic dances took the place of the aristocratic minuet, a dance difficult to learn, and not calculated to further what the Jacobins called "épanchements." All this, it need hardly be added, is propaganda rather than art, and belongs fitly to the social history of the Revolution rather than to the history of European culture. If one excepts the *music* of the "Marseillaise" (the words themselves could move only a very patriotic Frenchman) and perhaps some of the work of David, the only great artistic achievement of the period of the Revolution in France is the bitterly anti-revolutionary poetry of André Chénier.

The culmination, in a sense, of revolutionary propaganda is its new calendar. Almanacs had been from the beginning of the Revolution a favorite and successful method of spreading the word. Collot d'Herbois himself had won, with his *Almanach du Père Gérard*, a prize offered by the Paris Jacobins for a work to spread the new ideas in simple language. But for the Jacobins of 1794 it was not enough to print good republican moral counsels, after the manner of Franklin, at the appropriate dates and seasons. The whole calendar must be made over. The existing calendar perpetuated the frauds of the Christian church (Jesus himself was probably a good *sans-culotte*; all the nonsense stemmed from Paul), and was highly irrational and inconvenient. The new calendar, based on a report of Fabre d'Églantine, was adopted by the Convention in October,

1793. By it the year began on September 22 of the old calendar, and was divided into twelve months of thirty days each, leaving five days (six in leap years) over at the end of the last month. These five or six days were to be known as the *Sans-culottides*, and were to be a series of national holidays. Each month was divided into three weeks, called *décades*, the last day of each *décade* being set aside as a day of rest corresponding to the old Sunday. The months were grouped into four sets of three, by seasons, and given "natural" names, some of which are rather attractive—*vendémiaire, brumaire, frimaire* (autumn); *nivôse, pluviôse, ventôse* (winter); *germinal, floréal, prairial* (spring); *messidor, thermidor, fructidor* (summer). The days of the *décade* were named arithmetically—*primidi, duodi*, on to *décadi*. In place of the old saints' days, each day was dedicated to a suitable fruit, vegetable, animal, agricultural implement. The Sans-culottides were dedicated, the first to Genius, the second to Labor, the third to Noble Actions, the fourth to Awards, and the fifth to Opinion. This last was to be a sort of intellectual saturnalia, an opportunity for all citizens to say and write what they liked about any public man, without fear of the law of libel. The sixth Sans-culottide of leap years was dedicated to the Revolution, and was to be an especially solemn and grand affair. The republican era was to date from the declaration of the republic in September, 1792. When the calendar came into use, the year I had therefore already elapsed. In spite of its symmetry and its poetic months of budding and of mist, the new calendar was not a success, and Napoleon abandoned it in the year XII (1804). Workingmen preferred one day's rest in seven to one in ten; its terminology, appropriate to the climate of France, was singularly inappropriate to that of the Southern Hemisphere; it embodied a new cult, and that cult, though it profoundly influenced Christians then and since, failed completely to supplant Christian terminology. The calendar and its fate form in many ways a neat summary of Jacobin history.

II. EDUCATION

The Revolution hardly achieved what more unexcited democracies have failed to achieve, a distinction in practice between education and propaganda. In spite of the eloquence of their master Rousseau, the Jacobins were quite unwilling to allow the child to find his own way through trial and error. Their notion of education was pretty close to pure indoctrination. When the Convention decreed that free and compulsory education was the concern of the state, it passed on to local administrations the task of procuring suitable teachers for the new elementary schools. The administrations in turn consulted the "people" assembled in the Jacobin clubs. Many of the resulting debates have survived in the papers of these clubs. Almost universally, the first question as to a proposed candidate for a teaching position was directed towards his political orthodoxy and—what was much the same—his virtue. The opinion was commonly expressed that a good man could teach well even though he were ignorant. Only occasionally does a club admit that it "ought not to pass lightly over the question of talents."[6]

The Revolution had to the full the modern passion for education, the modern faith that in education lies an earthly salvation. Most modern beliefs centering on education originated in the eighteenth century, and were first raised to the power of stereotypes by the French Revolution. Almost rivaling Danton's "de l'audace, encore de l'audace, toujours de l'audace" in the hearts of his countrymen is his assertion that "after bread, the first need of the people is education." To any of its critics, the Revolution could always reply: "Our difficulties arise from the fact that we are forced to deal with men and women brought up with bad habits, superstitious, ignorant, and too old to learn better; give us a generation, and we will bring up the young as citizens of a democracy should be brought up, and all will be well." The argument has since been repeated.

The old bad education of monarchical France was destroyed as completely as possible. Education in old France had had all the diversity of the old régime. Dame schools and charity schools brought simple literacy, at least, within reach of some of the lower classes. Secondary education was wholly in the hands of the church, and was limited to nobility and bourgeoisie. The curriculum was strictly classical, and pedagogical methods had not yet been seriously affected by the work of Rousseau. Indeed, the great intellectual

[6] C. Brinton, *The Jacobins*, 132, 158.

effort of the Age of Enlightenment lay almost wholly outside teaching circles, and penetrated rather late into the formal academic world. By its confiscation of the property of the clergy and by its dissolution of monastic orders, the Constituent Assembly undermined the best part of primary and secondary education. The universities, headed by the ancient University of Paris, had undergone in the eighteenth century a decline similar to that of the great English universities in that same century, and their suppression by the Revolution was probably no great loss. None of the revolutionary assemblies succeeded in erecting a complete system of national education to replace the unsystematic institutions destroyed by the Revolution; none succeeded even in putting primary education on a broader quantitative basis than it had had during the old régime. Indeed, with the abolition of the teaching orders, the general economic crisis, the conservatism and timidity of the maiden ladies who used to run small private schools, it was probably harder to get a child taught his ABC's in 1793-1795 than it had been in 1788. Some practical improvement was made under the Directory, and it is but fair to add that the Convention itself laid down a platform that has subsequently been realized in most modern nations: free and compulsory primary education, and a system of state schools wholly separated from any organized Christian sect.

In secondary and in higher education the revolution has a more definite achievement. In place of the *collèges*, the clerically controlled secondary schools of the old régime, the Convention set up in each department an *école centrale*. These schools developed very successfully until they were abolished by the bureaucratic Napoleon. Their curriculum gave full attention to the sciences and mathematics, and to the so-called social sciences, as well as to the older philosophical and rhetorical subjects. They had adequate libraries and laboratories. Their students were given considerable freedom of choice as to subjects studied, and what is more astonishing, administrative work was kept at a minimum, and done by the teaching staff itself without political supervision. The cities which possessed these schools were very proud of them, and contemporary opinion is almost universal in their praise.[7]

[7] P. Sagnac, in Lefebvre, Guyot, and Sagnac, *La Révolution française*, 504.

In the field of higher education the revolution established special schools which were to have a distinguished career in the next century. The "École des travaux publics" became the "Ecole polytechnique" of today, one of the best technical schools in the world. The "École normale" of 1795 was hardly more than a series of lectures given by the greatest scholars and scientists of France to the more ambitious teachers of the new republic, but it contained the germ of the "École normale supérieure" which was—surprising as the fact will seem to an American—one of the important forces in the making of modern France. Three medical schools were founded—at Montpellier, at Strasbourg, and at Paris—which, incorporated in the higher education of the empire, became productive centers of medical research.

The true Jacobin, however, was always more interested in the culture of the heart than in the culture of the head. With all his devotion to the Enlightenment, he never trusted the free human intellect. Mere thinking never kept a man straight. Virtue must be sought in the communion of man with man. The republic has a perpetual job of adult education far more important than the ABC's. Its citizens must feel the mystic identity of the general will. The Terror was constantly preoccupied with a suitable cult, a suitable ritual, for the Republic of Virtue.

III. THE REVOLUTIONARY CULTS

Like so much else in the Terror, the origins of its ritualistic practices lie, modest but unmistakable, in the earliest days of the revolution. The Tennis Court Oath, the Bastille, the Fourth of August acquired symbolic values almost at once. This early symbolism hardly went beyond the placid and unsacrificing memorial spirit with which most modern nations celebrate their near past. The first clubs, however, began to introduce ritualistic devices of apparent Masonic origin, to surround themselves with busts of heroes, flags, emblems, framed copies of the Rights of Man and the Citizen, to assemble with intent to edify themselves and others. As the break between the Revolution and organized Christianity became inevitable, people consciously set to work to build up a visible Revolution as a substitute for the visible Church. to devise a revolutionary ritual as a substitute for the old ritual. The new ritual may have been in part the work of a Machiavellian few, superior and unbelieving themselves, but convinced of the necessity of religious practices for men in society. In part, too, it was the work of thousands of sincere, well-intentioned men, cut off by the Civil Constitution of the Clergy and its consequences from the normal solaces of Christianity, and driven to the difficult task of building themselves a new Church, a new set of religious habits. There is in revolutionary ritualistic devices more than a touch of that characteristic impotence of the self-educated dabbler that was the despair of the author of *Bouvard et Pécuchet*. They smell of the lamp of Enlightenment. They are too absurd to be dishonest. If they were concocted by would-be Machiavellis as opium for the people, they took revenge by dulling the wits of their own originators.

By the winter of 1793 the republican touch was on everything. One could not, at least in the towns, avoid republican costume, republican nomenclature. The old polite plural *vous* had given place—as earlier with the religious sect of the Quakers—to the singular *tu*. For *monsieur* and *madame* the use of *citoyen* and *citoyenne* was obligatory. Even the old complimentary epistolary formulas had given place to "salut et fraternité" and other Stoic phrases.[8] In daily meetings of the Jacobin clubs, civic services every *décadi*, festivals to celebrate victories at the front, festivals decreed by the Convention, festivals to honor the representative on mission —in these and in many other ways the faithful were brought into constant, indeed too constant, communion. The industry of local historians has provided the student of revolutionary cults with even more material than exists for the *cahiers* or the *maximum*. The revolutionists may, here as elsewhere, have aimed at standardization and centralization, but they certainly failed to achieve their ends. The most fantastic sort of divergencies may be seen in local revolutionary ceremonies. By a process of abstraction, however, it is possible to distinguish four main sources of these ritualistic practices.

The least important of such sources is immemorial—or at least

---

[8] Mme. de Roland concludes a letter to Brissot, January 7, 1791, "Adieu tout court. La femme de Caton ne s'amuse point à faire des compliments à Brutus."

pre-Capetian—folk-custom. The Jacobins were always planting "Liberty trees," which their counter-revolutionary enemies darkly conspired to cut down, deface, or defile. Sometimes these trees had to be protected from irresponsible animals and wicked men by iron pickets. Sometimes, after a counter-revolutionary had defiled the tree, the Jacobin club felt obliged to march in a body and cleanse the tree by a ritual of purification.[9] Around these trees, especially in spring, were held republican dances, and in the public squares and other open places rich and poor, young and old took part in simple civic meals, repasts meant to remind the participants of the primitive innocence of an early society. Spring dances, liberty tree, festival, all go back, indeed, like the maypole, to a Europe far older than the French monarchy.

Classical antiquity, and the classical spirit as interpreted by the eighteenth century, formed an important ingredient in the revolutionary cults. Plutarchian figures postured nobly on thousands of platforms. The trappings of republican Rome, much of the phraseology of its politics (usually misunderstood) filled the proceedings of the Jacobin clubs. Stoic apothegms made the stuff of many a republican sermon. From the long tradition of European classical culture was derived a tendency—it became almost an obsession—towards the personification of abstract ideas, towards the typification of human desires and habits. Goddesses of Reason surrounded by handmaidens were borne on floats in processions, lighted Torches of Knowledge, set fire to Tissues of Error. At Lyons there were carried in a procession a carpenter's plane to symbolize equality, busts of great Frenchmen and of foreigners worthy of being Frenchmen, a statue of liberty, tables inscribed with the laws, jars and baskets of food for the communal feast which was to mark the length of the celebration, and "other emblems of the present cult of Frenchmen."[10]

Many Jacobin religious forms seem to have a Protestant source, though it is probable that similarity of ethical aims between Jacobinism and Protestantism, rather than any actual borrowing, will account for the resemblance. Especially in the formal sessions of

---

[9] *La Vedette* (Besançon), June 29, 1792.
[10] *Journal républicain du Rhône-et-Loire,* 18 and 22 Ventôse, II.

the clubs is this resemblance marked. Like the Protestants, the Jacobins sang hymns, read responsively in their sacred books (Rousseau, the Constitution), listened to interminable sermons, founded Sunday schools, indulged themselves in *épurations* curiously resembling "experience meetings." Like the Protestants, the Jacobins in the end insist on salvation by faith alone. Good works may be achieved by the hypocrite. The searching, if metaphysical, eye of faith can never err.

Finally, as might be expected, the traces of that Catholic faith in which most of the revolutionists were brought up are everywhere. Sometimes the imitation of Catholic practice is so direct as to appear either childish or knavish. In a *Pratique des bons français*, imitated from old manuals of devotion, there appear: A republican invocation beginning "Chaste daughter of the heavens, O Liberty"; a republican salutation, "I salute you, *Sans culottides,* revered name"; a republican credo, "I believe in a Supreme Being, who has made men free and equal"; and "republican Ten Commandments." A familiar engraving, the "Pilgrimage of St. Nicholas" was parodied as "Pilgrimage of the patron of Liberty," with a *génie* capped with the liberty bonnet on a pedestal in place of the saint. Altars in confiscated churches became altars of Marat, altars of Lepeletier. In a little village near Beauvais there is actually mention of a "patriotic holy water font." A "patriotic sign of the cross" in the name of Marat, Lepeletier, Liberty, or Death appears in several provinces. Bertrand, *agent national* at Compiègne, told the faithful: "The priests in other days used to say, any parishioner who fails to come to mass three Sundays in a row risks excommunication. Well, let us say, any citizen who fails to come to our civic festivals will be denied employment, denied our friendship and confidence."[11] The list of such practices is endless, reaching its height perhaps at the "miracles" achieved by the "holy Guillotine."

The most familiar of revolutionary religious festivals is the often-described festival of the Supreme Being held at Paris on the 20 Prairial (June 8, 1794). Robespierre in one of his most famous and platitudinous speeches had dwelt on the necessity of belief in

[11] M. Dommanget, "La déchristianisation à Beauvais," *Annales révolutionnaires* (1920), XII, 447.

a Supreme Being if men were to be virtuous. "The idea of a Supreme Being and of the immortality of the soul is a continual reminder of justice, it is then social and republican."[12] His eloquence had secured from the Convention a decree setting up a whole series of national festivals, in one of which, "À la Maternité," one sees the forerunner of the American "Mother's Day." On the appointed day the Convention marched, carrying flowers and fruits and led by their president, Robespierre, to the garden of the Tuileries, where the people were already assembled. Robespierre preached; the people sang a republican hymn; Robespierre set fire to an artfully made cardboard Atheism, from the ashes of which there arose a presumably unharmed Wisdom (actually a bit scorched); Robespierre again delivered a brief sermon; and the whole crowd then marched across the city to the Champ de Mars, where the celebration finally ended in hymns, cries, and artillery salvos.

Now the slightest acquaintance with this ceremonial aspect of Jacobinism should be sufficient to show that here, at least, one of the great nineteenth-century generalizations about the Revolution is utterly false. The makers of the revolutionary creeds were neither ignorant nor contemptuous of history. They suffered, indeed, from rather an overdose of history. The great trouble with the revolutionary cults is that their syncretism is a syncretism based on too uncritical an acceptance of the past. Even from this short survey it should be clear that almost everything can be found in these revolutionary religious practices. The great apparent failure of Jacobinism as a religion was its inability to achieve a valid *form*, a symbolism and ritualism binding to believers and attractive to proselytes. Whether this failure depends on a more fundamental failure to achieve a valid *spirit*, to embody a new and effective theological idea, is a question that must be postponed to the conclusion of this study.

IV. THE THEORY OF THE TERROR

The Jacobin religion in its original form did not succeed in holding many people for a long time; but it did—and this point is essen-

---

[12] Robespierre, *Discours et Rapports*, ed. Ch. Vellay (Paris, 1908), 361.

tial for an understanding of the Terror—hold an elect few briefly in a psychopathic tension between this world and the next. Evidence is abundant that the ardent Jacobins were a minority, that the chosen were few. Figures are almost meaningless here; but the total enrollment of the popular societies in 1794 seems to have been about 500,000 in a population of 8,000,000 adult males.[13] Only a small proportion of the total membership seems to have had the warmth of true republicans, to have lived always "at the height of revolutionary circumstances." That the Terror was the work of an infinitely small number of Frenchmen is an unquestionable fact. Evidence is equally abundant that most of these terrorists talked, felt, and acted according to a frame of reference which must be called theological. For the true believer the devotional practices outlined in the previous section of this chapter were not absurd forms, but realities entering his life as inescapably as the weather. The devotional language of the Jacobins, their frequent accesses of collective emotion, their conviction of righteousness, their assurance that their opponents are sinners, direct agents of the devil, their intolerance, their desire for martyrdom, their total want of humor —all these are unmistakable signs of the theological temperament. It is possible to build up from the scattered records of what these Jacobins said and did a fairly systematic scheme of values cast into a form closely parallel to traditional Christianity. Mankind is divided into the saved and the damned. Salvation is achieved by grace. Grace is the free gift of a benign God. Though there are certain signs of election by which the elect may know one another, these signs are not the kind recognized in the world of law courts and laboratories. The saved are at eternal war with the damned. The regeneration of the race is ultimately possible, but can be achieved only by the conversion of the damned, or what is much more in accord with Calvinistic and Robespierrean theology, by their extermination.

In this theological background, the political theory of the Terror becomes comprehensible. Saint-Just, Couthon, Billaud-Varenne, and above all Robespierre, provide in their speeches and reports a considerable body of theory in justification of the Terror. Though there

[13] C. Brinton, The Jacobins, 42.

are certain divergencies in their thought, and a great deal of mere exhortative material in their speeches, they are in the main agreed on the simple outlines of the theory. They start with the distinction between constitutional government and revolutionary government. All the fine hopes of the Enlightenment, all the promises implied in Liberty, Equality, Fraternity will be realized under constitutional government. The free man under the constitution will do just what he desires to do. But constitutional government can be attained only through revolutionary government. The weaknesses and wickednesses of corrupt men make this transitional stage necessary. Surrounded by enemies from Pitt and Cobourg to the lurking moderate and the treasonous ultra, the republic can defend itself only by an apparent abandonment of the principles—notably that of individual liberty—on which it is based. Such an abandonment is, however, apparent, not real. For Citizen X is not really free when he commits an unrepublican act, or thinks an unrepublican thought. Freedom consists, not in doing what one wants to do, but in doing what is right. The general will of the republic is right. The Committee of Public Safety knows what that general will is. To obey the Committee, therefore, is to obey one's better self, to be really free. To disobey the Committee is to obey one's worse self, to be a slave. When the Committee interferes with a citizen selfishly following his particular and erring will it is, in Rousseau's words, forcing him to be free. When it cuts off the head of a very recalcitrant citizen, it is presumably also freeing him. Had not Bellarmine argued that it was a positive benefit to a heretic to kill him, because the longer he lived the more damnation he acquired?

Moreover, the use of force against the wicked, even the use, under the Terror, of force utterly unchecked by normal judicial procedure, is essential to protect the virtuous. The protection of judicial procedure must be denied the wicked, not only for the metaphysical reason that, as we have just seen, the wicked are not really to be considered as legal persons, but for the practical reason that the wicked are very clever and if given a chance will delude and destroy the innocent in no time. Ideally speaking, all men are potentially fit for true freedom. But in this present world thousands and thousands of men simply are wicked, irredeemably wicked. They corrupt good men as the rotten apples in a barrel corrupt the sound ones. The only way you can keep your apples at all is to separate the good ones from the bad, and throw away the bad. Surely the bad apple has no claim for other treatment? When one talks of the Rights of Man, one does not consider the bad man a man at all. Danton, Hébert, Hérault, Desmoulins—they were not men. A paradox? Robespierre himself asserted that the revolutionary government was "the despotism of liberty against tyranny."[14]

Now the anti-intellectualism of the late nineteenth and early twentieth centuries is doubtless right in maintaining that men do not normally guide themselves by theories, are not pushed to action by theoretical considerations. There was much jealousy, ambition, cupidity, hunger, and lust among the leaders and the followers of the Terror, more perhaps than this study has made clear. Yet it does seem absurd to pile upon the reproaches of Burke and Taine, that the Jacobins were led astray by a too simple devotion to abstract reason, the final and devastating argument that the Jacobins were not really following abstract reason at all, because such a pursuit is impossible. The truth would seem to be that for a few brief months the convinced Jacobins really were pursuing the ideal goal of their somewhat heterogeneous faith. That they did so with cold intellectual fervor is obviously false. The whole point is that their emotions were centered upon an abstract system of value-judgments, not in the tepid hope of vicarious satisfaction with which men usually devote themselves to such a system, but with a flaming, unreasonable desire of coming to grips with the promises of abstract felicity, with a passionate intention of acquiring virtue as other men acquire wealth. The men who made the Terror were compeers of the first Crusaders, of Savonarola, of Calvin.

Of course, the whole situation known as the Terror is more complex than the motives of Robespierre and his followers, more complex than any brief study can encompass. Analysis falsifies any historical situation. Water chemically analyzed into hydrogen and oxygen ceases to be water, but the separated elements can be reunited into water. To analyze a historical situation, however, is to

[14] Robespierre, *Discours et rapports*, 333. The two reports of 5 Nivôse and 18 Pluviôse, II, 311-346, contain the essentials of Robespierre's thought.

take apart something that can never be put together again. All that the historian can do ultimately is to make over a picture already a thousand times recopied, adding a touch here, a shade there, blurring over or omitting a detail or so. Now the picture of the Terror, thanks to the work of Aulard and his followers, contains an emphatic, indeed overwhelming, background of foreign and civil war; thanks to Mathiez, it has been completed with a touch of the class struggle. To drop the metaphor: into the historical situation known as the Terror there went certainly the desperate necessities facing men who wage a war in some measure not of their choice; there went the hatred of the poor for the rich, of the failure for the success; there went the relatively simple and eternal desire of men to rule other men; there went the desire of overeducated and inexperienced men to realize the paper Utopias of eighteenth-century thought; and there went the religious fanaticism of men borne in a frenzy of hope beyond the petty decencies of common sense. All this, and much more, is in the Terror. *But omit a single one of these elements, and you no longer have the Terror.* Modern historiography, with its pseudo-scientific bias, has emphasized the material circumstances, the economic motive, anything but the deliberate volition of men whose interests, ambitions, and ideas were in themselves varied and unpredictable compounds. The official explanation of the Terror, in the hands of either Aulard or Mathiez, is too naïvely mechanistic, too sure that men are reasonably selfish or reasonably altruistic, too unaware of the extent to which men prefer the illusions of art to the illusions of logic and the realities of the flesh. The conservative explanation of Taine or Cochin, though it errs in overemphasizing the elements of plot and idealistic conviction so neglected by the official school, errs in a way nowadays less fashionable and therefore less dangerous. The Terror, like much milder and less interesting political situations, is the interaction between a social environment and men consciously attempting to alter that environment. To oppose man and his environment, will and reality, ideas and interests, "plot" and "circumstances," to start out with the firm intention of proving that one element only in each of these pairs determined events, is to falsify everything. What you have is interaction, not opposition; reciprocal relationship, not a simple case of cause and effect. If this is unsatisfactory, if you still insist that either ideas made the Terror or the Terror made ideas, then you may abandon history and choose your favorite metaphysician. The choice is still substantially between Taine and Aulard.

Chapter Seven

EUROPE AND THE REVOLUTION: WAR

I. THE BORDER COUNTRIES

WITH THE DECLARATION of war, the French Revolution became a crusade. Revolutionary principles were spread through most of Europe by more or less well-organized minority groups, almost wholly composed of natives of the country in which they worked, and maintaining with revolutionary leaders in France relations the exact nature of which will probably never be determined. In certain countries bordering on France, however,—the Low Countries, the Rhineland, Savoy, Nice,—the victorious republican armies brought not only revolutionary propaganda, but revolutionary institutions. The policy of the Convention was frankly annexationist. All these border countries came within the so-called "natural frontiers" of France—Pyrenees, Alps, Rhine, Atlantic, and Mediterranean. All contained at least the nucleus of a Francophil party anxious to promote amalgamation with the republic. The process was broadly the same in Belgium, Mainz, Savoy, and Nice: occupation by French troops was followed in the key cities by organization of Jacobin clubs, composed of French officers and civil commissioners, and a suitable representation of trustworthy natives; these clubs would petition the Convention for annexation to France; natives of the region in question domiciled in Paris, frequently organized in clubs like the Savoyard *Club des Allobroges*, would make similar petitions; armed with this evidence of a popular desire for annexation, sometimes strengthened, as in the case of Savoy, by a request for annexation from an assembly elected under French bayonets, the Convention would incorporate the region in the French Republic; organization into departments followed, and the existing legislation in France, including, of course, that which abolished the remnants of feudalism, was applied to the newly acquired region. Save for short intervals when French armies were driven back, this whole border country remained part of France until the fall of Napoleon. The principle of nationality, as later understood, was, no doubt, violated in Belgium, in the Rhineland, and to a certain extent in Nice. Yet, especially after the French Republic ceased to persecute the Catholics, the annexed region seems to have been contented enough. The social and legal changes introduced by the French were, in the main, permanent.

The process of annexation varied somewhat according to the nature of the country annexed, and the circumstances under which annexation took place. Savoy was a small mountain country, almost wholly French-speaking, quietly and ingloriously ruled by its princes from Turin. The active French sympathizers—the Allobroges—were, as their fondness for the classical name of their native land would show, mostly educated merchants and professional men filled with eighteenth-century misunderstanding of the classics. But social conditions were not extremely different from those in nearby French Dauphiné and if the actual annexation was the work of a minority, the Savoyard peasant soon adapted himself to the new régime. The glories and profits of the French Riviera were hardly to be predicted in 1792. The county of Nice was poor, inhabited by a people of Italian stock, speaking a patois that was either Italian or Provençal, but certainly not French. The Jacobin club of Nice numbered very few Niçois, and was obliged to conduct in Italian a popular educational campaign in revolutionary principles.[1] But here again one need not assume the existence of a nineteenth-century indignation over the violation of nineteenth-century notions of nationality. Nice fitted quietly into the French Republic. In the Rhineland, French arms were not permanently successful until 1797, and the final organization of the left bank into departments had to await the peace of Campoformio. But the very first French invasion had seen the organization of a Jacobin club at Mainz, and the familiar process by which the Francophil minority petitioned the Convention for annexation. The minority at Mainz was a very distinguished one, numbering the most prominent members of the university faculty, and a good number of doctors,

[1] J. Combet, La société populaire de Nice (Nice, 1911), 405.

lawyers, and successful merchants.[2] But it was a minority, and it would seem that in the long run the French régime in the Rhineland rested largely on the peasantry, to whom the full ownership of the land was given.

In none of these countries were the methods of the French altogether in accordance with the benevolent notions of eighteenth-century philosophy. Most of these conquests are explicable enough in terms of human greed. But where the element of proselyting zeal enters, it is clear that the new god of the revolutionists is a vengeful and intolerant god. The treatment of Belgium is an excellent example of French methods in conquered countries at the height of the republican Revolution. Leopold's pacification of the Austrian Netherlands was apparently successful. The Belgian patriots, or "statistes," were ostensibly reconciled, and the real revolutionists, the pro-French "Vonckists," banished. A united "revolutionary committee of Belgians and Liègeois" was formed in Paris by these exiles, pamphlets were smuggled into Belgium, and plans made for organizing the country with French aid. These Vonckists moved into Belgium with the victorious Dumouriez, and under the general's supervision, attempted to organize an independent republic. But Dumouriez could control neither his army nor the civil agents of the government at Paris. Many of the Vonckists had learned wisdom from experience, were willing to compromise to some extent with their *statiste* opponents. But as the French armies swept over Belgium clubs were founded everywhere, filled with French officers and a few of the fierier Belgian Jacobins, and began to govern their districts as if they were constituted authorities. Their bitter attacks on the "despots with the cross and miter" aroused the whole country against the French.[3] Dumouriez, deserted by his War Office, was obliged to live off the land, and to make payments in *assignats*. By its decree of December 15, 1792, the Convention nominated four commissioners to supervise a new organization of Belgium, to confiscate church and royal lands, to impose taxes. Dumouriez might protest that the French ought not "to proclaim the sacred law of liberty and equality, like the Koran,

[2] K. Bockenheimer, *Die Mainzer Klubisten* (Mainz, 1896), 60-61.
[3] Pirenne, *Histoire de Belgique*, VI, 30.

sword in hand," but that is just what the Convention was doing.[4]
France had brought religious discord, civil disorders, confiscations,
billeting of soldiers. When Dumouriez was forced to retreat, most
Belgians greeted the allies as deliverers. But the French came back
victoriously into Belgium in 1794, and this time even less pretense
was made of consulting Belgian opinion. French agents had come
to feel that contempt for the Belgians which has survived to this
day among French common people. "The Belgian," wrote a French
commissioner, "understands only his mass and his money: the first
motive is even more important than the second."[5] This time it was
decided to annex Belgium outright, and divide it into departments.
The thing was done in 1795 with a minimum of effort, a minimum
of speeches, pamphlets, persuasion. The republic had outgrown its
youthful truculence of conviction. Henceforth the phraseology of
the new gospel was hardly more than a habit or a disguise. Regener-
ated France was improving, practically if not morally, upon the
foreign policy of Louis XIV.

II. GREAT BRITAIN

In parts of Europe untouched by French invasion the French influence is none the less clearly discernible in various forms of radical
agitation. In the more despotically governed countries, like Hungary and Sicily, these agitations took the form of conspiracies
among a chosen few. In England, they took a form not unlike that
which they had taken in France. But the London Corresponding
Society and its branches, unlike the Jacobin club, never succeeded
in capturing even a town government. Parliament and the ministry
were unaffected by the radical organizations. The history of the
French Revolution in England is a history of the failure of native
English revolutionists, though spurred on by emulation of their
French brothers, to affect the slightest change in the structure of
British government.

Fox and his friends were hardly revolutionists. Indeed, no group
in the British Parliament can be classified as having revolutionary
aims. Yet the French Revolution had a profound effect on the

[4] A. Chuquet, *Dumouriez* (1914), 156.
[5] Sorel, *L'Europe et la Révolution française*, III, 474.

balance of power in Parliament. Fox, though he regretted French violence, though he detested the Jacobin rule, could never bring himself to abandon the hope that all would turn out well in the end, and certainly could never be brought to feel that there was sufficient danger of Jacobin revolution in England to warrant repressive measures against individual freedom and civil rights. Most of the parliamentary Whigs, however, did not share Fox's romantic illusions on human freedom. They had, indeed, their own quite unromantic illusions, the illusions of fear. Whig lords, city bankers, solid borough members, all began to fear for their property and their security. Burke's rhetoric was beginning to take effect. Then came the execution of Louis XVI, the resemblance of whose fate to that of Charles I probably heightened rather than lessened Whiggish indignation, and England's entrance into the war against France. Social and political conservatism now became a patriotic duty against revolutionary France. In July, 1794, after long wavering, the Duke of Portland and the bulk of the Whig party in Parliament deserted Fox and opposition, Portland and three others accepting office in Pitt's cabinet. Fox remained with a mere rump of the old Whig party to form the sole opposition to the government—an opposition so impotent that in 1797 he and his followers "seceded" from a Parliament "that neither reason, experience, nor duty" could influence to oppose the government.[6] The union of the Portland Whigs and the Tories under the leadership of Pitt formed the new Tory party, by which, save for a brief interval, England was to be governed until 1830. This party could rely in the country on a coalition of most of the propertied classes—the old landed gentry as well as the new moneyed classes, or in Cobbett's terms, the landlords as well as the "fundlords." This coalition, so important for English social stability and hence for English manufacturing, was not altogether a natural and inevitable one, a product of British common sense; it was to a very large extent produced by a common fear of the French Revolution, regarded in England as a proletarian movement aiming at the destruction of private property.

The conversion of the Portland Whigs had come at the end of a

[6] C. J. Fox, *Speeches* (London, 1815), VI, 368.

determined campaign by Pitt against organized radical groups, and was partly effected by the alarms incident to that campaign. The London Corresponding Society had spread over London in twelve divisions, each of which met, discussed, and drew up revolutionary programs, ate and drank at the Bell, the Unicorn, or another tavern, and had affiliated societies in Sheffield, Manchester, Norwich, Stockport, Glasgow, Edinburgh, and smaller cities. A society called the "Southwark Friends of the People" was founded in that borough, and soon branched out all over London south of the Thames. The Stockport club was called the "Friends of Universal Peace and the Rights of Man." These clubs were composed mostly of respectable artisans, of small tradesmen, and a sprinkling of bright but not too well-born young men like Coleridge's friend Thelwall. The Constitutional Society and the Whig Friends of the People numbered many gentlemen, as well as richer members of the trading classes. In some of the Scottish societies the French pattern is perfectly reproduced: the societies of the "Friends of the Constitution" of Glasgow and Edinburgh numbered gentlemen like Maitland, brother of Lord Lauderdale, Lord Daer, Colonels Dalrymple and MacLeod, as well as humbler artisans. Just as in France, the inhabitants of the English and Scotch country districts were quite uninterested in political change. And again as in France, there is no sign that the very poor ever participated in the activities of these clubs.

The clubs circulated plans for an English constitution—that is, a real *written* constitution,—they celebrated the Fall of the Bastille, bought with their library funds the pamphlets of Paine and his imitators, and even the expensive volumes of Godwin's *Political Justice*, corresponded freely and vaguely with the Paris Jacobins, celebrated the triumph of "Gallic freedmen" at Valmy by demolishing "with considerable spirit" an effigy of Brunswick and drinking a "considerable number of excellent toasts."[7] Some traces of French ritualistic practices appear. Strikers at Alnwick erected a tree of Liberty in the market place. Members of the clubs called one another "citizen." The card of admission to the society at Sheffield was engraved with a female figure holding in one arm a spear with a

[7] P. A. Brown, *French Revolution in English History*, 64.

cap of liberty on its tip, her other arm resting on a pedestal carrying three books marked Milton, Sidney, Harrington.[8] The "British Convention" in Edinburgh began some of its reports with *"Vive la Convention"* and ended them with *"Ça ira"*; they even proposed to divide the country into departments.[9] Their activities in general, however, are markedly peaceful and convivial. They always disavowed any intention of using force, of attempting the violent overthrow of the monarchy. With the declaration of war against France the agitation loses its touch of conviviality. The clubs had not been popular with the mass of the people in peace time. In time of war, it was easy to persuade true Englishmen that the members of these popular societies were traitors. A lawyer named Reeves organized an "Association for Protecting Liberty and Property against Republicans and Levellers" (note the coupling of liberty and property) and began an active campaign against Jacobins all over the country. The government itself had begun isolated prosecutions in 1792. Thomas Paine had been obliged to flee to France to avoid arrest for the seditious libel of *The Rights of Man*. Safe in France, he sent a letter to the Attorney General in which he asked whether "Mr. Guelph, or any of his profligate sons, is necessary to the government of a nation?" This shocking sentiment elevated his crime from seditious libel to treason, and he was outlawed.[10] In August, 1793, Muir, a capable young lawyer and a leading figure among the Scottish agitators, was brought to trial before Lord Braxfield for sedition. His chief crime seems to have been promoting the circulation of Paine's pamphlet. He was sentenced to fourteen years' transportation. Similar treatment was given to another Scot, the Reverend Thomas Palmer of Dundee. Braxfield's conduct of both cases was obviously prejudiced; he held it against Muir that the latter had just been in France, and remarked in his summing-up "I never was an admirer of the French; but I can now only consider them as monsters of human nature." The "auld alliance" was pretty well dissolved.[11]

The war, the Braxfield trials, the growing indignation of most

[8] R. Birley, *The English Jacobins* (London, 1924), 22.
[9] W. L. Mathieson, *The Awakening of Scotland* (Glasgow, 1910), 136.
[10] M. D. Conway, *Life of Thomas Paine* (New York, 1909), I, 373.
[11] Howell, *State Trials*, XXIII, 231.

Englishmen at these traitorous lovers of things French, all spurred the English Jacobins into more determined action. A petition for reform, presented by the societies, and sponsored in Parliament by Francis and Grey, was turned down 282 to 41. The societies then rashly decided to try a convention, which met in Edinburgh in November, 1793, as the "British Convention of the Delegates of the Friends of the People associated to obtain Universal Suffrage and Annual Parliaments." This convention—an ominous name in 1793, when the great French Convention had already sat for a year—did much talking, and passed a resolution that if such conventions were in the future forbidden by act of Parliament, they would automatically assemble at a given spot and assert their rights. The Scottish authorities acted too quickly, however, and the leaders Skirving and Callender, Scotchmen, Margarot and Gerrald, delegates from London, were arrested and tried in 1794 by Judge Braxfield, from whom they received sentences of fourteen years' transportation.

So far the chief work of repression had been done in Scotland, less restricted in such matters by legal and historical tradition. Pitt, however, had by 1794 become genuinely frightened himself, or at least had come to the conclusion that to simulate fright would enable him to win over the Portland Whigs and give him power for life, and a free hand against France.[12] Whatever his motive, Pitt acted. In May, 1794, Hardy, Thelwall, Horne Tooke, and ten other members of the two chief London societies—the Corresponding Society and the Society for Promoting Constitutional Information— were arrested and tried for treason. Another joint convention was about to meet, in spite of the fate of the Edinburgh convention, and government spies had produced reports of arming among the radicals. The government apparently thought themselves justified in bringing the charge of treason, but the courts thought differently. Hardy, defended by the eloquent Erskine, was triumphantly acquitted and drawn through the West End in a coach by his friends. The other prisoners were shortly acquitted, and the State Trials of

[12] W. T. Laprade, *England and the French Revolution* (Baltimore, 1909), 144-148, maintains the latter hypothesis. His position is criticized by P. A. Brown, *French Revolution in English History*, 131. Since the problem rests ultimately on what went on inside Pitt's mind, it is insoluble. Professor Laprade would seem to imply that because Pitt got a thing, he had wanted it and planned for it, which is almost too great a compliment, even to a statesman.

1794 were over. Had Pitt brought a charge of seditious libel, he might well have secured convictions. But treason, with its necessary penalty of death, was too much for a London jury, even in 1794, to accept on government's assurance. Evidence proved the accused to have been active political reformers anxious to alter the existing régime. But there was no proof that the accused meditated violence, that they possessed arms enough to make revolt possible, that they wished to overthrow the monarchy.

The State Trials of 1794 show that the notion of individual rights had so far embedded itself in English law as to make it impossible for a government to take English lives arbitrarily. The public rejoicing at Hardy's release, coupled with public rejoicing over the burning of Paine in effigy, or the burning of Priestley's house in reality, gives evidence that even in moments of high tension one characteristic form of English freedom, that of mutual toleration among manifesting or celebrating groups, was still safe. It is unlikely, even in England, that the same persons could feast Hardy and burn Paine. But the years subsequent to 1794 marked a steady and successful encroachment by government on these sacred English liberties, until by 1799 Pitt was in most respects as absolute a ruler as anyone on the Continent. The whole governmental campaign against Jacobinism in Great Britain was pursued with a Machiavellian realism not to be reconciled with our present notions of the purity of British political life. Pitt was greatly aided here by his friend Dundas, who held the Home Office until July, 1794. *Agents provocateurs,* spies, subsidies to newspapers, assiduous cultivation of conservative clergymen, packing of juries—no possible means of suppression and counter-propaganda were neglected. The atmosphere at times seems like a burlesque of the current melodrama in France. Dundas and his nephew have actually been accused—unjustly, it would seem—of hiring a man named Watts as *agent provocateur*, and then abandoning him to be hanged for his provocations. A spy, J. B., reported a speech at a radical conference: "In the name of Mutius Scævola, Decius and Clodius, give me six determined fellows who shall be nameless. Give me only six whom I can confide in with daggers apiece, and the business is done!!! . . . Nothing is easier than access to the Chambers of the Aristo-

crats, when they are joyous over their cups, surfeiting and intoxi-
cating at the expense of the blood and treasure of millions of
British and Frenchmen—nothing is easier than access to them—and
thus—and thus—and thus!!!" (gives three dagger thrusts) "—the
death of such villains alarms the whole country. The *sans-culottes*
gather and the business is done."[13]

In 1795 the king, on his way to open Parliament, was stopped and
almost dragged from his coach by a mob. A shot was fired and
cries of "No war! Bread!" were heard. *Habeas corpus* had already
been suspended at the time of the State Trials. In this session of
Parliament were passed the Two Acts of 1795-96, by which it
became possible to speak or write, as well as to act treason, and
which forbade all large public meetings without special permit, and
classed lecture rooms as disorderly houses. The Mutinies in the fleet
at the Nore and the Irish rebellion, both of which were to a certain
extent decked out with French ideas, further alarmed the government. By this time English radicalism had had to confine itself to the
more curious and active of the working classes, had got itself mixed
up with freethinking and republicanism, was indeed laying the foundation for that interesting and none too well studied group of
nineteenth-century radicals, from Richard Carlile to Holyoake and
Bradlaugh, who relieve the respectability of Victorian England.
But Pitt would not tolerate even this slight menace to the ruling
classes. In 1799 the Two Acts were supplemented so that secret associations or federations, and even trade unions, were forbidden, press
censorship provided for, and registration of printing presses required. The England so admired by Montesquieu, Voltaire, and
other victims of Continental tyranny, was for the moment a very
effective tyranny herself.

The main influence of the French Revolution in England, as has
often been pointed out, was the hardening of all conservative elements into a rigid Toryism, and the postponement of reform of
Parliament for forty years. It is less often noted that the French
Revolution, together with Pitt's repression, virtually laid the basis
for the intellectual life of the English workingman, that it began
the education of these workingmen, that it made them, and helped

[13] For the foregoing details, see H. Furber, *Henry Dundas* (Oxford, 1931), 77-93.

to keep them, class conscious. Yet only a small part of the English working class—whether the "better" or the "worse" part is not for the historian to judge—accepted the new ideology. Most Englishmen were loyal subjects of the king, who was now old enough and domestically unfortunate enough to make an effective appeal to English sentimentalism. The oppressed were, in the French diction of the epoch, "proud of their chains"; a London mob of common people wrecked the house of the wealthy Lord Stanhope, a well-known champion of the rights of the common people. Now, though Pitt's government was extremely well-organized, and far better equipped to repress disorder than the government of Louis XVI, agitation for radical change in England was stopped so easily because that agitation had little effect on ordinary Englishmen, because in the words of Wilberforce's Yorkshire slogan of 1795 there were "Twenty King's Men to one Jacobin."[14] Yet there certainly were not twenty well-fed and prosperous Englishmen to one under-nourished and miserable Englishman at this turn of the century. The war, of course, gave a focus on which to concentrate emotional excitement and afforded Englishmen a heightened satisfaction in patriotism. Men in sheer want rarely revolt. The Englishmen who proposed toasts like "May the Wings of Liberty never flourish till they are washed in the blood of Despots" were suffering from imagi-nations that could be cured by patriotism, but certainly not by food and drink, of which latter they certainly had already had too much. Many sober and respectable Frenchmen underwent the madness of Jacobinism. Englishmen of a similar walk of life underwent the minor, and perhaps less bloody, madness of patriotism. English heads were not turned by the Republic of Virtue in the last decade of the eighteenth century. This is a strictly historical statement, and is not a sociological generalization to the effect that English heads are at all times peculiarly safe from being turned by anything.

III. CENTRAL AND EASTERN EUROPE

The internal history of Prussia was but slightly affected by the French Revolution. Frederick William had decided to combat the Enlightenment even before the Revolution broke out. The war,

[14] Mathieson, *England in Transition,* 53.

and rumors of active French propaganda, simply caused a tightening of the censorship. A few rash men like the Alsatian Leuchsenring, and the musician Reichardt, victim of some of the less heavy couplets of the *Xenien* of Goethe and Schiller, did indeed get into trouble with the Prussian police. There was no extensive "conspiracy" unearthed, though in 1796 some younger Prussian officials of the sort who later ably seconded Stein were arrested at the instigation of the grasping and reactionary governor of Silesia, Hoym, and kept in prison until the accession of Frederick William III in 1798. These young men—Zerboni, Leipsiger, Contessa—had been involved in a secret society, a "moral *Vehmgericht*" as they called it, which had attempted to liberalize the Silesian administration, and had attacked the evils of land-grabbing in newly acquired Polish territory. This *Vehmgericht* had in turn sprung from an earlier society called the "Euergetes," planned along Masonic lines. It was all very well-meant, very academic, very far from the Terror. Some actual trouble there was among the people, especially in this same province of Silesia, where the peasants protested bitterly against feudal restraints, and where the weavers struck, rioted, and were fired upon by the troops. Hoym, the governor, detected the influence of "evil ideas arising from French propaganda": agents reported that people said "we only wish the French would come."[15] On the whole, however, Prussia remained quiet during the French Revolution.

To some critics, indeed, Prussia was far too quiet. The Frederician state had great social and political weaknesses, and to leave this state untouched was a very different thing from leaving the English state untouched. Yet in 1794 Frederick William suffered the great Code, or *Landrecht*, initiated by his uncle, to be issued after long delay, and only after the very timid reforms of its makers, Carmer and Suarez, had been omitted. The proposed *Landrecht* had left feudalism untouched, had divided Prussians sharply into nobles, burghers, and peasants, had maintained the illegality of marriage between a noble and a member of another class (the original code provided for morganatic marriages, but this was struck out by Goldbeck, Carmer's successor), had presupposed the whole fabric

[15] G. P. Gooch, *Germany and the French Revolution* (London, 1920), 375-376.

of Prussian autocracy. But it did try to protect the judges by making them removable only by the courts, not by the crown, and in other minor ways attempted to put a legal limit on the king's authority. All this was destroyed by Frederick William, and the code as issued had no reforming value whatever. What may be called the breakdown of the morale of the Prussian ruling classes continued through the decade. The peace of Basel and the complicated intrigues of Prince Henry and the Pro-French party further involved the court of Berlin. The partitions of Poland brought to Prussia lands which had to be assimilated. That process brought renewed corruption and dissension. A royal order to Hoym can hardly be regarded as other than an invitation to land-grabbing: "to direct your attention so that in the new acquisitions *good German landlords* be maintained, and the lands, conferred in hereditary noble right, may not come again into possession of Polish owners." A consortium was formed by Hoym, Bischoffswerder, Rietz (the husband of the king's chief mistress), and others, and large profits made by resales of confiscated estates.[16]

In other parts of what is now Germany, the internal history of the period is not unlike that of most decades of the century. Everything depends on the local government, on the personality of the princelet, on his mistresses, on his ministers. In general, the enlightened middle classes were interested in the French Revolution and, until the Terror, more or less sympathetic. But there was no common German response to the Revolution, no threat of a serious German rising. "Here and there one finds plots, uprisings, resistance to magistrates or military officials; not the idea of the sovereignty of the people, however, but sheer hunger has produced them."[17] Just as in England, there was suffering enough, oppression enough, but no common revolutionary faith. The extreme subdivision of Germany, the social, economic, and intellectual backwardness of one of her greatest states, Austria, the prestige and real powers of the Junker class in another great state, Prussia, the lack of a social organization in which the new political ideas could be

---

[16] F. Mehring, *Zur preussichen Geschichte vom Mittelalter bis Jena* (Berlin, 1930), 286-287. Italics mine.
[17] K. T. Heigel, *Deutsche Geschichte*, I, 306.

propagated—all these factors contributed to prevent a revolution in Germany. Just as in England, however, the new ideas did penetrate into certain classes of society. But whereas in England French anti-clerical radicalism of the Jacobin type influenced a genuine working-class movement, in Germany only the milder liberalism of the monarchical experiment, of Mirabeau and Lafayette, got a foothold, and that among the prosperous merchants. Hamburg, as one might expect, was devoted to the French cause and celebrated the first anniversary of the fall of the Bastille in touching fashion. The merchants of the Senate could hardly be expected to approve the "Kannibalregiment" of the Terror, but at no time was Hamburg an active supporter of the imperial war on France, and indeed hardly did more in that war than her legal minimum as a member of the empire.[18]

In Austria the new emperor Francis II finally abandoned the promising, if occasionally rash, experiments of Maria Theresa and Joseph, and laid the foundations for the rule of Metternich. It is impossible to say how far the young ruler was influenced by fear of the French Revolution to take up a stand that now appears, in nineteenth-century terminology, reactionary. Francis was greatly influenced by his minister Thugut, who used to say of the Revolution "the axe alone can put out that fire."[19] Court society held the Revolution in horror. The emperor encouraged the activities of Alois Hoffman, who tried to make his *Wiener Zeitschrift* a major organ of European opinion hostile to the Jacobins. By the end of the century Vienna was pretty well established as the spiritual center of the opposition to new ideas and new institutions. Now, though much belligerently liberal historical writing has been obviously unfair to Metternich and his immediate predecessors, it is impossible to deny that the Austria of Francis II proudly maintained a privileged nobility, a strong Catholic Church, a peasantry in many regions still enserfed, and, what is equally important, a sufficiently coördinated public opinion in support of these things so that men could associate the two abstractions "Austria" and "reaction." Prussia under Frederick William II offered many a sight as horrifying

[18] A. Wohlwill, *Neuere Geschichte der Freie und Hansestadt Hamburg insbesondere von 1789 bis 1815* (Gotha, 1914), 135.
[19] Quoted in Denis, *La Bohème*, II, 17.

to liberal eyes as anything in the Austria of the time. But the diversity of Prussian opinion, the survival of Frederician traditions among the bureaucracy, the very scale of the personal intrigues of the court of Berlin, all prevented men from personifying Prussia as an enemy of things new.

Francis early began his policy of conformity with the wishes of the ruling classes of his dominions. His father had indeed surrendered to his rebellious subjects, but never without trying to save as many of Joseph's reforms as possible. Hardly a month after his accession, Francis quietly dropped Eger's projected continuation of peasant reforms. Where his father had shown much concern for the Magyar middle classes, Francis gave in completely to the nobles, cultivated them and flattered them, threw open to these Magyar gentlemen the holy of holies, high command in the Austrian army. His government in Hungary was "a respectful, caressing oppression, founded on spying and secret influence, but which succeeded only the more surely in making Hungary a province of Austria."[20]

Francis, like Metternich after him, was obsessed with the fear of secret societies, and blamed the revolutionary movement upon the wicked ideas of philosophers and *illuminati*. The Austrian censorship was among the most exacting and absurd in Europe. In 1795 Mozart's *Zauberflöte* was banned, not on the ground that its confused libretto reflects the simple hopes of eighteenth-century Freemasonry, but on the ground that it is specifically revolutionary propaganda—Pamina, for example, being Liberty, Papageno Aristocracy, the serpents the deficit, the priests of Sarastros the National Assembly, and so on.[21]

The Hapsburg lands really did not afford very fruitful ground for revolutionary propaganda. Social and economic conditions would seem to preclude any hope of sweeping reform, especially so soon after the failure of Joseph II. Revolutionary faith, however, was an enthusiasm not always consciously linked by its holders with social and economic conditions. Martinovics, Prandstätter, and their fellows might perhaps have been restrained from their Jacobin plots by a knowledge of the economic interpretation of history.

[20] Sayous, *Histoire des Hongrois*, 435.
[21] V. Bibl. *Der Zerfall Oesterreichs: Kaiser Franz und sein Erbe* (Vienna, 1922), 85.

Such knowledge was far from common in 1794. These two major plots do, however, show that French ideas had penetrated into Austria. They were, no doubt, much exaggerated, and possibly to no small extent initiated and developed, by police spies. But they do show that among the intellectuals, the more prosperous but not commercially grasping bourgeoisie, there was already a nucleus for what later came to be liberalism.

These Austrian and Hungarian conspirators were a small and rather naïve minority, not unlike the later Decembrists in Russia. Their names and callings are highly respectable—in Vienna, Prandstätter, judge, von Hebenstreit, officer, Baron von Riedel, professor, Count Hohenwart; in Budapest, Martinovics, ex-Franciscan, learned, trusted by Joseph II, thoroughly immersed in eighteenth-century humanitarian schemes, Hajnoczy, son of a Protestant minister, former official, Laczkovics, officer, Count Sigray, Szentmarjay, secretary in a noble family. Among these men there were, no doubt, some who opposed the old régime because they had been failures hitherto, because their own society had rejected them. Laczkovics, for instance, felt that he had been set aside from the straight line of military promotion by the jealousy of his superiors.[22] They belonged to groups hardly well-organized enough to be called Jacobin clubs, but certainly formed to circulate revolutionary literature, to provide meeting places for kindred souls. The Vienna Jacobins were accused of planting a tree of liberty in the Brühl, of singing "a song, in the highest degree revolutionary, composed in the spirit of liberty, provocative of plotting most dangerous to the state, and especially directed to the lowest classes." It is significant that these lowest classes jeered at their revolutionary friends exposed in the stocks.[23] A Hungarian Jacobin had translated the Marseillaise into Magyar, an offense for which he paid with his life. The trials both in Vienna and in Budapest were remarkable for secrecy, for the vagueness of the charge of conspiracy, and for the heavy penalties meted out—death, sixty years in chains, thirty-five years, exposure in the stocks, confiscation of property.

[22] H. Marczali, "Die Verschwörung des Martinovics," *Ungarische Revue* (1881), I, 15.
[23] Bibl, *Zerfall Oesterreichs*, 78; E. K. Blumml and G. Gugitz, *Von Leuten und Zeiten im alten Wien* (Vienna, 1922), 192.

If the Hapsburg policy towards new ideas seems scandalous to the modern liberal, Catherine's policy will seem almost fantastic. It is true that the higher Russian bureaucracy had quite recently acquired, not unaided by Catherine, a smattering of the vocabulary and stereotypes of the Enlightenment. Mme. Swetchine was brought up in the palace at Moscow, where her father was on the empress's private secretarial staff. She tells how, then about seven years old, she gave directions for illuminating her father's apartment, and, on the surprised official's return, exclaimed, "Oh, papa! Surely we must celebrate the fall of the Bastille, and the release of the poor French prisoners!"[24] But Catherine had attained and kept her power only by the complete surrender of political and economic power to the serf-owning, landed nobility. Under Catherine Russian serfdom was extended and crystallized into a fixed system. Her very bureaucrats were gentlemen, owners of souls. In spite of her Legislative Commission and her correspondence with Diderot and Grimm, she herself, and most of her servants, had little understanding of the economic or the emotional aspects of the philosophic movement which helped to make the French Revolution. Many Russian enthusiasts for the Enlightenment were like the landowner Struiski of Penza, who set up his own press to print his adaptations of Voltaire and other French poets, and who judged his serfs in strict, almost fanatical, accordance with European methods, himself reading the act of indictment, and making the speech for the defense. The questioning of the serf, however, was accompanied by torture, and Struiski kept a full arsenal for this purpose.[25]

To Catherine the attack of the Bastille, and especially the shocking *lèse-majesté* of the march of the women to Versailles, were unforgivable crimes. She did her best to stir up a European crusade against the French, wrote indignant and indelicate letters about the failure of the allies—"quelle cacade que ce duc de Brunswick est allé faire en Champagne!"—and flew into picturesque rages at Jacobin successes.[26] But Catherine was only morally concerned about a gen-

[24] V. O. Kluchevsky, *A History of Russia*, translated by C. J. Hogarth (London, 1931), V, 107.

[25] Kluchevsky, *Russia*, V, 109.

[26] Catherine to Grimm, October 31, 1792. *Pisma Imperatritsy Ekateriny* II K *Grimmu* (1774-1796), ed. Grot (St. Petersburg, 1878).

eral European order. Her practical interests lay in her own dominions, and these she attempted to seal up completely against French
influences. All Frenchmen in Russia were obliged to subscribe to a
special oath devised by Catherine, solemnly damning the Revolution and all its works, French diplomatic agents were dismissed, the
ports closed to French sailors, no objects of French origin, books,
letters, goods, works of arts, allowed to enter Russia, no Russian subject permitted to go to France. Catherine could find little at home to
suppress. She did, however, close down all Masonic lodges, most
of which were of the semi-mystic Martinist persuasion, and not very
earthly revolutionary, and brought to trial Novikov, of the *Gazette
de Moscou*, a mildly liberal journal with some four thousand sub-
scribers. Novikov was imprisoned in the Schlüsselburg. Radishchev,
whose *Voyage de St. Petersbourg à Moscou* had been approved by
the censor in 1785, and published in 1790, was exiled for this sentence: "It is not from the wisdom of the property-owners that one
may expect liberty, but from the very excess of slavery."[27] Paul,
though he altered his mother's foreign policy, maintained and en-
deavored to strengthen, her measures against things French. By
ukase he forbade the use of two perfectly good Russian words
(*grazhdanin* and *otechestvo*) because they translated *citoyen* and
patrie; in 1800 he similarly forbade all importation of printed matter of any kind, including music.[28]

IV. SOUTHERN EUROPE

The full impact of the French Revolution in Italy followed Bonaparte's successful invasion of 1796. Italy in 1789 was still a mere
geographical expression, and, though some states, like Tuscany
under Leopold, were much better governed than others, the general
economic level of the country was lower than that of North-
western Europe. Most of Italy, however, was free from the feudal
abuses so annoying in France. "Save perhaps in Naples and Sicily,
feudalism was, if not dead, at least dying, and the bourgeoisie already in possession of political power."[29] Even more, perhaps, than

[27] C. Larivière, *Catherine II et la Révolution française* (Paris, 1895), 208.
[28] K. Waliszewski, *Paul I*, English translation (London, 1913), 109, 115.
[29] F. Nitti, in *La vita italiana durante la rivoluzione francese e l'impero* (Milan,
1915), 268.

in Germany, French was the language of the educated minority, and French art and letters determined fashions. The first news of the Revolution, here as elsewhere, was welcomed by the "enlightened." Even Alfieri, later one of the most excited, if not the most profound, of the articulate enemies of the revolution, hailed its beginnings with an ode "Parigi sbastigliato" (Paris dis-Bastilled).

The more convinced proponents of revolutionary ideas soon organized themselves into clubs. In Italy, as in Central Europe, these clubs were forced by political conditions to organize secretly, and to indulge in what their conservative opponents regarded as conspiracies. Such a club was founded at Turin in 1793 from three smaller groups, which, as discussion groups or literary societies, may have antedated the Revolution. This club founded affiliated clubs—always in secrecy—in small Piedmontese towns. The Piedmontese Jacobins were betrayed to the police in May, 1794, by a faint-hearted brother, forty-eight of them imprisoned and three condemned to death. The French admiral Latouche had stopped at Naples with his fleet in December, 1792, and demanded an apology for what the French regarded as undue interference by the Neapolitan ambassador at Constantinople with a French mission to the sultan. The very unheroic Neapolitan government gave the apology, but Latouche's stay had been long enough to encourage the radicals of Naples to organize. A "Società degli amici della Libertà et del l'Eguaglianza" was founded in secrecy and plans were made for modernizing the unenlightened kingdom. The group split, quite in the French fashion, into a "Club Lomo," so-called from its motto, *Libertà o Morte,* willing to maintain a liberal monarchy, and a "Club Romo," with a motto *Repubblica o Morte,* determined to go the whole way to a republic. The Neapolitan Jacobins, like others scattered through Europe, were not always quite up to date in their knowledge of affairs at the fountainhead of their faith. They sent a complimentary address to Mackau, French ambassador in Naples in 1793, likening him to Lafayette, by that time regarded by good French republicans as a traitor.[30] These Neapolitan societies were elaborately organized to preserve secrecy. They were divided into sections, and members of one section were unknown to members of

[30] A. Franchetti, *Storia d'Italia dal 1789 al 1799* (Milan, 1911), 87, 153.

the others. Each section delegated certain members to a common body, and that body elected a kind of directorate, which alone knew the total membership of the society.[31]

Just as in Central Europe, the striking thing about these Italian revolutionists, at least to a twentieth century which considers revolutionists not quite socially respectable, is their high standing in their communities. The Jacobins of Milan numbered a duke, Serbellone (described, it is true, as of "mediocre intelligence"), a count, Porro, a distinguished jurist, Sopransi, lawyers, doctors, men of letters, professors.[32] Among Sicilian Jacobins were Dr. Giuseppe Ardizzone of Catania, "rich and popular," a nobleman, Di Blasi, who headed a conspiracy to seize the viceroy and proclaim an independent, democratic Sicily, Dr. Luigi Leo of Castelvetrano, guilty of possessing "heretical, magical, and erotic works," such as those of Luther, Calvin, Rousseau, Montesquieu, and Barthélemy de Saint-Hilaire.[33]

As will be evident from the above detail, the police all over Italy were zealous guardians of the established order, and all the governments, especially after August 10, 1792, attempted to prevent the spread of French ideas. The censors at Naples ordered a play called the *Corsair of Marseilles* to drop Marseilles from its title, which suggested the incendiary "Marseillaise," to change "I am not *free* to do so" to "I am not master of my person," and to change "I am going to breathe a moment in *freedom*" to "I am going to breathe a moment."[34] Measures like these seem a trifle alarmist. There was little sign that the Italian people as a whole were affected by the new ideas. Isolated troubles did break out, and occasionally the cry of "Let us do as the French have done" was heard, but these troubles, like the similar troubles in Silesia, have always a specific origin in local grievances or economic distress. Bread riots may further a revolution already begun, but they do not in themselves constitute a revolution. In Sardinia, indeed, there began in 1793 a serious rising directed against absentee government in Turin, and

[31] B. Croce, *La rivoluzione napoletana del 1799* (3rd ed. Bari, 1912), 196.
[32] A. Franchetti, *Storia d'Italia*, 246.
[33] F. Scandone, "Il giacobinismo in Sicilia," *Archivio storico siciliano* (1921-22), XLIV, 274.
[34] P. Hazard, *La Révolution française et les lettres italiennes* (Paris, 1910), 11.

in favor of the medieval *Stamenti,* or Estates. But this revolt against Piedmontese "foreigners" has no more to do with the French Revolution than has the very similar rebellion of the Belgian estates against Austria. Once the rebellion had broken out, the handful of true Jacobins on the island were encouraged to come out in the open, and by 1796 there is a Sardinian Jacobin party, headed by the nobleman Giovan Maria Angioi, judge of the Royal Udienza. Angioi, however, was even more powerless against the force of tradition than his Belgian parallel, Vonck, and Sardinia remained a picturesque and isolated bit of old Italy.

The immediate effect of the French Revolution in Italy was to promote Italian patriotism, and hence to encourage Italians to cling to old customs and institutions as against French novelties. Long French rule under Napoleon was to leave Italian patriotism and hatred for the French stronger than ever, but it was also to force upon Italy some, at least, of French institutions. Evidence of the growth of Italian patriotism, characteristically accompanied by that detestation of France which seems to be an abiding part of Italian patriotism, is abundant even before Bonaparte's invasion. The Sardinian peasants were worked up to a white fury against the French, pictured in popular verse as destroying altars and violating women. A dialect poem of 1793 says of the French:

> Issos adorant idolos de oro
> De attarzu et de ferru.
> Finzas su babbu ipsoro hant istestadu
> Franzesos malaitos!

(They adore idols of gold, of steel and iron. They have even killed their own father —Louis XVI—the cursed French!) [35]

In higher literary circles the same bitterness appears. The French hegemony, so fatal to eighteenth-century Italian literature, was broken, and Italian men of letters began to lay the foundations for the Risorgimento. Monti in his *Bassvilliana* repudiated the work of the *philosophes* and vindicated the Roman faith; Voltaire was "costui di Ferney l'empio e maligno Filosofante." [36] Alfieri, in his

---

[35] S. Deledda, "Motivi antifrancesi in Sardegna nel secolo XVIII," *Rivista d'Italia* (1925), XXVIII, 45.

[36] *Bassvilliana,* Canto III, lines 259-260.

Misogallo, after calling attention to Mirabeau's Italian name, Riquetti, adds "those who have been transplanted to France degenerate; but Frenchmen transplanted from France to any other land never get any better." The French language he declared to be "mono-aspri-vili-sillabi nasale."[37] Literature and simple peasant virtue had already made their characteristic modern alliance in patriotism. In Italy, perhaps, this patriotism involved at first rather more hatred of France and the Enlightenment than love of the Italian fatherland.

Spain was not a fruitful ground for revolutionary ideas, especially when these ideas had a French origin. The French had in increasing numbers penetrated into Spanish business life. There were nearly 14,000 French heads of families domiciled in Spain in 1791, almost all engaged in commerce. To the good Spaniard, these French were "money grubbers who had well-nigh monopolized the work in their towns."[38] Many of the upper classes had been touched by the Enlightenment. Charles IV was a benevolent eighteenth-century monarch, and his first ministers, Floridablanca and Aranda, both disposed towards moderate reform, the latter even Francophil. To the common people, however, French ideas were simply incomprehensible, Frenchmen themselves detestable atheists, destroyers of throne and altar. Godoy, who succeeded Aranda in 1792, provoked war with France by his clumsy efforts to buy the personal safety of Louis XVI, cousin of the Spanish king. The war was from the first extremely popular, though Spanish inefficiency and poverty made it a failure. Godoy by the peace of Basel succeeded in saving the kingdom from invasion. Measures against spiritual invasion had already been taken: a rigorous censorship had been established by Aranda, and furthered by the Inquisition. These measures were, of course, unsuccessful. The very few whom education, commercial position, or personal idiosyncrasy inclined towards new ideas were able to find out what was happening in France. There were the customary secret societies, rumored and real. San Sebastian was handed over to the French by Spanish Jacobins. There was a radical group in Burgos. On the whole, however, Spain was less

[37] Alfieri, Misogallo, sonnet 9, note: sonnet 31.
[38] M. Lafuente, *Historia general de España* (Barcelona, 1889), XV, 185.

affected by Jacobinism than any other country of Europe, save perhaps Russia. Even its reformers resisted the domination of France. A pamphlet of 1796, *Pan y Toros,* attacks the Spanish clergy as corrupt and pagan, the people as ignorant, the government as inefficient, all in the bitterest language; but it advocates the rebuilding of a new Spain without special reference to the French experiment.

V. CONCLUSION

Any study of the spread of the French Revolution in Europe must face the problem of how far a definite French propaganda, paid for and directed by the French government, really existed. Contemporaries talked much of French gold, of French agents, of an elaborate organization to subvert monarchical Europe. Sir John Acton, Neapolitan minister, wrote in 1792 that "from amongst the most refined scoundrels of the Jacobin Club in Paris three hundred are to be chosen to be sent in disguise through foreign countries, there to stir up the people and to obtain proselytes for their pernicious doctrine."[39] More extreme statements could be found. Newspapers like Hoffmann's *Wiener Zeitschrift* detected Jacobins behind every bush. The situation, moreover, has again become familiar to the modern world as a result of the Russian Revolution.

Of the more extreme and ridiculous of such reports it is sufficient to say that they are interesting elements of a history of public opinion, of a retrospective political psychology, but that they have nothing to do with fact. France had neither time, money, nor adequately educated men to produce an effective secret organization of European scope. The men in particular were lacking, and the new republic was hard put to it to build up an adequate public foreign service. Her new ambassadors, ministers, and consuls were, indeed, charged—or charged themselves—with the furthering of French interests through propaganda at their respective posts. There was nothing in principle very startling in this, save for the relative lack of subtlety with which these republican diplomats went about their work. Where the French armies went, there went naturally and easily enough a good deal of French propaganda which needed no special organization. The Convention had issued a decree in-

[39] Scandone, *Archivio storico siciliano,* XLIII, 298 note.

viting the whole world to join the Revolution. The government, the Jacobin clubs, the private newspapers did combine to send a lot of printed material into surrounding countries.

On the other hand, it is pretty clear that, where social and intellectual conditions favored it, the French Revolution propagated itself. Rarely does one find traces of Frenchmen among the radicals of the different countries; or when one does find a Margarot in England, a Romey in Italy, they are Frenchmen already established in these countries, not by any stretch of the imagination delegates of the French government. The prosecution in the Vienna and Budapest plots claimed to have linked Martinovics with Thomas Hardy, to have shown that the Convention had subsidized the Vienna and Budapest clubs. Modern historians have never found the links that were so clear in 1794.[40] The effective propagandist of the French Revolution was not the paid French agent; he was the discontented, ambitious, educated native. There is plenty of evidence that deliberate French propaganda, even in such favorable ground as Germany, was of little use in stirring up popular discontent. "Nothing more certain," wrote Harmer in 1796, "than that the internal situation in Bavaria is alarming; but this is not the revolutionary spirit, it is in no way the product of French agents who are operating there."[41] Perhaps the best organized and most determined effort made by the French to secure their ends by pure propaganda was this effort of 1796, centering above all in the upper Rhine valley. The energetic and well-financed campaign launched by the ex-marquis Poterat in Baden was a complete failure and the government of Baden remained in the hands of its Zähringen rulers.[42]

With the war and the Terror, indeed, the gap between French principles and French practice had become so much wider than the comfortable gap between word and deed commonly admitted in this world that not the most skillful propaganda could close it. Not Liberty nor Fraternity, and only a rather grim Equality, had ruled

[40] Marczali, *Ungarische Revue*, I, 17-18.
[41] R. Du M. Eckart, "Bayerische Zustände und die französische Propaganda im Jahre 1796," *Forschungen zur Kultur- und Litteraturgeschichte Bayerns* (1894), II, 211.
[42] K. Obser, "Poterat und die revolutionäre Propaganda am Oberrhein," *Zeitschrift für die Geschichte des Oberrheins* (1892).

with the guillotine. Even more strikingly to the rest of Europe was the aggressively nationalistic France of 1794 not the cosmopolitan France of good taste, good manners, and good intentions, the France where philosophy had made virtue attractive, attainable, and common. Once long ago the National Assembly had renounced conquests. It had annexed papal Avignon, but only on the repeated petition of the inhabitants of this very French enclave. The Convention on November 27, 1792, listened to a long report in which Grégoire showed how advantageous to both parties the annexation of Savoy by France would prove, how completely in accord with the law of nations, nature, and God. An obscure moderate, Pénières, rose to protest: "I maintain that it is not necessary to amalgamate two free peoples in order to secure their true union (murmurs). . . . In a little republic, each citizen, having more influence, has more interest in public affairs, takes part in them. In a big republic his influence is almost nil, and he neglects the public interest, lets himself be dominated . . ." (prolonged murmurs). Pénières, whose Rousseauistic orthodoxy is here irreproachable, was shouted down and the annexation voted by acclamation.[43] The republic was fast outgrowing Rousseau.

To the rest of Europe, at least, if not to Frenchmen, it was apparent that France had deserted the principles of eighteenth-century cosmopolitanism. Since France was highly successful, the inference was pretty obvious that those principles were no longer true, at any rate no longer useful. Cosmopolitanism must give way to nationalism. The psychological realities behind the abstraction are as old as Adam, but in its modern form nationalism was pretty completely dressed up in the decade of the French Revolution. Nature, to which the French had been proving themselves truer in their practice than in their theory, was on the side of diversity, idiosyncrasy, variation picturesque and profitable. The Germans should be very German, and expel the French, at least as a preliminary measure, from German courts and kitchens, academies and newspapers. Later they could be expelled from German lands. Many hatreds, many ambitions, many interests went to rouse European nationalities against the conquering France of the Revolution

[43] *Archives parlementaires*, LIII, 614.

and Napoleon. By a singular irony, these diverse and very concrete emotions centered themselves in the abstract principle most calculated to give the revolutionary principles of Liberty, Equality, and Fraternity a chance to do effective work on this earth. For if it is not being a Christian that matters, nor a gentleman, nor a commoner, nor even a man of virtue and feeling, but only being an Englishman, a German, an Italian, then within each separate state you have, indeed, a world as simple as the *philosophes* had imagined. Men, unequal as to wealth, talent, strength, goodness, are equal as to Englishness, Germanness, Frenchness. The earl and the brewer are brothers, if not yet, as was to be in nineteenth-century England, one and the same man.

Chapter Eight

THE THERMIDOREANS

I. THE NINTH THERMIDOR

THE REPUBLIC OF VIRTUE, so happily established by the elimination of the corrupt Dantonists and the traitorous Hébertists in the spring of 1794, ran its course in four troubled months. It was soon clear to the victorious Robespierre that there were still sinful men left alive, and that the republic could not be secure save in their deaths. No other explanation of the famous Law of 22 Prairial, drawn up by Robespierre, makes sense. This law split the Revolutionary Tribunal in four parts sitting simultaneously for greater speed of action, defined in conveniently vague terms the "enemies of the people" against whom it was directed, denied the accused right of counsel, reduced the number of jurors necessary for conviction, and gave to the Committees of Public Safety and General Security, and to the prosecuting attorney of the Tribunal, the right to send anyone, even a member of the Convention, before the Tribunal. Under the seven weeks' operation of the law, the average daily number of prisoners guillotined was increased tenfold. Now this law can scarcely be said to have an economic motive. The decrees of Ventôse did not need its help, having their own machinery for sorting out the suspects. In the bread-and-butter world men are agreed in calling normal, the Law of 22 Prairial simply has no place, is not to be understood. It belongs to the insane world where the heroic Robespierre could actually get things done. Granted that by a mystic intensity of faith the elect may know the damned without recourse to the unimportant, indeed often deceiving, realities of customary legal procedure, there is no reason why the procedure of the Tribunal should not be considered in the highest sense just. Granted that the continued earthly existence of the damned is a constant menace to the security of the republic, to put the damned to death is the duty of the guardians of the republic. These last steps of the journey to the earthly paradise lie through the greatest of dangers—the desertion of the false friends who have hitherto followed the road in the hope that they might turn the virtuous from it. One last effort, one final thrusting away of encumbrances, and the goal is reached.

This law destroyed Robespierre. The ferocity of its application undoubtedly helped disgust, or rather tire, the ordinary man with the revolution. Yet the actual fall of Robespierre was not directly brought about by the action of public opinion. The events of the Ninth Thermidor, even more than those of immediately preceding "revolutionary days" are matters of intrigue among the powerful few. Only *after* the Ninth Thermidor does public opinion assume a rôle, a rôle not altogether anticipated by the authors of the "day." The chief effective opposition to Robespierre and his aides, Saint-Just and Couthon—sometimes called the Triumvirate—lay in two groups, one within the great committees, the other among the representatives on mission. This opposition, in the face of the Law of 22 Prairial voted by a supine Convention, could not be open and parliamentary. It was organized and developed in secrecy, chiefly by Fouché.[1] Fouché was a man of great intelligence and no morals— as that word is commonly understood—and, of course, wholly incapable of losing himself in the Republic of Virtue. He had abandoned an ecclesiastical career for more certain preferment under the Revolution, and as representative on mission had been one of the most ruthless of dechristianizers. Robespierre had ticketed him with the Hébertists, and Fouché knew that he was marked for the guillotine. Recalled in disgrace from his mission, he made himself as obscure as possible, and set about cultivating a backstairs relationship with men he knew to be hostile to the existing government.

Some of the most important of these men were members of the government. Within the Committee of Public Safety, Collot d'Herbois and Billaud-Varennes, themselves Terrorists with a bloody record, had quarreled with Robespierre for reasons more

---

[1] The search for master-minds behind such events as the downfall of Robespierre is sometimes misleading. But it does seem that this is an authentic example of a political intrigue finally knotted together by one man. Fouché's rôle is very ably established in Madelin, *Fouché* (Paris, 1900).

personal than political. Other members, like Carnot and Cambon, had never been true Jacobins in the religious sense, had never regarded the Terror as more than a government of national defense. Meetings of the Committee grew more and more acrimonious, and in June and July Robespierre practically withdrew from it, planning eventually to purify it, with the aid of the majority he believed he possessed in the Convention, and reassume power. In one sense, then, he did not guide the Terror during those last terrible weeks— the Terror in this phase was simply the automatic working out of the Law of 22 Prairial. The Committee of General Security, jealous of the predominance of the other Committee, with which it was legally coequal, was, under the influence of Amar and Vadier, personal enemies of Robespierre, easily persuaded to join the plot— for plot it was, and no popular uprising. Finally, Fouché found at hand a number of ex-representatives on mission, like himself Terrorists identified with the dechristianizing movement so distasteful to Robespierre, and like himself living in daily fear of a final purification of the Republic of Virtue. Some of these, like Tallien and Fréron, had been guilty of financial extortions during their proconsulships, and knew that their victims might testify against them. Finally, the victories of the French armies served to assure the nameless deputies of the Center, upon whom the ultimate action of the Convention depended, that to attack the unity of the government was no longer to menace the sacred union of Frenchmen against the enemy.

Robespierre himself took the step that put the plot against him into action. On 8 Thermidor (July 26, 1794) he appeared before the Convention and delivered a long speech on the state of the country, filled with his usual moral aphorisms, but touching occasionally and vaguely on another conspiracy of wicked men, and demanding a final purification of the republic. The Convention listened with its usual docility, and voted that the speech be printed and distributed to the communes. Fouché and his fellow conspirators were ready. Hardly had the approving vote for publication been passed when opposition broke out in the open. Robespierre's threats had been so vague, his category of enemies of the republic so extended—he had more than hinted at the dissension within the Committees—that no one felt safe. Cambon rose and accused Robespierre of attempting to tyrannize over the Convention. Billaud-Varennes demanded that the speech be referred to the Committees before it was published. After a short debate, the Convention rescinded its previous vote approving the publication of the speech. Robespierre had lost his parliamentary majority.

That night Robespierre read his speech to the Jacobins, who gave it thunderous approval. Encouraged, he evidently hoped to recapture his majority and the next day, the Ninth Thermidor, he returned to the Convention, prepared to make specific accusations against his enemies, and demand that they be sent before the Revolutionary Tribunal. He never gave this speech. With the connivance of the president of the Assembly, Collot d'Herbois, he was shouted down, and his appeal to the "pure men" of the Center lost in the tumult. After a long session dramatic and disorderly even beyond the usual standards of crucial debates in the Convention, the decisive motion was made and carried. Robespierre, his brother Augustin, Saint-Just, Couthon, Lebas, Dumas, president of the Revolutionary Tribunal, and Hanriot, commander of the Parisian national guard, were sent before the Revolutionary Tribunal.

The Jacobins and the Paris Commune were still loyal to Robespierre. The only salvation for the Robespierrists lay in an armed insurrection of the Parisian populace—a step that hitherto had never failed of success. This time it failed, and the Revolution had run its course. Barras, appointed by the Convention to provide it with a military defense, actually succeeded in raising troops from the richer *sections* of the city. Robespierre, remembering perhaps how triumphantly Marat had been acquitted when he was sent before the Tribunal by his Girondin enemies, chose until the last to remain voluntarily under arrest—no Parisian jailer would have kept him against his will—and in this crisis refused to lead the insurrection. Without him the other leaders, released from prison by the men of the Commune, attempted to organize the uprising. The tocsin was sounded, and the square in front of the Hôtel de Ville was soon filled with loyal Robespierrists from the poorer sections. Hours passed, and nothing was done. Robespierre finally left his prison, and appeared at the Hôtel de Ville. His troops, discouraged by lack of action—perhaps also by a downpour of rain, though there is actually some doubt as to whether it rained or not—were melting away rapidly. About two o'clock in the morning a detachment of troops of the Convention led by one of the conspirators, Bourdon de l'Oise, appeared, and aided by a knowledge of the password used by the troops of the Commune, penetrated into the room where Robespierre and his colleagues were deliberating. In a brief scuffle, Robespierre was shot in the jaw and seized. Whether he attempted to commit suicide, or was shot by a gendarme who later took great credit for this exploit, will never be known. Lebas killed himself, Couthon was thrown down a staircase, and Augustin Robespierre leaped from a window and broke his thigh. Saint-Just stoically surrendered himself. The Convention, on learning of the insurrection, had outlawed its leaders, and they could therefore be executed without trial. Next day the maimed Robespierre and twenty-one of his followers were guillotined, to be followed within two days by most members of the Paris Commune.

The insurrection had failed primarily for lack of leadership. No doubt the Parisian populace had no longer the zeal for street-fighting that had won the Bastille, no doubt the more prosperous *sections* were alarmed at the socialistic tendencies of the Robespier-rists, no doubt, finally, that Barras did an excellent job in organizing the military defense of the Convention. Yet there was a nucleus of determined Jacobins strong in the tradition of success, and the immediate response to the tocsin was excellent. Hanriot, their military leader, showed himself incompetent. But so, too, faced with the necessity for action, did Robespierre. One can only conclude from the Ninth Thermidor, as from the other evidences of his speeches and his policies, that Robespierre was a talker, and no doer.[2]

II. THE REACTION IN PUBLIC OPINION

July 27, 1794—the Ninth Thermidor—has become a focal date in history. The fall of Robespierre is the dramatic crisis of the

[2] It is perhaps needless to say that the above account of the Ninth Thermidor differs from that of Mathiez, in spite of the prestige of his authority with all workers in the field. Mathiez does accept the conspiracy of Fouché, Tallien and their fellows, has indeed done much to throw light on it. But he refuses to admit that Robespierre failed in a crisis. For him, Robespierre remains to the end the wise leader of a democracy, defeated by unscrupulous foes and by the apathy of a proletariat not quite ripe for revolution. See Mathiez, *La Révolution française*, III, 222-223.

Revolution, the solution, in the high and primitive sense of the phrase, of its intrigue. The French Republic is not to be the Republic of Virtue. From now on something lofty, inhuman, terrible has gone out of the Revolution. Men have returned to their everyday virtues and vices. Common sense and common foolishness have resumed sway. The Thermidorean reaction has begun.

So at least the situation appears to the simplifying eye of history. Few historians, indeed, have been able to describe the last months of the Convention without betraying a let-down in their own emotions, without indicating their disgust or disappointment at the meanness of their subject. Needless to say that the spectators, and even more the actors, of Thermidor were unaware that the moment had become an epoch. "Days" had been the usual procedure of the revolution, and there was at first nothing to differentiate the Ninth Thermidor from the Second of June, or any other revolutionary "day." Certainly Tallien, Fouché, Fréron, and the other leaders who had contrived the fall of Robespierre had not consciously aimed at ending the Terror. Moved by fear of the guillotine for themselves, they were quite willing to continue using it for their enemies. Themselves terrorists, anti-Christians, proconsuls with bloody records in the provinces, they owed their prominence to the revolutionary government, and could hardly conceive any other form of the struggle for power than the one in which they had been so long immersed. Barère on the 10 Thermidor told the Assembly there must be no talk of "indulgence," that "the strength of the revolutionary government had centupled since power, remounting to its source, had secured a more energetic spirit and purer organs."[3]

For once, however, unorganized public opinion intervened directly in public affairs. No propaganda, no pressure group prepared the reaction against the Terror. All Paris behaved as the metaphoric language of sociology and political theory usually inaccurately describes social behavior: collective Paris felt an immense relief. The strain of life under the Terror had been too great for normal human beings. Those who were not cowed by the Jacobin dictatorship were exhausted by it. Political indifference, that mainstay of the modern state, had for months been impossible. Robespierre had come to stand to ordinary people for the

[3] *Moniteur*, XXI, 346.

guillotine, the *maximum*, bread lines, police spies, abolition of prostitution and gambling, curtailment of luxury, persecution of Christians, long, dull, pseudo-classic celebrations in honor of a remote and unsympathetic deity, above all for the almost indescribable tension of life in a society where neither dullness nor triviality is below suspicion. The end of Robespierre was to such people the beginning of normal times. On the 14 Thermidor the Paris police report notes, "People are asking for the total purification of the members of the Revolutionary Tribunal, which they are now calling the 'bloody tribunal.'" The report four days later significantly remarks, "Prostitutes are reappearing with their customary audacity."[4]

The political history of the Thermidorean reaction is thus closely tied up with its social history. Step by step the Convention was forced by public opinion, now increasingly worked on by moderate and even by royalist journalists, to undo the work of the last two years, to destroy the legal basis of the Jacobin commonwealth. Not without conscious irony, the leaders of the reaction seized upon much of the elaborate machinery by which the Jacobins had built up their power, and turned it against them. Newspapers, now again enjoying virtual freedom, attacked the "tigers thirsting for human blood" and rejoiced at the death of Cromwell-Robespierre. The theater became again the scene of political quarrels, where the hilarious Thermidorean youth were usually victorious over the glowering remnant of pure republicans, the "tail of Robespierre." Laharpe, just released from prison, added a few appropriate lines to his *Virginie* of 1788, and the piece was revived on the 25 Thermidor. Wild enthusiasm greeted Talma's reading of the inserted lines

> Un tyran démasqué n'est plus qu'un vil coupable;
> Il invoque la force, et la force l'accable.
> . . . .
> La vengeance publique insulte à son trépas:
> Il mourra dans la fange, on ne le plaindra pas.[5]

Plays definitely directed against the Jacobins begin to appear in

[4] A. Aulard, *Paris pendant la réaction thermidorienne et sous le Directoire* (Paris, 1898), I, 13, 20.
[5] A. Aulard, *Paris sous la réaction thermidorienne*, I, 39.

1795, *Tolérant, The Jacobins' Supper, The Club-Mania, The Mon-tagnards,* in which the patriots of 1794 are ridiculed or treated as villains of melodrama. The troop of the Théâtre de la Nation, released from the prison they had occupied since their unhappy performance of *Pamela,* became the heroes of a day. Actors who had taken active part in the Revolution, however, had a different time living down their past. Even Talma was accused of having been a terrorist, and of intriguing to have the troop of the Théâtre de la Nation guillotined, and was forced to recite the battle-hymn of the reaction, the "Reveil du Peuple."[6]

This "Reveil du Peuple," with music by Gaveaux, ran through Paris and the provinces as rapidly as had the "Marseillaise." It was the rallying-cry of the bands of youth organized by Fréron and other leaders to subdue the Jacobins by a judicious use of force. Not only, then, did the Thermidoreans borrow Jacobin publicity methods, but they also borrowed the Jacobin methods of direct action. Armed with sticks these members of the *Jeunesse dorée,* young men of wealth, not infrequently sons of the newly-rich war contractors, would range the streets of Paris, pick quarrels with articulate Jacobins, invade well-known Jacobin cafés and theaters, menace innocent bystanders whom nature or dress had made to look too virtuously republican, shout the slogans of the new dispensation.

Fashion, thus hastened by Thermidorean intent, went to almost logical extremes. That children should repudiate the ways of their parents is fit and proper enough, and history is full of the scorn of one generation for another. The French Revolution, however, here as elsewhere carried normal social processes to a caricatural intensity, quickened the almost imperceptible rhythm of change to a clear staccato. Men and women were in 1795 as nearly as possible all they had not been in 1794. To the puritan austerity of the Terror succeeded a very public search for the simpler and lusher pleasures. Theaters, cafés, and especially ballrooms, did a splendid business. Ballrooms were opened everywhere, even in a former cemetery, and everything possible done to lend excitement to the dance, as in the *Bal des Victimes* in memory of the guillotined of 1794. Good

[6] E. Lunel, *Le théâtre et la Révolution* (Paris, 1909), 136.

eating again became a French art, at least for those who could afford it. For the simple costume of the *sans-culottes*, male and female, were substituted clothes designed as successfully as ever clothes were to display the tastes and sex of the wearer. France had in the last few years run rapidly through Roman history, from Tarquin to the Gracchi and to Brutus, and the direct imitation of classical antiquity was natural enough for a France still republican in spite of the fall of Robespierre. Mme. Tallien, called Our Lady of Thermidor, launched the extremes of the fashion, appearing at Ranelagh "dressed as Diana, bust half bare, shod with cothurns and clad, if one can use that word, in a tunic which did not come below her knees."[7] Commonly, however, the robe reached the feet: it was on the generous display of the breasts that Thermidorean fashion chiefly relied to emphasize the pleasing fact that men and women are not anatomically identical. Classic influence was not by any means supreme. To the undisciplined desires of the newly-rich, to the jaded desires of the aristocratic survivors of the Terror, anything striking was good, and there arose an anarchy of taste in the minor arts of dress and decoration which gave earnest of the nineteenth century to come. Turbans, shawls, hats, "spencers" were imported from enemy England, and the Directory, in spite of the war, witnessed a curious revival of Anglomania. Blond wigs became a feminine fashion and Mme. Tallien had thirty such, hazel, golden, ash, yellow, reddish, and all shades in between. The fashion originated, it is claimed, in a way highly typical of Thermidorean society. Payan, a violent Jacobin, had said during the Terror that some shameless women had bought the hair of the aristocratic blond victims, and were wearing on their own heads this "so dear hair." In 1795, a reminder of that speech was sufficient to set everyone to wearing blond wigs—to the great benefit of the wigmaking trade.[8] The more eccentric members of such a society were encouraged to indulge themselves to the full, and produced two types much, but not very successfully, ridiculed in their own time, the masculine *incroyable* and the feminine *merveilleuse*. Both, in addi-

[7] Victor de Broglie, quoted in A. Mathiez, *La réaction thermidorienne* (Paris, 1929), 105.
[8] E. and J. Goncourt, *Histoire de la société française pendant le Directoire* (Paris, 1864), 408.

tion to eccentricities of dress, cultivated a bored manner, a lisping expiring speech in which all the consonants tended to sound alike, and an invincible distaste for the vulgarities of political democracy.

A hundred other details could be brought forward to show how completely the men of 1795 repudiated themselves of 1794—for, by and large, the Thermidoreans had once been Jacobins. The extremists, the leaders, of both groups are, indeed, separate, distinguishable, consistent: the surviving "suspects" had escaped the contagion of the Jacobin faith; and a few Jacobins were to escape the contagion of Thermidorean pleasures. But the bulk of Frenchmen had simply changed their minds and their tastes, so suddenly and so thoroughly that this change impressed even the politicians.

III. AMNESTY AND REPRESSION

Politically the Ninth Thermidor had been achieved by the union of the hitherto timid Center, or Plain, with certain Montagnards who had personal reasons for fearing Robespierre. Similar unions had occurred before, and always the Plain had lapsed into timid acquiescence with the violent proposals of the radical Montagnard minority. After Thermidor the Plain did not miraculously acquire courage and political skill. Rather, public opinion backed the naturally moderate Plain so strongly as to supply it with courage. Some of the anti-Robespierrist Montagnards, like Tallien and Fréron, were quick to see what was happening, and became advocates of clemency—for all save their recusant colleagues in terrorism. Step by step during the next fifteen months this alliance of moderates and repentant terrorists carried out the desires of the militant Thermidoreans, and laid the foundations for the bourgeois French state of subsequent history. This liquidation of the Jacobin venture in democratic republicanism was not accomplished without much stress and strain, without serious struggles with the Jacobin remnant and with the now frequently starving populace. The chronological ups and downs of the contest are less enlightening than its broader aspects.

First and most obvious among Thermidorean policies is that of amnesty, clemency towards political opponents. Liberty, people began to say, actually implies allowing a certain latitude of opinion.

Royalists, of course, could not be allowed liberty, but after all was there any use keeping a man in prison because he had forgotten to say "citoyen" for "monsieur," or refused to wear a liberty cap on the ground that it was not becoming to him? Moreover, arrest had been so easy during the Terror that many purely private grudges had helped to fill the prisons. Something like a jail delivery took place in Paris and in the provincial cities during the first few weeks after Thermidor. The great committees, now free from the "tyrant," sanctioned in five days, from the 18 to the 23 Thermidor, the release of 478 suspects at Paris.[9] The Convention legalized these measures by decreeing that all prisoners not clearly and formally suspects under the law of September 17, 1793—a law milder than the common practice of the Terror—were to be released, and that the revolutionary committees must furnish the evidence on which the remaining suspects were to be held.

In the spring of 1795 amnesty was extended to the surviving Girondins. Their case had cropped up in October previous as a mere incident in the party struggle between the old Jacobins and their opponents, but the friends of the imprisoned deputies refused to let the matter die, and in January, after many debates and committee reports, the sixty-seven survivors of the seventy-two who had secretly protested against the "day" of May 31, 1793 were released and amid public rejoicing reassumed their seats in the Convention. The Girondins were well on the way to their heroic apotheosis in the pages of Lamartine. Finally, in March, those Girondins who had actually taken arms against the republic and been outlawed were recalled. The next day, significantly enough, May 31 was dropped from the list of national holidays. The whole course of the Montagnard dictatorship had been repudiated.

By this time the Convention was carried away with the idea of complete pacification. Representatives, led by Ruelle, were sent to the west to treat with the remaining Vendéens and with the Chouans, less systematically organized royalist guerrillas who had begun to infest Brittany and its eastern borders. After direct negotiations with Charette, Stofflet, and other rebel leaders, these representatives, entrusted with full power by the Convention, issued a series

[9] Mathiez, *La réaction thermidorienne,* 31 note.

of pardons in which everything was yielded to the rebels—religious freedom, even for the non-juring clergy, return of property and full civil rights to the rebels, even the payment of actual money to the leading chiefs. In return, the rebels were to surrender their arms and return peacefully home. This pacification was, however, a mere truce, and the new government of the Directory found itself with a renewed civil war on its hands. The Thermidoreans had been too confident in the strength of good intentions. The Vendéens had not fought to end the Terror, but to restore the church and the crown. The Thermidoreans, most of whom were regicides, could hardly recall the Bourbons.

They did, however, make some attempt to restore religious toleration. Concession of religious freedom to the Vendéens meant that a similar concession could hardly be withheld from loyal France. By the decree of the 3 Ventôse, year III (February 21, 1795), a grudging toleration was granted to the Catholic Church. All sorts of restrictions were placed on the exercise of this freedom: the churches continued to belong to the state, and were simply made available to the Catholics when not needed by the municipality; priests were not allowed to appear in public in clerical costume; all public religious processions were forbidden; the expenses of the church must be met from voluntary contributions of the faithful. Boissy d'Anglas, in his speech in defense of the decree, made it clear that the Convention had by no means turned Christian. The Constituent Assembly, he said, had "made the mistake of estimating too slightly the strength of human enlightenment already achieved," and had not dared separate church and state. The result had been schism, the strengthening of "fanaticism" by persecution. "Religion thrives on martyrs, as love thrives on obstacles." Therefore, on purely pragmatic grounds, the Convention should allow complete freedom of belief, subject to the normal police power, and trust to time to destroy the Catholic superstition.[10] France in 1795, therefore, attained to separation of church and state, a condition under which numerous religious groups, Catholic, Constitutional, Protestant, Jewish, and numerous variants of "civic" cults managed to exist in a promising diversity until Napoleon by

[10] *Moniteur,* XXIII, 525-526.

the Concordat of 1801 reëstablished the Roman Catholic Church in France.

As amnesties were extended from suspects to Girondins, from Girondins to Chouans, from Chouans to refractory Catholics all over France, each successive amnestied group added weight to the reaction. Concurrently with the process of forgiving old enemies to the Right there went the process of proscribing old friends to the Left. For the rest of the life of the Convention, measures in favor of the conservatives may almost be said to alternate with measures against the radicals. The latter are of two types: those directed against the machinery of the revolutionary government, those directed against the persons of the terrorists.

Bit by bit the machinery of the Terror was dismounted. First, the two great committees were deprived of their dictatorial powers by requiring one-quarter of their personnel to be renewed each month, by restoring to the Convention the power of nominating other committees, by annulling the control exercised by the great committees over the executive commissions which had replaced the ministries, by establishing direct relations between each of the twelve executive commissions and the corresponding committee of the Convention, finally, by the raising of the committee on legislation to the level of the two great committees, so that henceforth the government is called the "Three Committees." The notorious law of the 22 Prairial was promptly repealed on the 14 Thermidor. The Revolutionary Tribunal was completely reorganized, and required to adopt something like normal methods of examining witnesses. It was hardly used save against the terrorists, and was abolished in May, 1795. Finally, by means of Thermidorean representatives sent out on mission, the machinery as well as the personnel of provincial administration was once again completely altered. Known terrorists were replaced by safe men, the clubs were filled with the new functionaries, the revolutionary committees gradually eliminated altogether. Briefly, it may be said that these changes handed the central government over to a moderate majority in the Convention, a majority pretty well controlled by a public sick of terror and experiment, and the actual administration to a nascent bureaucracy which, on the whole, was taken over nearly intact by Napoleon.

Not all the Jacobins had fallen with Robespierre and the Commune of Paris; not all had the wisdom or the cowardice to follow Fouché and Tallien into the reaction. Against these remaining Jacobins the Thermidoreans were to display at least as much violence, real and rhetorical, as the terrorists themselves had ever displayed. The White Terror was as barbarous as the Red. Fréron in his *Orateur du Peuple*, perhaps consistently enough consecrated by its author to carrying out the work of Marat, led the cry for blood: ". . . thou, Barère, who sowed the flowers of thy homicidal rhetoric o'er the innocent bodies of thy fellow citizens! Ah! 'Tis in vain the idea of Providence has been placed in men's hearts, if so much blood does not one day come back upon thee and thy accomplices."[11] The Convention had restored parliamentary immunity to its members as part of its revolt against the dreaded committees. Now it made no difficulty about revoking the parliamentary immunity of Jacobin deputies. Carrier was therefore tried, made full confession, convicted and executed in the winter of 1795. He has remained ever since the most infamous of the proconsuls, and the *noyades* of Nantes have become folk-history. Fouché, indeed, whose *mitraillades* of Lyons were quite as deadly, if not as picturesque, as the activities of Carrier, lived to become Duke of Otranto. The unfortunate Carrier was an earnest malefactor and an excellent scapegoat. The Convention was unanimous in decreeing his trial. Fouquier-Tinville and Hermann, both associated with the most active days of the Revolutionary Tribunal, soon followed Carrier. The professional politicians who had helped to overthrow Robespierre were more difficult to dislodge. Barère, Billaud-Varenne, Collot d'Herbois and the others of the Jacobin remnant had made the Ninth Thermidor possible. The closing of the Jacobin club in Paris by order of the Convention, and the stuffing of the provincial clubs with moderates, the prohibition of correspondence between clubs and of petitions in a collective name had, indeed, cut these leaders of the Left from their constituents, and they could hardly be considered a menace to public order. But the Thermidoreans still feared Jacobinism, even when it was reduced to phrases. The events of Germinal and Prairial, 1795, gave them an opportunity to rid themselves of the last of the rulers of '94, save for Carnot, whose title of "Organizer of Victory" saved him for the present.

To understand these abortive popular uprisings of the spring and summer of 1795, it is necessary to consider the economic aspects of the Thermidorean reaction. The victors of the Ninth Thermidor were forced by public opinion to abandon the half-socialistic measures of their predecessors; the real victors of that "day" were the business interests. The *maximum* was repealed in December, 1794. Saint-Just's decrees of Ventôse, with their purpose of redistributing the land to the rural poor, were abandoned, and what was left of the confiscated lands sold frankly to the capitalist class, not without considerable corruption and favoritism. Lands and other property of the now innocent victims of the Revolutionary Tribunal were restored to their families. The Bourse, or Stock Exchange, was reopened, and speculation once more became legal. Private property was again sacred. At the same time, more and more *assignats* were printed. Deprived of the support of the *maximum*, they sank with astonishing rapidity, and when the Convention was dissolved were worth only three or four per cent of their face value. The crippling, sometimes even the destruction, of organized charity by government confiscation of religious establishments completed the misfortunes of the poor. The Convention had, indeed, passed pious decrees guaranteeing the right to relief to all citizens, suppressing all private charities, and assuming poor relief as part of the state budget. "It is true," wrote a historian very favorable to the Revolution, "that these decrees were hardly executed save for their negative provisions."[12] The army supported many thousands of able-bodied males, and the demand for munitions, clothes, and food insured good business, if not prosperity. Many an entrepreneur, many a speculator flourished in these years, not all undeservedly. But the extraordinary inflation, the breakdown of public and private charity, the disorders and uncertainties in a society still far from stable, all contributed to the creation of a large class, in the cities at least, on the very edge of starvation. Nothing like precise statistics are available, but it seems not unlikely that the condition of the urban proletariat in the winter of 1794-95 was worse than at any time

[12] G. Pariset, *Études d'histoire révolutionnaire et contemporaine* (Paris, 1929), 65.

during the century. Even though the *maximum* had been repealed, a
system of rationing by bread-cards had to be continued. The police
reports at Paris for weeks are full of complaints of scarcity: "Pierre
. . . saw numerous citizens who got no bread, others who got but
one loaf, though their cards called for three."[13]

Twice these hungry poor of Paris, not unmindful of the more
literal meaning of equality and fraternity, attempted insurrections
against the Convention. On the 12 Germinal, year III (April 1, 1795),
a crowd of men, women, and children swarmed into the hall of the
Convention, crying for bread, attempting to make speeches at the
bar of the assembly, but in general abstaining from physical violence.
The manifesters were cleared from the hall by loyal troops. On the 1
Prairial following (May 20), a more angry mob invaded the hall,
were driven out, surged in again, attacked members, and finally
assassinated an inconspicuous deputy, Féraud, under the impression that he was the turncoat Fréron.[14] For hours the hall was filled
with a shouting, milling, drunken crowd, utterly without power
to do more than protest. Loyal—that is, conservative—national
guards from the richer quarters finally came to the rescue, and
order was restored. The Convention had held firm. After each invasion, however, it sacrificed some of its more active Jacobin members, presumably to discourage the others. The last of the great
committees—Collot d'Herbois, Vadier, Billaud-Varenne, and Barère
—were deported to Guiana after the insurrection of Germinal. Six
more obscure deputies, members of the "Crest," as the Mountain
was now called, were condemned to death without a real trial after
the insurrection of Prairial. The condemned six agreed to commit
suicide. Three succeeded in stabbing themselves to death; the other
three were guillotined after they had mutilated themselves. The
democratic party was destroyed. From this time on, the White
Terror had full sweep, especially in the valley of the Rhone. Everywhere the new Thermidorean proconsuls had arrested and imprisoned former terrorists. Now in Lyons, Aix, Nîmes, Toulon,
Marseilles, Tarascon, in many smaller places, suspected terrorists

---

[13] Aulard, *Paris pendant la réaction thermidorienne*, I, 439.
[14] A. C. Thibaudeau, *Mémoires* (Paris, 1824), I, 166. *Féraud*, pronounced in a tumult,
would sound like *Fréron*.

were dragged from prison by "companions of Jesus" and massacred, quite in the manner of September, 1792.

The insurrections of Germinal and Prairial failed chiefly because they were simply insurrections of the hungry and the suffering. Some organization, indeed, they had, achieved under the more obscure ward-heelers of the Dantons, Sergents, Panis, Momoros of old, but there is no evidence that the Jacobin deputies in the Convention, though they knew trouble was brewing, had shared in planning these risings. Quite the contrary, they had maintained a timid and scrupulous legality up to the last minute. Leaderless, the Parisian workmen were incapable of anything more than fruitless violence and disorder. Perhaps, as Mathiez maintained, the Jacobin deputies, who were all educated, middle-class gentlemen, had no real understanding of the plight of the workmen, no real capacity to lead them.[15] At any rate, the popular risings of 1795 are additional evidence in favor of the thesis that successful revolutions are not the product of physical suffering alone.

IV. PEACE WITH PRUSSIA AND SPAIN

By the spring of 1795 French armies had attained the "natural frontiers," had beaten back their enemies on every front, and invaded their lands. The republic had achieved what Louis XIV had failed to achieve. Somewhat disdainfully, the Thermidorean leaders, the Three Committees of the new government, looked about for overtures of peace. The relaxation from victory had proved more than the new armies of the *amalgame* could stand. As in 1793, after Jemappes, thousands of defenders of the fatherland simply deserted and returned to the fatherland. Out of a paper enrollment of 1,100,000 in all armies—the numbers have a modern look, and would have amazed Frederick II—only some 454,000 were actually under arms in March, 1795.[16] Under these circumstances, the Thermidoreans were willing to make peace, provided they found someone even more willing.

The Austro-Prussian alliance had never taken hold of the German imagination. It is a little surprising nowadays to note how rarely,

[15] Mathiez, *La réaction thermidorienne*, 258.
[16] G. Pariset, *La Révolution, 1792-1799*, in *Histoire de France contemporaine*, ed. E. Lavisse (Paris, 1920), 267. These were by no means all on fighting fronts.

even in Germany, the war of 1792-1794 was regarded as a united German effort against the hereditary enemy, France. If ordinary newspaper readers were indifferent, or perhaps a bit amazed, at this alliance, in the official world of the rulers it had never been really popular. Many, perhaps most, Prussian gentlemen distrusted Austria on what is called principle. After the second partition of Poland, they had an additional motive for hating the Austrians, the hatred of the cheater for his victim. The failure of 1792 had started spiteful rumors. Some Austrians believed Brunswick had deliberately lost the battle of Valmy as an accommodation to his brother Freemason, Dumouriez. The Austrian general Clerfayt did not dare start across the Rhine on the campaign of 1795, for fear of being attacked from the rear by the *Prussians*.[17] To this depth had the gossip and backbiting of tent and salon carried the allies of 1792.

Prussia, who was not responsible towards the empire for the left bank of the Rhine, who had less at stake, whose finances were completely disordered, in whose government many important men, like Frederick II's brother Henry, had never believed in the war against France, was the first of the great powers to treat for peace. Cessation of subsidies from England in the autumn of 1794 marked the end of Prussian participation in the war. Negotiations begun at Basel in the winter culminated in a treaty of peace arranged by Hardenberg on the Prussian side and Barthélemy on the French, and ratified by the Convention on April 14, 1795. Prussia's decision was, no doubt, hastened by the Polish situation. Russia and Austria had secretly come to an agreement on January 3 for a final partition of Poland, in which these two powers were to gain much more important accessions than Prussia. News of this agreement filtered into Prussian court circles easily enough, and was confirmed by the reports of Tauenzien, Prussian ambassador at St. Petersburg. The Prussian government hoped by concluding immediate peace with France to participate in the third partition of Poland on an equal basis with Austria and Russia. The peace of Basel publicly provided for the cessation of hostilities between France and Prussia, permitted France to occupy the left bank of the Rhine until a general peace, and offered the services of the King of Prussia to princes and

[17] Heigel, *Deutsche Geschichte*, II, 196.

states of the empire who might wish to conclude peace. By secret provisions, the Prussian government agreed to consent to French annexation of the left bank of the Rhine, in return for which France promised to assure compensation to Prussia for the actual *Prussian* possessions lost in French expansion to the Rhine. The diplomats who made the peace of Basel had obviously, in 1795, little acquaintance with the principle of nationality, and, of course, little regard for the moral code of the Enlightenment.

Spain was the second great power to beg off. The war along the Pyrenees had not been altogether without credit to Spanish arms, but in 1794 the French began to push the Spanish back, and had actually invaded northern Spain. Louis and his queen were dead, and the Bourbon dynasty in France seemed hardly to be restored by the Spanish Bourbons. The Spanish people were soon to show that they could resist the attempt to Gallicize them, but they had little heart in a crusade to reform their republican neighbors and restore monarchy in France. Godoy himself had perhaps as much influence as anyone on the Spanish side, and by 1795 he had decided to negotiate. The peace of July 4, 1795, also signed at Basel, was concluded between Barthélemy and Yriarte. It provided for French evacuation of Spanish territory and for the cession of the Spanish portion of the island of Santo Domingo to France—in view of the disordered state of that island, hardly a solid gain.

Tuscany, Saxony, Hanover, Hesse-Cassel were successfully detached from the coalition at this time, either by French victories or French diplomacy. An extraordinarily cold winter had frozen the lower Rhine, and facilitated a French invasion of Holland from a Belgium already overrun, a campaign in which the French cavalry achieved the surprising feat of capturing some Dutch ships frozen in the ice. The stadholder, committed to his English and Prussian allies, fled before the invaders, and left the Dutch republicans free to conclude a defensive and offensive alliance with the French "liberators." Of the major members of the First Coalition, only England and Austria remained, at the close of the Convention, at war with France. The Austrians, encouraged by the failure of the French general Pichegru in the Rhine campaign of 1795, still

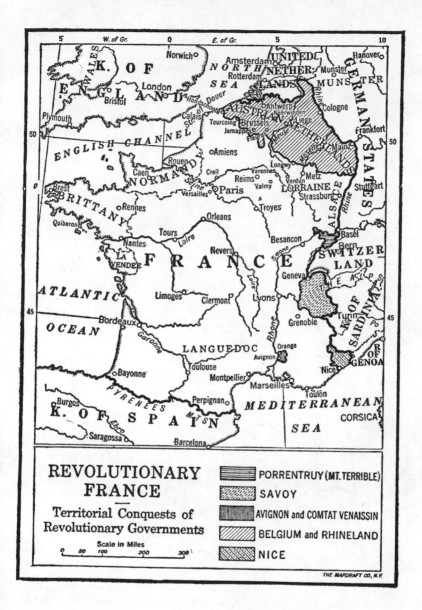

REVOLUTIONARY FRANCE

Territorial Conquests of Revolutionary Governments

Scale in Miles

PORRENTRUY (MT. TERRIBLE)

SAVOY

AVIGNON and COMTAT VENAISSIN

BELGIUM and RHINELAND

NICE

THE MAPCRAFT CO., N.Y.

had hopes of ultimate victory.[18] England could apparently still raise subsidies for Continental allies, and as long as the French were firmly established in the Low Countries, Pitt seemed to think these subsidies worth while.

A badly judged English enterprise did, however, give the Convention an opportunity to begin another important pacification, that of the Vendée. The generous amnesty negotiated by Ruelle had not been successful, and Vendéens and Chouans were again active. Royalist agents were everywhere. In conjunction with the English navy a force of *émigrés* landed on the south coast of Brittany to unite the scattered groups of western rebels against the republicans. The royalist army was bottled up on the narrow peninsula of Quiberon, and annihilated by the republicans under Hoche in July, 1795. Charette in retaliation deliberately massacred some thousand republican prisoners. Hoche set to work in earnest, and during the winter of 1795-96 completed the task of subduing the Vendée.

V. THE END OF THE CONVENTION

The Thermidorean Convention had thus gone far towards a general pacification, both internal and external. France had done so well in the scramble of national rivalries that the ordinary Frenchman might be expected to feel grateful to the men who had extended the boundaries and the prestige of their country. Patriotism, however, unlike more transcendental forms of faith, is rarely able to overcome the simpler forms of physical deprivation, such as cold and hunger. The Convention in its last month was as much detested by the sovereign people, who had elected it three years previously, as any of the numerous once-popular governments which have had the misfortune to endure into times of economic depression. Throughout these months the Convention had been working out a new constitution, for the paper constitution of 1793 had not been seriously considered by the victors of Thermidor. The constitution was now ready. The Convention had done its work. But how solve the transition to a new and legal government? At any rate, the mistake made by the National Assembly in denying its

---

[18] It is pretty clear now that Pichegru was already meditating the rôle of Monk, and that he deliberately neglected this campaign. G. Caudrillier, *La trahison de Pichegru* (Paris, 1908), 92. For a different view, see A. Meynier, *Les coups d'état du directoire* (Paris, 1928).

members the right to be elected to the Legislative Assembly must not be repeated. Such was the state of public opinion in 1795, however, that hardly a member of the hated Convention could expect to be elected again. There was always the danger that royalists might "conspire"—that is, vote and influence voting—and choose a body of men willing to recall the Bourbons. In fact, the royalist danger in 1795 was probably a real one. There was much talk of a possible restoration, from which the regicide Conventionnels must fear the worst. The dauphin, who had reigned as Louis XVII only in the hearts of the faithful, had died in prison (stories of escape and survival have no truth) and the new king, Louis XVIII, brother of Louis XVI, issued from exile in Verona a proclamation in which no concessions whatever were made to the Revolution. This tactless proclamation frightened many a conservative holder of confiscated lands, and made the royalist task of gaining converts in France much more difficult.

The Convention, however, alarmed by continued troubles in the Vendée and in Brittany, and by the recrudescence of royalist propaganda, decided to protect itself as far as possible. It passed two additional decrees providing for the obligatory election of two-thirds of the new legislative bodies from among the members of the Convention, and for enforcing this provision even if the required two-thirds were not chosen by the people. Many of the men who helped put these decrees through the Convention were vicious and corrupt, ex-terrorists now profiteers, who feared for their positions if true moderates gained control of the government; yet the committee in which the decrees originated was composed of former Girondins, most of whom were almost certain to be among the few Conventionnels voluntarily chosen for the new legislature.[19] In some measure, these decrees were a well-meant effort to avoid the mistake of the National Assembly.

Whatever their motive, the publication of the two decrees provoked a thoroughly Parisian mixture of laughter and fury. The representatives of the people were christened "les Perpétuels." Fury, however, proved stronger than laughter, and gave energy to the

[19] H. Zivy, Le 13 vendémiaire (Paris, 1898), 109.

organization of the last of the "days" the Convention was obliged to face. The new constitution was accepted after a half-hearted plebiscite not wholly free from the presence of the bayonet, but the additional decrees were actually voted down in Paris. Starting, as had the organization leading to the "day" of August 10, in the Paris *sections*—this time, however, in the wealthier and more conservative *sections*—an insurrection was carefully organized. Many of the national guard were won to the movement, and the Convention hastily rearmed some hardy old Jacobins of the slums of Saint-Antoine, and decreed that a committee of defense should be chosen to sit in permanence. Menou, commander of the troops in Paris, went over to the insurrection.

Unlike the insurgents of Prairial, these were not an unruly rabble, drunk with alcohol or Jacobinism. They were respectable bourgeois, mostly experienced national guards, mingled with some real royalists and aristocrats, well equipped, but not well led. They made the mistake of dividing their forces—some 25,000 all told—to attack the Tuileries, seat of the government, from both sides. One column was held on the left bank at the Pont-Neuf. The other advanced down towards the Rue Saint-Honoré from the north. Near the church of Saint-Roch it was met, for the first time in street-fighting of the Revolution, by a murderous artillery fire, and scattered in disorder. The Convention had entrusted its defense to Barras, and Barras had entrusted himself to the regular army. The insurrectionists outnumbered the troops loyal to the government by four to one, but they had no cannon. History has dramatized the 13 Vendémiaire, for Napoleon Bonaparte commanded the guns of the Convention. Yet Carlyle's almost too well-known phrase is misleading. The 13 Vendémiaire assured the Thermidorean majority in the Convention a continuance of power under the new constitution. Not by the cannonade of Saint-Roch, however, was "the thing we specifically call French Revolution . . . blown into space . . . and become a thing that was."[20] If there was ever a specific French Revolution, and if it was ever ended by a specific act, then the single bullet that broke Robespierre's jaw did more than Bonaparte's "whiff of grapeshot."

[20] Carlyle, *French Revolution,* Part III, book VIII, ch. II.

Chapter Nine

THE DIRECTORY

I. THE POLITICAL ASPECT

THE GOVERNMENT of the Directory was overthrown by Bonaparte in 1799. For years historians—even the republican ones—have continued to defend Bonaparte's act with almost as much uncritical earnestness as Bonaparte and his followers employed in 1799 to defend themselves. By the nineteenth century's favorite standard, the survival of the fittest, moreover, the Directory stood condemned. It had fallen because of its weakness, its corruption, its inept foreign policy, its financial incapacity. Waterloo, indeed, rarely provoked French historians to apply the standard of the survival of the fittest with quite the same rigor as did the events of 1799; but Napoleon, who was above so much else, was surely above Science? Twentieth-century historians, however, if only to give themselves something to do, have corrected their predecessor's one-sided estimate of the Directory.[1] It is pretty clear now that the constitution of 1795 was so molded by events and leaders that in 1799 the essential institutions of the Consulate and Empire were already in working order, and needed but slight alterations and additions to accommodate themselves to the much-praised Napoleonic internal stability. The financial policy of the Directory, seen in the light of modern experience of inflation, seems no longer a weak yielding to forces which firmness and wisdom might have overcome. Nor, in view of modern documentary studies, does the foreign policy of the Directory seem, as it seemed to Sorel, an intransigent chauvinism without regard for the realities of European politics.[2]

The basis of the government of the Directory was the constitution of the year III (1795), devised by the Thermidorean Convention to

[1] Their work is well summed up by one of their leaders, M. Guyot, in G. Lefebvre, R. Guyot, and P. Sagnac, *La Révolution française* (Paris, 1930), 285-464.
[2] A. Sorel, *L'Europe et la Révolution*, V, chap. I.

insure the continuance of middle-class rule, republican in form, but equally distant from the democratic republic desired by the Jacobins and the royalist restoration threatened by the *émigrés*. The suffrage once more, as in 1791, depended on a property qualification—the possession of wealth, landed or personal, subject to direct tax. Soldiers who had fought for the republic might vote even though they paid no direct tax. This provision excluded the urban and rural proletariat, but left an electorate of some five millions, instead of the six and a half or seven millions who would have qualified under universal suffrage.[3] Even allowing for the soldier vote, these figures would indicate that by 1795 property in France had been very greatly subdivided, that, though many peasants doubtless held very little land, too little to give them full support, yet most of them owned some, and paid a direct tax. After the year XII (1803-04) those attaining 21 years were to be registered as voters only if they could read, write, and practice a trade, industrial or agricultural, but this interesting anticipation of modern educational qualifications was never applied. For important offices, election in two degrees was maintained. To qualify as member of the assemblies which chose the national legislature and the higher local officials, it was necessary to own or lease land with an annual value, locally determined, of from 100 to 200 days' labor. The real power of franchise was thus restricted to a small number of wealthy men. The legislature was to follow American practice, and consist of two houses: a Council of Elders (*Anciens*) composed of 250 men at least forty years of age and either married or widowers, and a Council of Five Hundred, composed of 500 men at least thirty years of age, who need not be married. The good—and very likely mistaken —folk-notion that age and marital condition are directly correlated with political sobriety was thus formally incorporated in the constitution. The Ancients were to be the conservative check. Each council was to have one-third of its membership renewed annually. The executive was placed in the hands of five Directors, at least forty years of age, chosen by the Ancients from a list submitted by the Five Hundred, and holding office for five years. One new Director was to be chosen each year. The ministries were reëstablished,

[3] G. Pariset, *La Révolution*, 275.

and the ministers made responsible to the Directors. In local government the districts were abolished, and the cantons made much more important and given a municipal organization. The judicial system was further reorganized to secure judges who, though popularly elected, would prove satisfactory functionaries. Central control was maintained by continuing the national agents in the form of departmental agents of the Directors. Finally, the famous two decrees requiring the election of two-thirds of the new councils from the members of the Convention were added. In spite of electoral jockeying, only 374 of the necessary 500 Conventionnels were chosen by the sovereign people; the Convention itself thereupon chose the remainder.

The faults of this constitution, quite apart from the two decrees, are obvious. It separates the executive and the legislative so completely as to make rivalry between Directors and Councils inevitable and coöperation almost impossible. Once again the doctrinaire French failed to establish the parliamentary system and ministerial responsibility as practiced in England. Yet this criticism is not quite as valid nowadays as it was in the best days of parliamentary orthodoxy. The United States, with a most shocking separation of legislative and executive, has hitherto survived the mild forebodings of Bagehot and Bryce. The constitution of 1795 in actual practice showed a surprising adaptability to the stresses and strains of French politics, and was adjusted and altered in the four brief years of its life in a way far from doctrinaire or theoretical. On the whole the crucial political changes of these years, though they rightly bear the name of *coups d'état*, are, when compared to the great revolutionary "days," very little different from normal political changes in modern democratic states. The army, it is true, played an important part in the *coup d'état* of the 18 Fructidor, and a decisive part in that of the Eighteenth Brumaire. The politicians, however, were learning, and though their methods were still somewhat crude, though they themselves were often handicapped by a republican faith still unduly pure for this world, though economic distress sharpened the discontents of the working class, still the manipulation of the elections of the Year VI (1798) was a worthy forerunner of peaceful nineteenth-century methods.[4] There was nothing inevitable—save in the perhaps inadequate sense in which anything that has happened may be said to have been inevitable—in the intervention of the army and the subsequent military dictatorship. The historian must say that under the conditions of 1795-1799 a bourgeois government and society of typical nineteenth-century pattern, such as for instance was later established under Louis Philippe, might well have emerged without benefit of Napoleon.

In tracing the political evolution of the France of the Directory, the personalities of the Directors are of little importance. Of the original five, four—Reubell, Larevellière-Lépeaux, Carnot and Le Tourneur—were respectable bourgeois and good republicans, hard workers, desirous of establishing a middle-of-the-road government to give France peace and stability. The other, Barras, was an ex-noble, pleasure-loving, facile, plunged in the midst of that corrupt, mannered, promiscuous, excited, and barren society which dates from the Ninth Thermidor. Barras, not at all a typical republican, owed his election to the prestige he had gained on the 13 Vendémiaire, when he had been charged by the Convention with its defense. He alone retained his place as long as the government of the Directory lasted. Siéyès, chosen Director in 1799, helped overthrow a system which he was already known to hold in great contempt.

The new government was early faced with what it regarded—or wished the country to regard—as a serious danger from the radicals. This was the "Conspiracy of the Equals," led by Gracchus Babeuf, now canonized by orthodox socialists as the first truly class-conscious leader of the modern European proletariat. The incident has perhaps been given undue prominence because Babeuf's ideas approximate Marxian socialism more closely than those of any other revolutionary figure. He goes beyond the greengrocer's paradise of small property-owners proclaimed by Robespierre, and sets up as the true goal of the Revolution a communist society where private property is unknown. His immediate end, however, was the "restoration" of the still-born Constitution of 1793, and his *Analyse de la doctrine de Babeuf*, a manifesto in fifteen articles, does not go

[4] A. Meynier, *Les coups d'état du Directoire*, II, 43.

beyond the vague, economic equalitarianism of the Jacobins. Babeuf and his friends, organized as the Society of the Pantheon, clearly planned an insurrection against the Directory. The plan was mysterious, melodramatic, and perfectly futile. There seem to have been almost as many stool pigeons as genuine conspirators involved, and the government had no trouble in arresting Babeuf and his fellow conspirators in the spring of 1796. A radical attempt to persuade the troops in the camp at Grenelle, just outside Paris, to rise against the government produced a convenient riot, and the Directory was able to point out to France that there was clearly need for a strong government. A military commission made wholesale condemnations in the Grenelle affair. Babeuf was tried and condemned to death.

Three so-called *coups d'état*—they are hardly more than crude experiments with the machinery of change in a modern democratic state—sum up the subsequent political history of the Directory adequately enough. The danger to the state had first come from the Left, from Babeuf; now it was discerned from the Right, from the royalists. On the 18 Fructidor, Year V (September 4, 1797), the moderate republican group, led in the Directory by Reubell, Larevellière and Barras, overcame a reactionary group led in the Directory by Carnot and the newly-elected Barthélemy, who had negotiated the treaties of Basel in 1795. The reactionaries were a miscellaneous lot, ranging from Carnot, still at heart a republican, to General Pichegru, who was in the pay of Pitt and the Bourbons.[5] They were held together chiefly by a reactionary majority in the two councils elected in the previous spring, partly out of popular spite against the "perpetuals" of the Convention, partly by means of an excellently organized clerical-royalist political machine disguised under the name of *instituts philanthropiques* and spread through most of France by returned priests.[6] The conservatives were at last learning the ways of practical politics. Just how menacing this movement to the Right was to the new republic, just how far the victors of Fructidor were justified in their claim that they had

[5] A. Mathiez, "Le coup d'état du 18 fructidor," *Annales historiques de la Révolution française* (1929), VI, 539.

[6] For an example, see Caudrillier's study of the Institute in Bordeaux. G. Caudrillier, *L'association royaliste de l'Institut philanthropique à Bordeaux et la conspiration anglaise en France pendant la deuxième coalition* (Paris, 1908).

suppressed a "royalist plot" can doubtless never be decided. The latest historian of the subject, a member of the official republican school, concludes that, though there were certainly great differences of opinion between the new majority in the councils and the Directory, there was no important royalist plot. The movement to the Right was a perfectly constitutional one.[7]

The Directory, thanks to the aid of Augereau and his grenadiers, got the upper hand peacefully enough, banished Barthélemy, Pichegru and many of their adherents to Guiana—Carnot had saved himself by flight—and annulled, in a rump session of the councils, the election of 198 of their opponents. Special laws gave the Directory arbitrary powers over the press, the clergy, the émigrés. Armed with these powers, the government prepared the next year's elections with great care, establishing official government lists of candidates, using to the full the power and knowledge of functionaries, and controlling the press. The elections, much disputed—in some constituencies three separate lists of candidates claimed to have been chosen—tended on the whole to be a bit too Jacobinical for the government. True to its policy of the golden mean, the Directory set up a commission of five members to straighten up the electoral situation in accordance with the public welfare. The commission excluded 106 newly elected deputies, replaced 53 of them with opponents who had received fewer votes, and left the rest of the seats vacant. This harmless maneuver is dignified with the name of the "coup d'état of Floréal." The Directory had practically established a coöptative legislature closely allied with the executive —exactly the system of Napoleon's Consulate.

In the winter of 1798-99 the war turned badly against France. In spite of very real financial and political reforms, France was still subject to recurrences of severe distress. The inflation of 1793-1796 was not easily lived down, and all economic services were irregular. The elections of 1799 resulted in another defeat for the government. This time there was a recrudescence, under circumstances of national danger similar to those of 1793, of a demand for a Jacobin dictatorship.[8] Once again the clubs were opened, once again "trea-

[7] A. Meynier, *Les coups d'état du Directoire* (Paris, 1927), I, 198.
[8] A. Aulard, "Les derniers Jacobins," in his *Études et Leçons* (Paris, 1913), VII, 85.

son," "suspect," "levée en masse" became current coin of politics. On 30 Prairial, Year VII (June 18, 1799), a parliamentary revolution overthrew the dictatorial Directory issued from Fructidor, and set up a new Directory composed of Barras, Siéyès, Gohier, Roger-Ducos and Moulin. Once more the legislature, as on the Ninth Thermidor, was victorious over an unpopular executive. But the victors of this *coup d'état* of Prairial were far from united. Under the impulsion of their Jacobin friends, old and new, the councils passed two very radical measures—a forced loan on the rich, really a capital levy, and a law which permitted the authorities to take hostages in the families of notorious *émigrés* or suspects and hold them as guaranties for the good behavior of these enemies of the republic. Moderate men in politics and out were shocked by this apparent revival of the Terror. The army had been taking an increasing part in politics. Generals, retired, invalided, or simply off duty, had been candidates for office. There had even emerged, in 1798, a veterans' interest, and thanks to the efforts of Generals Marbot and Jourdan a very generous law was passed compensating the defenders of the fatherland for their efforts—a compensation deferred, however, until a general European peace. The military interest, then, was strong and well-organized. It had developed a hearty contempt for civilians, for lawyers and *pékins*. It was proud of its achievements, self-confident, aware that it was a revolutionary creation. Though, like all good armies, it was attached to order, discipline, inequality, though, in other words, it was a conservative force, it was quite hostile to royalism, regarded itself, indeed, as the mainstay of the republic. The army was thus the obvious instrument to set up the moderates again. All was ready for the Eighteenth Brumaire.

II. THE DIRECTORY AND THE ORGANIZATION OF FRANCE

The legend which describes Bonaparte as First Consul bestowing a life-giving order on a state languishing in incompetence is no longer tenable. "In spite of appearances, and the legend, half the road at least will have been got over somehow or other when Bonaparte takes the reins."[9] In place of the doctrinaire economic lib-

[9] R. Guyot, in Lefebvre, Guyot, and Sagnac, *Révolution française*, 318.

eralism of the Constituent Assembly, and the wild scramble of Thermidorean speculative liberalism, the next four years saw the gradual formation of a national economy, where laissez-faire was tempered with state intervention. Requisition of foodstuffs for the armies and the larger cities was maintained, and at times of crises bread lines reappeared in Paris and elsewhere. The government established a definite control over the foreign exchange and the stock market, and sought to prevent shocking speculative excesses. An unsuccessful attempt was made in 1796 to stabilize the paper currency. The *assignats* had depreciated to from one-three-hundredth to one-four-hundredth of their face value, and the government had long since been obliged to refuse to accept them at par. These *assignats* were now to be stabilized at one-thirtieth of their face value and exchanged on that basis for a new paper money, the *mandats territoriaux*. Holders of these *mandats* were to be given the privilege of using them to buy remaining nationalized lands—including some rich lands in newly acquired Belgium—at a price estimated by the government, without competitive bidding, first come first served. The *mandats* almost immediately depreciated to ten per cent of their face value. Under these conditions, the purchase of nationalized lands was a marvelous bargain, and the absence of competitive bidding an excellent opportunity for political graft. The best of the remaining lands were sold at ridiculous prices.[10]

After this unfortunate experience, however, the Directory returned to a metallic currency, and respectable French business men could count on the benefits of sound money. Inflation had been halted before it reached the extraordinary figures attained during the German inflation of the 1920's. The government continued in financial difficulties, however, and only the supply of precious metals obtained from victorious French armies in Holland, the Germanies and Italy, in addition to that obtained from trade, enabled it to avoid further use of fiat money. The Directory maintained a high tariff policy which gradually developed by agreement with dependent states and allies, into something very much like

[10] A wood in the Gers, bought for 3,000 livres (gold value), produced timber sold at once for 25,000 l.; a large hall in Lyons, bought for 20,000 l., was *rented* two days after for 25,000 l. M. Marion, *Histoire financière*, III, 426.

Napoleon's Continental system, a self-blockade of Europe against English goods.[11] Although this policy was partly inspired by a desire to injure England, and was therefore a war measure, there is in it a strong element of protectionism, of desire to use the power of the government to promote and protect the economic self-sufficiency of the nation-state. Finally, the Directory made a real attempt to promote French industry by encouraging invention, the useful arts, scientific research. Especially under the initiative of François de Neufchâteau, briefly a Director, subsequently Minister of the Interior, steps were taken towards establishing those services which a useful, if not too paternalistic, government can render an enterprising community—agricultural and industrial statistical bureaus, efficient poor relief, improvement of internal communications by canals and roads, industrial planning of all sorts. Already there appears in outline the bourgeois state of the nineteenth century, not by any means as devoted to a hands-off policy in economic life as certain economic theorists would have it.

Nor were the budgetary reforms of the Directory the work of a weak government. Ramel's budget of 1797 cut government expenditures from a thousand millions to some six hundred millions. This reduction was obtained partly by economies in the public services, but chiefly by a sweeping reduction in the interest charges of the public debt. One-third of the debt was consolidated and entered on the Grand-Livre of the public debt as a sacred charge; the other two-thirds simply ceased to receive interest, which was replaced by certificates later repudiated by the honest Consulate. Direct taxes were lowered, but a serious and not wholly unsuccessful attempt was made to collect back taxes, sometimes unpaid for years. In 1798 an important law laid the basis for a national system of assessment and collection of taxes by trained civil servants, under supervision of the Directory. The new system was a permanent improvement on the lax and unjust system of the old régime, and on the haphazard methods of amateur local politicians set up in the early years of the Revolution. Indeed, the whole Napoleonic bureaucracy exists as a nucleus under the Directory. "The Commissioners of the Directory serving in municipal and cantonal administrations were really

[11] E. F. Heckscher, *The Continental System* (Oxford, 1922), 56.

anticipations of the prefects and subprefects, named by the central government, and subject to recall by it."[12] Finally, the whole system of taxes, direct and indirect, was submitted to a careful revision and codification. Indirect taxes, unjust in their unequal incidence on rich and poor, but easy to collect, were increased. The failure of the campaign of 1798, the cutting off of revenues from conquered or protected states (the practical distinction is slight), the revival of party hatreds, all contributed to undermine some of this excellent work by the summer of 1799. Yet economically and financially, France seems further from breakdown on the eve of Eighteenth Brumaire than on several previous occasions since 1789. The Directory, without great courage or determination, had nevertheless managed to do a little better than simply keep things going; it had begun to put France in order.

III. THE FOREIGN POLICY OF THE DIRECTORY

The Thermidorean Convention had made peace with all the important enemies of France, save Austria and England. The Directory made in the first two years of its existence several efforts to conclude a general European peace, efforts which, in spite of the great authority of Sorel to the contrary, deserve to be considered sincere and not unreasonable.[13] Reubell, Alsatian by birth and an ardent advocate of French expansion in the Rhineland, was chiefly responsible for the foreign policy of the Directory in its early years. But he was limited by the opinions of various political circles, one of which, numbering Talleyrand and his banking friends, was very pro-English. Good children of the revolution, the Directors proposed to retain its conquests, which hitherto had been limited to the Gaul of antiquity. Moreover, they were bound by the Constitution of 1795—though French constitutions of the time were hardly very binding—to maintain intact French annexations in Belgium, Savoy, and Nice. They had allied themselves with Holland and with Spain, so recently enemies of the republic, and they intended to support these new allies. England had taken advantage of this situation to seize certain Dutch and Spanish colonies, the Cape of Good

[12] Meynier, *Les coups d'état du Directoire*, III, 126.
[13] R. Guyot, *Le Directoire et la paix de l'Europe* (Paris, 1911), 3.

Hope, Ceylon, Trinidad. In 1796, however, the twenty-seven-year-old Bonaparte began his extraordinary campaign in Italy and events in this region soon altered the whole military and diplomatic situation.

Napoleon Bonaparte has already appeared briefly in these pages at the siege of Toulon and at the Church of Saint-Roch on the 13 Vendémiaire. His rise to the rank of general at twenty-seven was not altogether astonishing in an age of revolution which had seen Saint-Just a Jacobin dictator at twenty-five. He was born at Ajaccio on the island of Corsica, just barely come under French rule, on August 15, 1769, the second son of a large family born to Carlo Buonaparte, a not very active lawyer and a persistent noble.[14] As the son of an impecunious nobleman, he was able to secure a military education in France at the king's expense, and at sixteen was commissioned a second lieutenant of artillery. Neither at school nor in garrison was he happy. His pride suffered from the contrast between his poverty and the wealth of his fellows, and from the scorn which his Italian ways and looks brought upon him. Indeed, the youthful Napoleon appears constantly as the romantic soul in rebellion, never, or rarely, as the calculating realist, as a figure rather Byronic than Machiavellian. The Prometheus in him was never wholly downed, even by the practical politician who guided himself by what the *gros paysan* would think of his policies, and at the Pyramids as at Moscow and on St. Helena, he was always bringing down the fire from heaven.

In these years Napoleon read, and even imitated, Rousseau, absorbed Raynal's *Histoire des Indes* and met its author in person, and (so he claims) read Goethe's *Werther* five times through. In these years, too, he was an ardent Corsican patriot, hoping to follow Paoli as a leader of his countrymen against the hated French. The death of his father brought on a crisis in family affairs, and Napoleon returned to Corsica to help his mother and his incompetent elder brother Joseph reconstruct the family fortune. He seems to have had hopes of achieving this end by literary success. The Revolu-

---

[14] Doubt has been cast by Jung and others on this date, and an attempt has been made to set back Napoleon's birth to the year 1768, in which case he was not born a Frenchman. The literature is summed up in A. Fournier, *Napoleon I*, ed. by E. G. Bourne (New York, 1903), 746-747.

tion found him in garrison again at Auxonne, with the Buonaparte clan still insecurely established.

The Revolution made Napoleon's career possible. But his first attempts to make use of the new opportunities met with apparent failure. He chose Corsica as the scene of his activities (though always maintaining a precarious hold on his commission in the regular army). There, after many shifts of fortune, and after some valuable experience in political manipulation and in minor *coups d'état*, he was defeated by the moderate Paoli, back in triumph from London, and with his whole family was banished from the island in 1793. But he left as a republican and a radical, and the new republican war gave his talents a wider scope than Corsica could ever have afforded. Politically he steered a careful course, avoiding the greatest extremes of Jacobinism, but preserving his orthodoxy. His brother Lucien, indeed, went the whole way, renamed himself "Brutus" Bonaparte, terrorized a little Provençal town, and after Thermidor came very near compromising the whole family. Napoleon's services at the siege of Toulon, however, had won him the gratitude of his superiors, and the Buonapartes survived the Terrors, both Red and White.

For Napoleon was an excellent officer of artillery. Even at school his teachers had acknowledged his mastery of his profession, though they regretted his pride, his temper, and his aloofness. Nor had his reading and his daydreaming centered wholly around Saint-Preux and Werther. He had mastered the chief strategists of his century, Saxe, Guibert, Bourcet, and had fought many a campaign in his mind. Bourcet, whose *Principes de la Guerre de Montagnes* was written about 1764 and circulated among trustworthy students and officers for years (it was not officially printed until 1888), had a very great influence upon Napoleon. The Italian campaign of 1796-97 illustrates several of the precepts of Bourcet, who advocated offensive warfare whenever possible, great mobility and rapidity, division of forces (*in mountainous country only*) for such rapidity of movement, sudden attacks to surprise and disconcert the enemy.

From the siege of Toulon in 1793 to the triumphant appointment as general in command of the army of Italy in 1796, Napoleon's fortunes continued to vary quite according to romantic formula.

A general in 1794, the fall of Robespierre deprived him of his commission, and sent him briefly to prison as a terrorist. At this depth in his career he claims to have contemplated offering his services as an artillery expert to the reforming Turkish Sultan Selim III. Acquaintance with Barras, and the good luck which Napoleon grandly discerned as his "star," gave him a chance to help save the Convention on the 13 Vendémiaire. He had now joined the corrupt set of officeholders, profiteers, and adventurers who were ruling a France quite sick of the Republic of Virtue. Marriage with Josephine Beauharnais, a former mistress of the Director Barras, sealed that alliance, and is commonly considered to have secured Napoleon the command of the army of Italy. The main campaign for 1796 was scheduled for the Germanies. Though Napoleon was known to entertain grand plans of offensive action, no one in authority seems to have taken his appointment as earth-rending. The campaign along the Riviera had slumbered peacefully in its lovely setting for years, and presumably would continue to do so.

The arrival of General Bonaparte (from now on the "u" is dropped) in the French camp was the signal for one of the most startling military campaigns in history. Within a few months Napoleon succeeded in placing himself between the Sardinians and the Austrians, beating them separately and driving them still farther apart, forcing an armistice on the Sardinians, crossing the Po where he was not supposed to, and outflanking the Austrians, entering Milan, and driving the Austrian army into the fortified town of Mantua. Four attempts to relieve the fortress were beaten back in a series of brilliant, if rather risky and unorthodox maneuvers, and on February 2, 1797, the garrison surrendered. As a result of Bonaparte's campaign the numerous petty states of Italy were available to the Directory as diplomatic stakes. North of the Alps, the campaign against Austria was a failure. Jourdan was beaten by the Archduke Charles, who was even younger than Bonaparte, and Moreau, the other leader of what was to have been a converging French march on Vienna, was forced to retreat through the Black Forest.

By the autumn of 1796 the Directory was not unwilling to negotiate for peace. England, sick of the war, suffering commercially from the beginnings of the Continental blockade, her famous fleets in mutiny, her finances disordered by Pitt's insistence on borrowing to meet war expenses, was also willing to negotiate. Lord Malmesbury, an able English diplomat, came to Paris in October, authorized by Pitt to negotiate a separate peace with France. Lord Grenville and the king, however, were able to exercise their influence against a peace with regicide France, and Malmesbury was tied down by rigid instructions not to allow Belgium to France. The negotiations were abandoned in December. In the summer of 1797, however, there was opened at Lille a conference between an English delegation headed by Malmesbury, and three representatives of the Directory, one of whom was Maret, friend of Talleyrand and future Duke of Bassano. The French claimed for themselves the "natural frontiers"—their conquests in Belgium, the Rhineland, Savoy, and Nice—and for their Spanish and Dutch allies the restitution by England of all colonial conquests. The English were apparently willing to concede a great deal, and peace might well have been concluded. The breakdown of negotiations seems to have been due less to directorial intransigeance than to complicated and unofficial intrigues between Maret and other agents of Talleyrand and the English, in which Maret deluded the English with false hopes, and in which Talleyrand probably made a good deal of money by speculation on a stock exchange very sensitive to rumors of war and peace. Of course, it is easy to point out that England could never have tolerated a France permanently installed in Belgium, and that even had the peace been made, even had Napoleon never come, England would sooner or later have gone to war to free the Low Countries. Yet too much credence need not be given this assumption. That England will always go to war to keep a major power out of the Low Countries has not yet taken on the validity of a scientific law. The definite occasion of the abandonment of the conference was the *coup d'état* of Eighteenth Fructidor, which cast upon the defeated Carnot, Barthélemy, and Pichegru the suspicion of being involved in an English plot, and gave the aggressive Reubel a new strength in foreign affairs.

With Austria the Directory—or rather General Bonaparte—made a kind of peace. After the fall of Mantua, Bonaparte had made a very risky stab straight across the Julian Alps towards Vienna, and thanks partly to the weakness and apathy of the army with which the Archduke Charles opposed him, had penetrated to within seventy-five miles of the Austrian capital. Here at Leoben, on April 18, 1797, he signed, without consulting his government at Paris, a preliminary peace, converted six months later, after much bickering and the customary consideration of all sorts of plans of territorial "compensations," into the formal treaty of Campoformio. Now, though the Directory wished above all to round out the natural frontiers of France towards the Rhine, and regarded Italy as just so much bargaining power, Bonaparte, Mediterranean by origin, romantic by age, temperament, and education, was already looking towards Turkey, Egypt, India. He had organized a Cisalpine Republic in Northern Italy, had evolved complicated plans for the future of Italy, had talked about reviving in Greece the memories of Sparta and Athens, had received a deputation of Mainotes from the Morea and informed them that "the French esteem the small, but brave Mainote people, who alone of ancient Greece, have maintained their freedom."[15]

The peace of Campoformio failed, therefore, because it was neither a German peace nor an Italian peace, because it was an unsatisfactory compromise between the ideas of the Directors and the ambitions of Bonaparte. It was quite an orthodox eighteenth-century peace, sacrificing the neutral republic of Venice to the principle of compensation. Austria ceded Belgium to France, recognized the new Cisalpine Republic, and received Venetia in exchange. In secret provisions France was granted the left bank of the Rhine as far as Andernach in return for Salzburg, and express provision was made that Prussia should not be compensated on the right bank for losses on the left. France by secret provisions made at Basel was already pledged to Prussia to secure her precisely this compensation. Reason of state is surely a higher form of reason. Finally, provision was made for a Congress to be held at Rastadt to extend this peace to the empire, and to settle the complicated problems involved by the cession of the left bank to France. The Congress was duly held, and mostly unduly failed. Campoformio was a truce, not a real

[15] Napoleon, *Correspondance* (Paris, 1859), III, 213.

peace, and by the time the Congress of Rastadt had settled down to work, the Second Coalition against France was formed, and ready to begin operations.

For the moment, however, France was at peace with all the world save England and England's perpetual ally, Portugal. There had, it is true, been bad feelings over Jay's treaty, whereby the United States accepted British notions of their rôle as neutrals, in spite of the sentimental ties which should have bound the new nation to its French ally. The attempt of the Directory to enforce the Continental blockade against English goods brought actual conflict with America, a sort of undeclared war limited mostly to privateers, which lasted through most of Adams's administration. The attempt of Talleyrand to extort bribes from commissioners of the young, and still relatively virtuous republic—the episode, familiar to readers of American history, of the "X Y Z papers"—further added to the bitterness on both sides. But the major war of 1798 was against England.

Now England usually got her Continental wars fought for her by paid allies. The allies had dropped off one by one, and Portugal alone remained of the famous First Coalition. On the other hand, England, protected by the Channel, was wholly out of French reach. An "Army of England" was formed, Bonaparte put at its head, and much talk made of an invasion of England. The French navy was incapable of protecting troops crossing the Channel, was not indeed in any shape to risk concentration in the Atlantic. For the navy, the Revolution had been a period of almost uninterrupted decline. Rigorous discipline is even more necessary on sea than on land, and the first days of Liberty, Equality, and Fraternity had injured the navy even more than the army. Moreover, ships are expensive both to build and to maintain. Ships could not protect Paris. Now, as a century earlier, the French were forced to choose between land and sea. They could not possibly spend men and money equally on both. They chose (did they after all have a choice?) the land. Something had to be done, however; an unoccupied military genius simply ceases to be a genius. England, impregnable at home, must be attacked in her empire.

Bonaparte's romantic Egyptian expedition set sail from Toulon on May 19, 1798, bearing some 35,000 soldiers and some dozens of experts and scholars about to found the ornamental science of Egyptology. This expedition will always be a touchstone for the estimation of Napoleon Bonaparte. To the cautious and the prosaic (wise after the fact of the naval disaster of the Nile) it will seem a reckless gamble, destined from the start to failure. To writers of a bolder disposition it will seem a daring stroke of genius, almost successful, and failing only by reason of unpredictable accidents. In the wide sweep of history, the expedition is a part of the long struggle between Europeans and non-Europeans in the Near East, and a culmination of French imperialist designs in that region dating in a sense from the Crusades, and quite precisely from the reign of Louis XIV, when Leibnitz, hoping to draw his attention from the Rhine, suggested to that monarch the occupation of Egypt. All through the eighteenth century the French were active in Egypt, more active, indeed, than the English, who were not fully awakened to the critical relation between India and Egypt until Bonaparte's expedition brought it inescapably to their attention.[16]

In the late nineties various schemes were circulated in French official circles, and a number of important people were occupied with the question of Egypt, notably Magallon, French consul general in Egypt, and Talleyrand, whose influence with the Directory may have proved decisive. Napoleon himself was full of Oriental ambitions, nourished by youthful daydreaming over the pages of Raynal's *Histoire des Indes*, and when it became clear that an invasion of England was impossible, he turned naturally enough to the Egyptian scheme. The hated English enemy was always in the background, even here; the army was told, just before embarcation, that it was still the army of England. Egypt, once in French hands, would be a stepping stone to India, where Tippoo Sahib, in revolt against the English tyrants, would extend a welcoming hand to Frenchmen, and where there had actually been a *Société des Amis de la Constitution de Séringapatam*. Moreover, the Isthmus of Suez

---

[16] F. Charles-Roux, *Autour d'une route: L'Angleterre, l'isthme de Suez et l'Egypte au XVIIIme siècle* (Paris, 1922), 367. This book and the same author's *Les origines de l'expédition d'Egypte* (Paris, 1910) establish in detail the diplomatic and economic background of the expedition; see also H. L. Hoskins, *British Routes to India* (New York, 1928), chap. III.

was the key to the best trade route to the Far East, and a short canal would make the owner of Egypt the mistress of world commerce. The prospects would have tempted a duller man than Napoleon.

There was no power in Egypt itself that could long oppose a good European army. Nominally a part of the Ottoman Empire, Egypt was wholly beyond the rule of Constantinople. The Mamelukes, originally a military bodyguard of the caliphs, formed a highly trained, and, as compared with the Janissaries in Turkey itself, a relatively uncorrupted military ruling caste. Their leaders, the beys, ruled as local lords, and exploited the helpless *fellaheen* in a way to which several millenniums of exploitation had quite accustomed the Egyptian common people. The Mamelukes made up a splendid body of cavalry, some 8,000 strong, but there was no other military force in Egypt, above all no adequate artillery, no trained infantry. Napoleon, having successfully dodged the English fleet, occupied Malta as a halfway station and took Alexandria on July 2. His trained troops, outnumbering the Mamelukes four to one, had little trouble in winning the Battle of the Pyramids, famous for one of Napoleon's characteristic bits of rhetoric: "Soldiers, from the summit of these pyramids forty centuries look down upon you!" The Mamelukes could be beaten in separate encounters, but it was difficult to crush them, since their mobility and skill enabled them to reform after each defeat. Cairo and Alexandria were in Napoleon's hands, however, and had all gone well at sea, the French could no doubt in time have reduced the country.

Disaster struck upon the sea. The French admiral Brueys, unable to get his biggest ships over the bar into Alexandria, and prevented by Bonaparte from following the Directors' order to seek safety in the Ionian Islands, drew up his fleet along the curving shore of Aboukir Bay, in a position he seems to have regarded as safe. Here on August 1, 1798, Nelson, who had played hide-and-seek with the French all over the Mediterranean, at last found his enemy. The French were not expecting the attack, and some of their crews were ashore. The English, though they had fewer ships than the French, accomplished the impossible by skillful and courageous handling of their ships, and by the genius of their leader, and actually turned Brueys's position so as to expose his ships separately to a deadly cross-fire. The French fleet was annihilated, only four ships escaping by flight.

Cut off for good and all from France, the expedition could not possibly succeed. Napoleon characteristically refused to admit defeat, and led his army to the Holy Land in the vague hope, perhaps, of carving out an independent principality for himself. Picturesque details like the pesthouse of Jaffa, the massacre of the Turkish prisoners, the siege of Acre were thereby added to the Napoleonic legend, but of permanent gains to France there could now be little hope. Back in Egypt, Napoleon decided that his star led him to France, where a new war had broken out; so he quietly departed on one of the two frigates still available. As commander-in-chief of the expedition he no doubt had legal power to leave, and furthermore the Directory had just sent for him (though it is not certain that he had received the letter).[17] Morally—at least to those who dislike Napoleon—it will seem that he deserted.

The Egyptian expedition itself played no small part in preparing for this new war of the Second Coalition. Turkey, whose sultan was legally suzerain of Egypt, was provoked into hostilities. French interference in the Levant, initiated by Bonaparte's seizure of the Ionian Islands on his partitioning of the helpless republic of Venice, was a direct defiance of Russia, whose new ruler, Paul, had reversed his mother's policy with respect to the Ottoman Empire, and was setting himself up as protector, curiously enough, of Turkey in the East, and Christianity in the West.[18] On both grounds, the English found it easy to persuade him to join the new coalition. Nor had the Directory been wholly pacific since the peace of Campoformio. Though the great days of republican propaganda were over, the French government was committed, partly through Bonaparte's initiative in Italy, to a policy of buffer republics in Holland and Italy. The necessity of maintaining communication with Italy led to interference in Switzerland, its conquest, and the formation of a Helvetian republic. In Italy, a convenient street-riot at Rome resulted in the death of the French general Duphot, come to wed

---

[17] G. Pariset, *La Révolution, 1792-1799*, 391.
[18] N. de Taube, "Paul I et l'ordre de Malte," *Revue d'histoire moderne* (1930), V, 162.

Désirée Clary, sister-in-law of the French ambassador, Joseph Bonaparte, herself once engaged to Napoleon, and later consoled with the hand of Bernadotte. The French, of course, interfered, helped expel the pope and set up a Roman republic. Austria was thoroughly alarmed by this continued French expansion into a peninsula she had been led to hope would be an Austrian sphere of influence, and was quite willing to listen to English proposals. By the autumn of 1798, the Second Coalition, composed of England, Austria, Russia, Naples, Portugal, and the Ottoman Porte, was constituted against France. An Anglo-Russian army under the Duke of York was to drive the French from the Low Countries, the Austrians under the Archduke Charles were to drive them out of Switzerland, and an Austro-Russian army under Suvorov was to drive them out of Italy.

The first sally of the allies, a Neapolitan invasion of the Roman republic, was a very sad failure. The Neapolitans were driven back into their own country, the king fled to Sicily, and under French protection the last of the Italian republics, the Parthenopean, was set up. The campaign of the Duke of York was disastrous, culminating in an English capitulation at Alkmaar. But in general the armies of the Archduke Charles and of Suvorov were spectacularly successful. In April, 1799, Suvorov's victory at Cassano destroyed the Cisalpine Republic, and made necessary the withdrawal of French troops from Naples, thus leaving the Parthenopean Republic on its own inadequate resources. In the summer the French were beaten north of the Alps at Zurich by the archduke, south of the Alps at Novi by Suvorov. Before autumn—and before Bonaparte's return—Masséna in Switzerland had succeeded in stopping the progress of the allies. Though Italy was lost to France, in October came the news that the Duke of York had surrendered. Holland, Belgium, the left bank of the Rhine were still secure. France was again at war with all Europe, but in no sense was her position as dangerous as it had been in 1792 and in 1793.

IV. EUROPE DURING THE RULE OF THE DIRECTORY

For most of Europe the years 1795 to 1799 brought no great internal changes. England continued in the way marked out by

Pitt in 1793-94, pursuing the war with France ardently enough, with only a slight lapse in 1797, restraining her own radicals firmly, gaining, in spite of the strain of war and war finance, in wealth and population. In Prussia, the death of Frederick William II and the accession of Frederick William III in 1797 had no great immediate consequences. Wöllner was indeed dismissed, the edict of religion revoked, and the reign of ostentatious piety ended. But the great reformation of Prussia was the work of the next decade. The Hapsburg dominions continued, under Francis II, to crystallize into a society anti-revolutionary in the exact sense of that rather loose term—a society whose aims, ideas, institutions are all an assertion of the opposite of the aims, ideas, institutions of revolutionary France. It is not that Austria remained, as the superior liberal historians of the last century put it, "reactionary" or "backward." On the contrary, she developed, evolved, an organized synthesis of traditional elements—feudal, Christian, dynastic, European—which, seen as a whole, seen, if you like, as Metternich's "system," is new. At the extremes of Europe, there is nothing of importance, from the point of European history, in the Spanish or the Scandinavian peninsulas.

In Holland, Switzerland, Italy, and Turkey the period of the Directory is of great importance. In Ireland and in Russia occur events which, though in a sense they are episodic, are yet so characteristic of the development of these two countries that they attain European importance.

The Convention finished by absorbing the "border countries"—Belgium, the Rhineland, Savoy, Nice. The Directory did not directly annex the regions immediately bordering their newly enlarged France, and into which, as if by a natural law of expansion, French armies poured. They adopted the policy of "buffer republics," French-dominated, "satellite" states set up between the great republic and its monarchic enemies. Holland, Switzerland, Italy were carved out into a series of republics with appropriately unreal and ineffective classical names—Batavian, Helvetian, Cispadane, Cisalpine, Ligurian, Roman, Parthenopean. None of these republics was *wholly* imposed from without: in none of them was there lacking a group of native citizens won to French ideas or French interests, and convinced that their new republic was a valid state. In general, however, such men were in a striking minority. In all the republics the majority remained indifferent, if not hostile, to the new régime. In all, the French constantly interfered in matters foreign and domestic. From all the French took, with due regard to their resources, money, works of art, and soldiers. In all the French occupation was to leave permanent trace in the destruction of what was left of feudalism, and in the accentuation, partly out of hatred for the French, of national solidarity.

Many of the defeated anti-Orange, or Patriot, party had fled from Holland to France in 1787, and since the outbreak of the Revolution had absorbed more French ideas than ever, had organized a "Club des Bataves," and had begun to circulate propaganda by pamphlets and journals smuggled into their native land. A Dutch legion accompanied the victorious French army in the invasion of Holland in 1795, and after the flight of the stadholder to England, these old "Patriots" formed a provisional government and negotiated a peace with France—for which they paid 100,000,000 florins, ceded strips of territory on the south, accepted a French garrison of 25,000 troops, and agreed to take *assignats* as legal tender. The banished Prince of Orange ordered colonial garrisons to receive British troops, and in this way the Cape and Ceylon passed permanently out of Dutch hands. Holland was obliged to join in the embargo on British goods. Finally, the Dutch navy, whose officers were almost wholly Orangist in sympathy, was beaten by the English at Camperdown in October, 1797, and never again played an important part in European history. In return for all this, the "Patriots" received a neat constitution on the latest French model—a Directory of five, a First Chamber of 64, a Second Chamber of 30, a neat system of local government by departments and circles which did not in the least coincide with the old provinces. All power was centralized in the national government. The historic federal Republic of the United Netherlands had become a unitary state. In actual political life, a series of *coups d'état*—again on the French model—altered the details of this system, and in 1798 Daendels, who had led the exiled Batavians in Paris, contrived to bring the new republic under the control of the moderates. These moderates assumed a somewhat equivocal—or perhaps merely consistently moderate—attitude during the Duke of York's unsuccessful campaign in North Holland, and were duly punished by Bonaparte, now First Consul. Augereau was sent in 1800 to supervise the installation of a very unified, undemocratic régime. The revolution in Holland had hardly meant more than a change of masters. No profound social change accompanied it. The "unitarians" who supported the Batavian Republic were not proletarians, and their triumphant French supporters were no longer the crusading Jacobins of the Republic of Virtue.

Swiss experience with the Revolution, though in some ways even more painful than that of the Dutch, was perhaps also more profitable. The aristocratic government at Berne maintained a precarious neutrality until 1797, and preserved itself from revolutionary infection. There was, of course, a "Club Helvétique" at Paris, formed chiefly of exiles from Fribourg and from Geneva, where the aristocrats had triumphed in 1781 and 1782 respectively. Many famous names are among them—Clavière, Girondin financier, Etienne Dumont, friend of Mirabeau and translator of Bentham, de Laharpe, liberal tutor of Alexander I. Yet their revolutionary propaganda had little success at home in Switzerland, where there was no court nobility, where privileged aristocrats and burghers perhaps outnumbered unprivileged peasants. By the year 1797, however, the Directory had been drawn by Bonaparte into an aggressive Italian policy, and the Swiss passes—especially the Simplon, over which a road was already projected—became necessary to France. Pretexts for intervention were easily found in disturbances engineered by French agents, an army was marched into Switzerland, rendered totally unable to defend herself by a long period of peace and neutrality, and, with the aid of the two leading Swiss revolutionists, de Laharpe and Peter Ochs of Basel, a Helvetian Republic set up. For the loose federal union of the cantons, a republic "one and indivisible" was, of course, established with a Directory and councils on standard French lines. In the next five years, the new republic was to enjoy six constitutions. The little cantons rebelled at this unification and into certain remote upland valleys the French rule hardly reached. The year 1799 saw disastrous fighting in Swiss territory between the Austro-Russian forces and the French, fighting which left miles of the Swiss countryside in ruins. The Helvetian Republic never took real roots in Switzerland, and Napoleon by the Act of Mediation restored the old Confederation at least in form. Yet the services of the French régime in making modern Switzerland possible were very great. "It proclaimed the equality of citizens before the law, equality of languages, freedom of thought and faith; it created a Swiss citizenship, basis of our modern nationality, and the separation of powers, of which the old régime had no conception; it suppressed internal tariffs and other economic restraints; it unified weights and measures, reformed civil and penal law, authorized mixed marriages (between Catholics and Protestants), suppressed torture and improved justice; it developed education and public works."[19]

The Italian republics, the Cispadane, later enlarged into the Cisalpine, and the Ligurian, in the north, the Roman in the center, the Parthenopean in the south were hardly more than instruments, of French foreign policy, and their boundaries, governments, and political prospects were subject to constant change. Bonaparte, indeed, talked much of Italian destiny from his almost regal court at Mombello in 1797, and did apparently force a reluctant Directory into extending the policy of founding buffer republics into Italy. He did bully the pope into territorial concessions, and permitted the establishment of a Roman Republic at a captive pope's expense. Only to initiates of the Napoleonic faith, however, will it seem that Bonaparte was an Italian patriot, that he really worked knowingly for a free and united Italy. In general, the main outlines of Italian experience have been recounted in Holland and Switzerland—French armies, a unified republic modeled on the government of the Directorate, and installed by the French with the aid of a small group of noisy but unrepresentative natives (they were commonly Masons, anti-clericals, enlightened children of their century, well-organized but definitely a minority), heavy indemnities in gold and works of art handed over to the French, application to the new republic of the social, legal, and political reforms achieved in France, alienation of the bulk of the population and growth of national feeling based

[19] W. Martin, *Histoire de la Suisse* (Paris, 1926), 187-188.

partly on violent hatred of the French. The Francophils in parts of Italy seem at times more than usually servile towards their masters. A Lombard school petitioned the Directory to be taught "the lovely language of the heroes of the Seine" instead of musty Latin.[20]

In the Cisalpine Republic trees of liberty were planted—and villainously cut down or "degraded" by anti-republicans—civic festivals were celebrated, Goddesses of Reason paraded through the streets, and similar manifestations of the new republican faith so heightened by the virtue and numerical smallness of the manifesters that the French Directory itself became alarmed, and interfered to suppress the "men of blood." The Roman Republic was endowed with a Constitution in whose terminology classicism ran wild—five consuls, a Senate, a Tribunate, comitiæ (electoral assemblies), prefects, and ædiles—but which was really simply another, and more authoritarian, copy of the French Constitution of 1795. Bonaparte appears to have had a hand in making this Roman constitution, and he may well have obtained ideas, as he certainly did names, for later use in France.

In this unheroic exploitation of Italy by French armies and by French stereotypes, the brief story of the Parthenopean Republic is tragic and simple. Nor is the rather artless spell which the Bay of Naples has long exerted over the transalpine mind altogether responsible for this distinction. The Parthenopean republic was set up, not without the aid of a French army, but certainly less palpably under French dictation than elsewhere. Its founders were singularly respectable men and women, noblemen, officers, artists, students, "idealists upon whose imaginations there smiled the promise of pure happiness for the human race, and who, thinking to embrace this cosmopolitan abstraction, ran up against the reality of Italy."[21] The reality of Southern Italy in 1799 was, indeed, sufficient to discourage all but the devotees of an immanent, if at present invisible, Nature —an ignorant and superstitious peasantry, an urban population in which workmen looked like beggars, and beggars looked like workmen, a powerful but hardly active clergy, an inefficient government unable to restrain banditry in the interior, an expensive court ruled

[20] A. Visconti, "Tendenze diverse della cultura nel 1774 e nel 1797," *Archivio storico lombardo* (1928), LV, 216.
[21] B. Croce, *Storia del regno di Napoli* (Bari, 1925), 219.

by Queen Marie Caroline, who inherited from her mother Maria Theresa the lust, but not the ability, to govern. When, a few months after the founding of the republic, the French troops under Macdonald were withdrawn to face Suvorov in the north, the proletarian royalist army gathered by Cardinal Ruffo, and known to itself as the "armata cristianissima" succeeded after hard fighting in compelling the republicans to surrender the city of Naples. Lord Nelson, entrusted by the fugitive king, Ferdinand, with full powers, used the English fleet to help in this overthrow, and did nothing to prevent—his enemies claim he actually promoted—the cruel measures of repression taken by the royalists. Eighty-four republicans were executed, and over a thousand exiled. The return of the monarch was celebrated by the death or exile of "prelates, gentlemen, generals, admirals, men of letters, scientists, poets, philosophers, jurists, noblemen, all the intellectual and moral flower of the nation."[22] Yet the very desperateness of this adventure in Utopia, the theatrical contrasts in which it abounded, the ferocity with which it was suppressed, gave it a symbolic after-life denied to the more prosaic republics of Northern and Central Italy. Ferdinand had made the gravest mistake of despots; he had created martyrs, had helped to form a myth to be used against him and his order. The Parthenopean Republic was the first earnest of a new Italy, a more-than-literary source of the Risorgimento.

In the history of Turkey this decade fulfills with striking neatness its apparent historic function as an age of transition. Now first appear the characteristic signs of what will be nineteenth-century Turkey—attempted reforms and continued abuses, internal disorders and external weakness, much individual intelligence, goodwill, and courage pretty well wasted in a society and a state increasingly conscious of being in decline. Many of the difficulties which now appear in striking evidence had been long developing; but the hammer-blows of the Russian armies in Catherine's two great wars seem to have shattered whatever held Turkey together, and to have brought out weaknesses hitherto not inescapably apparent.

In form an autocratic centralized monarchy, Turkey in 1789 was in reality a congeries of despotisms, in which the sultan was almost

[22] B. Croce, *Storia di Napoli*, 223.

powerless before the complexity of the machinery of government. Egypt, Tripoli, Tunis, and Algiers were now only nominally a part of the Ottoman Empire. In Anatolia and in Bosnia, and to a certain extent throughout the empire the ultimate military and financial power lay in the hands of a feudal fighting class, the *sipahi*, now much corrupted by opportunities for financial exploitation and governmental intrigue. The old territorial subdivisions of the central power had fallen into the hands of local lords, the *pashas*, recruited partly from the feudal landowners, partly from adventurers and politicians at Stambul and elsewhere. The pashas were extraordinarily independent of the central power, to which indeed they frequently owed their installation, and exploited their governments for what they were worth. Taxation, which was partly arbitrary, partly determined by a financial board in Stambul, was farmed out, and gave wide scope for quick enrichment and for petty tyrannies. Even at Stambul the central government was poorly organized, with a multiplicity of boards, and depended for coordination largely on the personality of the grand vizier. That officer was always in a position compared with which that of a French or English minister was security itself, for his tenure was at the mercy of harem plots, of the temper of the sultan, of the intrigues of his rivals, and even of distant pashas, and, finally, of the powerful military corps of the Janissaries.

The Janissaries play in the decline of Turkey a rôle inevitably to be compared with that of the Prætorian Guard at Rome. Actually the peculiar form taken on by the Janissaries in their final corruption is not quite like anything else in history, for in the end they formed a special interest transversing Turkish society almost from top to bottom, an impossible compound, if you will, of the Prætorians and Tammany Hall. Earlier a chosen band of soldiers of the sultan, taken in infancy from infidel families, brought up in fanatical devotion to Islam, sworn to celibacy, and living in barracks in strict military discipline, the Janissaries in 1789 were hardly to be recognized in their original constitution. Membership, and the emoluments of membership, had become, like offices under the French monarchy, hereditary and venal. Celibacy and barracks life were abandoned, and even the military requirements were maintained only in skeleton form. A given barracks might be staffed with a couple of veterans, a color-bearer, a cook, and a few orderlies, while a huge sum, allotted to maintain the equivalent of a European regiment, would go to the most varied collection of individuals, even to tailors and other artisans.[23] This strange band was held together only by solidarity of interests and by its attachment to its privileges. Naturally it was wholly conservative, and nicely organized by the accident of its historical accumulations to resist any kind of reform.

Turkish failure against Catherine was in itself a symptom of decay. In the next decade or so, other symptoms appeared with unmistakable clarity. Disbanded soldiers, outlaws, criminals, restless men of all sorts banded together and pillaged whole regions. These robber bands (mountain rebels, or simply mountaineers, taghli, from their retreats) were especially strong in Macedonia, but on a smaller scale they could be found almost everywhere. Worse yet, some of the leading pashas broke into open rebellion, like the famous Ali Tepelen in Albania, or like many of the great Anatolian lords, the dere beys, defied governmental attempts at reform. The most extraordinary of these men was really a robber baron whose success forced the sultan to recognize him as pasha. This was Pasvan Oglu, who seized Vidin on the Danube, beat off an army of 40,000 sent in 1796 to apprehend him, and another of 100,000 in 1798, and administered Vidin and its region not at all badly until his death in 1807. Egypt fell to Napoleon in 1798, and French troops invaded Syria. Early in the new century the heretic Wahabis of central Arabia captured holy Mecca, a serious blow to Ottoman prestige. Finally, the conquered Christian provinces were restless. The great revival of Balkan nationalism, especially in Serbia, barely began to stir in this decade. The Greek patriot Rhigas, however, now organized the first hetairia (revolutionary fellowship), translated the "Marseillaise" into modern Greek, and, distantly at least under the influence of the French Revolution, the movement for Greek independence was fairly begun.

It must not be supposed that all Turkey stood by helpless before

[23] O. von Schlechta-Wssehrd, Die Revolutionen in Constantinopel in den Jahren 1807 und 1808 (Vienna, 1882), 11.

this disintegration. As a matter of fact, there came to the throne in 1789 the first of the modern reforming sultans. Selim III was, for a product of the seraglio, a surprisingly open-minded and well-meaning young man. He lacked strength of character, however, was too fond of parading his liberalism, and in the end the forces of inertia proved too strong for him. His chief interest lay in military and financial reform, and no doubt he rightly found there the chief weakness of the Turkish state. He attempted to organize a new model army, with definite enlistments and promotions, uniforms, European arms (the bayonet instead of the scimitar, for instance), an adequate artillery, European training and discipline, and to pay for this army by special taxes earmarked for the purpose. The Janissaries and their innumerable allies in the government pretty effectively prevented his new army from attaining success. By 1799, after four years of the reform, Selim could summon barely a battalion of 1,600 men instead of the 12,000 he had planned, and these were ill disciplined and ill equipped. The new taxes went rather to favorites than to the army. Yet even this slight reform angered the conservatives. Selim, moreover, like Joseph II, offended by his extremes the delicate susceptibilities of his countrymen. He was said to have planned a school of European languages in Constantinople (a shocking impiety to a true Mohammedan), he traveled on Fridays, and he had a portrait of himself engraved in London, in spite of the Mohammedan law which forbade pictorial representation of the human figure.[24] His enemies brought about his fall in 1807, and postponed their difficulties for a while.

Both in Dublin and in Belfast—and the coupling is significant—the French Revolution was greeted with rejoicing. At the news of July 14, 1789, "volunteers swept through the streets in triumphal processions, while artillery discharged salvoes along the quays and great thoroughfares. Banners were carried displaying portraits of the French leaders and bearing such mottoes as 'Our Gallic brother was born 14th July 1789—alas! We are still in embryo!' "[25] The Irish Parliament had secured legislative independence in 1782, but as Catholics were excluded from the franchise by law, and the

[24] O. von Schlechta-Wssehrd, *Die Revolutionen in Constantinopel,* 68.
[25] R. Hayes, *Ireland and Irishmen in the French Revolution* (London, 1932), 12.

Presbyterians by social custom, Ireland continued under the rule of a minority of Anglican landowners. The promise of freedom brought by the French Revolution was eagerly accepted by Ulster Presbyterians, who had given many good radicals to the American republic, less eagerly by the mass of oppressed Catholics. Under Wolf Tone, son of a coachmaker, Protestant, educated for the bar, Protestant and Catholic were joined together in the Society of United Irishmen, who, after the declaration of war between England and France, committed themselves to complete secession from England. The United Irishmen were a secret society organized to spread propaganda and to attempt the political education of the Irish peasant. Under the leadership of Lord Edward Fitzgerald, second son of the Duke of Leinster, the society assumed a semi-military form. At the same time there came sporadic outbreaks in Ulster and northern Leinster between the militant Protestant "Peep o' Day Boys" and the Catholic "Defenders," outbreaks symptomatic of the profound and longstanding economic and cultural differences between the North and the South. Though these forced evictions, burnings and shootings were wholly contrary to the peace between Catholic and Protestant which the United Irishmen wanted, they did contribute to make Irish disorders evident to the English rulers. In 1795, Lord Fitzwilliam was sent over to Ireland as lord lieutenant, presumably to settle matters by granting to the Catholic gentry the right to sit in Parliament, a concession without which the franchise recently granted to Catholics would be useless. Fitzwilliam's mission has been the subject of endless dispute; it is quite possible that he exceeded his instructions by dismissing important figures in the Irish bureaucracy. At any rate he was recalled with the Catholics still unemancipated, and Ireland was given over by Pitt to its garrison.

With Fitzwilliam's recall the plan for an Irish rebellion gained precision. Plans were made for a French descent in Munster to serve as signal for an Irish rising. Hoche, a genuine republican, was given command, and in December, 1796, set out from Brest with some 15,000 soldiers. Bad weather and poor seamanship held the fleet off Bantry Bay, and separated Hoche wholly from his command. The French sailed off without touching Irish soil. Next year the rebellion began without French aid. The English government at Dublin acted quickly, however, arresting Thomas Emmet, Arthur O'Connor and other civilian leaders, taking Lord Edward Fitzgerald in a street-scuffle, and in general making use of their excellent spy and police service to stop trouble before it could develop seriously. In spite of these precautions, the Irish got temporary control of Wicklow and Wexford, formed a mob into a semblance of military order, and were only put down after a pitched battle at Vinegar Hill, June 21, 1798. Next year a French force of some 1,000 men under General Humbert did succeed in landing at Killala in Mayo, and maintained itself for a while against English troops much softened and undisciplined by service against unorganized civilians. But the illiterate peasants of Connaught hardly knew what Humbert was about, and refused to support him, making his surrender inevitable. Tone was caught on board a French ship attempting another raid in October, 1799, and hanged at once, adding another figure to the long and miscellaneous Irish martyrology.

The Rebellion of 1798 failed largely because Presbyterians and Catholics were not as united as the United Irishmen would have them, because the English machinery of repression was most effectively organized, because the bulk of Catholic peasants were uneducated, poor, suffering from economic ills, insufficiently lighted by hope of better days. It is probable that it failed also because the Catholic clergy, the only leaders who could make themselves understood to the poorer classes, were frightened by the attitude of the French Revolution to the church, and felt even England and Pitt less a menace to their faith than France and Tone. The rebellion is, however, a crucial factor in the subsequent history of Ireland. For the Rebellion, in Pitt's mind, meant that the union of Ireland and England was a necessary step; and the Union of 1801, forced upon an unwilling Ireland by intrigue and corruption, meant that true union would henceforth be impossible.

In Russia, the real importance of Paul I's brief reign (1796-1801) is usually overshadowed by the wealth of stories about his eccentricities, and by the dramatic circumstances of his assassination. Paul had been well educated, if not well brought up, had acquired a great admiration for Frederick II, and a great dislike and fear of his mother. He was a bright young man, vain beyond the common,

and certainly beyond most kings, extremely impatient, wholly un-
restrained by any discipline from above, afflicted, probably, with a
nervous instability always on the edge of insanity. Catherine seems
to have been on the point of arranging to pass over him and give the
throne to his son and her grandson, Alexander, when she died.[26]
Paul in his brief reign did two very important things: he began the
extension of Russian power to the south by means of friendly relations with Turkey, by espousing the cause of the Knights of Malta
against France, by entering into the Second Coalition to defend the
Levant from French aggression; and he began the modern emancipation of the Russian serf through imperial policy. Catherine's reign
had seen the low point reached by the serf; in spite of her "enlightenment," she had, for instance, permitted the extension of serfdom by
pripiska, to bastards, orphans, and sons of minor officials, a process
which went on all through the century. Paul's ukase of April 5, 1797,
made a modest beginning of reform, limiting the amount of labor
required from the serf to three days a week. Measures were taken
to limit the governmental action of Catherine's nobility. Paul's reforms—and they extended to absurd details of army drill—were met
by verbal acceptance and actual sabotage. His mental health, impaired at his accession, broke down under this subtle resistance, and
he became the tsar of tradition. Kluchevsky has admirably summarized his fate: "This participation of rancour and hysteria in the
Emperor's policy caused the latter to become a policy pathological
rather than political, and to comprise passing, impulsive moods
rather than thought-out ideas and well-pondered aspirations, and to
lead to the fact that the extensive reform program with which he
acceded gradually crumbled down to superficial, unimportant trifles,
and that the struggle with systems became mere persecution of individuals, and that the hostility to class privilege became merged into
suppression of elementary human rights, and that the notions of
equality and orderliness yielded to fits alternately of cruelty and
kindliness, yielded to the political "scenes" which mostly composed
his reign."[27] On March 23, 1801, a palace revolution ended the life

[26] K. Waliszewski, *Paul I* (London, 1913), 73.
[27] Kluchevsky, *Russia*, V, 125.

of this far from ordinary tyrant, and placed his handsome and apparently wholly normal young son Alexander I on the throne.

V. BRUMAIRE

Bonaparte, having deserted his army in Egypt, landed at Fréjus in the south of France on October 9, 1799. One month later he became, as First Consul, titular head of the republic, in actual fact its master. Now this sudden elevation lay in no simple "logic of history." The government of the Directory was not strikingly efficient, nor popular, but it was neither corrupt nor incompetent. It was a pedestrian, unimaginative, moderate government, quite capable of holding the new France together. French victories in Switzerland and in Holland had relieved the pressure towards executive centralization always attendant upon military defeat during this revolution. Power was not thrust upon Bonaparte by necessity. He seized it by an act of aggression. Many factors made that seizure possible. Moderates all over France were worried by such measures as the law of hostages and the forced loan, both put through by the new Jacobin thrust of 1799. The army, raised up by the Jacobin Carnot, had come to have a loyalty of its own, had come to detest the "lawyers" of the councils, to feel that the republic existed only through its fighting men. Siéyès, who still retained a mysterious reputation for political wisdom, had been raised to the Directory; and Siéyès still felt the itch for constitution-making. *Coups d'état* had come to be the accepted means of achieving political change, of redressing a balance bent too heavily to Right or Left. The last *coup* had gone too far to the Left. Most of those who aided Bonaparte can hardly have thought they were doing more than pushing the republic back again towards the Right.

Back in Paris—without any great popular acclaim—Bonaparte began sounding out the politicians and the generals. After some hesitations, he arranged a coalition with Siéyès. Two other Directors, Barras and Roger-Ducos, were won to the plot, thus making it possible to issue legally the administrative decrees necessary to begin the *coup*. On the pretext of danger from a Jacobin rising the councils were summoned to meet at Saint-Cloud, some miles outside Paris and safe from its mob. The three Directors in the plot then resigned, and the other two were arrested. When the councils met on the 19 Brumaire there was thus no Directory. Bonaparate had simply to appear before them, explain that the fatherland was in danger, and ask from the legal government of France power to remake that government. Just this sort of thing had already been successfully done in the buffer republics, at Amsterdam and at Milan. Bonaparte, whose talents were not parliamentarian, made a sad failure of his appearance before the Five Hundred. Challenged to disclose the pretended plot against the safety of the republic that made his proposed measures necessary, he could make no satisfactory reply. Cries of "Outlaw him" arose, and deputies swarmed towards him with outstretched daggers and flowing togas. Only the presence of mind of his brother Lucien, then president of the council, enabled him to escape in safety. All pretense of legality had now to be abandoned. Bonaparte had provided himself with troops, and these he now sent to clear the squabbling lawyers from the hall at the point of the bayonet. The lawyers left in unheroic haste. Later a rump council composed of friends of the conspirators was assembled, and voted to entrust power to these "temporary consuls," Bonaparte, Siéyès, and Roger-Ducos. At last the forebodings of Burke had proved true. After the Eighteenth Brumaire a single man, a soldier, ruled over twenty-five million free Frenchmen far more absolutely than Louis XVI had ruled over his enslaved subjects.

> Ma di dicembre, ma di brumaio
> cruento è il fango, la nebbia è perfida:
> non crescono arbusti a quell 'aure,
> o dan frutti di cenere e tòsco.[28]

[28] G. Carducci, *Odi Barbare: Per la morte di Napoleone Eugenio.*

Chapter Ten

THE ARTS AND SCIENCES IN REVOLUTIONARY EUROPE

I. DEFINITIONS

YOU CANNOT crib your new historian within the exacting confines of a chronology politically established. For social, economic, and intellectual history do not always fit into the time-scheme of political events. This is strikingly true of the period of the French Revolution. One cannot, following recent fashion, label the years from 1789 to 1799 the "purple decade," or "the roaring nineties." Good Tories might argue for the "red decade," but quite apart from the fact that revolutionary violence has subsequently been at least as intense and even more widespread, the epithet "red" is not aptly applied to the paintings of David, the poetry of Chénier and Cowper, or the music of Mozart and Haydn. Indeed, the simplest and hastiest of generalizations on the cultural achievements of these years of revolution would be that they were almost wholly conservative, conventional, mere patternings after earlier eighteenth-century models. Such a generalization would certainly have the support of statistics. A patient seeker after the Ph.D. in English Literature could no doubt establish that during this decade more poetry was written in the traditional form of the heroic couplet than in all other forms combined. Though *Lyrical Ballads* appeared in 1798, the poetry of Gifford was undoubtedly more widely read at the moment than the poetry of Wordsworth and Coleridge. In France, established canons of criticism were not even threatened with a Fourteenth of July or Fourth of August. In the widest sense, these changes go back to the beginnings of modern history in Renaissance and Reformation. They are still working themselves out in the contemporary world. One of their focal points, however, one of the periods of their greatest intensity as change, would appear to be the fifty years from 1780 to 1830.

The decade with which this study is concerned is a part of the transition between what historians of the arts have pretty well agreed to call neo-classicism and what they unanimously call romanticism. It is a transition singularly uneven in different countries and in different arts, but by 1800 the romantic spirit was almost everywhere well on the way to triumph, though the fact of that triumph was not yet apparent to conservative admirers of things Augustan.

Now "romanticism" is a Protean word, and one that has long been shuttled back and forth by critics with a cause to defend and enemies to slay. Perhaps it is impossible to give the word exact definition; or rather, you may give it any exact definition you like, and you can always dig up examples to fit your definition. Romanticism is conservative, even reactionary, in politics: there stand Burke, Chateaubriand, Maistre, Scott, the converted Schlegels, the repentant Fichte. Romanticism is liberal, even wildly radical in politics: there are Shelley, Byron, Heine, the mature Hugo, and Lamartine. Romanticism is philosophically realist (in the medieval sense): you may line up Hegel, Coleridge, Carlyle, Edgar Quinet. Romanticism is philosophically nominalist: in proof thereof call up Godwin, Robert Owen, Mill, Comte. Romanticism is a wild chase after the blue flower, and all romanticists are aflame with the desire of the moth for the star: Blake, Novalis, Berlioz, Shelley were crazy enough. Romanticism is pretty sensible after all: Scott and Hazlitt wrote sensibly, Southey at least lived sensibly, Chateaubriand sobered down and Byron was about to when he died, de Vigny remained a gentleman, and even in Germany Goethe lived to be ashamed of *Werther*.

Perhaps the best definition of romanticism is the works of the romantics, and an attempt will be made in the following pages to bring some of the earliest of them briefly before the reader. But the issue cannot wholly be dodged here. It would seem wise to give to the word romanticism a meaning that might include some of the opposites cited above, to stretch it to include the spirit of the age, the climate of opinion of the early nineteenth century. Very different men can manage to live in the same climate. In a real sense Carlyle and Mill were brother romantics.

For in spite of its multanimity, in spite of its lack of a single style or a single faith, the European world of the half-century or so following the French Revolution had at least one tenuous kind of unity, one determining and constant factor in its climate of opinion: change—change in manners, morals, institutions, business, art—was accepted as inevitable. Dispute might range from the desirability of a particular change to the metaphysical reality of all change. Most men came, indeed, to associate change with growth, with life. The nineteenth century found it difficult to conceive a static society, which is one reason why the idea of a Christian heaven had so little hold even over Christians. Now any change is, though in the most attenuate sense, a revolution of a sort. The nineteenth century was built upon revolutions. There is an intellectual attitude bred by this atmosphere of change, an intellectual attitude not quite like that of Plato, or Aquinas, or even of the Augustans of the previous century. This intellectual attitude is here called romantic. Without it, the doctrine of evolution, which almost served as a faith for the next century, could never have come into popular esteem.

The least ambiguous external manifestation of this intellectual attitude, the least confused with older habits of mind and with newer material diversions, is afforded by the nineteenth-century attitude towards history. Tory, liberal, radical, Scott, Hallam, Cobbett (and similarly in other countries), men of all shades of political opinion turned for justification to history. What all of them saw in history was a social *process*, a *growing*, which worked, and was working, slowly and mysteriously in human beings, altering them and therefore their mutual relations as life must alter any organism. History was no longer, as it had been to the eighteenth century, "philosophy teaching by example," a storehouse from which a past experience could be removed to serve again, a collection of old tools which might always prove handy. History became the living past, in the sense that every nationalist, every reformer, every defender of a pattern of values saw history as the birth and youth of his own particular cause—a cause now, of course, fully ripened to maturity.

The full implications of this attitude towards history—which we now see to involve a pretty complete acceptance of flux, or relativity —were not appreciated by the first generation of romanticism. Hegel, for instance, after providing in his dialectic an excellent formally and professionally philosophical translation of this romantic unrest, came to what he regarded as a safe stop in the Prussian state. Prussia, apparently, was one synthesis that did not immediately beget its antithesis. But Marx was to remedy that. This fate of the conservative Hegel may well serve as a type case. Romanticism was never successfully conservative in the narrow sense of the word which implies a refusal to accept any change whatever, and a study of the romantic use of history does but confirm what was already apparent in the romantic necessity for revolt. "But that intrinsically this thought was progressive, and even revolutionary, was unconsciously confessed by the parallelism in which Fichte, Hegel, and others with them placed the two revolutions, that of the French, which was political, and contemporary with it, that of the Germans, which was intellectual."[1] We are today still sufficiently good children of the nineteenth century so that heredity seems an undeniable fact. So when we see Hegel giving birth to Marx, Maistre to Comte, Coleridge to F. D. Maurice, we feel that the fathers of these radicals must themselves have had some radicalism in their constitutions. And rightly, for the Romantic Revolution was as real as the French and the Industrial Revolutions, and complemented rather than opposed them.

Romanticism is, no doubt, in part the rebellion of an educated but uncultivated middle class against the formalized taste and rules of an aristocracy. It is also in part the revulsion of human beings from a life overintellectualized, overrationalized, at once overcomplicated and oversimplified, towards a life more filled with the freshness, the uncertainty, and the consolation of emotion. It is, if you like, a return to the animal in man. But above all it is the acceptance of the inadequacy of any formal set of values, the free acceptance of the perpetual adventure which is the creation of values. Its logical end, perhaps, is the modern doctrine of relativity. Yet many who are called romanticists, and who do for certain great works deserve that name, sought to fix their own value systems with as much rigor of absolutism as did the Boileaus, the Popes, and the Johnsons from whom they rebelled. The great romantics were not quite Heracliteans, and whirl was never king in early nineteenth-century Europe. Shall we say, rather, a whole storm of little whirls?

[1] B. Croce, *History of Europe in the Nineteenth Century* (New York, 1933), 86.

II. THE FINE ARTS

On the whole, the full acceptance of romantic values had to await the working-out of the French Revolution. There is no more striking example of the lag of one aspect of the human spirit behind another than that provided by the fine arts in the decade 1789-1799. Politically a period of experiment, artistically the decade, especially in France itself, was marked by an almost pedantic patterning after the antique. True, the rigor of classical standards, the insistence on simplicity of form, the rejection of rococo ornament resulted in something new at least to contemporaries. The paintings of David do not resemble the paintings of Watteau. Yet in architecture and in the making of furniture the trend towards neo-classical simplicity had set in well before the outbreak of the Revolution. Architecturally, indeed, the eighteenth century is far from a triumph of rococo. Throughout its course are to be found buildings of an almost stark simplicity, put together conscientiously, if not always happily, from elements strictly classical. If the century saw the Zwinger at Dresden, Sans-Souci at Potsdam, if it saw the south of Italy covered with rococo churches, it also saw Santa Maria Maggiore at Rome, Saint-Sulpice at Paris, the royal palace at Berlin, and many other classic fronts which would have satisfied the taste of the First French Empire. Especially in England, Palladio was supreme during most of the century and rococo architecture never got a foothold. French furniture of the period of Louis XVI had already abandoned curves for straight lines, fantasy for geometry, and sought in classical archæology for its decoration. Its classicism was far from pedantic, however, and it succeeded in accommodating itself miraculously enough to the current taste for Oriental and other novelties, to the fragile, decadent grace of the last days of the court of Versailles.

With the French Revolution and the consequent return to a more-than-Plutarchian virtue, this tendency to imitation of the classic style was intensified into a pretty servile aping of republican Rome and Athens. Throughout the Western world the movement since known as "neo-classic" spread, until upper New York was grotesquely covered with Uticas and Syracuses, with Tullys, Scipios, and Semproniuses, and Doric fronts adorned a thousand American bank buildings. The style pervaded all the minor arts of decoration, and served well the purposes of republican propaganda. Its full bloom, however, came in the days of Napoleon, when the historical emphasis was appropriately shifted from republican Rome to the Rome of the Cæsars. In painting, the work of David has survived fashion, and his Mme. Récamier, his murdered Marat, his Rape of the Sabine Women, his Coronation of Napoleon are inevitable parts of a historical survey of the arts. Now that the contempt in which he was held by the ardent romantic colorists of the early nineteenth century has lost force, David's reputation as one of the founders of modern painting seems secure. A careful, though not pedantic, draftsman, a master of the art of grouping, a good observer, in his portraits frequently a notable realist, David is far from adequately summed up as a neo-classicist. His famous sketch of Marie Antoinette on her way to the guillotine fixes in a few strokes a painful rather than a tragic reality. (Perhaps reality is never tragic.)

In architecture the age produced no great monument. The sweep of the Rue Royale at Paris, blocked at one end by the Madeleine, an exact but somehow unfaithful enlargement of the Maison Carrée at Nîmes, at the other by the Palais Bourbon, is a good and familiar example of what neo-classic architecture could do. So, too, is the heavy Brandenburger Tor at Berlin. Sculpture followed logically the archæological interests of the eighteenth century in classical antiquity, retaining in the work of Canova a kind of softness and sentimentality lacking in architecture, acquiring in the work of Thorvaldsen a robust melancholy already a bit romantic. Neo-classic furniture is known accurately enough as the Empire style, though its beginnings date from the Revolution. Here everything is massive, simple, straight legged, upholstered in rather harsh yellows and browns, consciously avoiding fantasy and the grace of the boudoir, the grandeur that was Rome rather unhappily confined by the cabinetmaker. The pundit of the neo-classic style is the German archæologist and art critic Winckelmann, now somewhat dry and staled, but once capable of inspiring Goethe.

The vices of the style are apparent. Neo-classicism in the fine arts was a pedantic revival of an epoch in time and space that had little in common with the Northern and Western Europe of cold, damp winters, of Adam Smith and Cartwright, of a home-loving middle class fond of comfort and ill at ease in palaces, longing to find in fantasy, prettiness, and varied detail some solace for the dullness of their daily routine of life. The newly-rich of 1800 were for a time dazzled by the aristocratic prestige of the monumental and the simple; but their true spiritual home was to be in the mechanical finery of a revived and distorted Gothic. In the arts as in letters, neo-classicism was a discipline that could not long bind energies too great for it. Yet it was at least a style—in the plastic arts perhaps the last style the Western world has known, for the Victorian is less a style than a medley and the *style moderne* is still a luxury, if not an anarchy. For the last time in Europe and in America, cabinet-maker, architect, engraver, painter, sculptor of the late eighteenth and early nineteenth centuries still worked together in a harmonious scheme.

Some signs of the coming storm of romanticism are to be distinguished in the work of the period. The English landscape painters had already gone back to nature, not to the nature of the idyllic eighteenth-century convention, but to the homely England of rocks, trees, hedges and brooks from which Wordsworth leaped off into infinity. The work of the Norwich school and of Constable revived the landscape, and formed the basis for the frankly romantic work of the Fontainebleau school in the next century. In France, David's contemporary Prud'hon never accepted the neo-classic restraint, went back rather to an imaginary Greece than to a scholarly reconstructed Rome. His work is poetic in the romantic sense of the word,—indeed, the only sense in which the word can be applied to painting,—his figures graceful and a bit drooping, his light too caressing for this world. Prud'hon's Greece is the Greece of Longus, not of Pericles. Even before 1789, the Gothic revival had begun. Horace Walpole had built a supposedly medieval villa at Strawberry hill, and all through the 1790's an Englishman named Carter contributed to the *Gentleman's Magazine* a series of letters on "The Pursuits of Architectural Innovation," in which he upbraided irreverent restorers of England's medieval buildings, and suggested that, since the style was obviously English in origin, the uncomplimentary description "Gothic" be dropped in favor of the glorious adjective "English." Self-conscious and aggressive nationalism, in art almost an unknown thing in an eighteenth century whose taste was formed after that of Versailles, was beginning to take its place in the formation of the new romanticism.

Music is, of all the arts, the most difficult to fit into a synthesis at bottom sociological. Possibly music is above sociology. If the work of composers like Schubert, Berlioz, and Chopin is evidently a part of the world of de Musset, Heine, and Byron, if then their work is demonstrably romantic, the music of the decade from 1789 to 1799 is pretty clearly of another world. The French Revolution was not a revolution in music. Mozart is incomparably the greatest composer of the period, and much of his best music was written in this decade. Now, though Mozart was an experimentalist of genius, though often his harmony has a "modern" ring that shocked the orthodox of his day, he can hardly be labeled a preromantic, and, indeed, true romanticists to this day find him lacking in soulful depths. Haydn, too, belongs to eighteenth-century music. The Frenchmen—all minor people, Grétry, Méhul, Gossec, Gaveaux—wrote operas and provided the music for the *"chants nationaux"* of revolutionary propaganda, but always in the style of their unrevolutionary predecessors. Beethoven, in whom if you wish you may discern romanticism, did not ripen until the next decade. Program music—the attempt to imitate in music the world of nature, bird calls, moonlight, spring awakenings—is sometimes taken to be a specific sign of romanticism in music, and does indeed form a part of that appeal from the salon to field and forest which helped make the romantic movement. Unfortunately for those whose wish to synchronize the arts exactly with other forms of human activity, program music existed in the eighteenth century as well as in the nineteenth. Beethoven's cuckoo was not the first bird to sing in European music.

III. LETTERS

Although the French Revolution profoundly affected all European literature, other and earlier forces were at work in the decade from 1789 to 1799, and taken within its narrow chronological limits the decade has no especial significance in the history of literature.

If, however, the latter part of the eighteenth century and the first years of the nineteenth be taken as a transition between the Augustan security of Boileau and Pope and the romantic restlessness of Byron, de Musset, and Heine—a generalization in itself dangerously simple—then this decade is certainly an important element in the transition, especially in England and in Germany. Cultivated taste, the taste of the upper classes, still accepted Augustan standards. In England and Germany as in France and Italy, gentlemen knew their Latin if not their Greek. Addison and Pope, Boileau, Voltaire the dramatist, and their German imitators were still in high honor. Samuel Johnson the writer was still at least as important as Samuel Johnson the man. The minor poets—an Abbé Delille, for instance— still tried to write as Boileau had written or continued the insipidities of the Italian Arcadians, or turned, like the English Della-Cruscans, to rococo conceits.

The eighteenth century is not simply the era of common sense and good taste. Towards its end, however, even that sort of writing which is most fittingly reckoned as anticipative of romanticism— briefly, its bourgeois as opposed to its noble literature—seem to have reached an impotence almost as complete as that reached by neo-classic forms. Sentimental drama, a protest against the unities, and what is more important, against the classic concept of tragic guilt and punishment, reached in this decade with the plays of Kotzebue and the *Pizarro* of Sheridan a lachrymose puerility that makes a Delille or an Erasmus Darwin seem a well-rounded man. The novel had wandered off into the horrors of Gothic romance, or had gone beyond Rousseau and Richardson into a sentimentality one hopes is far less "natural" than is Augustan decorum. *"Sturm und Drang"* had stormed itself out, and both Goethe and Schiller were recovering from the excesses and the hopes of their youth. The essay form of the *Spectator* had been exhausted by countless imitators of Addison and Steele, and no new Defoe had risen to give life to middle-class prejudices. The generation of the Encyclopædists had done its work.

Yet the decade was not entirely barren, and in the major literatures the perspective of time has singled out some few great works. In France itself there is now little left. Frenchmen were forced to occupy themselves otherwise than with literature. Oratory and journalism—neither of which can often be included among the highest flights of the human spirit—did, indeed, flourish. For the rest, André Chénier alone has survived among the masters of French literature. Born in Constantinople of a Greek mother and a French father, Chenier had his Greek at first hand. He welcomed the Revolution with a fine ode on the *Jeu de Paume*, and entered political journalism on the side of the temperate revolutionaries. The excesses of the Terror disgusted him, and he enlisted openly against the Mountain. Arrested and tried as a suspect, he was guillotined in 1794 at the age of thirty-two. He has left some unforgettable poetry, elegiacs in the best tradition of the Greek Anthology, and passionate outbursts against the barbarians who were destroying his France. There is in Chénier, as in the painter Prud'hon, a softness alien to the deliberate Roman severity of neo-classic fashion, yet he cannot justly be labeled a pre-romantic. His masterpiece, perhaps, is *La Jeune Captive*, an elegy of faultless structure, of unforced harmonies, filled with a sadness quite pure of self-pity. Irony as well as hatred runs through the anti-revolutionary poetry of his prison days, but it is the controlled irony of a man sure of himself and of his value judgments, never the anchorless irony of the true romantic.

In English letters the publication of *Lyrical Ballads* in 1798 marks an epoch—a mark quite unnoticed at the time. In this anonymous joint publication, Wordsworth and Coleridge found themselves after a youthful groping among Rousseauistic sentimentality, Godwinian perfectibility, and French revolutionary optimism. To *Lyrical Ballads* Coleridge contributed the "Lay of the Ancient Mariner," dressed up in this edition with all sorts of obsolete spellings to recapture a suitably superstitious past, and three minor poems. Among Wordsworth's nineteen contributions are to be found many of his most quoted and most derided shorter poems— "Goody Blake and Harry Gill," "The Thorn," "We Are Seven," "Lines Written a Few Miles above Tintern Abbey." The two writers had little in common save a somewhat unstable friendship and a very intransigent scorn for contemporary English poets. Both threw over the heroic couplet, eighteenth-century diction, and common sense. Coleridge in the "Ancient Mariner" put a mystic dissatisfaction with the closed world of eighteenth-century rationalism into the old ballad form and told in consciously picturesque verse a wild tale belonging evidently enough to the cycle of the Wandering Jew. Coleridge later declared the moral purpose of the poem to be only too apparent, but wisely refused to commit himself further.[2] Wordsworth in the *Lyrical Ballads* exhibits most of his stock in trade: simple, willfully prosaic diction, subjects drawn like Crabbe's from commonplace lives, but unlike Crabbe's cast in a supernatural world where pettiness is very close to God, an ability to so relate natural objects to his own appetites as to make rocks and trees happy projections of William Wordsworth (pantheism is here an inadequate word staled by the intellect), a conviction that the kind of mental effort expended by physical scientists and their imitators in other fields is harmful, or at least useless. Wordsworth's

> One impulse from a vernal wood
> May teach you more of man,
> Of moral evil and of good,
> Than all the sages can

may be put with Goethe's *Gefühl ist alles* as good bald assertions of an anti-intellectualism which has persisted in various forms to the present day.

The *Lyrical Ballads*, as well as the early work of the other Lake poet, Robert Southey, was not acceptable to the critics. Canning, George Ellis, and other cultivated gentlemen mocked, in the *Anti-Jacobin*, at Wordsworth's simplicities, Coleridge's researches in another world, and Southey's humanitarian experiments, and lumped the three very unfairly together with the Della-Cruscans and Erasmus Darwin. The Lake poets, however, save perhaps Southey, have survived their parodists, and have attained in literary manuals the proud position of founders of English nineteenth-century poetry. There is no other great literary landmark in the decade. Burns had by 1789 given full measure of his abilities. His love of tunefulness, his egalitarian enthusiasms, his ready tears, his pleasing irresponsibility, all helped make up the romantic notion of a lyric poet. Blake's most productive period lies in this decade. Blake to his con-

[2] *Table Talk*, May 31, 1800.

temporaries, however, was a madman and it remained for a later generation to discern a higher sanity in his poetry. *Pride and Prejudice, Sense and Sensibility,* and *Northanger Abbey* were probably in their original form composed in the 1790's, but remained unpublished for more than a decade. And, though Miss Austen is to many the greatest English novelist, no one considers that she influenced the romantic movement. Crabbe, who continued through the decade to compose his Dutch paintings in verse, is equally apart from the movement.

In German letters the decade of the French Revolution is peculiarly one of transition. At its beginning Goethe, fresh back from the classical hypnotism of the Italian journey, and Schiller, immersed in the sobering study of Dutch history, were turning away from the now nearly extinguished furies of *Sturm und Drang,* and were beginning to feel that their own share in past eruptions had been less than earth-shaking. At its end, Tieck, Wackenroder, Novalis, Fichte, and the Schlegels were preparing to direct against the treasonous complacency of the Weimar group the renewed energies of German romanticism. In the interval, Goethe was at his most Protean intensity. The pigeonholer, even, indeed, the modest and well-meaning systematist, is helpless before the apparently contradictory efforts of his restless genius. *Torquato Tasso* has a background of pious devotion to the classicism of Renaissance Italy, but its theme is the stock romantic one of poetic genius pitted against the uncomprehending world. *Der Gross-Cophta* and *Der Bürgergeneral* are satires directed by eighteenth-century common sense against the wild aspirations of the French Revolution, and to one not brought up in the Goethe legend, do not add to the poet's reputation. The *Römische Elegien* are most classical in form of all Goethe's work. *Wilhelm Meister's Lehrjahre* is a grab-bag novel. Most of Goethe's interests crop up in its pages and in those of its sequel, *Wilhelm Meister's Wanderjahre,* but the romantic Mignon and the harpist made a true German longing for an unreal Italy the most influential element in the book. In *Xenien* Goethe and Schiller tried the effect of epigrammatic wit against a miscellany of critics, mostly decayed Augustans or retarded *Stürmer und Dränger* too sympathetic with Jacobinism. Classic art occupied Goethe greatly in these years. He worked on an appreciation of Winckelmann and his times, and collaborated with his friend Meyer in the publication of *Die Propyläen*, an art periodical devoted to the neo-classic cause. He busied himself with science, attempting to refute Newton through work in optics, and laying the basis for his work on the metamorphosis of plants. Goethe, in spite of the claims of his idolaters, hardly belongs to the history of science. He objected to the mechanistic assumptions of eighteenth-century science, and his scientific writings have been influential chiefly because of the philosophical assumptions—vitalistic, they are commonly labeled—contained in them. Finally, though the first part of *Faust* was not published until 1808, the subject was never wholly out of Goethe's mind during this decade, and his greatest work was slowly ripening from the *Urfaust* of his youth. When one considers that Faust, Mignon, Wilhelm Meister—all romantic figures—are the most abiding of Goethe's creations, that his philosophical influence has been almost wholly on the side of intuition, or the higher apprehension, and against eighteenth-century rationalism, that the expansive Germany of the nineteenth century adopted him as its greatest man of letters, one is obliged to conclude that, in spite of his devotion to neo-classic art, in spite of the Olympian pose of his later years, in spite of his dislike for the noisy young romanticists of the early nineteenth century, he himself is one of the great founders of European romanticism.

Schiller is a far simpler man than his friend. Made a professor at Jena in 1789 on the strength of his work in Dutch history, he devoted himself quietly to the history of the Thirty Years' War and to the philosophy of art. His *Über naive und sentimentalische Dichtung* is an attempt to make himself comfortable in a world of changing moral and æsthetic standards. In it he opposes "ancient" and "modern," "classic" and "romantic," "naïve" and "sentimental" in a way that has ever since been popular. Indeed, Spengler's opposition of Apollonian and Faustian is merely an embroidering of the same fundamental theme. The German genius, concludes Schiller, as later Spengler, is typically modern, romantic, and sentimental. The Schiller of the 1790's, however, was too sober a moralist, too safely established as a man, a Christian, and a citizen to venture into unplumbed depths, and his last work is the work of a satisfied sentimentalist—and a satisfied sentimentalist strikingly resembles a satisfied humanist. Schiller was led back to poetry through the study of history, and the Wallenstein trilogy began the series of historical dramas for which he is chiefly famous. To a foreigner, at least, they sound today a bit rhetorical, and their devotion to liberty and to the fatherland seems a bit remote in a world so much more complicated than the world of William Tell.

Neither Goethe nor Schiller, however, was young enough in the 1790's to lead a thoroughgoing revolt against common sense. That task fell to Tieck and his friends, and was not well under way until the next decade. Wackenroder's *Herzensergiessungen eines kunstliebenden Klosterbrüders* is indeed an outpouring of a heart sick of the dogmatic assurances of neo-classic art, and will do very well as a starting point for the study of the German romantic school. Such a study, however, lies wholly outside this decade. Soon the search for the blue flower was on for fair, to lead to medieval Catholicism, to an Athens uncorrupted by Macedon and Rome, to the murmuring forest depths of Teutonic Germany, to elfin happiness and Titanic despair, to magic ecstasy and an opium Nirvana.

IV. PHILOSOPHY

To the unphilosophical mind, the history of philosophy seems an almost perfect illustration of Talleyrand's famous aphorism, *plus ça change, plus c'est la même chose*. Metaphysics would seem to have no other choice than an oscillation between the poles known in medieval times as realism and nominalism and today, by a confusing shift in terminology, as idealism and realism. Men by nature addicted to each sort of metaphysics have probably existed at all moments of European history, but the climate of opinion may usually be discerned as tending towards one pole or another. Now the climate of philosophical opinion in the eighteenth century was clearly nominalist, in spite of the clever stroke by which Berkeley converted Locke's nominalism into a radical assertion of the idealistic thesis that thought alone makes the world real. Towards its end, the skepticism of Hume began to disturb contemporaries. And the position of Hume is really an abandonment—a reluctant one, but still an abandonment—of metaphysics. For him, even that iron law of causation with which nominalist and idealist alike bound the world together was simply a trick of the human memory. Hume never denied that the law of causation, that the whole process of logic, was a useful and therefore necessary way for men to make themselves comfortable in this world. What he did deny was that this process was in any way absolute, in any way outside and above the experience of the individual. In another way, the French Revolution further unsettled men's minds, and by its apparent failure cast a doubt on the philosophical certainties of the Encyclopædists who appeared to have fathered the Revolution. But doubt has never yet proved a satisfactory state of mind for large numbers of men. Theology, metaphysics, or science has hitherto always emerged victorious over skepticism and the despair with which skepticism is apparently always accompanied.

To Kant is commonly given the credit for rescuing metaphysics from its destroyer Hume, and for founding the modern idealistic school. With two qualifications, the statement may stand. In the first place, neither Hume nor the French Revolution wholly destroyed eighteenth-century nominalism. In France, Kant was virtually unknown until well into the nineteenth century, and the Directory and the Consulate saw a flourishing school of *idéologues* who continued the work of the Encyclopædists. In England, Bentham kept alive the traditions of Lockian empiricism. It is true that Bentham indignantly repudiated the word "metaphysics" as he repudiated the phrase "natural rights." He retained, however, the psychological convictions behind both the word and the phrase, and certainly has little in common with Hume. Bentham, in fact, was an absolute metaphysical nominalist, who thought he made his own position more convincing by labeling his idealist opponents "metaphysicians"—one of the favorite tricks of English philosophers. In the second place, Kant himself was not so much an idealist as the starting point from which later idealists like Schelling and Hegel began. Kant always disliked mysticism and illuminism, which he was fond of calling *Schwärmerei*. He had always a respect for clarity and precision of thought—though to the uninitiate he seems rarely to have attained them—and thought of himself as the savior rather than the destroyer of eighteenth-century thought. He had none of the contempt for the natural sciences characteristic of many of the romanticists. In ethics and politics he remained a child of his age, a meliorist and an individualist, very far from the Hegelian surrender of the individual to the omnivorous state.

Kant, like his fellow countryman Goethe, is a complex, frequently a contradictory, figure, and both men have proved rich mines for subsequent commentators. Kant was, merely by avocation, a distinguished astronomer, who helped evolve the nebular hypothesis, an anthropologist, and one of the first and most optimistic of planners who schemed for international peace. Kant's conclusion, that if Europe were all republican it would all be peaceful, seems today a rather pathetically characteristic fragment of the Enlightenment. In so brief a study as this, however, it is impossible to do more than point out what seems to have been Kant's chief influence on European thought. That influence, on the whole, has been on the side of romanticism. Kant was a kindly man, convinced that the world can be made a much better place for human beings than it actually is, a man who, like Adam Smith, represents the riper wisdom of his century, the union of rationalism with sturdy middle-class ethics, and with an imaginative sense of human interdependence. For such a man, a metaphysics was an essential. Skepticism is never a kindly attitude, and your real skeptic has in him a touch of cruelty. Nor is skepticism a satisfactory ground from which to start the reformation of mankind.

Kant had to seek certainty. He found it, at the end, in God, where it is happily always to be found. But he was too good a child of his age to start with God; the eighteenth century had to earn its Revelation by earnest mental effort. Kant, therefore, starts with men, and finds in human nature the way to the absolute. Men know by sensibility (*Sinnlichkeit*), understanding (*Verstand*), and reason (*Vernunft*). Now Hume was right to this extent: the kind of knowledge we attain through sensibility and understanding *alone* is purely contingent, is changing, uncertain, knowledge of phenomena. The most thorough application of the understanding to the study of physics, for instance, cannot give us absolute truths. But reason is there to save us. Kant finds salvation in reason in two ways (at least they seem to be two ways to the uninitiate, though to the Kantian they are one and the same). One way is clear and unavoidable, the way of the *Kritik der praktischen Vernunft*. However bewildering and uncertain the world revealed to us by the operations of the understanding, however impossible of solution the problems of the one and the many, subject and object, *phenomenon* and *noumenon*, however relative the laws of natural science appear, when we turn to ethics uncertainty and relativity vanish. The moral law is unchanging, and duty no phenomenon, but an enduring and timeless absolute. The categorical imperative is not dictated to us by our sensibility or by our understanding, but by our reason. Reason reconciles liberty and necessity (a task certainly beyond the powers of logic). Kant's ethics are in specific content quite in accord with traditional Protestant ethics, and the categorical imperative itself is but a restatement of the Golden Rule. But truth had been saved for metaphysics, and doubt banished to the more profitable fields of natural science.

Kant's second way of salvation through reason is somewhat less clear. One can defend the position that the *Kritik der reinen Vernunft* is as destructive of what ordinary men regard as sure knowledge as anything Hume ever wrote. Yet Kant could not wholly give up pure reason. Synthetic judgments *a posteriori* and synthetic judgments *a priori* are somehow reconciled, logic is immaculately conceived of reason, and this contingent world tied to eternity.[3]

For the average educated man, at least, this distinction between understanding and reason was the great achievement of Kant. Reason in the Kantian sense became a weapon to be used against the narrow, stultifying reason of the *philosophes*. Now, whatever the limitations of this latter type of reason (logic is probably a better word for it than the Kantian understanding), however many the fields of human activity into which it cannot profitably go, this kind of reason does, when properly employed, attain objectivity—frequently so great a degree of objectivity, measured by common

[3] I apologize for this irreverent treatment of Kant, and especially for the heretical suggestion that he *started* with psychology. Kant himself wrote steadily on the level of metaphysics, and I have perhaps erred in trying to write about him on a different level. Yet if intellectual history is to differ at all from formal special histories of given disciplines, that difference must appear in the greater attention paid by intellectual history to what the inexpert makes of the expert.

agreement of men, that to disagree with its results is to risk the accusation of insanity. Kantian reason, though it may well be a higher and more valuable kind of human awareness, must, judged by its actual results, have a considerable degree of subjectivity. However completely Kant made the subjective objective, his followers, especially among laymen, were able to explain the wildest aberrations as the infallible dictates of *Vernunft*. The shocking consequences of the killing of an albatross by the Ancient Mariner may thus be fully in accord with *Vernunft* if not with commonsense. To the romanticist, the higher court thus set up in Kantian terminology was inevitably presided over by the romanticist himself, preferably in the form of his higher ego. To objectors who might assert that this was a very private court, the reply could always be made that *Vernunft* prefers privacy, that at any rate the validity of its judgments is not to be decided by the mere number of those who accept them. The Kantian philosophy does not merely assert that men make non-logical judgments; it asserts that certain of those judgments *transcend* logic, that they are higher, better, more universal. The word transcendental was seized upon by the romanticists with delight, and became, especially in America, the symbol of a philosophical mysticism Kant himself would hardly have accepted.

The direct influence of the French Revolution is more discernible in political philosophy than in metaphysics. The decade was full of political discussion, not merely on the plane of personalities and policies, but on the plane of principles. Political ideas are to be found even in the newspapers of the time. A brief outline of what may be called Jacobin political theory has already been given.[4] For the rest, there is little new in French political theory of the time. Siéyès was an able pamphleteer, who focused the class consciousness of the bourgeoisie in his *Qu'est-ce que le Tiers Etat?* and produced for the Consulate a paper constitution which Napoleon converted into a first-class dictatorship. But Siéyès was hardly an original thinker. Condorcet is appropriately tagged the last of the Encyclopædists, and his *Esquisse d'un tableau historique des progrès de l'esprit humain*, written in outlawry as a Girondin,

[4] See above, pp. 158-163, Chap. VI, Section IV, "The Theory of the Terror."

is a tragic testament of eighteenth-century belief in human perfectibility. Anti-revolutionary writing in France is, until Maistre, merely journalism. Joseph de Maistre's *Considérations sur la France* is an earnest of his later work as the great theorist of the ultramontane reaction, and however alien it may seem to prevailing tendencies of modern thought, is a serious attempt to construct from current events a system of political and theological values. Maistre was a Savoyard civil servant of noble blood, who until the Revolution had lived quietly and usefully in his native land, untouched by the heresies of the new thought of the age. The invasion of Savoy by the French drove him into exile and into philosophy. The rest of his life was an attempt to reconstruct a world that had been pulled down about his head. He found the origin of the Revolution in the Encyclopædists' theories of human perfectibility, in their ruthless undermining of established institutions, and especially the church. But the actual course of the Revolution presented to Maistre a striking contrast between the tragic greatness of events and the pettiness of the actors in them, a contrast not to be explained by the shallow logic of ordinary cause and effect. The Revolution was to Maistre a miracle. It was the intervention of an avenging God in the affairs of his erring children. The Christian doctrine of atonement holds that sin can be wiped out only by suffering, and that the innocent must suffer for the guilty. The generation of Voltaire had heaped up a mountain of sin which could be leveled only by a cataclysm. The guillotine avenged the sins of the fathers upon the children. The very horrors of the Revolution are a proof of the existence of a living God, a sign to its survivors that they must return to the Catholic Church.[5]

Though in Germany and Italy the intellectual ferment of the Revolution produced much interesting political writing, though in this decade such men as Gentz, Fichte, and Cuoco began their work, it is in England that the debate over the French Revolution attained its greatest importance for the historian of political thought. The Revolution stirred Edmund Burke from party politics into political philosophy. The question as to whether the Burke who

[5] This is almost exactly the position taken by Berdyaev towards the recent Russian Revolution.

had defended the American revolutionists was a different man from the Burke who attacked the French revolutionists need not here be debated, though to the sympathetic student of his career there is no inconsistency between the younger and the older man. The *Reflections on the Revolution in France* was published in 1790 and assumed even in that year of optimism a determined opposition to the political methods, aims, and ideas of the revolutionists, and predicted with uncanny accuracy the course of events which was to lead through the Terror to Napoleon. Burke's subsequent pamphlets, the *Appeal from the New to the Old Whigs* and the *Letters on a Regicide Peace* added fury but little substance to his work. Burke's bitterness has alienated many mild liberals, and his polemical purpose did, indeed, obscure for him the incompetence of the old régime against which the Revolution was directed. Yet Burke's writings on the French Revolution, once their prejudices and hatreds have been discounted, provide perhaps the best statement of the position of the enlightened conservative to be found in modern political writing. Burke's fundamental ethical assumptions are at the opposite pole from those of his century. He fully accepts the pessimistic Christian doctrine of original sin. Man, the animal man of private sensations and emotions, is not, as Rousseau claimed, good, but, as St. Paul said, wicked. Left to themselves men are stupid, selfish, cruel, overreaching. Yet somehow these wicked men manage at times to live together on this earth without tearing each other apart, and life, if not joyous, is at least not death. Men in society are miraculously better than a knowledge of their attributes as individual animals would lead one to expect. Civil society—church, state, family, law, custom, even, Burke adds in defiance of a century which gave to the word a supremely dyslogistic sense, even prejudices—save man from himself. Civil society is thus of divine institutions, an essential part of God's rule.

Now the individual is not tied to society by what the eighteenth century called reason, but by habit, by emotions like patriotism and loyalty, by the final achievement of faith. The institutions of any given society—that is, the objective realizations of human habits, emotions, faiths—can always be called in question by the faculty of reason. Anyone can devise with words whole sets of institutions that sound much better than any existing ones. But if you say to common men, give up your existing institutions, give up your unreasonable allegiances, and adopt these excellent institutions our reason shows to be perfect, you can, if you are clever and insistent enough, sometimes get them to turn against their institutions and allegiances, but you will not get them to follow the schemes of reason. On the contrary, stripped of what makes them men,—their dumb, unreasoning loyalty to their leaders, their fixed allegiance to old laws, their consoling certainty that their daily routine is a status rather than a habit,—they will show themselves beasts. This is substantially what has happened in France. The *philosophes* have destroyed the old régime, but anarchy, and no new régime, has followed. Now anarchy cannot last, and a new régime will eventually emerge in France. But it will be a régime established by force, a dictatorship built up by the strongest, but not necessarily the best, elements of society. Now Burke was an adopted Englishman, a Protestant, and in some ways a good child of the century of common sense. He did not, therefore, carry out his authoritarianism to the kind of logical extreme later reached by Maistre. He did not regard even English civil society as perfect, though in a passion against France he sometimes talked as though he did. Change is as necessary to the Western man as permanence. But you must "reform in order to conserve." You must proceed slowly, prepare men's minds for the change, attack but one problem at a time, and frame your changes in accord with the whole past of human experience. You must never stir men up to disloyalty, never persuade them to a ferocious discontent against their rulers. Above all, you must never expect impossible perfection, for perfection is inhuman. Heaven is not for mortals, and on this earth men will never be free, equal, and brothers. Burke seems to us modern devotees of the economic interpretation of history to have exaggerated the influence of the *philosophes* in producing the French Revolution, to have failed to realize that the irrational allegiances of Frenchmen had been sapped, not by words, but by facts. Yet his work is thoroughly modern in its insistence on the limitations of pure logic in politics, and, save for orthodox republican Frenchmen who have never forgiven him his intellectual leadership of the European crusade against the First Republic, is universally regarded as a storehouse of political wisdom.

Burke's pamphlets stirred up numerous replies, some of which would, if space permitted, merit analysis. Mackintosh's *Vindiciæ Gallicæ* is a temperate defense of the Revolution from a point of view much like that of later English liberalism. Mary Wollstonecraft not only replied to Burke, but in her *Rights of Woman* went a step beyond her century, and made one of the earliest contributions to the feminist movement. Her husband, William Godwin, composed his *Political Justice* with one eye to the refuting of Burke, though the work is a full-fledged political philosophy in its own right. *Political Justice* is important as the most uncompromisingly logical development of eighteenth-century assumptions as to human perfectibility—and Godwin was no logic-ridden Frenchmen, but an East Anglian, a member of a race supposedly devoted to common sense in politics. Godwin carried to their natural conclusion in philosophical anarchism the assumptions that the individual is by nature virtuous and reasonable, that his private judgments are the only possible form of successful human adaptation to a universe in constant flux, and that evil is a maladjustment resulting from the social and political compulsion which attempts to arrest this flux by imposing laws and institutions on the individual. Even the involuntary compulsion of the orchestra following the leader's baton seemed to him beneath human dignity. State, church, and family were, of course, swept away, education reduced to the removal of inhibitions, and the individual left free to obey his unerring conscience. *Political Justice* bore fruit in the *Queen Mab* of its author's son-in-law Shelley, a consequence which hardly redeems it from sterility.

By far the most influential of the replies to Burke was the *Rights of Man* of Thomas Paine. Paine's book is hardly more than a restatement of the natural rights philosophy of his Girondin friends, a philosophy untroubled by the paradoxes concerning the tyranny of liberty over despotism which emerge from the theorists of the Mountain. But it is a restatement so cannily eloquent, so adapted to the hopes and fears of the common man, that it became one of the bibles of nineteenth-century political radicalism in Europe and

America. Paine, a humble East Anglian of Quaker stock who had knocked about on two continents, had what Burke had not, a first-hand acquaintance with people for whom the Revolution was more than a matter of words. He knew why tradesmen hated noblemen, and knew that for them natural rights were no metaphysical abstractions, but a concrete code for economic protection and domestic security. The *Rights of Man* contains an inconsistency that was to afflict most nineteenth-century radicalism, and has not yet been wholly cleared up by those who cling to eighteenth-century political traditions. Paine's work is based on the assumption that the common man, given freedom of opportunity and a proper education, can work out his own salvation. Paine distrusts authority, asserts that that government is best which governs least, and most cheaply. At the same time he distrusts the rich and powerful, and notably in the second part of the *Rights of Man* looks to the government to protect the common man by far-reaching schemes of a sort which would now be called economic planning, even state socialism. The dilemma is, intellectually at least, not insoluble. You may say that government should intervene in order to equalize the conditions of competition, in order to enforce the rules of the game. But such an intervention will certainly cost money, will certainly be an act of authority. Paine himself never carried the problem even as far as this.

V. SCIENCE

As an attempt to discern the workings of a natural order not directly affected by man's desires, science ought not to be concerned with value judgments, and the history of science, unlike the history of art and letters, ought not to present such vague oscillations as that between classicism and romanticism. To the non-scientist, it may perhaps seem that science is not wholly free from the rule of fashion, that its directives have some of the coloration of widely held and not strictly scientific concepts. Thus eighteenth-century science may be considered as mechanistic in its assumptions, and nineteenth-century science as guided by the concept of organic growth. However this may be, the decade from 1789 to 1799 does not, in the history of science, mark any striking change in directives. The decade was productive enough, but its achievements are a straightforward continuation in the course of previous achievements. Its history need, therefore, involve nothing but a record of work done. In chemistry, the decade is an extremely important one, for it marks the definite establishment of the modern science. The Englishman Priestley had already discovered the existence of a gas necessary to animal respiration, which he called "dephlogisticated air" but it remained for Lavoisier to realize the importance of this discovery, and to fit into chemistry the Newtonian principle that matter does not change in amount. Lavoisier analyzed water into two gases possessing the ordinary properties of matter, and named them oxygen and hydrogen. Burning he explained as a rapid oxidation, and thus freed chemistry from the concept of a "phlogiston" with negative weight. Chemistry was now ready for straight mathematics and the atomic theory.

In the older mathematical sciences of physics and astronomy, the decade capped the achievement of the century with a series of great works of synthesis. Of these the most striking is the *Système du Monde* of Laplace, and its continuation the *Mécanique celeste*. Laplace filled out the Newtonian system into a rounded whole, extended and completed the infinitesimal calculus, and, taking up a suggestion thrown out by Kant, developed the nebular hypothesis, according to which the solar system was evolved from a rotating mass of incandescent gas. Beyond the nebulæ he refused to go, and a Creator is significantly absent from his work. Two other Frenchmen, Lagrange and Monge, made in the decade significant contributions to mathematics. In the *Traité de géometrie descriptive* (1799) Monge invented a science at once practical and theoretical. Lagrange's differential equations reduced the theory of mechanics to general formulas from which special formulas for particular problems may be derived, and his work in physics forwarded the study of kinetic energy. Two Italians, Galvani and Volta, made possible the science of electrochemistry. Galvani in 1786 had discovered that the leg of a frog contracted under the influence of a discharge from an electrical machine, and later obtained the same effect when a nerve and muscle were connected with two dissimilar metals in contact. Volta in 1800 produced his pile, a primitive battery composed of a series of zinc and copper disks separated by wet paper, and thus proved that Galvani's effect could be produced without the use of an animal substance.

The origins of modern geology also lie in the late eighteenth century. Buffon had already had trouble in reconciling his study of natural history with the book of Genesis. William Hutton published in 1785 his *Theory of the Earth*, in which he pointed out that stratification of rocks and the embedding of fossils were processes still at work, and that the existing face of the earth could be explained by the long-continued past action of such processes. His work was continued by his countryman William Smith, who was able to establish geological periods by noting the relative ages of fossils in different strata. The Frenchman Cuvier extended the biological aspect of the science by comparing the structures of existing animals with those of fossils, thus establishing the fact of biological continuity. At the beginning of the next century, Lamarck was thus in a position to unite the work of geologists and paleontologists into a genuine theory of evolution. Lamarck's basic hypothesis, that organic variation is the result of the will of the organism to adapt itself to its environment (there is the familiar illustration of the lengthening of the giraffe's neck by its desire to reach up into trees for food), implies the inheritance of acquired characteristics, and was discredited by the work of Darwin. Moralists, at least, have refused to let Lamarck die, and in our own day Mr. Shaw has cried loudly "Back to Lamarck." Lamarck's main work, and indeed most of the synthesis of biological and geological discoveries just analyzed, was not completed until the early nineteenth century. But the foundation was laid in the decade of the French Revolution. Moreover, the year 1798 saw the publication of a book which, though not the work of a biologist, had a major place in the formation of the Darwinian theory. Malthus's *Essay on Population* is almost as important for the history of the biological sciences as for the history of economic thought. Malthus's main thesis is a denial of eighteenth-century optimism as to the perfectibility of man. Life on earth is a constant struggle for survival among organisms which breed in geometric progression while their means of subsistence tends to increase in simple arithmetic progres-

sion. Man, as well as other organisms, is subject to this law of population. The negative checks of war, pestilence, starvation, abortion
and infanticide, and the positive check of abstinence from sexual
intercourse operate to keep the human population at a subsistence
level. Any great improvement in man's control over nature will
simply encourage breeding, and bring population back again to the
old level. Darwin was struck with the Malthusian concept of a
ceaseless struggle for the means of existence, and in the *Essay on
Population* found a starting point for his life work in the problem:
given this struggle, what determines the survival of one organism
rather than another? Finally, the decade is one of great importance,
not merely for genetics, but for the more descriptive studies of
botany, zoölogy and physiology, as well as for the study of medicine. From the old *Jardin du roi*, transformed in the midst of the
Revolution into the *Muséum d'histoire naturelle* there came much
valuable work by Daubenton, Fourcroy, Lamarck, Geoffroy Saint-
Hilaire and others. The *idéologues*, inspired by Condillac, devoted
themselves to physiology and medicine, and the work of Cabanis,
Bichat, as well as the German Haller is of great importance.

The social sciences—not yet so christened—are more properly
considered under the older label of political philosophy. Yet two
of these sciences, both with somewhat more claim to alliance with
the natural science than have history, law, and political theory,
made definite progress in this period. In economics, Malthus's *Essay
on Population* formed one of the starting points of the economics of
scarcity which even today maintains itself as orthodox, and the
ideas of Adam Smith were given increasing circulation by a number of minor writers. In psychology, Cabanis, Pinel and Bichat
brought the resources of physiology to the study of human behavior, and sought to base their work strictly on experimental
methods. Notably in the clinical study of insanity they did much to
banish the older notions of demonic possession, and to substitute
gentleness and medical treatment for the harsh violences with which
the insane were customarily treated. These *idéologues*, so scorned
by Napoleon, were among the founders of the modern study of
abnormal psychology, a study which has singularly increased our
understanding of Napoleon himself.

VI. CULTURE AND THE FRENCH REVOLUTION

There still remains, as the heritage of the bitter polemical writing which has made up so much of the historiography of the Revolution, the notion that the revolutionists themselves were cocksure barbarians with a contempt for all that had gone before them, and that in the realm of human culture they destroyed far more than they built. The type anecdote is the one which relates how Lavoisier was sent to the guillotine—his income came from the hated institution of tax-farming—with the remark that "the republic has no need of savants." Now the Terror, as this study has been at some pains to establish, was a brief paroxysm of collective madness, in which much that was precious perished. The Jacobin was a destroyer of idols, even when the idols were works of art. Many a masterpiece of medieval sculpture or architecture was broken up by the fanatic's hammer. Yet if one goes to the abundant literature of the Revolution in the provinces, one is struck by the fact that in almost every town there were men who sought, more often successfully than not, to protect works of art from the iconoclast. When one reflects that the bulk of French ecclesiastical art was Gothic, and that the generation of 1789 had been taught that Gothic art was an inferior and barbarous art, one is obliged to conclude that many of the revolutionists had a real feeling of piety towards the past, that they wished to preserve the continuity of human culture.

Moreover, the Terror is not the whole Revolution. The preceding pages should give ample evidence that even in France the decade from 1789 to 1799 is culturally far from sterile. The truth is that the revolutionists had a rather pathetic faith in the possibilities of cultural progress, and that they did much to further it by creating institutions. Their achievement in education, if not in actual institutions quite up to their grand ideals, remains far from negligible. For science they had a thoroughly modern reverence, and the great Napoleonic achievement in this field is based on foundations laid by the Revolution. The metric system, which has proved an indispensable tool for modern science, was gradually elaborated throughout the decade. A committee created by the Constituent Assembly in 1790, composed of Borda, Lagrange, Laplace, Monge and Condorcet, was directed to consider the problem of weights and measures and reported in 1791 that the basis of the new system should be taken from the meridian of the earth. In 1800 the work was capped by the final adoption of the meter and the kilogram throughout the republic. The full extension of the decimal system was accomplished only because the Revolution had given so complete a shock to old ways. England, sheltered from revolutionary violence, continues today the complicated bookkeeping of pounds, shillings, and pence. The scientific establishments of the Revolution have almost all proved their worth by long survival; the Museum of Natural History, already mentioned, the School of Public Works (later the Polytechnique), the National Institute, created by one of the last votes of the Convention, are all revolutionary foundations.

In art, the earlier revolutionists were, theoretically at least, strongly in favor of liberty, and the old privileged corporations—the Comédie Française, the Academy—were abolished. Yet these bodies were soon revived, and the spirit which had abolished them was not a spirit hostile to art itself. The accession to power of a new class, the dispersal of a nobility of connoisseurs, brought to light many crudities of taste. But neither Jacobin intransigence nor Thermidorean exuberance could wholly destroy the traditions of good taste in France. It is impossible to draw from a study of the French Revolution the sweeping conclusion that periods of civil disturbance are periods of cultural sterility. Politics, even in times of revolution, never completely absorbs human energies, and the history of culture is never wholly determined by political history. The decade of the Revolution is not a great period in the history of French art and letters, though in science it forms a part of one of the most productive eras in French thought. Its relative barrenness in the arts, however, would seem to be the result rather of too close an adhesion to old standards than of any anarchic pursuit of new standards. Russian experience since 1917 also suggests that political revolutionaries find it comforting to be aesthetic conservatives, accepting what they take to be the artistic standards of those they have thrown out of power.

Chapter Eleven

CONCLUSION

I. THE CHANGE IN INSTITUTIONS

IT IS NOT EASY to distil from the pageantry of narrative history the undramatic realities of change as they affected the lives of ordinary men. The drama of the "days" of the Revolution has, if told with any skill at all, something of the immediacy of experience. A summary of the "results" of the Revolution can hardly avoid generalities which may hang together well enough, but which seem abstract and unreal. Yet one cannot avoid the conclusion that Frenchmen, and to a less degree all Europeans and Americans, led in 1799 lives they could not have led in 1789, that the differences were concrete, important, no mere matter of formulas. Some attempt must here be made to seize that reality of change, to answer the question as to what the decade of the French Revolution did to ordinary men. Since the heart of the movement is, after all, French, the answer must concern itself with Frenchmen. But it must not be forgotten that the French Revolution sooner or later came to influence all Western civilization. French armies, even during this decade, brought to parts of the Low Countries, Germany, and Italy many of the institutional changes made in France itself, and neither Burke nor Maistre was able to stop the spread of French ideas. Finally, one of the most tangible kinds of change in modern history, —the change summarized in the phrase "Industrial Revolution"— though a good deal of it belongs to this decade, lies outside the field of this study.

France in 1789 had no elected assembly. In 1799 she had had the recent experience of four more or less representative assemblies, and was about to try another. The Revolution had given France for the first time, not a constitution—for to anyone but a most determined quibbler the France of the old régime had had a constitution—but what can be loosely called parliamentary government.

That government, reduced to mere form under Napoleon, was revived under the *Charte* of 1814, and has persisted to the present day. Now, though the electoral qualification has varied, did vary in these ten years, between universal manhood suffrage and a more or less high property qualification, the fact is that since 1789 the ordinary French middle-class man has had the vote, that France has been a political democracy in the nineteenth-century sense of the term. Such a democracy has not achieved the Utopian results once hoped for by earnest theorists, but it has been a very different thing from the closed government of Versailles. Ultimate political decisions have not been made by a small council of royal advisers, but by the agreement of hundreds of thousands, even millions, of Frenchmen. French democracy has not always behaved politically the way Anglo-Saxon theorists thought their own democracy behaved, but only the very doctrinaire will deny that modern France has a democratic tradition. The government of France since 1789 has been a government by discussion: and that has involved parliaments, parties, the press, political stereotypes, pressure groups, mass contagions—all the phenomena so familiar today, so unknown to the Frenchman of 1788.

The régime begun in 1789 has proved a much more efficiently centralized governmental machine than the one it replaced. De Tocqueville was perhaps the first important historian to point out that the Revolution really achieved what the Capetians had striven for in vain, the concentration of power in the central government. By the end of the Revolution the old conflicting political jurisdictions, *province, généralité, baillage, gouvernement, sénéchaussée, seigneurie*, and many others, had given place to the unified hierarchical system of *commune, arrondissement, département*; the tangled jurisdictions of *seigneurs, haute, moyenne*, and *basse justice, parlements, présidiaux*, and the numerous special courts had all been united into one system of justice, with a *Cour de Cassation* as supreme court of appeal; the special fiscal privileges of nobles, priests, and corporations had been swept away; internal tariffs, salt taxes, *taille, capitation, vingtième, don gratuit, grosses fermes*, feudal dues—all the hodgepodge of taxation under the old régime—had given place to a simple, unified financial system; the bewildering variety of weights and measures had been supplanted by the metric system; the old customary law of the North and the written law of the South had been united in a new code; the medieval guilds had been abolished; and the church had been stripped of the special privileges which had made it an *imperium in imperio*. Even in 1799 the foundation had been laid for that modern hierarchy of *fonctionnaires* (civil servants) which was never to escape control from Paris as completely as the *intendants* had escaped control from Versailles. Aided by modern transportation and by universal education, the new régime was able to reduce French provincialism to a mere sentiment cultivated largely for the tourist trade, to make France perhaps the most completely unified great nation in the world today.

Obviously, to the ordinary Frenchman these political changes meant a great deal. They meant that he had acquired certain civil rights—the right to trial by jury in many cases, in all to trial in a court which recognized no social and political privileges; the right, if he possessed a certain income, to vote; the right, whether he were Catholic, Protestant, Jew, or Deist, to worship in public with his fellows; the right, subject to property laws on the whole determined in the interests of the landed classes, to pursue any occupation he pleased—and could afford; the right to hold a commission in army or navy; the right, subject to a censorship never again quite as arbitrary as, if sometimes even more effective than, the censorship of the old régime, to form and discuss opinions in the press and on the platform. Such rights, formulated in a hundred Bills of Rights in Europe and America, have never in practice proved quite as absolute as they are declared to be on paper. But their very formulation leaves a tremendous gap between the world of Louis XIV and the modern world.

Again, the new régime made certain kinds of economic activity easier than they had been under the old régime. Here—as, indeed, throughout this summary—the change must not be understood to have been catastrophic. The Revolution matured, rather than initiated, really important changes. The career of John Law had shown that money could be made with great rapidity—and lost also— under the old régime. But on the whole the France of 1799 was a very much more favorable country for the business man than the France of 1789 had been. Political changes, and especially the new system of taxation, made the conduct of business on a national scale much easier. To take a very simple example: it was almost impossible under the old régime to manufacture and market bushel measures from a single center when the definition of a bushel varied from town to town; under the metric system, grain measures could be made on a large scale and sold all over France. A single code of commercial law was equally indispensable for modern business, and the Revolution provided one. The abolition of guilds gave the entrepreneur a freer labor market, and supplanted fixed standards for goods with the modern adage of "caveat emptor." Complete laissez-faire was never to rule in France, but when the government interfered with business, as in imposing tariffs on imports, or in providing subsidies to certain manufacturers, or in improving commercial or agricultural standards by education, research, prizes, expositions, it usually interfered to the benefit of the entrepreneur. Even more important, perhaps, than any specific institutional change was the social change which made business wholly honorable, which set a premium upon the acquisition of wealth, which accustomed men to innovation and the career open to talents.

In agricultural life, still the backbone of all French life, the Revolution was decisive. The long process, begun in feudal times, of making France a land of small independent peasant proprietors and free tenants was virtually completed by the Revolution. After 1789, even where the peasant was a tenant, he held on a strictly commercial basis, and exploited his holding as his own enterprise. The Revolution did not so much eliminate an agricultural proletariat as strengthen an agricultural middle class. Thus the agricultural laborer commonly had rather the status of the American "hired man" than that of the English agricultural laborer or that of the Eastern European semi-serf. Great farms worked wholly by paid labor hardly existed. The typical farm was owned by a peasant who exploited it with the aid of his family and, if the scale of the holding permitted, a few hired men. Social distinctions between owner and laborer were never very rigid, and in spite of the scarcity of land the laborer might rise to ownership. The forbidding of entail and the other restrictions on the free testamentary disposal of land made by the revolutionary, or Napoleonic, code have further operated to maintain in France, at least until the "economic miracle" of the 1950's, a class of small or middling and very conservative peasants with a low birth rate. (This last is important, not only as explaining French fear of more populous neighboring states, but as contributing, by reducing the supply of mobile labor, to the failure of France until just yesterday to achieve rapid economic growth.) The industrial expansion of France since the end of World War II has been accompanied by, indeed reinforced by, an unexpected rise in the birth rate. In turn, French agriculture is being modernized. There are beginnings of consolidation of small and scattered plots of land. There are rather more than beginnings of mechanized farming. The "peasants" who protested low prices in 1961 at department chef-lieux did so in tractors or in motor cars. Farmers are no longer self-sufficient. In a sense, then, the social and economic institutions fixed on France by the great Revolution are, after nearly two centuries, giving place to new ones, truly "revolutionary" once more in their implications.

But for those two centuries, the great French Revolution paradoxically helped to perpetuate in France a *relatively* small-scale industry and a *relatively* stationary and balanced rural economy which was little more than the later manorial system liberalized and adapted to a money economy. When in addition one reflects on de Tocqueville's conclusion that administratively the Revolution did but perfect the work of the old régime, one is tempted to the final paradox that, in spite of the melodramatic horrors of events in France, the French Revolution has *in the long run* proved even more revolutionary in its effects on other countries than in its effects on France. For abroad the ideas of 1789, adopted by a rising middle class, helped remake Germany and Italy, helped reconcile the new industrial England to the old England; adopted by the working classes in the industrial countries and altered to suit their needs, these ideas helped stiffen their resistance to what they considered exploitation by a new set of feudal overlords. In France the tradition of the Revolution remained, but only as a tradition and a consolation; the realities of French life, in spite of surface changes in governmental forms, were sober, pedestrian, and, in a century so ridden with change as the last, relatively unchanging.

Again, the ordinary Frenchman of 1799 found himself in a world the educational possibilities of which were far different from those of 1789. Democracy had definitely set before itself the goal of universal education. Illiteracy had become a stigma instead of an ordinary accompaniment of humble life. And what is more, education had ceased to be the monopoly of religious orders, and was acquiring more and more of a secular cast. Universal education, like Bills of Rights, has not yet, and certainly had not in 1799, quite lived up to its paper promises. But the lad who passes through the discipline of the little schools so touchingly inscribed with the revolutionary trinity of "Liberty, Equality, Fraternity" is a very different lad from the illiterate peasant of the old régime, or even from the more privileged lad who had learned to read, write, and obey God and king in dame schools and church schools.

Another revolutionary institution which by 1799 had become inescapably a part of the life of the ordinary Frenchman was universal military service—an institution which during the next century spread to most parts of the civilized world. Universal military service has not had in manuals of democratic historians quite the attention given universal suffrage, universal education, and other benign universalities, but the origins and development of them all are inescapably the same. Neither in medieval nor in early modern times was fighting the occupation of the common man. In the Middle Ages a military caste, in early modern times mercenary armies officered by gentlemen, fought pretty continuously, but on a rather small scale. Since the famous mobilization of French men and money in 1793, modern wars have been somewhat more discontinuous, but they have directly touched every citizen.

The social structure of France was no less directly affected by the Revolution than the political structure. Broadly speaking, one may say that in spite of the ups and downs of Empire and Restoration, France has been since the great Revolution almost as fully a social democracy as the United States. A common background of eighteenth-century political philosophy has perhaps done more to furnish a similar social background in the two republics than devotees of the Turner school of American uniqueness have been willing to admit. For the French Revolution really did destroy the old French aristocracy, and only its shadow was ever revived—and that chiefly for the benefit of newly enriched bourgeois with marriageable children. In England and in Germany there is still distinguishable among the lower classes a certain deference towards their superiors. In France and in America that feeling is dead. One may take as a symptom of much else (the social historian must rely mainly on such symptoms) the fact that in France and in the United States policemen are commonly regarded as potential tyrants not quite amiably ridiculous, and that in England policemen are commonly liked and respected. Englishmen easily acquire a feeling for social gradations which in an American seems forced, and in a Frenchman a pose. The distinction is subtle, but the question of social equality in a society based on physical and economic inequalities is inevitably a question dealing with imponderable self-valuations made by ordinary men. The vague notion that somehow one man is as good as another may or may not be a desirable thing, may or may not be, in the face of the fact of economic and other inequalities, an important thing, but it is a concrete inheritance of the revolutionary movements of the late eighteenth century.

II. THE CHANGE IN IDEAS

The exact relationship between ideas and institutions is certainly a matter of debate, but fortunately it is a debate which can be disregarded here. Whether changes in ideas produce changes in institutions, or whether the reverse is true, at any given moment the two exist together and interact one upon the other. Not even an economic institution is independent of the thoughts and emotions of the human beings who live under it. Some eighteenth-century thinkers undoubtedly underestimated the place of emotion, prejudice, habit, faith in the relation between the individual and society, but that is a fault that can hardly be committed in the twentieth century. Now just as the Frenchman of 1799 lived in a society institutionally quite different from that of 1789, so he lived in a society cemented by quite different ideas and emotions from that of 1789. One fact stands out quite clearly, and must form the basis of any discussion of the reality of the change in ideas effected by the French Revolution.

Burke was right, and his worst fears have been realized. The French Revolution did destroy, as completely as it can be destroyed, the nexus of loyalties which had once made the old régime an authority. It might be more accurate to say that the French Revolution merely made evident to all a work of destruction begun long before, but the fact of that destruction was undeniable in 1799. Frenchmen had ceased to feel the authority—and a true authority must be *felt*, that is, emotionally incorporated as a projection of the individual's personality—of the God of St. Paul, St. Louis, and even Louis XIV. We have all of us today been so much affected by this abandonment of the Christian God, we are all of us such good children of the eighteenth century, that only by a difficult leap of the imagination can we live again even for a moment in the old world of ideas. But in this old world men really did believe that a concrete hell and a concrete heaven were a part of sense-experience, that life on this earth is a fleeting transition to eternity, that such a life is inevitably one of misery, that, however, there are rigid rules of conduct for such a life, conformity with which will be rewarded with eternal bliss, disobedience of which will be punished by eternal damnation. Remnants of such ideas still exist among us, but recognizably as remnants, not as parts of a completely unified system. Furthermore, these remnants have been forced to accommodate themselves to a more general frame of reference which is, for the modern world, new and revolutionary. (The old Greeks would have found it in some respects familiar.) To describe in detail this frame of reference, this new nexus of loyalties, would involve the impossible task of analyzing the whole of contemporary civilization. But its essential characteristic may be not unfairly stated as an assertion of the possibility of the harmonious satisfaction here on earth of what are assumed to be normal human appetites. Men may fairly expect good bodily health, adequate and pleasing food and drink, comfortable shelter, congenial and not excessive work, a satisfactory sex-life, an opportunity for recreation and æsthetic pleasures. In achieving this life, men are to find a guide, or if you prefer, an authority, not in any supernatural being constituted of elements wholly different from the elements which make up the world of their appetites, but, at bottom, in those appetites themselves as they have borne fruit in science, art, and common sense.

Now the French Revolution, though it helped in the process of destroying the authority of organized Christianity—a process begun long before—was by no means destructive of authority in general. No one new authority grew up to take the place of Christianity, but several competing authorities gained strength from the Revolution. Heaven was not successfully brought to earth, but a good deal of the earth was brought to the newer ideas of heaven. Since every man could not attain his desires directly, most men were obliged to attain theirs vicariously by submitting themselves to some transcendental authority, be its transcendence of ordinary sense-experience ever so slight. Men's value-patterns tended, indeed, to considerable diversity, the wilder romanticists professing to believe that their own were unique, unshared and unsharable. Actually the diversity of these value-patterns, or authorities, or faiths (the three phrases merely describe the same thing from different approaches), has been much exaggerated by critics who see the modern world about to disintegrate for lack of a single authority. Most Europeans arrived at a working compromise between new aspirations and old beliefs. It is quite possible to describe briefly a value-pattern held by most Frenchmen after 1799, to show what modifications the French Revolution made in vulgar notions of teleology. To ordinary Frenchmen, the new heaven took a form perhaps most easily analyzed in that revolutionary trinity which replaced the Christian trinity. The French Revolution simply did not make possible for all men the good life of the senses. It was forced to atone for the inadequacies of the sense-life of its followers by providing them with the consolations of another life. "Liberty, Equality, Fraternity" came to stand to Frenchmen—and in somewhat different forms to most Europeans and Americans—for the new heaven.

Liberty soon ceased to mean—if, indeed, it had ever meant—that a man might do at any given moment exactly what he pleased. It meant, as it had meant to Rousseau, that a man must do at any given moment what he ought to do, what the higher part of his nature which helped make up the General Will told him to do, that to be truly free was to obey, not a human master, but a master miraculously evolved from common human experience. In practice, no doubt, this meant that liberty consisted in doing what the majority of his fellows were doing, and Rousseau's General Will, descending from metaphysics to the world of politics, has meant to the common man that the majority is always right. But this is no more than the usual process by which abstractions do their work among men.

Equality, too, was early lifted into another world—if, indeed, it had ever belonged in this one. To the middle-class Frenchman who had chiefly benefited by the revolution, equality did not by any means imply that men are physically, intellectually, or in any concrete way identical. Notably, it did not mean that men should possess even roughly equal shares of wealth. It meant that the noble and priestly privileges of the old régime should no longer be recognized in law, nor in society. It meant above all what has since been called equality of opportunity, that any one man should find no artificial barriers in the way to developing his own talents, especially when those talents lay towards the acquisition of wealth. It meant also, perhaps, that, however much Frenchmen might differ in strength, beauty, intelligence, or wealth, they were, as Frenchmen, equals, sharing alike in a common wealth.

In this last sense, the notions of liberty and equality were fused with that of fraternity to form the religion of *la patrie* in which are centered so many of the vicarious satisfactions of modern Frenchmen. Fraternity had meant to the hopeful eighteenth century the outpouring of its favorite virtue, benevolence, upon all human beings, and more especially upon the downtrodden and the distant—on peasants, Chinamen, and South Sea Islanders. The Revolution started by preaching fraternity among peoples, and a common crusade against wicked governments. (This distinction between a people and its government has often proved very convenient.) It ended, however, by confining true fraternity to Frenchmen and French subjects. This new brotherhood of Frenchmen was, even more than the brotherhood of Christians, a purely spiritual matter. One shared one's exaltation, but not one's goods, among the brethren. The religion of nationalism has not as yet produced a St. Francis. Yet it is undeniable that modern nationalism—and here

France is merely a pattern for other nations—has most of the attributes of a religion, and that notably it provides the patriot with an extension of his personality into a mystic world where no desire is ever thwarted (or realized either, from the point of view of the unbeliever).

That strange force which gives life to mere words has today pretty well gone from "Liberty, Equality, Fraternity." Yet once they commanded the passion of devout followers; once they were mixed with the awareness men have of food and drink, of clothes, women, music, money, and peace. If men on this earth might be sorted into just and unjust, and if their emotional responses to "Liberty, Equality, Fraternity" could be registered by some subtle statistical method, then perhaps it might be found, after all, that the just outnumbered the unjust among the followers of the revolutionary trinity. Surely there is no use now in repeating attacks, Anglo-Saxon or French, on the sins of the terrorists against liberty, or against fraternity, or in damning the French Revolution as a wicked piece of authoritarian leveling. The moral aspirations behind the phrase "Liberty, Equality, Fraternity" are not greatly different from the moral aspirations of Buddha, of Christ, of Socrates. Nor is the moral failure of the French Revolution more dismal than the numerous moral failures to which the race should by now be accustomed. At any rate, the realities of the French Revolution lay deeper than its slogans. Its real aspirations were perhaps not altogether moral ones.

What has become of hell? The fact is that the idea of hell has become extremely attenuate in most modern faiths. Presumably all that the most ardent French nationalist can say is that not to be a good Frenchman is hell. That is, hell has become again, as it was for the Greeks, a mere negative, a not-sharing in the delights of the elect. This attenuation of the idea of hell has not necessarily brought with it a greater spirit of toleration among men of differing value-patterns (faiths). On the contrary, it may seem to the pessimist that the modern man, and particularly the more bitter nationalist, since he is not certain that his enemy will suffer in another world, is especially eager to inflict as much suffering as possible upon him in this. Of course, what really explains the absence of hell from modern faiths is the persistence, through all the shocks of the Revolution, of the eighteenth-century belief in the natural goodness of man. Belief in a Christian hell implies belief in the doctrine of original sin, and both beliefs call for a considerable expenditure of the mystic imagination. The limited mystic capacities of the modern men have been almost wholly exhausted upon the idea of Progress.

The real changes in ideas marked by the French Revolution are not quite what the textbooks of the Third Republic make them out to be. The Revolution did not bring freedom of thought—the *philosophes* had long enjoyed an inefficient censorship far more favorable to the dispersal of ideas than an indifferent freedom. The Revolution did not immediately encourage political experimentation —its general European influence lay precisely in the other direction, and put a stop to a good deal of the work of the enlightened despots. The Revolution was no burgeoning of the human spirit, delighted with its emancipation, into the heights of artistic achievement—in general, it was a period of artistic conformity. The real significance of the Revolution for intellectual history is that it made necessary a new series of value-judgments to orientate the triumphant bourgeois among the ruins left by the *philosophes*. Some attempt has been made above to describe the theological aspect of these new value-judgments. To go much further would be to trespass on later volumes in this series. But it must be pointed out that even in 1799, the outlines of nineteenth-century intellectual—or if you prefer, spiritual—values are pretty well blocked out. The typical nineteenth-century conformist built his safe universe partly with the aid of the French Revolution. This universe still exists, though it seems now a trifle unsafe. Briefly, the "higher" life of the nineteenth-century middle-class European comprised more or less active participation in the religious life of some Christian sect, and a complete misunderstanding of traditional Christianity; patriotism, not infrequently allied with Christian reminiscences, so that God, who had once been Jehovah, became especially and exclusively disposed in favor of Englishmen, or Frenchmen, or Germans, according to need; a moral code in its more general passages close enough to the traditional code of European Christianity, but with an emphasis on thrift, labor, solvency, solid rather than luxurious living, sobriety, and female chastity which stems from Protestant capitalism as well as from the French Revolution; a set of abstractions varying somewhat according to the nationality and social position of their owner, but all involving some equivalent of "progress," and nearly all some equivalent of "Liberty, Equality, Fraternity"; a robust faith in economic individualism, an absolute assurance that government interference in business will always prove harmful; adherence to some form of parliamentary government, assumed to be the sole reasonable form of government, and transcending the old-fashioned divisions of monarchy, aristocracy, democracy; æsthetic standards tending generally towards the picturesque, the violent, the improbable, the pathetic, the unattainably perfect—in short, towards the romantic; a conviction that, however much order is necessary in moral and political life, anarchy is the natural condition of æsthetic life. This is the compromise made by the nineteenth-century with the Utopian hopes of 1789.

The French Revolution was, however, an act of rebellion. If by 1799 there had begun to emerge from it the somewhat troubled bourgeois synthesis typical of the nineteenth century, there was also formed in this decade a tradition of rebellion which has sometimes adapted itself to certain aspects of bourgeois order, but which is none the less a pretty clear tradition in its own right. You may call it, if you like, the tradition of '93, as opposed to the tradition of '89. In its purest form it inspired Continental radicals throughout the century, and is even discernible in England in men like Charles Bradlaugh. Certain elements of it were taken over by the working-class movement, and helped to make up the socialist tradition. Both these forms must be briefly analyzed.

The pure radical tradition is a pretty faithful reproduction of the aims of Robespierre. This Jacobin legend sets up a republican form of government, based upon universal manhood suffrage (but usually hostile to female suffrage, fearing clerical influence); universal compulsory education wholly in the hands of lay authority; theoretical religious freedom, based upon a firm conviction that religious freedom will mean the end of the Roman Catholic Church; in practice, certain restrictive measures such as dissolution of religious orders and closing of church schools, calculated to hasten the extinction of superstition; an economic order based on private property and private enterprise, but so regulated by taxation and other forms of state action as to prevent the accumulation of large fortunes; a unified nation-state impatient of regional differences within itself, regulating its relations with other independent nation-states by open diplomacy based on the universal principles of morality; a patriotism in theory tolerant of other patriotisms, in practice quite easily converted into an aggressive nationalism; an industrious population untempted by luxury, virtuous, its artistic life untouched by aristocratic decadence; in short, the greengrocer's paradise of Robespierre.

The socialists took over from the Jacobins their hostility to the Roman Catholic Church, or to the more privileged Protestant churches like the Anglican and the Lutheran, their republicanism, and, what is more important, their tradition of direct action. Jacobin political tactics—the organization of pressure groups, ceaseless propaganda, street manifestations and other forms of violence, use of ritual and other religious practices to maintain the cohesion of the group, belief in the necessity of a temporary "dictatorship" of the elect—all this was a valuable school for European socialism. It is significant that Marx, Jaurès, and other socialist leaders were careful students of the first French Revolution. In Babeuf and his conspiracy of the Equals—which at the time hardly played a con picuous part in French politics—later socialists discerned a full-fledged proletarian revolt, and Babeuf was incorporated in socialist mythology. From pure Jacobinism socialism differed above all in its complete repudiation of private property, and in its thoroughgoing espousal of the concept of a class struggle. But the debt of modern socialism to the French Revolution is immense. In the simplest sense—and simplicity has its hold over the ordinary man—the one is the direct heir of the other. For the French Revolution promised men equality—not equality before God, but equality on earth. If the prosperous bourgeois was able easily enough to gloss over the principle of equality with a consoling metaphysics, for the poor man equality continued to mean what it seemed to mean to common sense—that all men should have an equal share of this world's goods. In practice the French Revolution destroyed a social and political hierarchy buttressed by the Christian tradition (as an economic hierarchy this older hierarchy had already been undermined, which, briefly, is why the French Revolution was a success). In place of the older hierarchy it set up a new middle-class one, hastily buttressed by the curious amalgamation of old traditions and new ambitions which served the nineteenth century as an authority. But this buttress was weak in a fundamental point: it necessarily incorporated the egalitarian ideas with which the bourgeoisie had appealed to the lower classes for aid. It asserted in outright print the "self-evident truth" that all men are created equal. It was founded on the romantic faith in indefinite progress, in a "natural" order hostile to fixed hierarchies, in the virtues of rebellion and unrest. Its very faith in universal education made inevitable the spread of these ideas to the very lowest classes. Hitherto, at least, this process has not stopped, and through socialism the French Revolution is still at work in the modern world.

III. SUMMARY

The temptation to explain the whole subsequent history of France by the great Revolution is thus not easily to be resisted. French politicians and French historians—the two terms are not quite synonymous—are even now still moved by the principles of 1789. Elsewhere, save perhaps in that other product of the eighteenth century, the United States, politics employs a vocabulary less archaic. Even the Jacobin dictatorship seems today, among the varied contemporary dictatorships, a bit old-fashioned, and rather deceptively heroic. So many competing myths have grown up in recent years that the myth of the French Revolution has been crowded out. Other promises seem to us more golden than "Liberty, Equality, Fraternity," other threats more menacing than the guillotine of the Terror.

Even in France, the political conflicts of the nineteenth century were not mere repetitions of the great Revolution. No sensible man would now maintain with Taine that the Constituent Assembly was responsible for Sedan. Socialism, Utopian and Marxian, the unpredictable fact and legend of Napoleon, the almost equally unpredictable fact of Bismarck, and a hundred other novel elements went to produce the France of 1870. The struggle between bourgeois and proletariat is, no doubt, dimly outlined in the opposition between Girondins and Montagnards. Certain portions of the machinery of nineteenth-century French government—the bloc system, the tradition of a unicameral legislature, the problem of *scrutin de liste* or *scrutin d'arrondissement*, governmental manipulation of elections, and so on—are in part inheritances of the great Revolution. The bitter hatred between clericals and anti-clericals is an earlier inheritance made fatal by the Revolution. Yet the realities of social and economic life, even the realities of bureaucratic administration, are deeper than the startling changes of *coups d'état* and political revolutions, and it is now clear that, however unstable France as a *government* has been since 1789, France as a *society* has, in so restless a century as the last, been singularly stable.

The French Revolution must not, then, be regarded as a complete key to modern history, either in France or in the Western world. Its abiding significance is twofold: as drama and as faith. As drama, the French Revolution is to be seen as unique in space and time, as a not ignoble struggle among men bearing the full, complex burdens we call human nature, and comparatively unsupported, for the moment, by the stays we call (as we are optimists or pessimists) convention or tradition. In this drama we shall not find laws, but we may find meaning, and we shall certainly find ourselves. As faith, the French Revolution becomes comprehensible to the sociologist, to the seeker after laws.

For Jacobinism is one of the three major movements of modern times which have the essential characteristics of a fully-developed *active* religion among Western peoples: a rigid but alluring eschatology, a comforting determinism, a proselyting zeal undisturbed by the logical difficulty of reconciling free will and determinism, an uncompromising intolerance, a willingness to kill, a rigorous moral code, a lack of common sense (as well, of course, as of other supports of daily life, such as cowardice, laziness, avarice, and the like). Now an *active* religion is—or at least always has been—short-lived. No considerable body of men has had the physical and moral resources necessary to maintain life at such an extraordinary tension. All active religions tend to become inactive within a generation at most. The wise, experienced, and consistently inactive religious institution known as the Roman Catholic Church has always been threatened by outbreaks of active religion. Until Luther, at least, such outbreaks were tamed, strait-jacketed with laws and institutions, made harmless. St. Francis, perhaps the most radical of all these rebel leaders, lived to see his own Order well on the way to respectability, learning, and wealth. Since the Reformation, the great outbreaks of active religion have taken place outside the Church of Rome. Of these the earliest, Calvinism, has long since been sobered into partial conformity with a world not to be permanently transcended or denied. The second, Jacobinism, has in contemporary France made its compromise with the flesh, has, indeed, so thoroughly absorbed the lessons of experience that, especially to its devotees, it seems hardly a faith at all, gives, indeed, few of the routine consolations even an inactive religion should provide. The third, Marxism, would appear to the outsider to be entering the inactive stage, at least in the Russia of Khrushchev. Even in China, Marxism seems not quite the active, millennial, Utopian faith it was for the Old Bolsheviks. The modern West seems for the moment to have run out of active religions; its great surrogate or secular religion is nationalism, democratic or totalitarian, the most disturbing and persistent of our inheritances from the decade of the French Revolution.

BIBLIOGRAPHICAL ESSAY

Bibliographical Essay

(Revised as of November, 1958; supplemented October, 1962)

I

A NOTE ON HISTORIOGRAPHY

THE FOUNDATION of the Third Republic brought a new impetus to the study of its origins in the great Revolution. The first fruits of this study were, however, hardly favorable to the revolutionary tradition. Indeed, from the publication of its first volume in 1878 Taine's famous *Origines de la France Contemporaine* has remained a focus for anti-revolutionary opinion. Embittered by the disasters of the Franco-Prussian War, Taine, by training and temperament a historian of literature and of ideas, set himself to explain those disasters—or rather, to find someone to blame for them. The origins of his tragic contemporary France he found clearly in the France of Louis XVI. No orthodox republican has painted a darker picture of the old régime than did Taine. All the old clichés are there— the peasant who paid four-fifths of his income in taxes and feudal dues, the unbelieving bishop wasting the revenues of his diocese in worldly splendor, the starving parish priest, the great nobleman intriguing his way through the artificialities and parasitic ambitions of Versailles, the well-meaning king imprisoned in a round of empty etiquette. The old régime was thus to Taine a thoroughly unsatisfactory society, a society that *had* to be reformed. But the re- formers who prepared the way for the Revolution were to him the products of this corrupt régime, were formed intellectually in a perverse and faulty philosophy at least as old as Descartes. The heart of Taine's work lies in the discussion of what he called *l'esprit classique*. His argument is at bottom almost identical with Burke's. The French *philosophes* turned from the difficult realities of political life to a cloudland of right reason. Inheriting from the classic art of Racine and his peers (but not, since Taine had the full nineteenth- century reverence for natural science, not from the science of Galileo and Newton) a tendency to pursue the abstract, the typical, the universal, and to neglect the individual, the concrete, the particular, they built up a system of "natural rights" utterly unreal in this contingent world. Once the financial incompetence of the old government gave them an opportunity, the disciples of the *philosophes* tried to embody these abstractions in concrete institutions. The result was the "spontaneous anarchy" of 1789-1792, an anarchy from which France was only temporarily rescued by the Jacobin dictatorship of 1793-1794. Since this dictatorship was based wholly on force, was, indeed, an attempt to realize the abstract Utopia of the *philosophes* by methods quite un-Utopian, it had to give way to the more mundane, but still unduly rigid and unnatural, dictatorship of Napoleon. Taine's actual narrative is very full, and is based on considerable research among the archives. He paid much attention to what was going on in the provinces, and definitely freed himself from reliance on the *Moniteur* and similar official sources. Aulard, of course, thought his documentation faulty, and devoted a book, *Taine, historien de la Révolution française,* to pointing out his errors. Many of these errors are trivial misprints, and are far from undermining Taine's work. At most, one can say that Taine was deliberately on the hunt for instances of Jacobin violence, and that if in a given region he found a single atrocity in a long period of comparative quiet, he noted the atrocity and forgot the quiet. Taine was quite clear as to what was wrong with his contemporary France, but he was not at all clear as to how to right it—did not, perhaps, intend to embody in his work a positive program. The historian of English literature had a great admiration for English practical political sense, and the reader of the *Origines* gathers that he felt the salvation of France to lie in an abandonment of revolutionary ideology, and in an acceptance of a bourgeois society governed by successful men of affairs, reverential toward the past, and distrustful of philosophers and lawyers.

Aulard is also a product of 1870, but of the hopeful and aspiring elements in the new republic. He was early established in the first chair of History of the Revolution at the Sorbonne, and from that point of vantage founded the official school of professional academic historians which has ever since been identified with French higher state education. He was a child of the age when history was consciously setting itself up as a scientific discipline with its own special technique for the criticism and use of sources, and to the end of his long life maintained that he and his disciples had a monopoly on the scientific, objective history of the Revolution. To an outsider, his starting point appears to have been at least as much a passionate desire to defend the Revolution against Taine as a disinterested devotion to scientific truth. Aulard edited from 1887 until his death in 1927 the *Révolution française,* a learned journal devoted to the monographic study of the subject. In addition to a vast amount of research embodied in articles and monographs, he found time to produce a general history of the Revolution, the *Histoire politique de la Révolution française.* Aulard wrote good dull French, but he had a contempt for literary skill, which he did not possess, and which he apparently regarded as more damaging to historical objectivity than partisan zeal, of which he possessed a great deal. The book is clear, but hard to read with sustained interest. It is, as the title indicates, strictly political history, and is based on "official" sources—the speeches, reports, and newspaper accounts composed by the revolutionists themselves. Aulard had the distrust of memoirs common to most historians of his time—especially the memoirs of men hostile to the Revolution, like Gouverneur Morris, upon whom Taine had greatly relied. He disavowed general ideas smacking of the "philosophy of history," a pursuit still much in discredit among professional historians, yet his *Histoire politique* is based on a broad generalization which seeks to explain the Terror in terms of what Cochin has called the "thesis of circumstances." According to Aulard, the Terror was simply a government of national defense, a dictatorship forced on the Mountain by pressure of foreign and civil war. He attempts to trace a sort of informal graph in which the high points of intense terrorism—the September Massacres, the great Terror of 1793-1794—coincide exactly with the high points of success for the enemies of revolutionary France—the Prussian invasion of 1792, the Vendéen revolt, the treason of Dumouriez. There is, however, one serious discrepancy which even Aulard cannot neglect. The greatest danger to France had been met by December, 1793, and the spring of 1794 was a triumph for republican arms at home and abroad. Yet the greatest activity of the guillotine came in the late spring and early summer of 1794. There is a six months' lag of Terror behind victory which cannot easily be explained by the thesis of circumstances alone.

Aulard's ablest pupil, Albert Mathiez, broke with his master early in the present century, and founded his own review, the *Annales révolutionnaires,* now the *Annales historiques de la Révolution française.* Mathiez, too, was a professional historian of rigorous training, and he accomplished an immense amount of monographic research chiefly in ecclesiastical and economic history. During the 1920's he did, however, set himself to write a brief popular account of the Revolution, which he had carried down to the beginning of the Directory when he died suddenly in 1932. The quarrel with Aulard, which continued with great bitterness until the latter's death, was superficially centered on the personalities of Danton and Robespierre. Both historians felt that modern France needed a revolutionary hero and, of course, a villain. Aulard found the hero in Danton, robust patriot and man of common sense, the villain in Robespierre, vain, pedantic, empty idealist who sacrificed the revolution to his hierophantic ambitions. Mathiez found the hero in Robespierre, far-seeing democrat and practical social reformer, the villain in Danton, corrupt and sensual schemer, ready to betray the Revolution and to line his own pockets. Actually Danton and Robespierre were merely symbols of a difference that went far deeper than personalities. Aulard saw the world—and therefore the Revolution— with the desires and emotions, the value-scheme, of a good republican bourgeois, anti-clerical, intensely patriotic, in economics and in ethics an individualist of the old school. He sought in the Revolution for a myth which would serve the bourgeois Third Republic as our own myth of the American Revolution has served us. Mathiez, of humble Franche-Comtois peasant stock, saw the world and the Revolution with class-conscious proletarian desires and emotions. As anti-Catholic as his master, he doubted the adequacy of the individualistic, ethical-society principles of Aulard, and felt the need of a more imaginative popular faith. Nationalism in its modern form he distrusted. Though he always denied that he was a party socialist, he accepted the economic interpretation of history pretty straight from the cruder Marxians and was a bitter critic of Girondin *laissez-faire*. Mathiez accepted Aulard's explanation of the Terror as the product of foreign and civil war, but he added to that explanation an element which quite transformed it. Briefly, that element is the class struggle. The dictatorship of the Terror was not only a government of national defense, it was also a *premature dictatorship of the* proletariat. Of the two sentiments which supported this dictatorship, bourgeois patriotism and proletarian solidarity, the first was, in a France still untouched by the Industrial Revolution, infinitely the stronger. With the victories of 1794, the need for a government of national defense ceased, and in the spring and early summer of 1794 the Terror was used by Robespierre, Saint-Just, and their colleagues wholly as a dictatorship of the proletariat —witness the decrees of Ventôse. Selfish bourgeois interests proved too strong for the democratic republic, and with Robespierre fell this first and incomplete experiment in socialism. Mathiez, it will be seen, has at least given an explanation of the six months' lag of Terror behind victory, and he has given the Terror positive aims. Mathiez was preceded in the economic interpretation of the Revolution by the socialist political leader Jean Jaurès, who, in the leisures of parliamentary life, composed an *Histoire socialiste de la Révolution française* in the early years of the present century. Jaurès's book abounds in new materials for social history, and breaks new ground in such special subjects as price fixing and the agrarian program of the Robespierrists. It is not a well-proportioned study, and not good reading. The best of Jaurès's work has been absorbed into the work of Mathiez and his disciples.

What has happened since 1939, if it has not quite united as *bons républicains* all official historians of the great revolution, has relegated the polar opposition Aulard-Danton and Mathiez-Robespierre to the history of historical writing. The Fourth Republic indeed refused quite as firmly as did the Third to accept Robespierre unanimously as a national hero, a figure like Washington, above contest. But the very great success of Communism among French intellectuals, and the consonance of the economic interpretation of history with the spirit of our time, even among non-Communists, has given the work of Mathiez a currency denied to that of Aulard, which now looks most old-fashioned. Georges Lefebvre, who succeeded Mathiez in the chair at the Sorbonne and who continued quietly but firmly during the rule of Pétain to maintain the republican tradition of the study of the revolution, and Ernest Labrousse, perhaps the leader of the official school today, are both well grounded as economic historians, both convinced that at bottom the revolution was somehow a rising of the economically deprived, oppressed, or at least unjustly hindered.

As Aulard was the founder of the official republican school, so Taine was the founder of what may be called the royalist, or at least anti-revolutionary, school. Its ablest representative was Augustin Cochin, whose early death in battle in 1916 cut short a most promising career. Cochin never wrote a complete history of the Revolution, but his brief *Sociétés de pensée* is at least a complete philosophy of the Revolution. Cochin here and in the posthumous *Sociétés de pensée en Bretagne* (1926) analyzes in the work of Taine, and modifies as the basis of his own work, what he called the "thesis of plot (*complot*)." The word "plot" is unfortunate, since it suggests the melodramatic conspiracies so dear to unbalanced conservative historians from the Abbé Barruel to Mrs. Nesta Webster. Neither Taine nor Cochin really means anything much stronger than "plan" or "the conscious social purpose of a determined minority." Briefly, Cochin opposes to Aulard's "thesis of circumstances" an explanation of the Terror as the dictatorship of a pressure group inspired by the work of the *philosophes* to attempt the realization of heaven on earth. The Jacobin, casting aside the traditional values on which human conduct is based, and especially the Catholic tradition, sought to make men act according to a pattern of behavior he had worked out from his reading and discussion in the "*sociétés de pensée*." When it became evident that men would not so act, he was obliged to try and force them to so act—hence, the Terror. Cochin's originality lay above all in the care with which he traced the rise of this revolutionary group, the formulation of its aims in the period preceding 1789, its manipulation of the elections to the States-General in Brittany, its growth into a political party. Cochin, a good Catholic bourgeois, contrasted the "*petite ville*" of the Jacobins with the "*grande ville*" which was Catholic France rooted in historical tradition. He grants that the "*grande ville*" was somewhat disorganized in 1789, that the old régime was maladjusted to a growing society. But he insists that the Revolution was at bottom the triumph of the "*petite ville*" over the "*grande ville*," of a determined, unscrupulous minority over a poorly organized, politically innocent majority, that the Terror therefore was no mere government of national defense, not even a popular "tyranny" in the Greek sense, but the attempted and necessarily violent rule of a disciplined group of fanatics over sensible men caught unawares by the thoroughly modern political tactics of the Jacobins. The Terror was not accidental, but planned.

Cochin clearly regarded the old régime less unfavorably than had Taine. There remained, however, for the anti-revolutionary historians the further step of discovering, not only that the Revolution was bad, but that it was unnecessary. That step was taken most conspicuously in 1928 by M. Pierre Gaxotte, whose *Révolution française* had a phenomenal sale in a France disturbed by difficulties inherited from the war of 1914-1918. As for the Revolution itself, Gaxotte accepts the "plot" thesis of Taine and Cochin, decking it out in the latest historical and political fashions. With extraordinary cleverness, he laid hold of the patient labors of Mathiez, and turned them against the republicans. The "plot" was inspired not only by the writings of the *philosophes,* but by the communistic ambitions of the proletariat. Well-meaning bourgeois radicals accepted in 1793 as they accepted in 1924 the dangerous slogan "no enemies to the Left," and France was drawn into the communistic experiments of the *maximum,* the decrees of Ventôse, the cult of *décadi.* The experiment was, of course, a failure, which should be adequate warning against similar experiments in 1928. Gaxotte's account of the Revolution, though clear and sprightly, is not markedly original. He was avowedly not a research historian, but a popularizer. His apology for the old régime is newer. That the old régime was really a pretty good society had long been a tenet of avowed royalists, and the thesis had recently been given a scholarly cast in 1926 in the *Ancien régime* of M. Funck-Brentano. Gaxotte gives the government of Louis XVI almost a clean bill of health. France was economically prosperous, growing richer throughout the eighteenth century. The lack of standardization under the old régime insured a healthy regional independence, and left the individual much freer than he can be under the centralized modern régime. The pretended abuses are seen on further analysis to be largely myths invented by the revolutionists to justify themselves. The feudal dues were very light, and the weight of taxation certainly no heavier than under the war-burdened Third Republic. The famous *lettres de cachet* were almost wholly used as means of enforcing family discipline in the upper classes. The censorship of thought certainly did not prevent the extraordinary outburst of the Enlightenment. Indeed, the old régime was too easygoing, too tolerant of its enemies. The Revolution was not the rising of an oppressed majority against intolerable misery, but the regrettable victory of a small group of narrow, grasping, envious, unchristian upstarts over a society decently organized in a hierarchy humane, Christian, and French.

The old opposition between those who love and accept and those who hate and reject the great French Revolution remains one of the real, and as such oppositions go among civilized peoples, one of the most simple and clear-cut, of human polarities of sentiment. Though the opposition is obviously most intense in France—the famous phrase *les deux France* is not mere rhetoric—it runs throughout our Western culture, and therefore throughout the contemporary world. For the French Revolution, even more than the American Revolution or the great and comparatively rapid changes in men's ability to control natural resources which we call the industrial and scientific revolutions, has come to symbolize a very great change in what men make intellectually and emotionally of the universe they live in, and of their own kind. The men who achieved the French Revolution came in the end to attempt the forceful destruction of organized Christianity in France; and though the compromises of all sorts since then made between the religion of Christianity and the religion of the Enlightenment have not only softened this opposition of world-views, but quite naturally have made many men of good will reluctant to spell out their opposition, the fact remains that *traditional* Christianity finds it at least as hard in mid-twentieth as in late eighteenth century to accept in all its cosmic range the optimistic, materialistic, this-worldly, egalitarian and rationalistic democracy of the American and French Revolutions—let alone a "democracy," that of the Soviet Union, whose adherents claim to be in the *true* tradition of the eighteenth-century Enlightenment. The French Revolution, in short, is still going on, all over the world. It is no wonder that historians still differ over it.

After one hundred and seventy years, then, the French are still in the midst of their great Revolution. Yet not even the French, let alone the rest of us, are quite fighting the battles of the 1790's, or even those of the 1870's. Three generations of faithful research have added to our supply of facts—yes, even of "objective" knowledge. Time has not for most of us put the French Revolution into a category like that of the neolithic revolution of prehistoric times, or even of that "chemical revolution" which was contemporaneous with the French Revolution, revolutions which do not involve our deeper sentiments about the universe, or in the too current term, our "value judgments." Yet even so, time has nevertheless softened some acerbities, buried some problems. In troubled France itself, one can at least say that the relation between newer current troubles and those of 1793 seems less immediate than it did to the generation of Taine and Aulard. The rise of a strong Catholic group willing to accept some of the aims of social democracy, the discredit into which royalism of the school of Maurras has fallen through its compromises with Hitler's Germany, the mediating implications of "neutralism," all this, added to the many recently arisen difficulties of the French Union and—who knows?—possibly the slow accumulation of historical knowledge, have taken some of the clarity out of partisan absolutism. To go from Aulard to Lefebvre, Labrousse, or Godechot, or from Taine to Latreille, is an agreeable reminder that historical writing, and good manners among historians, may make progress after all.

Yet the balance is always precarious. Daniel Guérin, a splinter-group Marxist who has found in the *bras nus* of his *La lutte des classes sous la première république* (1946) the *real* proletarian heroes of 1793, well beyond the bourgeois Robespierre, is as terrible a simplifier as any of his predecessors. The recurrent, or merely threatening, crises of the Fifth republic may yet bring into fashion as bright, readable and opinionated an enemy of the great French Revolution as was Pierre Gaxotte in the 1920's. There is something about a revolution like the French that carries into time an indestructible passion. No one has written more wisely about the French Revolution than an Athenian who lived several thousand years before Robespierre: "And revolution brought upon the cities of Hellas many terrible calamities, such as have been and always will be while human nature remains the same. . . . When troubles had once begun in the cities, those who followed carried the revolutionary spirit further and further, and determined to outdo the report of all who had preceded them by the ingenuity of their enterprises and the atrocity of their revenges. The meaning of words had no longer the same relation to things, but was changed by them as they thought proper. Reckless daring was thought to be loyal courage; prudent delay was the excuse of a coward; moderation was the disguise of unmanly weakness; to know everything was to do nothing. Frantic energy was the true quality of a man. . . . The lover of violence was always trusted, and his opponent suspected. He who succeeded in a plot was deemed knowing, but a still greater master in craft was he who detected one. On the other hand, he who plotted from the first to have nothing to do with plots was a breaker-up of parties and a poltroon who was afraid of the enemy. . . ."[1] Historical time does not greatly alter the pathology of revolutions, nor yet provide a satisfactory prophylaxis.

II

BIBLIOGRAPHY

THE FIRST EDITION of this working bibliography was published in 1934. Since history is in some sense a cumulative study—perhaps in more ambiguous senses a "science"—it is true that some work published in the twenty-five years since this bibliography was first compiled has superseded earlier work, put that work "out of date." This fact, and the Procrustean bed printer and publisher cannot avoid making, means that in the present revised version many works cited in the first have had to be omitted to make place for new ones. Yet historical writing never quite loses its value for historians: a historical bibliography of 1934 cannot be outdated in 1959 in anything like the sense that a bibliography

---

[1] Thucydides, III, 82 (Jowett's translation).

of nuclear physics of 1934 would be outdated in 1959. A book like H. M. Stephen's *French Revolution* (1886-1891), for instance, even one as recent as C. D. Hazen's *French Revolution* (1932) have had to be omitted from this bibliography. But no historian, no research worker, indeed no general reader, should conclude that the work of Stephens and Hazen can now be written off as valueless. The wise and certainly the cautious will want to supplement this edition with the earlier one for any given piece of research or planned reading.

Bibliographical aids

The indispensable tool for the student who wishes to do any advanced work in the field is P. Caron, *Manuel pratique pour l'étude de la Révolution française* (Paris, 1912; new ed., 1947). An admirably chosen *brief* bibliography is in R. R. Palmer, *A History of the Modern World*, rev. ed. (New York, 1956), pp. 918-920. Good working bibliographies are abundant, for example, in G. Lefebvre, *Peuples et Civilisations*: XIII, *La Révolution française*, 2nd ed. (revised and augmented) (Paris, 1957), and in G. P. Gooch, "The Study of the French Revolution" in his *Maria Theresa and Other Studies* (New York, 1951). The latter is a brief critical historiographical study, for which see also Paul Farmer, *France Reviews Its Revolutionary Origins* (New York, 1944). Pieter Geyl hopes to follow his admirable *Napoleon: For and Against* (New Haven, 1949) with a *The French Revolution: For and Against*. More exhaustive lists can be found in A. Martin and G. Walter, *Catalogue de l'histoire de la Révolution*, 5 vols. (Paris, 1936-1955); G. Walter, *Bibliothèque nationale: Répertoire de l'histoire de la Révolution française, travaux publiés de 1800 à 1940*, vol. I: *Personnes* (Paris, 1941); vol. II: *Lieux* (Paris, 1951); a third volume arranged according to subject matter is promised; and in L. Villat, *La Révolution et l'empire, 1789-1815*, 2 vols. (Paris, 1936; new ed., 1940-1942), vol. I: *Les assemblées révolutionnaires, 1789-1799*.

For European and world history of the decade, the first bibliographical source remains *A Guide to Historical Literature*, ed. by W. H. Allison, S. B. Fay, and others (New York, 1931). A completely revised edition, covering works published through 1956, is now in process under the auspices of the American Historical Association and will be published shortly. For current work, see the standard *International Bibliography of Historical Sciences*, ed. by the International Committee of Historical Sciences (Zurich, New York, etc., 1926-). Two recent works of synthesis escape the concentration on France so common in older studies, and contain in footnotes and chapter bibliographies admirable bibliographical coverage: Jacques Godechot, *La Grande Nation*, 2 vols. (Paris, 1956), and R. R. Palmer, *The Age of Democratic Revolutions*, vol. I, "The Challenge," scheduled for publication by the Princeton University Press, 1959. Most of the national historical bibliographies cited in P. Roberts, *The Quest for Security, 1715-1740* (New York, 1947), are useful for this period also. To them should be added *Bibliographie annuelle de l'histoire de France*, published by the Centre national de la recherche scientifique at Paris. Volumes covering the years 1955 and 1956 have appeared.

Local history is very well covered for this period, and can be most useful for students of certain problems. There is no complete guide to these rich materials, but in spite of lapses in war and postwar years, the following sequence will provide the student with lists of periodicals devoted to local history and with topical subdivisions: E. Saulnier and A. Martin, *Bibliographie des travaux publiés de 1866 à 1897*, 2 vols. (Paris, 1932-1938); G. Brière and P. Caron, *Répertoire méthodique de l'histoire moderne de la France*, covering work appearing from 1898 to 1913; P. Caron and H. Stein, *Répertoire bibliographique de l'histoire de France*, listing work appearing from 1920 to 1931; and the *Bibliographie annuelle de l'histoire de France*, 1955 and 1956, listed just above. The missing years, or some of them, will probably be covered eventually.

Finally, the French are at work on that most useful tool for the historian, a very complete biographical dictionary, unfortunately so far completed only for the letters A-D, *Dictionaire de biographie française* (Paris, 1933-).

Printed source materials

These are abundant for the Revolution in France. P. B. Buchez and P. C. Roux, *Histoire parlementaire*, 40 vols. (Paris, 1834-1838), a still convenient miscellany; the *Réimpression de l'ancien Moniteur*, 31 vols. (Paris, 1843-1845); the *Archives parlementaires*, ed. J. Mavidal, E. Laurent and others, Series I, 1787-1799, 82 vols. (Paris, 1879-1913), an attempt to piece together from various sources (not acknowledged in the earlier volumes) the debates of the revolutionary assemblies, and at present stopping at January 4, 1794; and many of the other newspapers of the time enable the student to follow the debates of the various assemblies. B. F. Hyslop, *A Guide to the General Cahiers of 1789, with the texts of unedited cahiers* (New York, 1936), is a guide to these remarkably rich documents. See also Miss Hyslop's work in French: *Répertoire critique des cahiers* (Paris, 1932); *supplément au répertoire critique des cahiers* (Paris, 1953), and "Les cahiers de doléances de 1789," *Annales historiques de la Révolution française* (1955), XXVII, 115-123, with still more materials. Aulard's great collections are still most useful: A. Aulard, *Recueil des actes du comité de salut public,* 26 vols. (Paris, 1889-1925); and *Paris pendant la réaction thermidorienne et sous le directoire,* 5 vols. (Paris, 1898-1902). There is a fairly complete list of printed minutes of Jacobin clubs from all over France in C. Brinton, *The Jacobins* (New York, 1930).

Good source books are E. L. Higgins, ed. and tr., *The French Revolution as Told by Contemporaries* (Boston, 1938), and J. H. Stewart, *A Documentary Survey of the French Revolution* (New York, 1951), fully translated, and L. G. W. Legg, *Select Documents Illustrative of the History of the French Revolution,* 2 vols. (Oxford, 1905). More than a source book, Leo Gershoy's excellent Anvil paperback, *The Era of the French Revolution, 1789-1799: Ten Years That Shook the World* (Princeton, 1957), is a brief running account illustrated by readings.

The period is rich in contemporary drawings, paintings, caricatures. A fine choice is reproduced in A. Stern, *Propyläen Weltgeschichte,* vol. VII (Berlin, 1929), and in Marcel Reinhard, *Histoire de France,* vol. II (Paris, 1954). For a guide to this field, consult A. Monglond, *La France révolutionnaire et impériale; Annales de bibliographie méthodique et descriptive des livres illustrés,* 7 vols. (Grenoble, 1930-1953).

General studies

F. Mignet, *History of the French Revolution,* English trans. (London, 1913), first published in 1824 by a young Orleanist, the first and in many ways still the best brief, detached narrative; L. A. Thiers, *History of the French Revolution,* English trans., 5 vols. (London, 1895), long a "classic" of the subject, now somewhat old-fashioned: the point of view is that of moderate constitutionalism; T. Carlyle, *The French Revolution,* ed. by C. R. L. Fletcher, 3 vols. (New York, 1912), a grand sermon, with vivid bits of narrative writing, and on the whole remarkably accurate within the limits of its sources, chiefly memoirs; J. Michelet, *Histoire de la Révolution française,* rev. ed., 9 vols. (Paris, 1883-1887), comparable only to Carlyle, a Gallic rhapsody to balance a Scotch sermon, Michelet's sacrifice to his mystic God the People, lyrically written, with striking flashes of common sense; L. Blanc, *Histoire de la Révolution française,* 12 vols. (Paris, 1847-1862), the first socialist history, rehabilitating Robespierre and emphasizing economic factors, detailed and substantial, still useful; H. A. Taine, *Les origines de la France contempo-*

raine, rev. ed., 12 vols. (Paris, 1899-1914) (where no critical remarks are made, see the previous "Note on Historiography"); A. Aulard, *The French Revolution, a Political History,* English trans., 4 vols. (New York, 1910); J. Jaurès, *Histoire socialiste de la Révolution française,* ed. A. Mathiez, 8 vols. (Paris, 1922-1924); Lord Acton, *Lectures on the French Revolution,* new ed. (London, 1925), not the best of Acton, but typical of his extraordinary mixture of Liberalism, Catholicism, and scientific devotion; A. Mathiez, *The French Revolution; The Thermidorean Reaction,* English trans., 2 vols. (New York, 1928-1931); A. Cochin, *Les sociétés de pensée et la démocratie* (Paris, 1920); P. Gaxotte, *The French Revolution,* English trans. (New York, 1932); P. Kropotkin, *The Great French Revolution,* English trans. (London, 1909), by the Russian anarchist, a book of much interest for the skill and liveliness with which it narrates the great revolutionary days, and with much material on social and economic history not elsewhere so attractively presented; N. Webster, *The French Revolution* (London, 1919), an extreme example of high-Tory history which sees the whole Revolution as a series of interlocking conspiracies among a relatively few villains, Orleanists, Freemasons, *illuminati, philosophes,* etc.; G. Lefebvre, *La Révolution française,* vol. XIII of *Peuples et civilisations,* 2nd ed. (Paris, 1957), admirably balanced, and covering Europe as well as France (an earlier version, by G. Lefebvre, R. Guyot, and P. Sagnac, Paris, 1930, is still useful). A useful collection of Lefebvre's articles, *Études sur la Révolution française* (Paris, 1954), ranges widely over the whole period. M. Göhring, *Die Grosse Revolution,* 2 vols. (Tübingen, 1948-1950), a very objective study by a contemporary German scholar, who promises a third volume of notes and bibliographies; R. Mousnier and E. Labrousse, *Histoire générale des civilisations*: V, *Le 18ᵉ siècle: révolution intellectuelle, technique et politique, 1715-1815* (Paris, 1953), containing M. Labrousse's major effort at an *oeuvre de vulgarisation.* Willy Andreas, *Das Zeitalter Napoleons und die Erhebung der Völker* (Heidelberg, 1955), is an admirable general study, nearly a third of which deals with the years before 1799.

Two volumes of the Lavisse series, Lavisse, ed., *Histoire de France contemporaine*: I, *La Révolution, 1789-1792,* by P. Sagnac; II, *La Révolution, 1792-1799,* by G. Pariset (Paris, 1921), are still essential for work at the graduate level. Two standard American textbooks are L. Gershoy, *The French Revolution and Napoleon* (New York, 1933), and L. R. Gottschalk, *The Era of the French Revolution* (Boston, 1929). A standard British textbook is J. M. Thompson, *The French Revolution* (Oxford,

1943). There are a number of brief popular accounts, such as A. Goodwin, *The French Revolution* (London, 1953); J. M. Thompson, *Robespierre and the French Revolution* (in the "Teach Yourself History" series, London, 1952); and the readable, old-fashioned-liberal S. Matthews, *The French Revolution*, rev. ed. (New York, 1923).

The student who wishes to "keep up" with the field must follow the learned quarterly *Annales historiques de la Révolution française*. This is the sole survivor of various periodicals devoted to the study of the Revolution, an account of which can be found in P. Caron, *Manuel pratique pour l'étude de la Révolution française*. Economic and other difficulties have over the years caused some irregularities in the publication of the *Annales historiques*, but it keeps appearing courageously.

Special studies, primarily political

For the "background" or "causes" of the Revolution consult the bibliography in the previous volume of this series, Leo Gershoy, *From Despotism to Revolution* (New York, 1944). G. Salvemini, *The French Revolution*, translated by I. M. Rawson (London, 1954), by the distinguished Italian fighter against Fascism, deals with the transition from political agitation to action. A. Cochin, *Les sociétés de pensée en Bretagne, 1788-1789*, 2 vols. (Paris, 1926), though limited to a single province, is a significant contribution to the study of the transition from ideas to action. G. Martin, *La franc-maçonnerie française et la préparation de la Révolution*, 2nd ed. (Paris, 1926), is a fair-minded treatment of a difficult and important subject. R. Priouret, *La franc-maçonnerie sous les lys* (Paris, 1953), a revisionist study, minimizes the influence of the lodges on the Revolution. One of the central problems of the Revolution is handled from the point of view of political ideas as well as from that of political machinery in H. Hinze *Staatseinheit und Föderalismus im alten Frankreich und in der Revolution* (Stuttgart, 1928). A general political view can be found in J. M. Thompson, *Popular Sovereignty and the French Constitutional Assembly* (Manchester, 1952).

One of G. Lefebvre's best general studies is *The Coming of the French Revolution*, trans. R. R. Palmer (Princeton, 1947), originally written for the 150th anniversary of 1789. Lefebvre's *La grande peur de 1789* (Paris, 1932) remains the best study of this important phase of the Revolution. A recent local study is H. Diné, *La Grande Peur dans la généralité de Poitiers* (Paris, 1951). The consequences of August 4 are best studied in S. Herbert, *The Fall of Feudalism in France* (London, 1921), an able summary of the work of Aulard and of P. Sagnac's classic, *La législation civile de la Révolution française* (Paris, 1898). On the *annus mirabilis* see also F. Braesch, *1789: l'année cruciale* (Paris, 1941), and A. Soboul, *1789, l'an un de la liberté* (Paris, 1950). M. Garaud, *Histoire générale du droit privé français: La Révolution et l'égalité civile* (Paris, 1953), analyzes the changes in such law initiated in 1789.

L. B. Pfeiffer, *The Uprising of June 20, 1792* (Lincoln, Neb., 1913), is an adequate monograph. Though without scholarly trappings, A. Mathiez, *Le dix août* (Paris, 1931), has the authority of a monograph, and is one of Mathiez's most readable books. F. Braesch, *La commune du dix-août* (Paris, 1911), though in some ways the uninspired doctoral dissertation at its worst—lengthy, shapeless, dull—is an indispensable source of information. See also P. Sainte Claire-Deville, *La Commune de l'an, II* (Paris, 1946). The final disorders of 1792 are conveniently summed up in P. Caron, *Les massacres de Septembre* (Paris, 1935), and in the same writer's *La première terreur, 1792: les missions du conseil exécutif provisoire et de la commune de Paris* (Paris, 1950).

L. Mortimer-Ternaux, *Histoire de la terreur,* 8 vols. (Paris, 1863-1881), must not be omitted as the first study of the subject made from the archives. It is bitterly hostile to the Jacobins, and paints a very black picture indeed. From an opposite political bias, Mathiez approached the Terror, and also consulted the archives. He made some of his most important contributions in the realistic (if not quite "objective") study of the Terror, notably: *La conspiration de l'étranger* (Paris, 1918); *Un procès de corruption sous la terreur; L'affaire de la compagnie des Indes* (Paris, 1920); *La corruption parlementaire sous la terreur,* 2nd ed. (Paris, 1927). Mathiez's Protean labors are completely recorded, moreover, in the handy "Bibliografía de A. Mathiez" by R. Caillet-Bois in the *Boletín del Instituto de Investigaciones Históricas* (Buenos Aires, 1932), 268.

R. R. Palmer, *Twelve Who Ruled* (Princeton, 1941), is a scholarly and readable account of the great Committee of Public Safety. See also the same author's bibliographical study, "Fifty Years of the Committee of Public Safety," *Journal of Modern History* (1941), XIII, 375-397. L. Jacob, *Les suspects pendant la Révolution, 1789-1794* (Paris, 1952), treats the whole topic of revolutionary repression. D. Greer, *The Incidence of the Terror* (Cambridge, Mass., 1935), breaks new ground in the statistical study of the social and economic status of victims of the repression. New interpretations of phases of the Terror can be found in H. Calvet, "Une interprétation nouvelle de la loi de prairial," *Annales historiques de la Révolution française* (1950), XXII, 305-319, and G. Lefebvre, "Sur la loi de prairial," *Annales historiques de la Révolution française* (1951), XXIII, 225-256, and (1952), XXIV, 253-255, and in R. Baehrel, "Epidémie et terreur: histoire et sociologie," *Annales historiques de la Révolution française* (1951), XXIII, 113-146.

On the machinery of the Terror the clear survey of P. Mantouchet, *Le Gouvernement révolutionnaire* (Paris, 1912), is essential. H. Wallon, *Histoire du tribunal révolutionnaire,* 6 vols. (Paris, 1880-1882), based on the archives, is in point of view and in historiographical importance much like the work of Mortimer-Ternaux. Special studies are numerous: G. Belloni, *Le comité de sûreté générale de la Convention* (Paris, 1924), praised by Aulard, damned by Mathiez; A. Ording, *Le bureau de police du comité de salut public* (Oslo, 1930), by a pupil of Mathiez, whitewashing the Robespierrists of dictatorial aims; C. Richard, *Le comité de salut public et le fabrications de guerre* (Paris, 1921); P. Robin, *Le séquestre des biens ennemis sous la Révolution* (Paris, 1929); J. D. Godfrey, *Revolutionary Justice. A study of the organization, personnel and procedure of the Revolutionary Tribunal* (Chapel Hill, 1951), an excellent monograph; J. B. Sirich, *The Revolutionary Committees in the Departments of France* (Cambridge, Mass., 1943), and the same author's "The Revolutionary Committees after Thermidor," *Journal of Modern History* (1954), XXVI, 329-339, form a major contribution. On the *armées révolutionnaires* there is a recent monograph, R. C. Cobb, *Les armées révolutionnaires des départements du Midi* (Toulouse, 1956).

On the role of the Jacobin clubs, see L. de Cardenal, *La province pendant la Révolution: histoire des clubs jacobins* (Paris, 1929); C. Brinton, *The Jacobins* (New York, 1930); G. Walter, *Histoire des Jacobins* (Paris, 1946).

For the great day that ended Jacobin rule, see L. Barthou, *Le neuf thermidor* (Paris, 1926). Later political disturbances can be studied in G. Lefebvre, *Les Thermidoriens* (Paris, 1937), and his *Le Directoire* (Paris, 1946). There is a good general survey, M. Reinhard, *La France du Directoire,* 2 vols. (Paris, 1956); also P. Bessand-Massenet, *La France après la terreur, 1795-1799* (Paris, 1946), and a careful monographic treatment, A. Meynier, *Les coups d'état du Directoire,* 3 vols. (Paris, 1932). Babeuf and the "Equals" figure in almost all histories of socialism. J. R. Talmon, *The Rise of Totalitarian Democracy* (Boston, 1952), deals with Babeuf, but is rather intellectual than political history. E. Belfort Bax, *The Last Episode of the French Revolution* (London, 1911), is straightforward social-democratic history. There is an excellent recent study: D. Thomson, *The Babeuf Plot* (London, 1947).

The "counter-revolution," Vendée, the emigration are subjects treated inevitably with partisan passion, rarely, however, at all disguised. Donald Greer, an American, has applied the neutrality of statistics, as in his earlier work on the incidence of the Terror, in *The Incidence of the Emigration* (Cambridge, Mass., 1951). On the Vendée, there is L. Dubreuil, *Histoire des insurrections de l'Ouest,* 2 vols. (Paris, 1924-1925), scholarly, and for the work of one of the "official" school very fair-minded indeed; C. Le Goffic, *La Chouannerie* (Paris, 1930), especially good on the military side, but covering the whole subject; E. Gabory, *L'Angleterre et la Vendée,* 2 vols. (Paris, 1930-1931), thoroughly sound, and refreshingly fair toward the English, especially in view of the noticeable Anglophobia of such recent historians as L. Madelin in his *La contre-révolution sous la Révolution* (Paris, 1935); G. Walter, *La guerre de Vendée, sociologie d'une contre-révolution* (Paris, 1953), based on a "sociology" of the pro-revolutionary kind; E. Vingtrinier, *Histoire de la contre-révolution,* 2 vols. (Paris, 1924-1925). Together with F. Baldensperger, *Le mouvement des idées dans l'émigration française,* 2 vols. (Paris, 1925), this last makes a pretty satisfactory history of the emigration and supersedes the work of E. Daudet.

No one has greatly added to the work of A. Vandal, *L'avènement de Bonaparte* (Paris, 1903), I, on the situation in 1799.

The constitutional history of the period is summarized and related with other aspects of the Revolution in so broad a way as almost to belie its title in M. Deslandres, *Histoire constitutionnelle de la France de 1789 à 1815* (Paris, 1932). Even more complete a handbook is J. Godechot, *Les institutions de la France sous la Révolution et l'Empire* (Paris, 1951).

For the Revolution in the French colonies, the literature is listed, and earlier work incorporated, in J. Saintoyant, *La colonisation française pendant la Révolution,* 2 vols. (Paris, 1930), a sober, if thoroughly patriotic, study. The monographs of E. Rusch, *Die Revolution von St. Domingue* (Hamburg, 1930), C. L. Lokke, *France and the Colonial Question, 1763-1801* (New York, 1932), and G. Debien, *Esprit colon et esprit d'autonomie à Saint-Domingue aux XVIIIme siècle,* 2nd ed. (Paris, 1954), should be noted.

Religious history

The great work here is P. de la Gorce, *Histoire religieuse de la Révolution française,* 5 vols. (Paris, 1909-1923), written by a Catholic, indeed, but gently written, without unacknowledged prejudices, scholarly, and never dull. The same virtues appear in the work of another Catholic historian, A. Latreille, *L'église catholique et la Révolution française,* 2 vols. (Paris, 1946-1950). Another recent study is Canon J. Leflon, *La crise révolutionnaire* (Paris, 1949), vol. XX of A. Fliche and Y. Martin, eds., *Histoire de l'Eglise*. For Protestantism, there is an American monograph, B. C. Poland, *French Protestantism and the French Revolution, 1685-1815* (Princeton, 1957), a thorough survey, covering much more than the decade of the actual Revolution. For the Jews, see H. M. Sachar, *Course of Modern Jewish History* (Cleveland, 1958).

Other recent studies: C Ledré, *L'Eglise de France sous la Révolution* (Paris, 1949); J. Hérissay, *La vie religieuse à Paris sous la Terreur* (Paris, 1952); M.-H. Jette, *La France religieuse du XVIIIᵉ siècle, de la Révolution et de l'empire* (Paris, 1956); W. Gurian, "L'influence de l'Ancien Régime sur la politique religieuse de la Révolution," *Revue internationale d'histoire politique et constitutionnelle* (1956), XXIV, 259-277.

On the anti-Christian side, the work of Mathiez is typical: *La question religieuse sous la Révolution* (Paris, 1930), and also Aulard's *Christianity and the French Revolution*, English trans. (London, 1927). (The "revolutionary cults" are considered below under the heading "social history.") There is a remarkable bibliography at the end of chap. XV, "Les problèmes religieuses," in J. Godechot, *La grande nation* (Paris, 1956), II, 534-535.

Military history

This is a difficult subject indeed for the historian seeking "objectivity." There is an abundant literature, of which the following is a sampling: A. Latreille, *L'oeuvre militaire de la Révolution* (Paris, 1914); A. Chuquet, *Les guerres de la Révolution,* 11 vols. (Paris, 1886-1896), each volume of which has a separate title, *La première invasion prussienne, Valmy,* etc., a warmly patriotic and "republican" work. The best available single work, in English, is R. W. Phipps, *The Armies of the First French Republic,* 4 vols. (Oxford, 1926-1939), conscientiously compiled from secondary sources, a bit conservative, and thoroughly English. Perhaps the most sensible writing on the subject is to be found in two clear, brief essays by S. Wilkinson: *The French Army before Napoleon* (Oxford, 1915); *The Rise of General Bonaparte* (Oxford, 1930). From the side of the opponents of France two works may be especially distinguished: J. W. Fortescue, *History of the British Army,* IV, *1789-1801,* 2 parts (London, 1906), and the co-operative work of various Austrian military historians called *Krieg gegen die Französische Revolution, 1792-1797,* 2 vols. (Vienna, 1905). An important monograph on a special phase of military history is G. Michon, *La justice militaire sous la Révolution* (Paris, 1922). On naval history A. T. Mahan, *Influence of Sea Power upon the French Revolution and Empire, 1793-1813,* 10th ed. (New York, 1898), remains the best. Of recent work, there is R. S. Quimby, *The Background of Napoleonic Warfare: the Theory of Military Tactics in 18th Century France* (New York, 1957); M. Lauerma, *L'artillerie de campagne française pendant les guerres de la Révolution* (Helsinki, 1956); J. Godechot, *Les commissaries aux armées sous le Directoire,* 2 vols. (Paris, 1937); M. Bourdet-Pléville, *Surcouf; sa vie et la guerre de course* (Paris, 1951); M. Reinhard, *Le grand Carnot,* 2 vols. (Paris, 1950-1952); C. Brinton et al., "Jomini" in E. M. Earle, ed., *Makers of Modern Strategy* (Princeton, 1944).

Economic history

F. L. Nussbaum, *Commercial Policy in the French Revolution* (Washington, 1923); C. Poisson, *Les fournisseurs aux armées sous la Révolution* (Paris, 1932); E. Pollio, "Le commerce maritime pendant la Révolution," *La Révolution française* (1931), LXXXIX, 289 ff.; G. Lefebvre, "Le commerce extérieure en l'an II," *La Révolution française* (1925), LXXVIII, 133 ff.; and many of Mathiez's articles in the *Annales révolutionnaires* and its successor, the *Annales historiques de la Révolution française,* deal with commerce and the business world.

On financial and monetary history, M. Marion, *Histoire financière de la France depuis 1715,* 5 vols. (Paris, 1914-1932), remains authoritative, though its monetary theory—or prejudices—is mid-19th century. It should be corrected by S. Harris, *The Assignats* (Cambridge, Mass., 1930). Most detailed and scholarly is F. Braesch, *Finances et monnaies révolutionnaires,* 5 vols. (Nancy, 1934-1936). G. Pariset, *Études d'histoire révolutionnaire* (Paris, 1929), is composed mostly of valuable material on economic history omitted (from lack of space presumably) from his volume in the Lavisse series. C. E. Labrousse has pioneered the study of prices, scarcities, economic deprivation, and their relation to revolutionary activity in two major works: *Esquisse du mouvement des prix et des revenus en France au XVIIIᵉ siècle* (Paris, 1932) and *La crise de l'économie française à la fin de l'ancien régime et au début de la Révolution,* vol. I (Paris, 1944). A second volume of the latter is promised. Mathiez's best work is *La vie chère et le mouvement sociale sous la Terreur* (Paris, 1927). It is complemented from new materials in W. F. Shepard, *Price Control and the Reign of Terror,* University of California Publications in History, no. 45 (Berkeley, 1953), and attacked from a heretical Marxist position in D. Guérin, *La Lutte des classes sous la 1re république: Bourgeois et "bras nus,"* 2 vols. (Paris, 1946). See also G. Rudé, "Prices, Wages, and Popular Movements in Paris during the French Revolution," *Economic History Review* (1954), VI, 246-267. An old but not yet superseded book is E. Levasseur, *Histoire des classes ouvrières et de l'industrie en France depuis 1789,* 2 vols. (Paris, 1903). On the "social services," poor relief, and the like we have two works by S. T. McCloy, *Government Assistance in Eighteenth-Century France* (Durham, 1946) and *The Humanitarian Movement in Eighteenth-Century France* (Lexington, Ky., 1957).

On the urban proletariat there is G. M. Jaffe, *Le mouvement ouvrier à Paris pendant la Révolution* (Paris, 1924), which is concerned with the difficulties in applying the *loi le Chapelier* under the Constituent Assembly; A. Mathiez, "La Révolution et les prolétaires," *Annales historiques de la Révolution française* (1931), VIII, 479, his last word on the subject; J. de la Monneraye, *La crise du logement à Paris pendant la Révolution* (Paris, 1928); E. Soreau, "Les ouvriers en l'an VII," *Annales historiques de la Révolution française* (1931), VIII, 117.

On matters rural, G. Lefebvre's impressive doctoral dissertation, *Les paysans du Nord pendant la Révolution* (Lille, 1924), far transcends local history in importance, and points the way to further work. His *Questions agraires au temps de la terreur,* 2nd ed. (Poitiers, 1954), though mainly a collection of documents, has useful critical introductions, and sets in a more reasonable light the famous decrees of Ventôse. Two of M. Lefebvre's articles are admirable summings-up of our knowledge: "Recherches relatives à la vente des biens nationaux," *Revue d'histoire mederne* (1928), III, 188, and "La place de la Révolution dans l'histoire agraire de la France," *Annales d'histoire économique et sociale* (1929), I, 506. There are also reliable articles by E. Soreau, "La Révolution française et le proletariat rurale," *Annales historiques de la Révolution française* (1932), IX, 28 and following. See also O. Festy, *L'agriculture pendant la Révolution française* (Paris, 1947); L. Chevalier, *Les paysans, étude d'histoire et d'economie rurale* (Paris, 1947); M. Bouloiseau, "Elections de 1789 et communantés rurales en Haute-Normandie," *Annales Historiques de la Révolution française* (1956), XXVIII, 29-47, on materials for study of socio-economic life of rural communities. There are good recent studies of supply: R. Werner, *L'approvisionnement en pain de la population du Bas-Rhin et de l'armée du Rhin pendant la Révolution* (Strasbourg, 1951), with extensive documentation; R. B. Rose, *The French Revolution and the Grain Supply,* Nationalization Pamphlets in the John Rylands Library, *Bulletin of the John Rylands Library* (Manchester, 1956), XXXIX, 171-187; R. Cobb, "Le ravitaillement des villes sous la Terreur: La Question des arrivages (septembre 1793)," *Bulletin de la Société d'histoire moderne* (1954), ser. 11, X, 8-11; A. Rémond, *Études sur la circulation marchande en France aux XVIII*ᵉ *et XIX*ᵉ *siècles,* I, *Les prix des transports marchands de la Révolution au 1*ᵉʳ *Empire* (Paris, 1956).

For a broad view of modern French economic history, see S. B. Clough, *France: A History of National Economics, 1789-1939* (New York, 1939).

Social history

The most useful collection of information for the student of social history is still the volumes of the brothers Goncourt, E. and J. de Goncourt, *Histoire de la société française pendant la Révolution; Histoire de la société française pendant le Directoire,* 3rd ed. (Paris, 1864). There is also W. A. Schmidt, *Tableaux de la Révolution française,* 3 vols. (Leipzig, 1867-1871), a classic collection based on police reports. Most of such history is, of course, fragmentary. The following seem to be of the greatest significance: J. Tiersot, *Les fêtes et les chants de la Révolution française* (Paris, 1908); M. Dommanget, *Le symbolisme et le prosélytisme révolutionnaires à Beauvais et dans l'Oise* (Beauvais, 1931), a work raised above local history by its wide use of a general knowledge of revolutionary symbolism; E. F. Henderson, *Symbol and Satire in the French Revolution* (London, 1912); G. G. Andrews, "Making the Revolutionary Calendar," *American Historical Review* (1931), XXXVI, 515; P. Mantouchet, "La vie à Paris sous la Terreur," *Révolution française* (1930), LXXXIII, 203 ff.; G. Lefebvre, "Foules révolutionnaires," in his *Études sur la Révolution française* (Paris, 1954), 271-288, an interesting attempt to complete the now outmoded G. Lebon. Two popular books dwelling on the luxuries and scandals of the Directory are L. Madelin, *La France du Directoire* (Paris, 1933), and M. Minnigerode, *The Magnificent Comedy* (New York, 1931). On the arts, education, and social services there is a large special literature. A sampling of recent work: Cornwall B. Rogers, *The Spirit of Revolution in 1789* (New York, 1949), a study of popular songs; David L. Dowd, *Pageant-master of the Republic: J.-L. David and the French Revolution* (Lincoln, Neb., 1948); J.-A. Rivoire, *Le patriotisme dans le théâtre sérieux de la Révolution* (Paris, 1950); S. J. Idzerda, "Iconoclasm during the French Revolution," *American Historical Review* (1954), LX, 13-26; E. W. Cason, "L'Abbé Gregoire and Education as an Agency of Social Change," *Developments in Education*, Florida State University Studies, no. 9 (Tallahassee, 1953).

Social history is the best rubric for the work of L. L. T. Gosselin (G. Lenôtre, *pseud.*), *Paris révolutionnaire. Vieilles maisons, vieux papiers*, 6 vols. (Paris, 1901-1930), and many others, some of which are translated into English. Lenôtre was a conservative antiquarian scholar fascinated by the melodrama of the Revolution, which he does not minimize. In a sense, the best social history of the Revolution remains Anatole France's novel *The Gods Are Athirst* (many editions).

Biography

An enormous field, especially if memoirs (autobiographies) are added. For these latter see P. Caron's *Manuel pratique* listed above and the original *Cambridge Modern History*, vol. VIII. The following is a mere sampling, in which preference is given to the latest scholarly work. J. J. Chevallier, *Barnave; ou, des deux faces de la Révolution, 1761-1793* (Paris, 1936); E. Ellery, *Brissot de Warville* (Boston, 1905), which has stood up as the best life; J. S. Schapiro, *Condorcet and the Rise of Liberalism* (New York, 1934); A Cento, *Condorcet e l'idea di progresso* (Firenze, 1956), with good bibliography; L. Barthou, *Danton* (Paris, 1932), in praise of the great statesman, and proving conclusively (if only by its existence) that Mathiez has labored partly in vain; Mathiez's own writings on Danton, bitterly hostile, are extensive—perhaps *Danton et la paix* (Paris, 1919) and *Autour de Danton* (Paris, 1926) will do as samples; K. Pfister, *Danton* (Munich, 1947); R. Arnaud, *La vie turbulente de Camille Desmoulins* (Paris, 1928); L. Sauvel, *Hoche* (Paris, 1947); D. G. Loth, *Lafayette* (London, 1952); L. R. Gottschalk's great study of Lafayette has not yet reached his French Revolutionary activities and there is no thorough biography of him available—but see S. W. Jackson, *Lafayette, a Bibliography* (New York, 1930); L. Jacob, *J. Le Bon* (Paris, 1933); L. R. Gottschalk, *Jean Paul Marat* (New York, 1927), certainly one of the most interesting books written by an American on the subject of the French Revolution; G. Walter, *Marat* (Paris, 1933); G. Martin, *J.-P. Marat* (Paris, 1938); H. Belloc, *Marie Antoinette*, 2nd ed. (New York, 1924), an excellent book—Belloc is always at his very best on French Revolutionary subjects, relatively free from his political and social eccentricities, and his literary talents fully turned on; L. de Loménie and son, *Les Mirabeau*, 5 vols. (Paris, 1879-1891), the classic treatment; J. J. Chevallier, *Mirabeau* (Paris, 1947); O. J. G. Welch, *Mirabeau, A Study of a Democratic Monarchist* (London, 1951); D.

Walther, *Gouverneur Morris, témoin de deux révolutions* (Lausanne, 1932), English trans. (New York, 1934). On Robespierre the output is large, and very wide-ranging in its judgments on the man. The old life by E. Hamel, *Histoire de Robespierre,* 3 vols. (Paris, 1865-1867), is still a quarry for popularizers. The two volumes of J. M. Thompson, *Robespierre* (Oxford, 1953), are sympathetic yet not worshiping, the best single study. See also R. S. Ward, *Robespierre, a Study in Deterioration* (London, 1934), hostile, and R. Korngold, *Robespierre and the Fourth Estate* (New York, 1941), M. Bouloiseau, *Robespierre* in the "Que sais-je" series (Paris, 1957), and J. Massin, *Robespierre* (Paris, 1956), which deals with the "ignoring" of Robespierre by official France (his bicentenary came in 1958); G. Huisman, *La vie privée de Madame Roland* (Paris, 1955)—but here her memoirs, edited by Carl Becker, are best; A. Ollivier, *Saint Just et la force des choses* (Paris, 1954); E. N. Curtis, *Saint-Just, Colleague of Robespierre* (New York, 1935); J. H. Clapham, *The Abbé Siéyès* (London, 1912), still best; G. Lacour-Gayet, *Talleyrand,* 4 vols. (Paris, 1928-1931), the scholarly life, fundamentally hostile—as are most French lives, including L. Madelin, *Talleyrand* (Paris, 1944); for defenses of Talleyrand, see C. Brinton, *The Lives of Talleyrand* (New York, 1936), and D. Cooper, *Talleyrand* (London, 1947); P. V. Vergniaud, *Vergniaud* (Monaco, 1949), and C. G. Bowers, *Pierre Vergniaud, Voice of the French Revolution* (New York, 1950), the latter adulatory indeed.

Dissemination of the Revolution

In the original edition of this bibliographical essay, several pages were devoted to what was then very scattered material. Two major works now enable the student to organize his work in this important field, and dispense us here from repetitions. They are J. Godechot, *La grande nation; L'expansion révolutionnaire de la France dans le monde de 1789 à 1799,* 2 vols. (Paris, 1956), a thorough study indeed, whose bibliographies, which are very full, by no means Gallocentric, are given at the end of each chapter; that on pp. 127-132 is most important, though all should be consulted; and the forthcoming work of R. R. Palmer, *The Age of Democratic Revolutions,* 2 vols., of which the second will be most useful for bibliographical help in this field.

Of very recent work, the following may be noted: H. Voigt, *Die deutsche jakobinische Literatur und Publizistik, 1789-1800* (Berlin, 1955); W. von Groote, *Die Entstehung des Nationalbewusstseins in Nordwest-deutschland, 1790-1830* (Göttingen, 1955); H. Acton, *The

Bourbons of Naples, 1734-1825 (London, 1956); A. Heriot, *The French in Italy, 1796-1799* (London, 1957); C. Zaghi, *Bonaparte e il Direttorio dopo Campoformia* (Naples, 1956), important for 1797-1798, well documented from archives; R. R. Palmer, "Recent Interpretations of the Influence of the French Revolution," *Cahiers d'histoire mondiale* (1954), II, 173-195.

National histories

The decade 1789-1799 has little precise meaning in the history of any country but France. Here, then, it will be possible only to indicate the major works which deal with the whole or with part of this decade in each important country.

H. Pirenne, *Histoire de la Belgique*, 6 vols. (Brussels, 1900-1926), of which volumes V and VI are germane here—a work already classical; G. H. Dumont, *Histoire des Belges* (Brussels, 1954); P. J. Blok, *History of the People of the Netherlands*, English trans., 5 vols. (New York, 1898-1912), V, dull but accurate and substantial; J. A. Houte et al., *Algemeene geschiedenis der Nederlanden*, vol. VII, *1748-1795* (Utrecht, 1955), a modern scholarly collaborative work; W. Oechsli, *History of Switzerland, 1499-1914* (Cambridge, 1922), certainly the best in English; W. E. H. Lecky, *History of England in the Eighteenth Century*, new ed., 7 vols. (New York, 1892), VI, VII, very full in this revolutionary decade, a history reflecting Victorian stability and confidence; a delayed volume of the Oxford History of England, dealing with the later eighteenth century, should be published soon, and will be authoritative; J. H. Rose, *Life of William Pitt*, 2 vols. in 1 (New York, 1924), the best available, very readable, thorough, and with easily discountable patriotic attachments for Pitt; W. L. Mathieson, *The Awakening of Scotland, 1747-1797* (Glasgow, 1910), excellent; for Ireland there is still only Lecky; A. E. Richardson, *Georgian England* (New York, 1931), and D. Hartley and M. M. Elliott, *Life and Work of the People of England. The Eighteenth Century*, 2 vols. (London, 1931), both good examples of the use of illustrations and careful details in social history; J. B. Williams, *A Guide to the Printed Materials for English Social and Economic History, 1750-1850* (New York, 1926), in which the reader can pursue an important subject beyond the scope of this volume; K. Biedermann, *Deutschland im XVIIIten Jahrhundert*, 4 vols. (Leipzig, 1880), the work of a sentimental liberal, still very interesting, and still best for *Kulturgeschichte*; K. T. von Heigel, *Deutsche Geschichte vom Tode Friederichs des Grossen bis zur Auflösung des alten Reichs*, 2 vols. (Stuttgart, 1899-

1911), one of the very best of such histories, modern, professional, never cheaply popular, but never dull; V. Bibl, *Der Zerfall Oesterreichs: Kaiser Franz und sein Erbe* (Vienna, 1922), violently partisan against the old régime, not to be used without caution, but containing a good deal of new material; G. S. Ford, *Hanover and Prussia, 1795-1803* (New York, 1903); F. Meinecke, *Das Zeitalter der deutschen Erhebung, 1795-1815,* 2nd ed. (Bielefeld, 1913), fully up to the high standard of his other work; H. Brunschwig, *La crise de l'état prussien à la fin du XVIIIe siècle* (Paris, 1947); C. A. Gulick, *Austria from Hapsburg to Hitler,* 2 vols. (Berkeley, 1948); E. Denis, *La Bohème depuis la Montagne Blanche,* new ed., 2 vols. (Paris, 1921), sound and well established; R. J. Kerner, *Bohemia in the Eighteenth Century* (New York, 1932), a very important monograph, centered on the years 1790-1792, and using sources some of which have been destroyed by fire in Vienna; E. Sayous, *Histoire générale des Hongrois,* 2nd ed. (Paris, 1900), still the best reasonably detailed account in a Western tongue; F. Eckhart, *Short History of the Hungarian People* (London, 1931); R. H. Lord, *The Second Partition of Poland* (Cambridge, Mass., 1915), a beautifully neat monograph which disposes of the whole subject; O. Halecki, *A History of Poland,* 2nd ed. (New York, 1956); K. Waliszewski, *Romance of an Empress* (New York, 1894), *Story of a Throne,* 2 vols. (London, 1895), *Paul I of Russia* (London, 1913), constituting a consecutive history of Russia in some detail, and still the best available in English for political and diplomatic history; V. O. Kliuchevsky, *History of Russia,* English trans., 5 vols. (New York, 1911-1931), IV, V, a somewhat personal interpretation, but well backed up, and essential for the student of economic and social history; K. Stählin, *Geschichte Russlands,* 4 vols. (Stuttgart, 1923-1939); B. J. Hovde, *The Scandinavian Countries, 1720-1865,* 2 vols. (New York, 1948); R. N. Bain, *Gustavus III and His Contemporaries,* 2 vols. (London, 1894), with many defects of presentation, but based on original sources; A. Franchetti, *Storia d'Italia dal 1789 al 1799* (Milan, 1907), good detailed account, by no means yet outmoded; C. Tivaroni, *Storia critica del risorgimento italiano 1735-1870,* 9 vols. (Turin, 1888-1897), of which volume II deals with this period, still best as *Kulturgeschichte*; but for Italy in this decade see especially the bibliographies in J. Godechot, *La grande nation,* and E. Rota, ed., *Questioni di storia del Risorgimento* (Milan, 1951); A. Ballesteros y Beretta, *Historia de España y su influencia en la historia universal,* 9 vols. (Barcelona, 1918-1941); N. Jorga, *Geschichte des Osmanischen Reiches,* 5 vols. (Gotha, 1908-1913), V; F. Schevill, *History of the Balkan Peninsula from the Earliest Times* *to the Present Day* (New York, 1922), though not so much a history as a survey, will through its bibliography introduce the reader to a subject not in itself very important for this particular decade.

International relations

Two great classics study the influence of the Revolution on European international relations; both are diplomatic histories in the grand manner, not mere *précis* of negotiations: H. von Sybel, *Geschichte der Revolutionszeit,* rev. ed., 10 vols. (Stuttgart, 1897-1900), English trans., 4 vols. (London, 1867-1879); A. Sorel, *L'Europe et la Révolution française,* 8 vols. (Paris, 1895-1904). Von Sybel is bitterly prejudiced against the French, but without his spadework Sorel's book would have been much harder to write. The most striking of the many scholarly researches which have modified the conclusions of Sorel is R. Guyot, *Le directoire et la paix de l'Europe* (Paris, 1911), which shows French foreign policy under Reubell in a much more favorable light. The latest scholarly work, with good bibliographies, is A. Fugier, *Histoire des relations internationales,* vol. IV: *La Révolution française et l'empire Napoléonienne* (Paris, 1954). From the mass of modern monographic writings the following may be mentioned: G. Michon, "Robespierre et la Guerre," *Annales révolutionnaires* (1920), XII, 265-311; E. D. Adams, *The Influence of Grenville on Pitt's Foreign Policy* (Washington, 1904); C. Ballot, *Les Négotiations de Lille* (Paris, 1910); E. W. Lyon, *Louisiana in French Diplomacy, 1759-1804* (Norman, Okla., 1934); D. Gerhard, *England und der Aufstieg Russlands* (Munich, 1933); S. S. Biro, *The German Policy of Revolutionary France,* 2 vols. (Cambridge, Mass., 1957); P. Rain, *La diplomatie française,* vol. II: *1789-1800* (Paris, 1950); P. R. Rohden, *Die Klassische Diplomatie, von Kaunitz bis Metternich* (Leipzig, 1939); W. Real, "Der Friede von Basel," *Basler Zeitschrift* (1951), L, 27-112; (1952), LI, 115-228; B. Narbonne, *La Diplomatie du Directoire et Bonaparte* (Paris, 1951); J. Dechamps, "Lord Erskine et l'opposition Wigh de 1792 à 1815," *Annales historiques* (1948), XX, 97-116; J. Godechot, "Le Directoire vu de Londres," *Annales historiques* (1949), XXI, 311-336; (1950), XXII, 1-27.

An excellent summary of the European situation in this decade is A. Wahl, *Geschichte des europäischen Staatensystems, 1789-1815* (Munich, 1912). For the beginnings of economic methods of waging war, earlier portions of E. J. Heckscher, *The Continental System* (Oxford, 1922), are valuable. In the co-operative *Cambridge History of British Foreign Policy,* 3 vols. (Cambridge, 1922-1923), the first volume deals very thoroughly and completely with the period as seen through English eyes. H. Oncken, *Die historische Rheinpolitik der Franzosen* (Gotha, 1922), though chronologically it extends far beyond this particular period, is essential to a modern understanding of the subject. Foreign relations are also treated in many of the works listed under the heading "National histories" above.

Intellectual history

For the broad interpretation of the French Revolution and its place in our Western culture, the forthcoming work of R. R. Palmer, *The Age of Democratic Revolutions,* will be of major importance. See also many of the works mentioned in the "Note on Historiography" above; and A. Cobban, *The Myth of the French Revolution* (London, 1955); C. Brinton, *The Anatomy of Revolution,* Vintage paperback ed. (New York, 1957); the same author's *French Revolutionary Legislation on Illegitimacy* (Cambridge, Mass., 1934) attempts a large generalization from a small case history; J. L. Talmon, *The Rise of Totalitarian Democracy* (Boston, 1952); C. S. Lewis, *De descriptione temporum* (London, 1955), finds the "great divide" in modern history is *not* the French Revolution; E. Cassirer, *The Question of J.-J. Rousseau,* English trans. with introduction by Peter Gay (New York, 1954); F. Meinecke, *Weltbürgertum und Nationalstaat* (Munich, 1928); *Encyclopedia of the Social Sciences* (New York, 1930-1934) article, "Declaration of the Rights of Man and the Citizen," with bibliography; O. Vossler, "Studien zur Erklärung der Menschenrechte," *Historische Zeitschrift* (1930), CXLII, 516; B. Shickhardt, *Die Erklärung der Menschen-und-Bürgerrecht von 1789-1791 in den Debatten der Nationalversammlung* (Berlin, 1931); G. McNeil, "The Anti-revolutionary Rousseau," *American Historical Review* (1953), LVIII, 808-823; A. Cobban, *Rousseau and the Modern State* (London, 1934); M. Leroy, *Histoire des idées sociales en France de Montesquieu à Robespierre* (Paris, 1946); G. Lefebvre, "La Révolution française et le rationalisme," *Annales historiques de la Révolution française* (1946), XVIII, 4 ff.; R. Derathé, *Rousseau et la science politique de son temps* (Paris, 1950); G. G. Granger, *La mathematique sociale du marquis de Condorcet* (Paris, 1956); L. M. Gidney, *L'influence des États-Unis sur Brissot, Condorcet, et Mme. Roland* (Paris, 1930); H. Peyre, "The Influence of Eighteenth-Century Ideas on the French Revolution," *Journal of the History of Ideas* (1949), X, 63-87; A. Lichtenberger, *Le socialisme et la Révolution française* (Paris, 1899); H. T. Parker, *The Cult of Antiquity and the French Revolution* (Chicago, 1937); L. P. Williams,

"Science, Education, and the French Revolution," *Isis* (1953), XLIV, 311-330; A. Favre, *Les origines du système métrique* (Paris, 1931); P. Farmer, *Lavoisier et la Révolution française* (Paris, 1956); F. E. Manuel, *The New World of Henri St. Simon* (Cambridge, Mass., 1956). Burke is central to the study of antirevolutionary ideas. His work can be studied conveniently in R. J. S. Hoffman and Paul Levack, *Burke's Politics: Selected Writings* (New York, 1949). See also A. Cobban, *The Debate on the French Revolution* (London, 1950); P. R. Rohden, *Joseph de Maistre als politischer Theoretiker* (Munich, 1920); Golo Mann, *Secretary for Europe; the Life of Friedrich Gentz*, Eng. trans. (New Haven, 1946); P. H. Beik, *The French Revolution Seen from the Right* (Philadelphia, 1956); F. Baldensperger, *Le mouvement des idées dans l'émigration française*, 2 vols. (Paris, 1924).

Romanticism can hardly be confined to this brief decade. See later volumes of the series, and H. E. Hugo, ed., *The Romantic Reader* (New York, 1957), and for the origins especially, P. Trahard, *La sensibilité révolutionnaire* (Paris, 1936); A. Viatte, *Les sources occultes du romantisme*, 2 vols. (Paris, 1928); A. Monglond, *Le préromantisme français* (Grenoble, 1930); I. Babbitt, *Rousseu and Romanticism* (Boston, 1919).

Supplement, October, 1962

George F. Howe and others, eds., *The American Historical Association's Guide to Historical Literature* (New York, 1961); see before, p. 303. The periodicals *Historical Abstracts* and the less expensive *Historical Abstract Bulletin*, 800 Micheltorena St., Santa Barbara, California, are now available and essential for historians of the modern world. Hans Beyer and others, *Aufklärung und Revolution* (Bern, 1960), volume IX of the *Historia Mundi*, is a conventional Europe-centered collaborative scholarly work on the period from the early eighteenth century to 1815 with classified bibliographies useful especially for smaller countries. J. Steven Watson, *The Reign of George III, 1760-1815* (New York, 1960), volume XII of *Oxford History of England*, a long awaited volume, with bibliographies.

Thanks to the impulse given by the late Georges Lefebvre, and the continued support of scholars like J. Godechot, A. Soboul, M. Bouloiseau and W. Markov, the *Annales historiques de la révolution française* has had a new lease of life. It is nowadays far from Gallocentric, covering work in German, Russian, Italian, English and other languages. This periodical remains, of course, firmly Leftist and pro-French Revolution.

It is nowadays indispensable for the researcher, especially for its coverage of French local history during the great Revolution, a most fertile field even for the general historian. Proofreading remains uncertain, witness "Charles Parkin, *The moral bases of Burk's political thouth,* Cambridge University Press, 1956 . . . *publiée par Firzwillimer et Bourke.*" See *Annales historiques de la révolution française,* XXXI (1959), 76. Many of the serial publications of source materials have been resumed during current French prosperity, and new ones added. For example, *Oeuvres complètes de Maximilien Robespierre,* publication of which by the Société des études Robespierristes was begun in 1912, are still not quite "complete"; but volume IX, consisting of the speeches, September 1792 to 1793, appeared in 1958. The researcher once more must go to the post–World War II volumes of the *Annales historiques de la révolution française* to keep up with these and other continuing publications. Alfred Cobban, *The Myth of the French Revolution* (London, 1955); R. R. Palmer, "Sur la composition sociale de la Gauche à la Constituante," *Annales historiques de la révolution française,* XXXI (1959), 154-156; Cobban's reply and Palmer's final word, *Annales historiques de la révolution française,* XXXI (1959), 387-391, give interesting evidence of the continued polemical vitality of the French Revolution—and of its historians. W. Markov in a brief review of the three-volume *Oeuvres choisies de Jean-Paul Marat* published in Moscow by the Academy of Sciences of the USSR in 1956 gives a useful set of leads to Soviet-sponsored work in the French Revolution, mostly in Russia. See *Annales historiques de la révolution Française,* XXX (1958), 87-89.

Bernard Faÿ, *La grande révolution, 1715-1815* (Paris, 1959); the "plot" thesis lives on, as do haters of the great Revolution. Paul Sethe, *Die grossen Tage: Von Mirabeau zu Bonaparte* (Frankfurt am Main, 1953), a very good and very readable account of the great *journées.* Eugène Tarlé, *Germinal et Prairial* (Moscow, 1959), in French, by the late Russian historian, specialist in the period. Albert Soboul, *Les sans-culottes parisiens de l'an II. Mouvement populaire et Gouvernement révolutionnaire; 2 juin 1793-9 thermidor an II* (Paris, 1958), a major monograph on an important subject, Marxist in view. M. J. Sydenham, *The Girondins* (London, 1961), based on latest interpretations. G. Lefebvre, *Les Thermidoriens* (Paris, 1960), new edition with up-to-date bibliography. Marcel Garaud, *La révolution et la propriété foncière* (Paris, 1959), volume two of the thorough history of French *droit privé* begun in 1953; see before, p. 308. Jacques Godechot, *La contre-révolution: doctrine et action, 1789-1804* (Paris, 1961), a major study of a field little worked of late years. Leo Gershoy, *Bertrand Barère: A Reluctant Terrorist*

(Princeton, N.J., 1962), a major study of a major figure. Jean Massin, *Marat* (Paris, 1960), in a not unfriendly tone treats Marat as a "prophet." Auguste P. Herlaut, *Deux témoins de la terreur: Le citoyen Dubuisson; Le ci-devant Baron de Haindel* (Paris, 1958), volume I of his *Autour d'Hébert,* from the documents, on two interesting minor characters. Louis Jacob, *Hébert, le Père Duchesne, chef des Sans-Cullotes* (Paris, 1960), the best and probably the kindest biography of this important figure.

Joseph Fayet, *La Révolution française et la science, 1789-1795* (Paris, 1960); the emphasis on revolutionary vandalism annoyed French leftist historians, but there is much solid work in this book. Louis Trénard, *Histoire social des idées, Lyon de l'Encyclopédie au Préromantisme* (Paris, 1958), a well-documented study. Jean Gaulmier, *Un grand témoin de la Révolution et de l'Empire, Volney* (Paris, 1959), a doctoral thesis on a comparatively neglected figure, the last of the *philosophes.*

E. Wangermann, *From Joseph II to the Jacobin Trials* (Oxford, 1959); Denis Silagi, *Ungarn und der geheime Mitarbeiterkreis Kaiser Leopolds II* (Munich, 1960), two useful additions to our knowledge of the effect of the French Revolution in the Hapsburg dominions.

A. Soboul, *Précis d'histoire de la Révolution française* (Paris, 1962). A good up-to-date summary, vigorously Marxist.

Index

INDEX

Revised January, 1970

harper ✦ torchbooks

American Studies: General

HENRY ADAMS Degradation of the Democratic Dogma. ‡ *Introduction by Charles Hirschfeld.* TB/1450

LOUIS D. BRANDEIS: Other People's Money, *and How the Bankers Use It. Ed. with Intro. by Richard M. Abrams* TB/3081

HENRY STEELE COMMAGER, Ed.: The Struggle for Racial Equality TB/1300

CARL N. DEGLER: Out of Our Past: *The Forces that Shaped Modern America* CN/2

CARL N. DEGLER, Ed.: Pivotal Interpretations of American History
Vol. I TB/1240; Vol. II TB/1241

A. S. EISENSTADT, Ed.: The Craft of American History: *Selected Essays*
Vol. I TB/1255; Vol. II TB/1256

LAWRENCE H. FUCHS, Ed.: American Ethnic Politics TB/1368

MARCUS LEE HANSEN: The Atlantic Migration: 1607-1860. *Edited by Arthur M. Schlesinger. Introduction by Oscar Handlin* TB/1052

MARCUS LEE HANSEN: The Immigrant in American History. *Edited with a Foreword by Arthur M. Schlesinger* TB/1120

ROBERT L. HEILBRONER: The Limits of American Capitalism TB/1305

JOHN HIGHAM, Ed.: The Reconstruction of American History TB/1068

ROBERT H. JACKSON: The Supreme Court in the American System of Government TB/1106

JOHN F. KENNEDY: A Nation of Immigrants. *Illus. Revised and Enlarged. Introduction by Robert F. Kennedy* TB/1118

LEONARD W. LEVY, Ed.: American Constitutional Law: *Historical Essays* TB/1285

LEONARD W. LEVY, Ed.: Judicial Review and the Supreme Court TB/1296

LEONARD W. LEVY: The Law of the Commonwealth and Chief Justice Shaw: *The Evolution of American Law, 1830-1860* TB/1309

GORDON K. LEWIS: Puerto Rico: *Freedom and Power in the Caribbean. Abridged edition* TB/1371

HENRY F. MAY: Protestant Churches and Industrial America TB/1334

RICHARD B. MORRIS: Fair Trial: *Fourteen Who Stood Accused, from Anne Hutchinson to Alger Hiss* TB/1335

GUNNAR MYRDAL: An American Dilemma: *The Negro Problem and Modern Democracy. Introduction by the Author.*
Vol. I TB/1443; Vol. II TB/1444

GILBERT OSOFSKY, Ed.: The Burden of Race: *A Documentary History of Negro-White Relations in America* TB/1405

CONYERS READ, Ed.: The Constitution Reconsidered. *Revised Edition. Preface by Richard B. Morris* TB/1384

ARNOLD ROSE: The Negro in America: *The Condensed Version of Gunnar Myrdal's* An American Dilemma. *Second Edition* TB/3048

JOHN E. SMITH: Themes in American Philosophy: *Purpose, Experience and Community* TB/1466

WILLIAM R. TAYLOR: Cavalier and Yankee: *The Old South and American National Character* TB/1474

American Studies: Colonial

BERNARD BAILYN: The New England Merchants in the Seventeenth Century TB/1149

ROBERT E. BROWN: Middle-Class Democracy and Revolution in Massachusetts, 1691-1780. *New Introduction by Author* TB/1413

JOSEPH CHARLES: The Origins of the American Party System TB/1049

HENRY STEELE COMMAGER & ELMO GIORDANETTI, Eds.: Was America a Mistake? *An Eighteenth Century Controversy* TB/1329

WESLEY FRANK CRAVEN: The Colonies in Transition: 1660-1712† TB/3084

CHARLES GIBSON: Spain in America † TB/3077

CHARLES GIBSON, Ed.: The Spanish Tradition in America + HR/1351

LAWRENCE HENRY GIPSON: The Coming of the Revolution: 1763-1775. † *Illus.* TB/3007

JACK P. GREENE, Ed.: Great Britain and the American Colonies: 1606-1763. + *Introduction by the Author* HR/1477

AUBREY C. LAND, Ed.: Bases of the Plantation Society + HR/1429

JOHN LANKFORD, Ed.: Captain John Smith's America: *Selections from his Writings* ‡ TB/3078

LEONARD W. LEVY: Freedom of Speech and Press in Early American History: *Legacy of Suppression* TB/1109

---

† The New American Nation Series, edited by Henry Steele Commager and Richard B. Morris.
‡ American Perspectives series, edited by Bernard Wishy and William E. Leuchtenburg.
a History of Europe series, edited by J. H. Plumb.
§ The Library of Religion and Culture, edited by Benjamin Nelson.
‖ Researches in the Social, Cultural, and Behavioral Sciences, edited by Benjamin Nelson.
° Harper Modern Science Series, edited by James A. Newman.
 Not for sale in Canada.
+ Documentary History of the United States series, edited by Richard B. Morris.
# Documentary History of Western Civilization series, edited by Eugene C. Black and Leonard W. Levy.
A The Economic History of the United States series, edited by Henry David et al.
¶ European Perspectives series, edited by Eugene C. Black.
** Contemporary Essays series, edited by Leonard W. Levy.
* The Stratum Series, edited by John Hale.

2

ARNOLD M. PAUL: Conservative Crisis and the Rule of Law: *Attitudes of Bar and Bench, 1887-1895.* New Introduction by Author
TB/1415

JAMES S. PIKE: The Prostrate State: *South Carolina under Negro Government.* ‡ *Intro. by Robert F. Durden*
TB/3085

WHITELAW REID: After the War: *A Tour of the Southern States, 1865-1866.* ‡ *Edited by C. Vann Woodward*
TB/3066

FRED A. SHANNON: The Farmer's Last Frontier: ...*Agriculture, 1860-1897*
TB/1348

VERNON LANE WHARTON: The Negro in Mississippi, 1865-1890
TB/1178

American Studies: The Twentieth Century

RICHARD M. ABRAMS, Ed.: The Issues of the Populist and Progressive Eras, 1892-1912 +
HR/1428

RAY STANNARD BAKER: Following the Color Line: *American Negro Citizenship in Progressive Era.* ‡ *Edited by Dewey W. Grantham, Jr. Illus.*
TB/3053

RANDOLPH S. BOURNE: War and the Intellectuals: *Collected Essays, 1915-1919.* ‡ *Edited by Carl Resek*
TB/3043

A. RUSSELL BUCHANAN: The United States and World War II. † *Illus.*
Vol. I TB/3044; Vol. II TB/3045

THOMAS C. COCHRAN: The American Business System: *A Historical Perspective, 1900-1955*
TB/1080

FOSTER RHEA DULLES: America's Rise to World Power: 1898-1954. † *Illus.*
TB/3021

JEAN-BAPTISTE DUROSELLE: From Wilson to Roosevelt: *Foreign Policy of the United States, 1913-1945. Trans. by Nancy Lyman Roelker*
TB/1370

HAROLD U. FAULKNER: The Decline of Laissez Faire, 1897-1917
TB/1397

JOHN D. HICKS: Republican Ascendancy: 1921-1933. † *Illus.*
TB/3041

ROBERT HUNTER: Poverty: *Social Conscience in the Progressive Era.* ‡ *Edited by Peter d'A. Jones*
TB/3065

WILLIAM E. LEUCHTENBURG: Franklin D. Roosevelt and the New Deal: 1932-1940. † *Illus.*
TB/3025

WILLIAM E. LEUCHTENBURG, Ed.: The New Deal: *A Documentary History* +
HR/1354

ARTHUR S. LINK: Woodrow Wilson and the Progressive Era: 1910-1917. † *Illus.*
TB/3023

BROADUS MITCHELL: Depression Decade: *From New Era through New Deal, 1929-1941* ∧
TB/1439

GEORGE E. MOWRY: The Era of Theodore Roosevelt and the Birth of Modern America: 1900-1912. † *Illus.*
TB/3022

WILLIAM PRESTON, JR.: Aliens and Dissenters: *Federal Suppression of Radicals, 1903-1933*
TB/1287

WALTER RAUSCHENBUSCH: Christianity and the Social Crisis. ‡ *Edited by Robert D. Cross*
TB/3059

GEORGE SOULE: Prosperity Decade: *From War to Depression, 1917-1929* ∧
TB/1349

GEORGE B. TINDALL, Ed.: A Populist Reader: *Selections from the Works of American Populist Leaders*
TB/3069

TWELVE SOUTHERNERS: I'll Take My Stand: *The South and the Agrarian Tradition. Intro. by Louis D. Rubin, Jr.; Biographical Essays by Virginia Rock*
TB/1072

Art, Art History, Aesthetics

CREIGHTON GILBERT, Ed.: Renaissance Art ** *Illus.*
TB/1465

EMILE MALE: The Gothic Image: *Religious Art in France of the Thirteenth Century.* § 190 illus.
TB/344

MILLARD MEISS: Painting in Florence and Siena After the Black Death: *The Arts, Religion and Society in the Mid-Fourteenth Century.* 169 illus.
TB/1148

ERWIN PANOFSKY: Renaissance and Renascences in Western Art. *Illus.*
TB/1447

ERWIN PANOFSKY: Studies in Iconology: *Humanistic Themes in the Art of the Renaissance.* 180 illus.
TB/1077

JEAN SEZNEC: The Survival of the Pagan Gods: *The Mythological Tradition and Its Place in Renaissance Humanism and Art.* 108 illus.
TB/2004

OTTO VON SIMSON: The Gothic Cathedral: *Origins of Gothic Architecture and the Medieval Concept of Order.* 58 illus.
TB/2018

HEINRICH ZIMMER: Myths and Symbols in Indian Art and Civilization. 70 illus.
TB/2005

Asian Studies

WOLFGANG FRANKE: China and the West: *The Cultural Encounter, 13th to 20th Centuries. Trans. by R. A. Wilson*
TB/1326

L. CARRINGTON GOODRICH: A Short History of the Chinese People. *Illus.*
TB/3015

DAN N. JACOBS, Ed.: The New Communist Manifesto and Related Documents. 3rd revised edn.
TB/1078

DAN N. JACOBS & HANS H. BAERWALD, Eds.: Chinese Communism: *Selected Documents*
TB/3031

BENJAMIN I. SCHWARTZ: Chinese Communism and the Rise of Mao
TB/1308

BENJAMIN I. SCHWARTZ: In Search of Wealth and Power: *Yen Fu and the West*
TB/1422

Economics & Economic History

C. E. BLACK: The Dynamics of Modernization: *A Study in Comparative History*
TB/1321

STUART BRUCHEY: The Roots of American Economic Growth, 1607-1861: *An Essay in Social Causation.* New Introduction by the Author.
TB/1350

GILBERT BURCK & EDITORS OF Fortune: The Computer Age: *And its Potential for Management*
TB/1179

JOHN ELLIOTT CAIRNES: The Slave Power. ‡ *Edited with Introduction by Harold D. Woodman*
TB/1433

SHEPARD B. CLOUGH, THOMAS MOODIE & CAROL MOODIE, Eds.: Economic History of Europe: *Twentieth Century* #
HR/1388

THOMAS C. COCHRAN: The American Business System: *A Historical Perspective, 1900-1955*
TB/1180

ROBERT A. DAHL & CHARLES E. LINDBLOM: Politics, Economics, and Welfare: *Planning and Politico-Economic Systems Resolved into Basic Social Processes*
TB/3037

PETER F. DRUCKER: The New Society: *The Anatomy of Industrial Order*
TB/1082

HAROLD U. FAULKNER: The Decline of Laissez Faire, 1897-1917 ∧
TB/1397

PAUL W. GATES: The Farmer's Age: *Agriculture, 1815-1860* ∧
TB/1398

WILLIAM GREENLEAF, Ed.: American Economic Development Since 1860 +
HR/1353

J. L. & BARBARA HAMMOND: The Rise of Modern Industry. || *Introduction by R. M. Hartwell*
TB/1417

3

ROBERT L. HEILBRONER: The Future as History:
*The Historic Currents of Our Time and the
Direction in Which They Are Taking America*
TB/1386
ROBERT L. HEILBRONER: The Great Ascent: *The
Struggle for Economic Development in Our
Time* TB/3030
FRANK H. KNIGHT: The Economic Organization
TB/1214
DAVID S. LANDES: Bankers and Pashas: *International Finance and Economic Imperialism in
Egypt. New Preface by the Author*
TB/1412
ROBERT LATOUCHE: The Birth of Western Economy: *Economic Aspects of the Dark Ages*
TB/1290
ABBA P. LERNER: Everbody's Business: *A Reexamination of Current Assumptions in Economics and Public Policy* TB/3051
W. ARTHUR LEWIS: Economic Survey, 1919-1939
TB/1446
W. ARTHUR LEWIS: The Principles of Economic
Planning. *New Introduction by the Author°*
TB/1436
ROBERT GREEN MC CLOSKEY: American Conservatism in the Age of Enterprise TB/1137
PAUL MANTOUX: The Industrial Revolution in
the Eighteenth Century: *An Outline of the
Beginnings of the Modern Factory System in
England°* TB/1079
WILLIAM MILLER, Ed.: Men in Business: *Essays
on the Historical Role of the Entrepreneur*
TB/1081
GUNNAR MYRDAL: An International Economy.
New Introduction by the Author TB/1445
HERBERT A. SIMON: The Shape of Automation:
For Men and Management TB/1245
PERRIN STRYER: The Character of the Executive: *Eleven Studies in Managerial Qualities*
TB/1041
RICHARD S. WECKSTEIN, Ed.: Expansion of World
Trade and the Growth of National Economies ** TB/1373

Education

JACQUES BARZUN: The House of Intellect TB/1051
RICHARD M. JONES, Ed.: Contemporary Educational Psychology: *Selected Readings* **
TB/1292
CLARK KERR: The Uses of the University TB/1264

Historiography and History of Ideas

HERSCHEL BAKER: The Image of Man: *A Study
of the Idea of Human Dignity in Classical
Antiquity, the Middle Ages, and the Renaissance* TB/1047
J. BRONOWSKI & BRUCE MAZLISH: The Western
Intellectual Tradition: *From Leonardo to
Hegel* TB/3001
EDMUND BURKE: On Revolution. Ed. by Robert
A. Smith TB/1401
WILHELM DILTHEY: Pattern and Meaning in History: *Thoughts on History and Society.°
Edited with an Intro. by H. P. Rickman*
TB/1075
ALEXANDER GRAY: The Socialist Tradition: *Moses
to Lenin °* TB/1375
J. H. HEXTER: More's Utopia: *The Biography of
an Idea. Epilogue by the Author* TB/1195
H. STUART HUGHES: History as Art and as
Science: *Twin Vistas on the Past* TB/1207
ARTHUR O. LOVEJOY: The Great Chain of Being:
A Study of the History of an Idea TB/1009
JOSE ORTEGA Y GASSET: The Modern Theme.
Introduction by Jose Ferrater Mora TB/1038

RICHARD H. POPKIN: The History of Scepticism
from Erasmus to Descartes. *Revised Edition*
TB/1391
G. J. RENIER: History: *Its Purpose and Method*
TB/1209
MASSIMO SALVADORI, Ed.: Modern Socialism #
HR/1374
GEORG SIMMEL et al.: Essays on Sociology,
Philosophy and Aesthetics. *Edited by Kurt
H. Wolff* TB/1234
BRUNO SNELL: The Discovery of the Mind: *The
Greek Origins of European Thought* TB/1018
W. WARREN WAGER, ed.: European Intellectual
History Since Darwin and Marx TB/1297
W. H. WALSH: Philosophy of History: In Introduction TB/1020

History: General

HANS KOHN: The Age of Nationalism: *The
First Era of Global History* TB/1380
BERNARD LEWIS: The Arabs in History TB/1029
BERNARD LEWIS: The Middle East and the
West ° TB/1274

History: Ancient

A. ANDREWS: The Greek Tyrants TB/1103
ERNST LUDWIG EHRLICH: A Concise History of
Israel: *From the Earliest Times to the Destruction of the Temple in A.D. 70 °* TB/128
ADOLF ERMAN, Ed.: The Ancient Egyptians: *A
Sourcebook of their Writings. New Introduction by William Kelly Simpson* TB/1233
THEODOR H. GASTER: Thespis: *Ritual Myth and
Drama in the Ancient Near East* TB/1281
MICHAEL GRANT: Ancient History ° TB/1190
A. H. M. JONES, Ed.: A History of Rome
through the Fifgth Century # Vol. I: *The
Republic* HR/1364
Vol. II *The Empire:* HR/1460
SAMUEL NOAH KRAMER: Sumerian Mythology
TB/1055
NAPHTALI LEWIS & MEYER REINHOLD, Eds.:
Roman Civilization *Vol. I: The Republic*
TB/1231
Vol. II: The Empire TB/1232

History: Medieval

MARSHALL W. BALDWIN, Ed.: Christianity
Through the 13th Century # HR/1468
MARC BLOCH: Land and Work in Medieval
Europe. *Translated by J. E. Anderson*
TB/1452
HELEN CAM: England Before Elizabeth TB/1026
NORMAN COHN: The Pursuit of the Millennium
*Revolutionary Messianism in Medieval and
Reformation Europe* TB/103
G. G. COULTON: Medieval Village, Manor, and
Monastery HR/102
HEINRICH FICHTENAU: The Carolingian Empire
*The Age of Charlemagne. Translated with a
Introduction by Peter Munz* TB/114:
GALBERT OF BRUGES: The Murder of Charles the
Good: *A Contemporary Record of Revolutionary Change in 12th Century Flanders
Translated with an Introduction by James
Bruce Ross* TB/131
F. L. GANSHOF: Feudalism ° TB/105
F. L. GANSHOF: The Middle Ages: *A History of
International Relations. Translated by Rém
Hall* TB/141
W. O. HASSALL, Ed.: Medieval England: *A
Viewed by Contemporaries* TB/120
DENYS HAY: The Medieval Centuries ° TB/119
DAVID HERLIHY, Ed.: Medieval Culture and Society #
citey # HR/134

ℋistory: Renaissance & Reformation

History: Modern European

EUGENE C. BLACK, Ed.: European Political History, 1815-1870: *Aspects of Liberalism* ¶ TB/1331

ASA BRIGGS: The Making of Modern England, 1783-1867: *The Age of Improvement* ° TB/1203

D. W. BROGAN: The Development of Modern France ° Vol. I: *From the Fall of the Empire to the Dreyfus Affair* TB/1184 Vol. II: *The Shadow of War, World War I, Between the Two Wars* TB/1185

ALAN BULLOCK: Hitler, A Study in Tyranny. ° Revised Edition. *Illus.* TB/1123

EDMUND BURKE: On Revolution. *Ed. by Robert A. Smith* TB/1401

E. R. CARR: International Relations Between the Two World Wars. 1919-1939 ° TB/1279

E. H. CARR: The Twenty Years' Crisis, 1919-1939: *An Introduction to the Study of International Relations* ° TB/1122

GORDON A. CRAIG: From Bismarck to Adenauer: *Aspects of German Statecraft. Revised Edition* TB/1171

LESTER G. CROCKER, Ed.: The Age of Enlightenment # HR/1423

DENIS DIDEROT: The Encyclopedia: *Selections. Edited and Translated with Introduction by Stephen Gendzier* TB/1299

JACQUES DROZ: Europe between Revolutions, 1815-1848. ° *a Trans. by Robert Baldick* TB/1346

JOHANN GOTTLIEB FICHTE: Addresses to the German Nation. *Ed. with Intro. by George A. Kelly* ¶ TB/1366

FRANKLIN L. FORD: Robe and Sword: *The Re-Louis XIV* TB/1217

ROBERT & ELBORG FORSTER, Eds.: European Society in the Eighteenth Century # HR/1404

C. C. GILLISPIE: Genesis and Geology: *The Decades before Darwin* § TB/51

ALBERT GOODWIN, Ed.: The European Nobility in the Enghteenth Century TB/1313

ALBERT GOODWIN: The French Revolution TB/1064

ALBERT GUERARD: France in the Classical Age: *The Life and Death of an Ideal* TB/1183

JOHN B. HALSTED, Ed.: Romanticism # HR/1387

J. H. HEXTER: Reappraisals in History: *New Views on History and Society in Early Modern Europe* ° TB/1100

STANLEY HOFFMANN et al.: In Search of France: *The Economy, Society and Political System In the Twentieth Century* TB/1219

H. STUART HUGHES: The Obstructed Path: *French Social Thought in the Years of Desperation* TB/1451

JOHAN HUIZINGA: Dutch Civilisation in the 17th Century and Other Essays TB/1453

LIONAL KOCHAN: The Struggle for Germany: *1914-45* TB/1304

HANS KOHN: The Mind of Germany: *The Education of a Nation* TB/1204

HANS KOHN, Ed.: The Mind of Modern Russia: *Historical and Political Thought of Russia's Great Age* TB/1065

WALTER LAQUEUR & GEORGE L. MOSSE, Eds.: Education and Social Structure in the 20th Century. ° *Volume 6 of the Journal* of Contemporary History TB/1339

WALTER LAQUEUR & GEORGE L. MOSSE, Ed.: International Fascism, 1920-1945. ° *Volume 1 of the* Journal of Contemporary History TB/1276

WALTER LAQUEUR & GEORGE L. MOSSE, Eds.: Literature and Politics in the 20th Century. ° *Volume 5 of the* Journal of Contemporary History. TB/1328

WALTER LAQUEUR & GEORGE L. MOSSE, Eds.: The New History: *Trends in Historical Research and Writing Since World War II.* ° *Volume 4 of the* Journal of Contemporary History TB/132?

WALTER LAQUEUR & GEORGE L. MOSSE, Eds. 1914: *The Coming of the First World War* ° *Volume3 of the* Journal of Contemporary History TB/130?

C. A. MACARTNEY, Ed.: The Habsburg and Hohenzollern Dynasties in the Seventeenth and Eighteenth Centuries # HR/140?

JOHN MCMANNERS: European History, 1789? 1914: *Men, Machines and Freedom* TB/141?

PAUL MANTOUX: The Industrial Revolution i the Eighteenth Century: *An Outline of th Beginnings of the Modern Factory Syster in England* TB/107?

FRANK E. MANUEL: The Prophets of Paris: *Turgot, Condorcet, Saint-Simon, Fourier, an Comte* TB/121?

KINGSLEY MARTIN: French Liberal Thought i the Eighteenth Century: *A Study of Politic Ideas from Bayle to Condorcet* TB/111?

NAPOLEON III: Napoleonic Ideas: *Des Idée Napoléoniennes, par le Prince Napoléon-Lou Bonaparte. Ed. by Brison D. Gooch* ¶ TB/133?

FRANZ NEUMANN: Behemoth: *The Structure an Practice of National Socialism, 1933-1944* TB/128?

DAVID OGG: Europe of the Ancien Régime, 171? 1783 ° *a* TB/127?

GEORGE RUDE: Revolutionary Europe, 178? 1815 ° *a* TB/127?

MASSIMO SALVADORI, Ed.: Modern Socialism TB/137?

HUGH SETON-WATSON: Eastern Europe Betwee the Wars, 1918-1941 TB/133?

DENIS MACK SMITH, Ed.: The Making of Ital? 1796-1870 # HR/135?

ALBERT SOREL: Europe Under the Old Regim? *Translated by Francis H. Herrick* TB/112?

ROLAND N. STROMBERG, Ed.: Realism, Natura ism, and Symbolism: *Modes of Thought an Expression in Europe, 1848-1914* # HR/135?

A. J. P. TAYLOR: From Napoleon to Lenin: *Hi torical Essays* ° TB/126?

A. J. P. TAYLOR: The Habsburg Monarchy, 180? 1918: *A History of the Austrian Empire an Austria-Hungary* ° TB/118?

J. M. THOMPSON: European History, 1494-178? TB/143?

DAVID THOMSON, Ed.: France: Empire and R? public, 1850-1940 # HR/138?

ALEXIS DE TOCQUEVILLE & GUSTAVE DE BEAUMONT Tocqueville and Beaumont on Social Refor? *Ed. and trans. with Intro. by Seymo Drescher* TB/134?

G. M. TREVELYAN: British History in the Nin? teenth Century and After: 1792-1919 ° TB/12?

H. R. TREVOR-ROPER: Historical Essays TB/126?

W. WARREN WAGAR: Ed.: Science, Faith, an MAN: *European Thought Since 1914* # HR/136?

MACK WALKER, Ed.: Metternich's Europe, 181? 1848 # HR/136?

ELIZABETH WISKEMANN: Europe of the Dictator 1919-1945 ° *a* TB/12?

JOHN B. WOLF: France: 1814-1919: *The Rise a Liberal-Democratic Society* TB/30?

Literature & Literary Criticism

JACQUES BARZUN: The House of Intellect TB/10?

W. J. BATE: From Classic to Romantic: *Premises of Taste in Eighteenth Century England* TB/1036

VAN WYCK BROOKS: Van Wyck Brooks: The Early Years: *A Selection from his Works, 1908-1921* Ed. with Intro. by Claire Sprague TB/3082

ERNST R. CURTIUS: European Literature and the Latin Middle Ages. *Trans. by Willard Trask* TB/2015

RICHMOND LATTIMORE, Translator: The Odyssey of Homer TB/1389

JOHN STUART MILL: On Bentham and Coleridge. *Introduction by F. R. Leavis* TB/1070

SAMUEL PEPYS: The Diary of Samual Pepys. ° *Edited by O. F. Morshead. 60 illus. by Ernest Shepard* TB/1007

ROBERT PREYER, Ed.: Victorian Literature ** TB/1302

ALBION W. TOURGEE: A Fool's Errand: *A Novel of the South during Reconstruction. Intro. by George Fredrickson* TB/3074

BASIL WILEY: Nineteenth Century Studies: *Coleridge to Matthew Arnold* ° TB/1261

RAYMOND WILLIAMS: Culture and Society, 1780-1950 ° TB/1252

Philosophy

HENRI BERGSON: Time and Free Will: *An Essay on the Immediate Data of Consciousness* ° TB/1021

LUDWIG BINSWANGER: Being-in-the-World: *Selected Papers. Trans. with Intro. by Jacob Needleman* TB/1365

H. J. BLACKHAM: Six Existentialist Thinkers: *Kierkegaard, Nietzsche, Jaspers, Marcel, Heidegger, Sartre* ° TB/1002

M. BOCHENSKI: The Methods of Contemporary Thought. *Trans. by Peter Caws* TB/1377

CRANE BRINTON: Nietzsche. *Preface, Bibliography, and Epilogue by the Author* TB/1197

ERNST CASSIRER: Rousseau, Kant and Goethe. *Intro. by Peter Gay* TB/1092

FREDERICK COPLESTON, S. J.: Medieval Philosophy TB/376

F. M. CORNFORD: From Religion to Philosophy: *A Study in the Origins of Western Speculation* § TB/20

WILFRID DESAN: The Tragic Finale: *An Essay on the Philosophy of Jean-Paul Sartre* TB/1030

MARVIN FARBER: The Aims of Phenomenology: *The Motives, Methods, and Impact of Husserl's Thought* TB/1291

MARVIN FARBER: Basic Issues of Philosophy: *Experience, Reality, and Human Values* TB/1344

MARVIN FARBER: Phenomenology and Existence: *Towards a Philosophy within Nature* TB/1295

PAUL FRIEDLANDER: Plato: *An Introduction* TB/2017

MICHAEL GELVEN: A Commentary on Heidegger's "Being and Time" TB/1464

GLENN GRAY: Hegel and Greek Thought TB/1409

K. C. GUTHRIE: The Greek Philosophers: *From Thales to Aristotle* ° TB/1008

W. F. HEGEL: On Art, Religion Philosophy: *Introductory Lectures to the Realm of Absolute Spirit.* || *Edited with an Introduction by J. Glenn Gray* TB/1463

W. F. HEGEL: Phenomenology of Mind. ° || *Introduction by George Lichtheim* TB/1303

MARTIN HEIDEGGER: Discourse on Thinking. *Translated with a Preface by John M. Anderson and E. Hans Freund. Introduction by John M. Anderson* TB/1459

F. H. HEINEMANN: Existentialism and the Modern Predicament TB/28

WERER HEISENBERG: Physics and Philosophy: *The Revolution in Modern Science. Intro. by F. S. C. Northrop* TB/549

EDMUND HUSSERL: Phenomenology and the Crisis of Philosophy. § *Translated with an Introduction by Quentin Lauer* TB/1170

IMMANUEL KANT: Groundwork of the Metaphysic of Morals. *Translated and Analyzed by H. J. Paton* TB/1159

IMMANUEL KANT: Lectures on Ethics. § *Introduction by Lewis White Beck* TB/105

WALTER KAUFMANN, Ed.: Religion From Tolstoy to Camus: *Basic Writings on Religious Truth and Morals* TB/123

QUENTIN LAUER: Phenomenology: *Its Genesis and Prospect. Preface by Aron Gurwitsch* TB/1169

MAURICE MANDELBAUM: The Problem of Historical Knowledge: *An Answer to Relativism* TB/1338

GEORGE A. MORGAN: What Nietzsche Means TB/1198

H. J. PATON: The Categorical Imperative: *A Study in Kant's Moral Philosophy* TB/1325

MICHAEL POLANYI: Personal Knowledge: *Towards a Post-Critical Philosophy* TB/1158

KARL R. POPPER: Conjectures and Refutations: *The Growth of Scientific Knowledge* TB/1376

WILLARD VAN ORMAN QUINE: Elementary Logic *Revised Edition* TB/577

WILLARD VAN ORMAN QUINE: From a Logical Point of View: *Logico-Philosophical Essays* TB/566

JOHN E. SMITH: Themes in American Philosophy: *Purpose, Experience and Community* TB/1466

MORTON WHITE: Foundations of Historical Knowledge TB/1440

WILHELM WINDELBAND: A History of Philosophy *Vol. I: Greek, Roman, Medieval* TB/38 *Vol. II: Renaissance, Enlightenment, Modern* TB/39

LUDWIG WITTGENSTEIN: The Blue and Brown Books ° TB/1211

LUDWIG WITTGENSTEIN: Notebooks, 1914-1916 TB/1441

Political Science & Government

C. E. BLACK: The Dynamics of Modernization: *A Study in Comparative History* TB/1321

KENNETH E. BOULDING: Conflict and Defense: *A General Theory of Action* TB/3024

DENIS W. BROGAN: Politics in America. *New Introduction by the Author* TB/1469

CRANE BRINTON: English Political Thought in the Nineteenth Century TB/1071

ROBERT CONQUEST: Power and Policy in the USSR: *The Study of Soviet Dynastics* ° TB/1307

ROBERT A. DAHL & CHARLES E. LINDBLOM: Politics, Economics, and Welfare: *Planning and Politico-Economic Systems Resolved into Basic Social Processes* TB/1277

HANS KOHN: Political Ideologies of the 20th Century TB/1277

ROY C. MACRIDIS, Ed.: Political Parties: *Contemporary Trends and Ideas* ** TB/1322

ROBERT GREEN MC CLOSKEY: American Conservatism in the Age of Enterprise, 1865-1910 TB/1137

MARSILIUS OF PADUA: The Defender of Peace. *The Defensor Pacis. Translated with an Introduction by Alan Gewirth* TB/1310

KINGSLEY MARTIN: French Liberal Thought in the Eighteenth Century: *A Study of Political Ideas from Bayle to Condorcet* TB/1114

BARRINGTON MOORE, JR.:Political Power and Social Theory: *Seven Studies* ‖ TB/1221
BARRINGTON MOORE, JR.: Soviet Politics—The Dilemma of Power: *The Role of Ideas in Social Change* ‖ TB/1222
BARRINGTON MOORE, JR.: Terror and Progress—USSR: *Some Sources of Change and Stability*
JOHN B. MORRALL: Political Thought in Medieval Times TB/1076
KARL R. POPPER: The Open Society and Its Enemies *Vol. I: The Spell of Plato* TB/1101 *Vol. II: The High Tide of Prophecy: Hegel, Marx, and the Aftermath* TB/1102
CONYERS READ, Ed.: The Constitution Reconsidered. *Revised Edition, Preface by Richard B. Morris* TB/1384
JOHN P. ROCHE, Ed.: Origins of American Political Thought: *Selected Readings* TB/1301
JOHN P. ROCHE, Ed.: American Political Thought: *From Jefferson to Progressivism* TB/1332
HENRI DE SAINT-SIMON: Social Organization, The Science of Man, and Other Writings. ‖ *Edited and Translated with an Introduction by Felix Markham* TB/1152
CHARLES SCHOTTLAND, Ed.: The Welfare State ** TB/1323
JOSEPH A. SCHUMPETER: Capitalism, Socialism and Democracy TB/3008
PETER WOLL, Ed.: Public Administration and Policy: *Selected Essays* TB/1284

Psychology

ALFRED ADLER: The Individual Psychology of Alfred Adler: *A Systematic Presentation in Selections from His Writings. Edited by Heinz L. & Rowena R. Ansbacher* TB/1154
ALFRED ADLER: Problems of Neurosis: *A Book of Case Histories. Introduction by Heinz L. Ansbacher* TB/1145
LUDWIG BINSWANGER: Being-in-the-World: *Selected Papers. ‖ Trans. with Intro. by Jacob Needleman* TB/1365
ARTHUR BURTON & ROBERT E. HARRIS: Clinical Studies of Personality Vol. I TB/3075 Vol. II TB/3076
HADLEY CANTRIL: The Invasion from Mars: *A Study in the Psychology of Panic* ‖ TB/1282
MIRCEA ELIADE: Cosmos and History: *The Myth of the Eternal Return* § TB/2050
MIRCEA ELIADE: Myth and Reality § TB/1369
MIRCEA ELIADE: Myths, Dreams and Mysteries: *The Encounter Between Contemporary Faiths and Archaic Realities* § TB/1320
MIRCEA ELIADE: Rites and Symbols of Initiation: *The Mysteries of Birth and Rebirth* § TB/1236
HERBERT FINGARETTE: The Self in Transformation: *Psychoanalysis, Philosophy and the Life of the Spirit* ‖ TB/1177
SIGMUND FREUD: On Creativity and the Unconscious: *Papers on the Psychology of Art, Literature, Love, Religion.* § *Intro. by Benjamin Nelson* TB/45
J. GLENN GRAY: The Warriors: *Reflections on Men in Battle. Introduction by Hannah Arendt* TB/1294
WILLIAM JAMES: Psychology: *The Briefer Course. Edited with an Intro. by Gordon Allport* TB/1034
C. G. JUNG: Psychological Reflections. *Ed. by J. Jacobi* TB/2001
KARL MENNINGER, M.D.: Theory of Psychoanalytic Technique TB/1144
JOHN H. SCHAAR: Escape from Authority: *The Perspectives of Erich Fromm* TB/1155

MUZAFER SHERIF: The Psychology of Social Norms. *Introduction by Gardner Murphy* TB/3072
HELLMUT WILHELM: Change: *Eight Lectures on the I Ching* TB/2019

Religion: Ancient and Classical, Biblical and Judaic Traditions

W. F. ALBRIGHT: The Biblical Period from Abraham to Ezra TB/102
SALO W. BARON: Modern Nationalism and Religion TB/818
C. K. BARRETT, Ed.: The New Testament Background: *Selected Documents* TB/86
MARTIN BUBER: Eclipse of God: *Studies in the Relation Between Religion and Philosophy* TB/12
MARTIN BUBER: Hasidism and Modern Man. *Edited and Translated by Maurice Friedman* TB/839
MARTIN BUBER: The Knowledge of Man. *Edited with an Introduction by Maurice Friedman. Translated by Maurice Friedman and Ronald Gregor Smith* TB/135
MARTIN BUBER: Moses. *The Revelation and the Covenant* TB/837
MARTIN BUBER: The Origin and Meaning of Hasidism. *Edited and Translated by Maurice Friedman* TB/835
MARTIN BUBER: The Prophetic Faith TB/73
MARTIN BUBER: Two Types of Faith: *Interpenetration of Judaism and Christianity* ° TB/75
MALCOLM L. DIAMOND: Martin Buber: *Jewish Existentialist* TB/840
M. S. ENSLIN: Christian Beginnings TB/5
M. S. ENSLIN: The Literature of the Christian Movement TB/6
ERNST LUDWIG EHRLICH: A Concise History of Israel: *From the Earliest Times to the Destruction of the Temple in A.D. 70* ° TB/128
HENRI FRANKFORT: Ancient Egyptian Religion: *An Interpretation* TB/7
MAURICE S. FRIEDMAN: Martin Buber: *The Life of Dialogue* TB/64
ABRAHAM HESCHEL: The Earth Is the Lord's & The Sabbath. *Two Essays* TB/828
ABRAHAM HESCHEL: God in Search of Man: *A Philosophy of Judaism* TB/80
ABRAHAM HESCHEL: Man Is not Alone: *A Philosophy of Religion* TB/83
ABRAHAM HESCHEL: The Prophets: *An Introduction* TB/142
T. J. MEEK: Hebrew Origins TB/6
JAMES MUILENBURG: The Way of Israel: *Biblical Faith and Ethics* TB/13
H. J. ROSE: Religion in Greece and Rome TB/5
H. H. ROWLEY: The Growth of the Old Testament TB/10
D. WINTON THOMAS, Ed.: Documents from Old Testament Times TB/8

Religion: General Christianity

ROLAND H. BAINTON: Christendom: *A Short History of Christianity and Its Impact on Western Civilization. Illus.* Vol. I TB/131; Vol. II TB/13
JOHN T. MCNEILL: Modern Christian Movements. *Revised Edition* TB/140
ERNST TROELTSCH: The Social Teaching of the Christian Churches. *Intro. by H. Richard Niebuhr* Vol. TB/71; Vol. II TB/7

8

9

RUDOLF BULTMANN and KARL KUNDSIN: Form Criticism: *Two Essays on New Testament Research. Trans. by F. C. Grant* TB/96
WILLIAM A. CLEBSCH & CHARLES R. JAEKLE: Pastoral Care in Historical Perspective: *An Essay with Exhibits* TB/148
FREDERICK FERRE: Language, Logic and God. *New Preface by the Author* TB/1407
LUDWIG FEUERBACH: The Essence of Christianity. § *Introduction by Karl Barth. Foreword by H. Richard Niebuhr* TB/11
C. C. GILLISPIE: Genesis and Geology: *The Decades before Darwin* § TB/51
ADOLF HARNACK: What Is Christianity? § *Introduction by Rudolf Bultmann* TB/17
KYLE HASELDEN: The Racial Problem in Christian Perspective TB/116
MARTIN HEIDEGGER: Discourse on Thinking. *Translated with a Preface by John M. Anderson and E. Hans Freund. Introduction by John M. Anderson* TB/1459
IMMANUEL KANT: Religion Within the Limits of Reason Alone. § *Introduction by Theodore M. Greene and John Silber* TB/FG
WALTER KAUFMANN, Ed.: Religion from Tolstoy to Camus: *Basic Writings on Religious Truth and Morals. Enlarged Edition* TB/123
JOHN MACQUARRIE: An Existentialist Theology: *A Comparison of Heidegger and Bultmann.* ° *Foreword by Rudolf Bultmann* TB/125
H. RICHARD NIERUHR: Christ and Culture TB/3
H. RICHARD NIEBUHR: The Kingdom of God in America TB/49
ANDERS NYGREN: Agape and Eros. *Translated by Philip S. Watson* ° TB/1430
JOHN H. RANDALL, JR.: The Meaning of Religion for Man. *Revised with New Intro. by the Author* TB/1379
WALTER RAUSCHENBUSCHS Christianity and the Social Crisis. ‡ *Edited by Robert D. Cross* TB/3059
JOACHIM WACH: Understanding and Believing. *Ed. with Intro. by Joseph M. Kitagawa* TB/1399

Science and Mathematics

JOHN TYLER BONNER: The Ideas of Biology. Σ *Illus.* TB/570
W. E. LE GROS CLARK: The Antecedents of Man: *An Introduction to the Evolution of the Primates.* ° *Illus.* TB/559
ROBERT E. COKER: Streams, Lakes, Ponds. *Illus.* TB/586
ROBERT E. COKER: This Great and Wide Sea: *An Introduction to Oceanography and Marine Biology. Illus.* TB/551
W. H. DOWDESWELL: Animal Ecology. *61 illus.* TB/543
C. V. DURELL: Readable Relativity. *Foreword by Freeman J. Dyson* TB/530
GEORGE GAMOW: Biography of Physics. Σ *Illus.* TB/567
F. K. HARE: The Restless Atmosphere TB/560
S. KORNER: The Philosophy of Mathematics: *An Introduction* TB/547
J. R. PIERCE: Symbols, Signals and Noise: *The Nature and Process of Communication* Σ TB/574
WILLARD VAN ORMAN QUINE: Mathematical Logic TB/558

Science: History

MARIE BOAS: The Scientific Renaissance, 1450-1630 ° TB/583
W. DAMPIER, Ed.: Readings in the Literature of Science. *Illus.* TB/512

STEPHEN TOULMIN & JUNE GOODFIELD: The Architecture of Matter: *The Physics, Chemistry and Physiology of Matter, Both Animate and Inanimate, as it has Evolved since the Beginnings of Science* TB/584
STEPHEN TOULMIN & JUNE GOODFIELD: The Discovery of Time TB/585
STEPHEN TOULMIN & JUNE GOODFIELD: The Fabric of the Heavens: *The Development of Astronomy and Dynamics* TB/579

Science: Philosophy

J. M. BOCHENSKI: The Methods of Contemporary Thought. *Tr. by Peter Caws* TB/1377
J. BRONOWSKI: Science and Human Values. *Revised and Enlarged. Illus.* TB/505
WERNER HEISENBERG: Physics and Philosophy: *The Revolution in Modern Science. Introduction by F. S. C. Northrop* TB/549
KARL R. POPPER: Conjectures and Refutations: *The Growth of Scientific Knowledge* TB/1376
KARL R. POPPER: The Logic of Scientific Discovery TB/576
STEPHEN TOULMIN: Foresight and Understanding: *An Enquiry into the Aims of Science. Foreword by Jacques Barzun* TB/564
STEPHEN TOULMIN: The Philosophy of Science: *An Introduction* TB/513

Sociology and Anthropology

REINHARD BENDIX: Work and Authority in Industry: *Ideologies of Management in the Course of Industrialization* TB/3035
BERNARD BERELSON, Ed., The Behavioral Sciences Today TB/1127
JOSEPH B. CASAGRANDE, Ed.: In the Company of Man: *Twenty Portraits of Anthropological Informants. Illus.* TB/3047
KENNETH B. CLARK: Dark Ghetto: *Dilemmas of Social Power. Foreword by Gunnar Myrdal* TB/1317
KENNETH CLARK & JEANNETTE HOPKINS: A Relevant War Against Poverty: *A Study of Community Action Programs and Observable Social Change* TB/1480
W. E. LE GROS CLARK: The Antecedents of Man: *An Introduction to the Evolution of the Primates.* ° *Illus.* TB/559
LEWIS COSER, Ed.: Political Sociology TB/1293
ROSE L. COSER, Ed.: Life Cycle and Achievement in America ** TB/1434
ALLISON DAVIS & JOHN DOLLARD: Children of Bondage: *The Personality Development of Negro Youth in the Urban South* ‖ TB/3049
ST. CLAIR DRAKE & HORACE R. CAYTON: Black Metropolis: *A Study of Negro Life in a Northern City. Introduction by Everett C. Hughes. Tables, maps, charts, and graphs* Vol. I TB/1086; Vol. II TB/1087
PETER E. DRUCKER: The New Society: *The Anatomy of Industrial Order* TB/1082
CORA DU BOIS: The People of Alor. *With a Preface by the Author* Vol. I *Illus.* TB/1042; Vol. II TB/1043
EMILE DURKHEIM et al.: Essays on Sociology and Philosophy: *with Appraisals of Durkheim's Life and Thought.* ‖ *Edited by Kurt H. Wolff* TB/1151
LEON FESTINGER, HENRY W. RIECKEN, STANLEY SCHACHTER: When Prophecy Fails: *A Social and Psychological Study of a Modern Group that Predicted the Destruction of the World* ‖ TB/1132